# A history of Seafaring

# A history
## based on

506 illustrations 150 in colour

contributors

GEORGE F.BASS · ARNE EMIL CHRISTENSEN
OLE CRUMLIN-PEDERSEN · KEITH DeVRIES
MICHAEL L.KATZEV · ALEXANDER McKEE
PETER MARSDEN · MENDEL L.PETERSON
ENRICO SCANDURRA · PETER THROCKMORTON
JOSEPH W.SHAW · FREDERICK VAN DOORNINCK
RICHARD C.VAN GEMERT · ROBERT C.WHEELER

# of Seafaring

## underwater archaeology

edited by
## George F. Bass

WALKER AND COMPANY · NEW YORK

©1972 Thames and Hudson Ltd, London

All rights reserved. No portion of this work may be
reproduced without permission except for brief passages
for the purpose of review

Library of Congress Catalog Card Number: 72–81455

ISBN: 0–8027–03909

First published in the United States of America in 1972
by the Walker Publishing Company, Inc.

Printed and bound in Great Britain

# Contents

# Introduction

MAN LIVES ON A PLANET which is nearly three-quarters covered by water. Most of this forms large oceans and seas, but even our land masses are crossed and broken by rivers and streams or dotted with lakes. Sometimes a barrier to movement, water has more often served to facilitate contacts between different geographical areas. The earliest civilizations in Mesopotamia and Egypt owed their existence largely to the rivers which served as highways connecting the far reaches of each country. The spread of Neolithic cultures and ideas from the Near East to Greece, Italy and farther west was more often than not by sea – a pattern continued in Classical times when Greeks and Phoenicians seldom travelled far inland through neighbouring lands, but sailed great distances to reach foreign coasts and islands in the Mediterranean and beyond.

The part played by ships in the story of man's progress cannot be overestimated. It would be impossible to consider the history of Western civilization without the spread of ideas, men and goods by sea, or the decisive sea battles which more than once reversed the fortunes of major powers. Indeed, it now seems that before there were either farmers or shepherds there were sailors; before man settled in villages and began to make pottery, he had learned to construct some sort of sea-going craft.

The reason for the great importance and antiquity of seafaring is a simple one. Wherever water is present, the most efficient method of moving materials in any quantity is by floating them in some sort of water craft. A North American birch-bark canoe 35 feet long, as we shall see, carried about 8,000 pounds, including the weight of eight men. The same cargo would require 35 porters if carried over land, assuming that each man could carry 180 pounds for a day! Add a sail, and efficiency becomes even greater. Arne Emil Christensen, one of our authors, has elsewhere compared the 34-ton cargo of a small Norwegian sloop, sailed by only two men and a boy, to 110 sledgeloads, or 340 packs for horses. During Roman times, it cost more to cart a large quantity of grain just 75 miles than to ship it from one end of the Empire to the other by sea. And sometimes the cargo of a vessel consisted of such heavy pieces that it could not have been carried any distance by either men or beasts of burden; there is, for example, the case of an Egyptian queen nearly 35 centuries ago who moved a pair of stone obelisks totalling 700 tons in weight the length of Egypt on the Nile. Then, too, a boat may be paddled or sailed in most cases at a greater average speed than can be attained by a man on foot or an animal-drawn cart or wagon. Lastly, of course, there are many places which, before the invention of aircraft, would have been inaccessible except by water.

This is a book about the development of the ships and boats which have affected the history of Western civilization. It concentrates – and this is a new departure – on the ships themselves, and is not dependent on literary descriptions or artistic representations of ships, which are often unreliable. We have, needless to say, taken due account of the latter, for they have contributed materially to our knowledge of seafaring down the ages, but there can be no substitute for the study of the remains of actual ships of each period of history. We have only to reflect how relatively little we could say about the construction of Greek temples, Roman theatres, medieval castles, or Colonial American houses without the physical remains of such structures, to realize the truth of this.

The book could not have been written even a dozen years ago. The remains of a Bronze Age ship in the Mediterranean were excavated for the first time in 1960. The first examples of Classical Greek ships, here described, were not found and excavated until after the book was put in hand. While we had some clues concerning the design of Imperial Roman ships, from finds on land and in rivers and lakes, and from pieces of their hulls brought to the surface of the Mediterranean by the early aqualung divers twenty years ago, we knew nothing of Late Roman and Byzantine ship construction until the 1960s. Only now are we beginning to see where and when the revolutionary change from Graeco-Roman methods of hull-first construction to our modern method of skeleton-first construction took place. We have been familiar with the design of Viking ships from land burials for quite a considerable time, but knowledge of their later development and the first-hand study of northern medieval ships has resulted largely from discoveries of shipwrecks made during the past dozen years. The first Venetian galley was discovered only in 1963, the *Vasa* was raised from Stockholm Harbour in 1961, and research on sunken fur-trade canoes in North America did not begin until 1960. Even more recent have been the studies of shipwrecks of the Spanish Armada. The results of this modern archaeological research are contained in the pages that follow, and a unique feature on this book is that each of the contributors has worked on the actual remains of ships from the area, and of the period, about which he writes.

The archaeology of ships of the later periods might be considered less important than those of more remote antiquity, for we have many contemporaneous paintings and, commonly in the case of ships built since the eighteenth century, the actual shipwrights' plans. But even here, the sixteenth-century *Vasa* presented some surprises in ship design, and many of the plans for early ships and boats in North America simply have not survived. Further, salvaged items of cargo and personal property often reveal facts of commerce and life on water not known from still extant bills of lading or logs.

Owing to the fortunes of archaeology, there are certain gaps in the story. Ships of the Far East are not discussed only because no shipwrecks of that area have as yet been located and excavated. A chapter on Arab shipping might well have followed that on Byzantine ships, but the excavation of the first Arab shipwreck (at Sharm-el-Sheikh) was completed by an Israeli team after the book was ready to go to press. At the time of writing, a seventeenth-century French merchantman is being excavated by the Canadian Historic Sites Service, and there are plans for a complete excavation of the eighteenth-century Dutch East Indiaman *Amsterdam* at Hastings. Had the results of these and other projects been available, Alexander McKee's chapter with its emphasis on British warships might have been differently conceived.

Finally, it was necessary to decide how far to carry our history of seafaring. The raising of the American Civil War ironclad *Cairo* and the excavation of the Missouri River steamer *Bertrand*, to name but two examples, have shown the value of archaeological research on ships recent enough for photographic records to be available. However, the introduction of steam propulsion for water transport seemed a logical point at which to draw the line.

The world of nautical and underwater archaeologists is so small that it has been my pleasure to know personally all of the authors (DeVries, Katzev, Shaw, and Van Doorninck as former students at the University of Pennsylvania). I began and finished the editing at the University Museum in Philadelphia, but much of the work was done while I was a visiting scholar at St John's College, Cambridge, on a fellowship from the American Council of Learned Societies. This enabled me to make frequent visits to London to consult with Mr Thomas Neurath of Thames and Hudson, and to seek the ready advice and help of Mr Eric Peters who worked as hard as I to make the book what it is, but whose major contributions to all aspects of the volume would remain anonymous except for these inadequate words of thanks. I owe also a great debt to Miss Ruth Rosenberg for understanding so well the story we wished to tell in her final selection and lay-out of the pictures, and to the patience and hard work of Mrs Vanessa Whinney and other members of the Thames and Hudson picture research department. Colleagues and scholars who provided me and the other authors with information and illustrations are far too numerous to be thanked adequately here, but the sources of the illustrations will be found elsewhere in the book. Finally, I wish that I might thank Walter Neurath for asking me to undertake this task, and I am especially saddened that he did not live to see the book past its first stages of conception.

GEORGE F. BASS

1

# The earliest seafarers in the Mediterranean and the Near East

GEORGE F. BASS

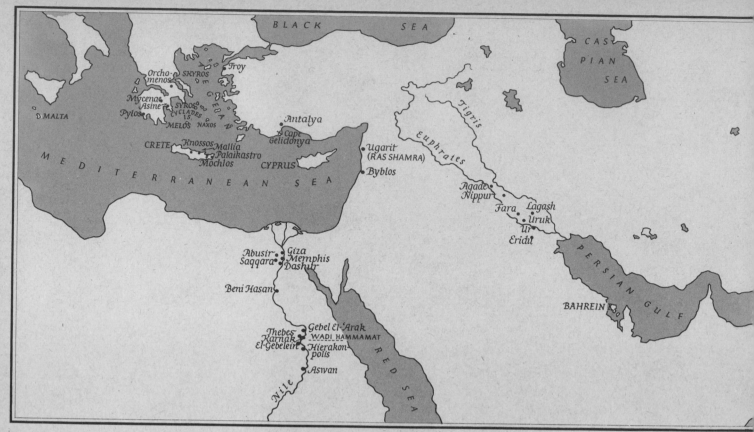

6  *By 3000 BC, seafarers had crossed the Aegean and the Adriatic, sailed the open seas between Egypt and Crete, and ventured into the Red Sea and Persian Gulf. Named on this map are places with which the present chapter is primarily concerned*

### Third Millennium BC

*Mesopotamia and the Indus Valley.* Our knowledge of water transport in the third millennium BC is greatly increased by documents written in Sumerian and, somewhat later, Akkadian; although not linguistically related, both languages were inscribed on clay tablets in cuneiform characters. Both continued in use throughout the period covered by this chapter.

13    The necessity for canals in Mesopotamia for irrigation is well known, but these canals formed at the same time the most important highways for transporting goods. Grain from the fields, stone and timber brought by river from distant mountains, and metals imported from overseas by way of the Persian Gulf, all ended up on canals. From there they were conveyed to the great temples by barges and boats which were tied up to poles at various quays. Such craft were paddled, propelled by punting poles, or sometimes towed from the canal banks. The crew of a river boat is listed on a clay receipt for its oil rations:

2 boat-towing men, 2 men at the outside rope, 1 man watching the depth, 2 men walking the deck, 5 able-bodied workers, 1 scribe = 13 men

The importance of these crews to the temple economy is evidenced by a list of the people attached to the temple of Bau at Lagash. About 125 men, or a tenth of the entire temple population, were rowers, steersmen, or sailors, and in addition there were various slaves and porters for moving cargoes; many of these boatmen were foreigners.

Business documents from the Third Dynasty of Ur, about 2000 BC, list some of the materials of which boats were made, including pitch for coating their hulls, material for caulking, and hides for covering leather skiffs. Most of the small boats, we know from cylinder seal carvings, continued to have the high prow and stern of the previous millennium. Sometimes the hulls seem shorter and more U-shaped than those of earlier examples, but this may be due to the cramped space available to the engravers. Models from Ur, in silver and in bitumen, are long canoe-like craft with benches and, in one case, six pairs of paddles.

Larger vessels set sail for such places as Magan, on the Persian Gulf, and Melukhkha, somewhere on the coast of Oman, to obtain timber and other raw materials. Perhaps it was to protect these interests that King Shar-Gani-sharri sent out a naval expedition to conquer the coasts and islands of the Gulf during the last part of the millennium.

Certainly the most important of these foreign ports was in a land called Dilmun: 'Ships of Dilmun' brought ivory, timber, gold, copper, and lapis lazuli to the great cities of Ur, Lagash, and Agade. This bountiful land has

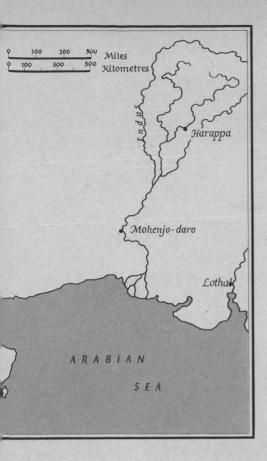

potamia, the 'Ubaidians (see above), were driven out by the Sumerians, and that they fled to the coasts of the Arabian Sea, to form the Indus Valley civilization.

*Egypt.* Our knowledge of boats and ships during the Old Kingdom in Egypt (*c.* 2780–2280 BC), the time of the building of the Great Pyramids, is enhanced by numerous models, stone reliefs, and written documents. Even the remains of an entire ship, dismantled and buried near the Pyramid of Cheops, has been uncovered and is being reassembled; perhaps intended for sacred pilgrimages by the king in the afterworld, the large vessel (over 140 feet long) preserves in carved wood at stem and stern the appearance of bound bundles of papyrus from an earlier era.

The painted stripes on earlier predynastic clay models had surely represented the ropes or lines used to lash papyrus bundles together, and Old Kingdom tomb reliefs now show such craft actually being built. They were depicted usually as small boats for hunting and fishing in quiet Egyptian marshes. The type has had a long life; Egyptian 'vessels of bulrushes' were mentioned nearly two thousand years later by Isaiah, and similar primitive reed boats have been seen recently in the Sudan and elsewhere. The Old Kingdom examples retained the 'sickle-shaped' hulls we have seen in Gerzean representations, but another early form is suggested by a hieroglyphic sign that occurs in the word for boat or skiff. This represents a papyrus-bundle boat with its bow bent back sharply, and its stern cut off, a type also observed by modern travellers in the Sudan.

cf. 23

7

8

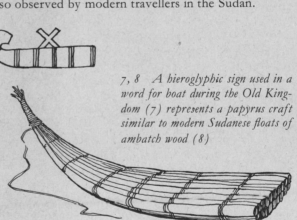

*7, 8 A hieroglyphic sign used in a word for boat during the Old Kingdom (7) represents a papyrus craft similar to modern Sudanese floats of ambatch wood (8)*

Wooden hulls, made with planks, copied the 'spoon shape' or 'sickle shape' of the papyrus boats; centuries later their sterns were often carved with plant motifs only slightly reminiscent of their papyrus prototypes. Contemporary reliefs show that both types, wooden and reed, were sometimes paddled, with crews facing forward and kneeling, and sometimes rowed, with crews seated and facing aft. Steering seems at first to have been effected by men holding long spear-shaped paddles over one or both sides of the boat near the stern, but soon it

21

15

usually been identified as the island of Bahrein in the Persian Gulf; although the island is itself not rich in raw materials, it may well have been an exchange centre. The noted Sumerologist Samuel Kramer, however, has proposed that this country of 'great dwellings', this 'dock-yard-house of the (inhabited) land', 'the place where the sun rises', represents, rather, the great Indus Valley civilization to the east of Sumer.

Although there is strong evidence against this identification, recent archaeological research has shown the importance of sea trade in that area. A number of Harappan ports have been located on the Gujarat coast of the Arabian Sea, the best known being that at Lothal (see Chapter 4, p. 89). Here a huge artificial dock of baked brick, together with a warehouse for storage of cargoes, has been excavated by S. R. Rao. Seven stone anchors, five from the dock itself, represent two primitive types: two are simple pierced stones, but five have additional pairs of holes to hold sticks for digging into the sea or river bottom. Five terracotta models from the site included two sailing ships, and three river 'barges'.

Representations of boats painted or scratched on pottery, as well as on a seal, have been found at Lothal and at other Harappan sites. Most have the high prow and stern so typical of even the earliest boats in Mesopotamia. This accords with an extension of Kramer's theory, for he believes that the original settlers of southern Meso-

10

was discovered that it was more efficient to attach the paddle to the hull and rotate it on its own axis by means cf. 18 of a tiller attached to the paddle handle.

Although some of the wooden hulls were no larger than their papyrus counterparts, others, built for the open sea, were quite sizeable; a cedar vessel built during the reign of Snefru of Dynasty IV was said to be 100 cubits, or 172 feet, long. Expeditions along the eastern Mediterranean coast, to obtain cedar from Lebanon for unforested Egypt, are suggested as early as Dynasty II; and not far from Byblos a Dynasty IV boat crew left its name on an axe-head found near the port.

Actual seafaring ventures were also recorded during the Old Kingdom. A Dynasty V relief shows ships filled 16 with Syrian captives greeting King Sahu-re, and the same pharaoh sent a fleet southward to Punt on the Somali coast. An inscription on the wall of the tomb of one Khnemhotep, in the following dynasty, indicates that he was a steersman who made eleven voyages to myrrh-rich Punt.

It is from reliefs that we know the principal features of early Egyptian ships, many of which continued into the second millennium BC. The mast was usually, though 15, 16 not always, a bipod which straddled the hull rather than being stepped directly in the longitudinal centre as in single-masted ships. This was to spread the weight over the weak hull, as is done today in the double-masted reed boats of Lake Titicaca in Peru. The mast was supported by a forestay and numerous backstays, but shrouds were not needed and do not appear. When the ship was floating or being paddled downstream, against 9 the prevailing wind on the Nile, the mast was lowered

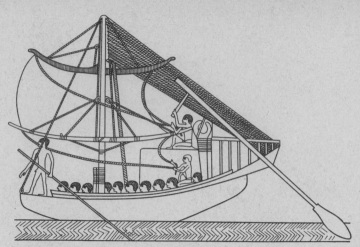

10 Relief in the tomb of Ipi at Saqqara, c. 2500 BC. A helmsman holds both the braces to the upper yard and the tiller; a man below controls the lower braces. Note the single forestay and numerous backstays, and the crutch for lowering the mast

9 Relief in the tomb of Abibi, at Saqqara, of c. 2500 BC, showing men lowering a typical bipod mast of the Old Kingdom

into a crutch near the stern. An upper and a lower yard usually spread the tall, narrow sail, but sometimes spars, instead of a lower yard were used to hold the lower edge of the sail in place. Crew members controlled the sail by 10 means of lines (braces) from the upper, and occasionally the lower, yard.

Running from stem to stern was a huge cable, called 16 today a 'hogging truss', which was tightened in the centre of the ship by means of a stick thrust through two strands of the cable and turned so as to twist and shorten

it. The purpose of the cable was to hold up the ends of the ship so that they would not sag, especially when a wave was passing beneath the hull amidships. The strong skeletons of most ships now prevent this sagging, or 'hogging', but Egyptian ships were built without keels. Lacking large timbers, the Egyptians built up their ships from small pieces of wood carefully joined together, a cf. 20 method compared by Herodotus two millennia later to that of building a wall of bricks. After the hull was completed, frames (ribs) and a sort of keel were inserted, as well as a series of thwarts which sometimes protruded from the sides of the hull. The strength of the ship, however, depended mainly on the strength of its shell, which was held together partly by the pressure of the surrounding water, much as an arch stands from its own weight. An additional latticework of cable was some- times wrapped completely around the hull, below the 16 gunwale, to provide additional strength.

*The Aegean.* The Early Bronze Age in the Aegean, basi- cally the third millennium BC, is divided into three geo- graphical areas to which archaeologists have given distinctive names: Early Minoan on Crete, Early Helladic on the Greek mainland, and Early Cycladic in the islands of the Cyclades. International trade and sea traffic were intense at this time, perhaps spurred on by the search for and barter in metals. Copper and bronze implements become more and more common, and jewellers' techniques in gold and silver show a striking similarity from southern Russia through Asia Minor to Mesopotamia, and out across the Aegean.

Early Cycladic sailors ventured between the coasts of Asia Minor, Crete and the mainland of Greece, as far north as Troy in the east and the Northern Sporades in the west. Outside the Aegean, Cycladic exports have come to light as far away as the Dalmatian coast and Sicily. The long boats used by these island traders are known to us through incised pictures on terracotta objects called 'frying pans' by archaeologists. (What purpose they served is not known; about the only thing we can be certain of is that they were not frying pans.)

They are low vessels, with high prows topped by ensigns of fish. Below each fish hangs a tassel, like those seen before on Egyptian Gerzean vases; the over-all shape of the vessels, of course, is much more like the 'foreign boats' depicted in the early period of Nile travel. More than twenty oars or paddles are represented on each side of many of the 'frying pan' ships, but there is never evidence of a mast. Did the Cycladic people go through a long stage of rowed seafaring before they began to use sails, as did their later Scandinavian counterparts (see chapter 7)?

11 Long boats used in the Cycladic Islands during the Early Bronze Age were frequently incised on terracotta objects. Typical features are the fish ensigns with tassels below, high stems, horizontal protrusions at stern, and many oars

Three lead models of these Cycladic boats, up to about 16 inches in length, were discovered on the island of Naxos. For thirty years they remained unnoticed in the Ashmolean Museum, Oxford, until their recent publication by Colin Renfrew. Each boat is made of three strips of metal: a flat bottom piece, sharply turned up at the prow and more gently at the stern, and two side pieces. This seems to indicate that the actual boats were plank-built, perhaps with a hull formed of a hollowed-out log with planks added to the sides to give greater depth. On the other hand, they may have been skin-covered instead.

A similar type of boat is known from an Early Minoan clay model from Palaikastro on Crete; the typical high prow and low stern represent features which will continue into the sea-going sailing ships of Middle Minoan times. Another Cretan clay model, from Mochlos, seems to represent a much smaller boat with thole pins for attaching oars as on many modern Aegean boats which are not fitted with rowlocks.

The coastal Early Helladic people must also have had ships and boats, but we know virtually nothing about them. One crude representation, scratched on a vase from Orchomenos in central Greece, shows a boat almost identical to those on Cycladic 'frying pans'; vertical strokes may in this case represent a mast, but it is possible that they are merely accidental scratches.

12 An Early Bronze Age clay model from Palaikastro, Crete, now in the Heraklion Museum. Except for the lack of fish ensign and tassel, it is remarkably like the Cycladic long boats of the same period. Note thwarts inside the hull

## 2000-1600 BC

The first four hundred years of the second millennium BC cover roughly the time of the Middle Kingdom in Egypt (and an Intermediate period of internal disorder which separates it from the New Kingdom), the Middle Bronze Age in the Aegean, and the Isin Larsa and Old Babylonian periods in Mesopotamia.

*Mesopotamia.* Our knowledge of shipping during the Old Babylonian period comes mainly from cuneiform tablets. Grain, oil, fruit, vegetables, cattle, fish, milk, wool, stone, bricks, shoe leather, as well as people, are mentioned as being carried by boat along the Mesopotamian canals. 'Road maps', naming the canals like our modern avenues, are preserved for us in clay. The rivers served as highways, but travel by towed barge

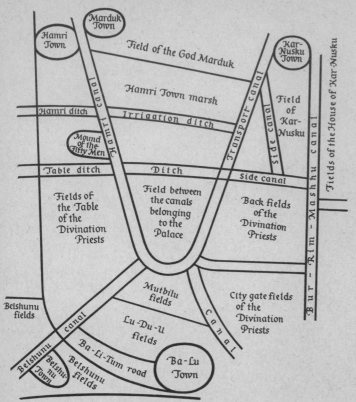

Marduk Town
Hamri Town
Field of the God Marduk
Kar-Nusku Town
Hamri Town marsh
Hamri ditch
Irrigation ditch
Field of Kar-Nusku
Mound of the Fifty Men
Table ditch
Ditch
side canal
Fields of the House of Kar-Nusku
Fields of the Table of the Divination Priests
Field between the canals belonging to the Palace
Back fields of the Divination Priests
Belshunu fields
canal
Mutbilu fields
City gate fields of the Divination Priests
Belshunu Town
Belshunu nu Town
Belshunu fields
Ba-Li-Tum road
Lu-Du-U fields
Ba-Lu Town
Bur-Rim-Mashhu canal
Transport canal
Spis canal
Hamri canal
Canal

13 *By 2500 BC an elaborate canal system linked the major cities of Mesopotamia, as well as supplying water for farming. A map inscribed on a clay tablet at Nippur, c. 1500 BC, names the canals in cuneiform script, here translated into English*

against the current was slow; the 85-mile trip between Lagash and Nippur took sixteen or seventeen days upstream, but only four or five down.

From the first half of the second millennium are numerous tablets documenting laws which controlled the busy canal traffic. At Eshnunna, an Amorite-controlled state, archaeologists found laws declaring how much should be paid for the hiring of different sizes of boats, and the rates at which boatmen were to be paid for a day's work; the captain, as now, was responsible for his boat:

If the boatman is negligent and causes the sinking of the boat, he shall pay in full for everything the sinking of which he caused.

The most famous of these laws are, of course, contained in the slightly later Code of Hammurabi. These state that the pay for caulking a boat of sixty *kur* (7260 litres) shall be two shekels of silver, but if the boat leaks within a year, the workman must do the entire job over again at his own expense. The rates for rental are defined as before, as is the fact that the boatman must pay for the boat and cargo if he sinks it through carelessness. But the laws of salvage were already in effect: if the boatman finds the sunken boat, he must pay only one-half its value. Even the laws of right-of-way were strikingly modern:

If a rowboat rammed a sailboat and has sunk (it), the owner of the boat whose boat was sunk shall in the presence of god set forth the particulars regarding whatever was lost in his boat and the one in charge of the rowboat which sank the sailboat shall make good to him his boat and his lost property.

Clay tablets tell us also about the boats themselves, and we have the words for large ships and small ships; sailing ships, rowed boats, and towed barges; passenger ships and cargo ships; empty ships and fully laden ships; repaired ships and disabled ships; royal ships and divine ships; and so on. The largest of these usually had a capacity of 120 *kur* (14,520 litres) although 60-*kur* boats were more common, and at least one giant 300-*kur* vessel is mentioned. Armas Salonen, a Finnish cuneiform scholar, has made a detailed study of the texts dealing with ships and boats, and has determined the numbers of side planks, bow planks, stern planks and thwarts normally used in each size of boat down to those of 10-*kur* capacity; these last, for example, used only fifteen or sixteen side planks and 600 treenails in their construction, while the larger 120-*kur* ships required between forty-three and forty-six side planks and 7,200 treenails each! Salonen believed that some of the words referred to parts of ribs, but Lionel Casson has more plausibly suggested that the boats at that time were not built with frames and that the words more likely meant the clamps and tenons, of types used contemporaneously in Egypt, which held the edge-joined planks together. As today in Iraq, the boats were smeared inside with fish oil to soften the wood, and were coated outside with waterproof asphalt.

Maritime trade continued with foreign lands such as Dilmun which supplied copper ingots and luxury items like ivory, precious stones, eye paint, and 'fish-eyes' (perhaps pearls) in return for woollen garments, leather, and barley from agricultural Babylonia. Shipwrecks must have been common, and the grateful sailors who made the round trip safely offered tithes or dedicated silver models of their ships to the gods who had protected them. Divine protection, however, was not enough for the businessmen who offered the capital to finance overseas ventures; often they accepted lesser profits by refusing to enter into full partnership with the seafaring merchants, thus avoiding risk of sharing a loss at sea. Such tragedies are reflected in the legendary story of Adapa which vividly tells us, in a fourteenth-century BC version, how 'the sea was like a mirror. But the south wind came blowing and submerged me, causing me to go down to the home of the fish.'

*Egypt.* The finest models of Nile boats come from the tomb of Meket-re, an Egyptian nobleman buried at Thebes about 2000 BC. Discovered and studied by H. E. Winlock, the boats are now in the Metropolitan Museum,

17–19
14, 15

New York, and the Cairo Museum. Four of the models represent a bright yellow boat used by Meket-re to make inspection trips on the Nile. Two of them, it seems, are travelling upstream with sails raised as if to catch the north wind, but the other two are rowed downstream with masts and sails lowered. The boat, estimated to be between 40 and 50 feet long by the size of human figures on board, does not have the 'hogging truss' of the ships we have seen earlier, but instead a longitudinal beam running the length of the vessel just below deck level. From this beam run ten cross beams on either side, and between them are the deck planks; the deck planks could be removed to allow the rowers to stand at a lower level

*14, 15 The models of Meket-re's light green yacht (or funerary barque) clearly exhibit a shape based on earlier papyrus craft. Details of steering oars and tabernacle are below*

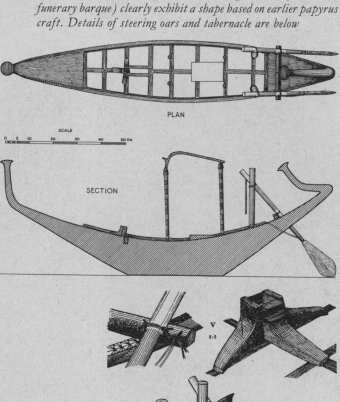

PLAN

SCALE
0 5 10 20 30 40 50 CM.

SECTION

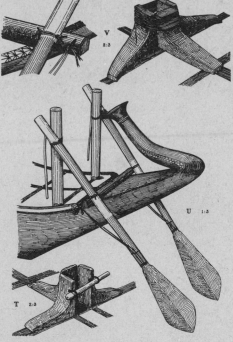

or to sit on the thwarts. The extremely tall and narrow sail of the Old Kingdom Nile boats has now been replaced by a sail markedly broader than it is high, proportions that remain standard into later periods. The mast is supported by stays and shrouds, and the upper yard is raised by means of eight halyards; the lower yard is supported by numerous lifts. The large, single steering oar ran from the top of a tall rudder post directly through a notch at the stern of the vessel, and was rotated by the steersman using a tiller. A vault-like cabin of fabric over a light wooden framework could be moved from near the stern to a point amidships when the mast was down and the ship was being rowed. A crew of twenty-one men, including captain, helmsman, look-out holding a forked pole at the bow, and eighteen rowers, was larger by five men than when the boat was sailing without oars.

A kitchen boat, almost identical in construction, accompanied Meket-re on his travels. This vessel, represented by one sailing model and one rowed model, contains jars of beer and wine, joints of meat, and men engaged in baking bread. Also represented, by four models, is Meket-re's yacht, with the nobleman himself seated under a deck awning during what has the appearance of a pleasure cruise; stem and stern are curved up in a manner reminiscent of tied papyrus bundles, so that it was not possible to run the steering oar directly over the stern, and the steering was done by a pair of oars, one on either side of the stern. A smaller sporting boat, for netting birds and harpooning fish, had a single steering oar running from rudder post over the starboard side at the stern, and a light wicker cabin covered with rugs. Lastly, a pair of papyrus-bundle boats, each paddled by only two men, pull a trawl net between them in order to catch fish.

Meket-re's fleet contained boats made both of planks and of papyrus bundles, the traditional materials used previously in the Old Kingdom. Now, in Dynasty XII, we have representations of boatwrights at work on each type of construction. A relief from the tomb of Ukhhotep, of the twentieth century BC, shows a boatbuilder tightening the binding around one end of a papyrus boat of the typical shape used for hunting and fishing. On a wall in the tomb of Khnemhotep at Beni Hasan, boatbuilders fit together short planks in the manner described much later by Herodotus.

How such short planks were held together in a vessel whose strength depended on its shell is known from actual boats of Dynasty XII excavated at Dashur. Here the planks are joined edge to edge both by wooden pegs and by carefully cut 'dovetail-shaped' tenons sunk into the surfaces of the planks; thwarts protrude through the hull for additional lateral support. The tools used in such construction – adzes, axes, drills, chisels and gravers – are known from Dynasty XII accounts of the dockyard workshop at This (Papyrus Reisner II).

Overseas voyages continued, but the journey to Punt required first the arduous overland trip from the Nile Valley to the Red Sea. Records of Dynasty XI recount

19

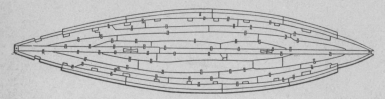

*16    The plan of one of the two boats found buried at Dashur,
dating from c. 2000 BC, clearly shows the Egyptian technique
of constructing hulls from numerous short planks held together
with mortise-and-tenon joints*

how sailors marched to the sea, to build their ship, by
way of the Wadi Hammamat, a route for sailors since
Neolithic times. The long trip was later avoided when a
canal was dug, probably during the reign of Sesostris III
(1878–1842 BC), from the eastern branch of the Nile to
the north end of the Gulf of Suez.

Traffic with Punt must have been considerable, if we
may judge from the contemporary, but fabulous, Tale
of the Shipwrecked Sailor: the only survivor of a storm
in the Red Sea which sank his 180-foot ship, he was
marooned on an island for only four months before
being rescued by another passing Egyptian ship.

The earlier trade with Syria was also maintained, but
whether or not the 'Byblos' ships used in the trade were
Syrian or only Egyptian ships built for the Byblos route
is an open question. Unfortunately, no representations
of such ships have been discovered.

*The Aegean.* Minos of Crete was, according to Thucydides, the first ruler to possess a navy, and the excavation
of the unfortified 'Palace of Minos' at Knossos seems to
bear this out. It, and other unwalled palaces on the
island, surely depended on a fleet for defence. The
nature of the fleet, however, is unknown for we have
no evidence of warships in the Middle Minoan period.
Perhaps ships played the dual role of troop transports
and merchantmen.

Minoan trade goods (pottery) have been found in
Italy, Greece, Asia Minor, Egypt, and on the Syro-
Palestinian coast. Probably it was the contact with Egypt
that led to the type of ship crudely engraved on Middle
22    Minoan gems: the frequent high prow and low stern
continue the Aegean tradition of the Early Bronze Age,
but instead of multitudes of oars we now see, for the
first time, mast, square sail and standing rigging. Oars
were still used, however, with a maximum number of
fifteen shown on the side of one representation (Professor Sp. Marinatos, using the common figure of 5 feet
between rowers, estimates this ship to have been about
65 feet long if additional length is allowed for bow and
stern).

Sails are sometimes so poorly carved on the gems that
they seem to be deck awnings, but in other cases an
upper and lower yard is clear. Stem and stern often end
in a characteristic fork, sometimes resembling a bird in
flight on the bow. Some of the gems depict a crescent-

shaped hull of the type associated with later 'round'
merchant ships.

From the Greek mainland, during the Middle Helladic
period, we have nothing. Widely published, but greatly
restored, ships on a vase from Iolkos have been con-
vincingly compared by K. DeVries to fish painted on a
vase of the period in the Nauplion Museum.

## 1600–1000 BC

*Egypt.* Sea and river traffic is well documented in the
Egyptian New Kingdom (1570–1085 BC). Large, sea-
going vessels are best known from Deir el-Bahari, where
stone temple reliefs represent an expedition sent to Punt
by Queen Hatshepsut. Stevedores carry ebony, myrrh    24
trees, ivory, gold and other precious commodities up
the gangplanks of moored ships, while other ships approach under oar as their sails are furled. Hogging trusses
still support the ends of the ships, and deck beams protrude through the sides of the hulls as earlier. The sails
are so broad that the upper and lower yard of each is
made of a pair of long, tapering poles lashed together at
their ends. The mast, stepped in the centre of each ship,
is held by two forestays and one backstay; on its top is
a metal cap with holes through which some of the running rigging passes, calling to mind the great friction on
lines in this era preceding the use of blocks.

On the same temple are reliefs depicting a different
venture of similar grand proportions. The queen ordered
two huge obelisks to be carved from the quarries at    17
Aswan and shipped down the Nile to Karnak, where
one of them still stands. Each obelisk weighed about
350 tons and was nearly 100 feet high; the barge needed
to support them was immense. Not one but eight hogging trusses, side by side, held the ends of the vessel;
three rows of thwarts protruded through the sides of
the hull. The steering oars, two on each side, have been
estimated to have weighed 4 or 5 tons apiece. Naturally
such a vessel could not be rowed: it was towed by
twenty-seven smaller boats, each manned by thirty oarsmen – a total of 810 men!

By great good fortune, we have also from the New
Kingdom a number of unique nautical documents on
papyrus. One (Papyrus Leiden I 350 Verso), a scroll of
1239 BC, is a ship's log recording the downstream journey of a Nile boat. The log consists of messages, sent by    26
hand to a high priest in Memphis nearly every two days,
telling of the progress of the voyage. Daily rations of
bread are recorded and these show that the crew varied
between twenty-six and forty members; some of these
people leaving and boarding may have been passengers,
but they too received food. Food other than bread was
perhaps bought by crewmen along the river bank, as is
shown in a painted tomb scene.

Another papyrus (Papyrus Turin 2008 and 2016),
almost a century later, resembles a purser's accounts in
its description of a ship's cargo.

Even dockyard records are preserved. In these we
read how foreign-type or foreign-owned ships were re-

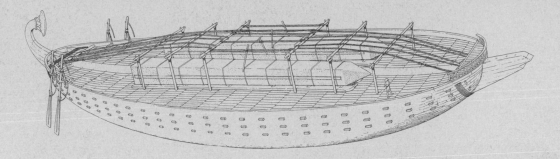

17 *A modern reconstruction of the barge on which Queen Hatshepsut shipped two huge obelisks down the Nile from Aswan to Karnak based on a fragmentary relief at Deir el-Bahari, c. 1500 BC*

fitted or constructed in an Egyptian dockyard, near Saqqara, where many of the workmen bore Semitic rather than Egyptian names.

Perhaps the most interesting of the papyri is that in which Wen-Amon, an official of the Temple of Amon at Karnak, describes his voyage to Byblos in order to obtain wood for building a ceremonial barge. The decline in Egyptian power by this time, around 1100 BC, is indicated by the misfortunes of the poor traveller who is robbed, insulted by the Prince of Byblos, and, finally, after being blown off course to Cyprus on his return voyage, threatened with death by the local populace.

We do not know what Wen-Amon's ship looked like, but Egyptian ships had by this time greatly changed in appearance. On a relief at Medinet Habu, commemorating Ramesses III's successful naval battle with the enigmatic Peoples of the Sea (1190 BC), the pharaoh's ships no longer have a lower yard on their sails, the rowers sit behind protective washboards, the masts are topped by crow's-nests from which men direct the archers, and the sails seem to be furled by means of brails. Most of the new features are seen also on the ships of the northern Sea Peoples, suggesting that Egyptians were now learning techniques from Aegean shipwrights, to whom they may earlier have taught the use of sails.

*The Aegean.* Minoan pottery continued to reach overseas ports during the first two centuries of the Late Bronze Age (1600–1400 BC), but even more of the pottery in Egypt and the Near East came from the Greek mainland; it might seem that Mycenaean Greeks were now the dominant Aegean seafarers. Pottery, however, is misleading as a clue to ancient trade patterns; return goods – perhaps including perishable grain, cloth, spices, and unworked metal and ivory – have left few traces to suggest the nationalities of the ships which carried them. Nevertheless, Minoan colonies in the Aegean islands and on the coast of Asia Minor attest a continuing maritime role for Crete. And it is precisely at this time that the

18

*18   Relief in the temple of Ramesses III at Medinet Habu, Thebes, commemorates the Pharaoh's victorious naval battle against invading 'Sea Peoples'. The low Egyptian ships, with lion-headed prows and protruding thwarts, are rowed. Ships of the invaders, with high stem and stern posts ending in duck heads, are without oars. The Peleset (Philistines in later days) wear feathered headdresses; the horned helmets are being worn by the Sherdern (who may have been Sardinians)*

land of Keftiu (almost certainly Crete) and even 'Keftiu ships' are most frequently mentioned in Egyptian texts.

After 1400 BC, and the destruction of Knossos, there can no longer be doubt of Mycenaean (Late Helladic) naval prominence. Mycenaean colonies appear throughout the Aegean islands and along the Asia Minor coast; trading posts are established as far east as Ras Shamra (Ugarit) and as far west as Scoglio del Tonno in Italy; and Mycenaean pottery is abundant from the Delta up the Nile, along the Syro-Palestinian coast, and in Sicily – never far from sites accessible to ships.

It is only later, however, from the final years of Mycenaean civilization, that we can learn anything at all about Mycenaean ships. Shortly before the destruction of the Palace of Nestor at Pylos (c. 1200 BC) a Mycenaean scribe details oarsmen 'to go to Pleuron'; were they part of a last defensive contingent? One tablet lists thirty men, possibly the crew of one ship.

A vase from the same region, but from the following century, shows a ship with many of the features that will 19 be common in the succeeding Geometric period (see chapter 2, p. 41): high vertical prow and high curving stern, latticed platforms fore and aft, steering oar with tiller, fence-like vertical lines along the side, and a slight protrusion of the keel which will become a fully-fledged ram in the later period; the fish ensign on the bow must trace its origin to the ensigns of Early Cycladic ships.

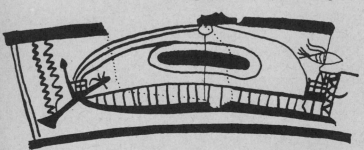

*19–21  Mycenaean ships painted on twelfth-century BC vases. Those from Pylos (19) and Asine (20) show elements which continue into the Iron Age. That from Skyros (21) has the duck head and mast top common to ships of the Sea Peoples*

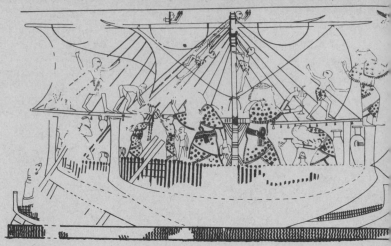

*22  A Syrian merchant fleet stops at an Egyptian port of the fourteenth century BC. Seven ships, one with a crow's-nest, are tied up, their cargoes being unloaded by porters. Two ships, on the left, have just arrived still under sail. Egyptian shopkeepers*

A ship on a contemporary vase painting from Asine 20 has a square sail seemingly made of small squares of fabric, similar to those of Geometric ships. If the ram-like protrusion at one end of the ship is, as I suspect, a steering oar, then the bow now shows the horn-like curvature also prominent in Geometric representations. The vertical lines may be oars, or crudely drawn 'fencing'.

Little can be learned from even cruder paintings and stone engravings from Greece, but a twelfth-century ship from Skyros, painted on a Late Helladic vase, is 21 strikingly like the ships of the Sea Peoples on the Medinet Habu relief.

Throughout the second millennium, anchors were of stone. Honor Frost has studied examples from Byblos, Mallia on Crete, and Malta: those for rocky bottoms are simply stones pierced to receive hawsers; others, usually flat, have additional holes for wooden stakes which catch in sand; and a third type, flat and roughly triangular, has a hawser hole at the top and two holes near the base for stakes. Two anchors of this last type, which could be used on a rocky or sandy sea bed, have been found recently on Cyprus. They probably date to 25 between 1400 and 1200 BC, and that they were for Cypriot ships is proved by the Cypro-Minoan sign carved into one of them.

*Syria*. For the Near East in the Late Bronze Age we turn from Mesopotamia to the Syrian coast. Here the Canaanites, later to be known as Phoenicians, played an active maritime role that has been strangely minimized by modern scholars. Aegean pottery from Egypt and the Syro-Palestinian coast has been adduced only for Minoan and Mycenaean shipping, and perishable trade goods have been ignored. Copper ingots, more valuable than pottery but not so lasting, have been regarded as typical Minoan trade goods because of an Egyptian tomb

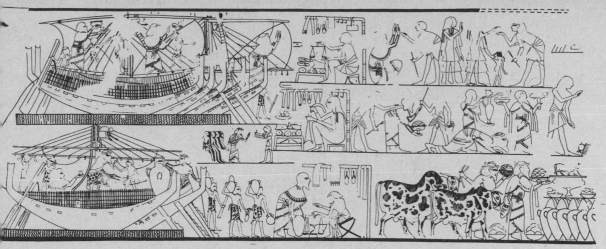

*inspect and weigh the assortment of merchandise, including jars of wine or oil, two humped bulls, metal vases, and bowls filled with precious material; they offer, in return, sandals, food, and textiles for sale*

28 painting of such ingots arriving from 'Keftiu'; a dozen such paintings, however, refer to the ingots as being Syrian, and in one case even brought to Egypt on a Syrian ship.

Canaanite ships, it seems, were large and numerous. A thirteenth-century BC letter requests the king of Ugarit (Ras Shamra) to equip one hundred and fifty ships, a contingent half again as large as that sent by the king of Mycenae to Troy. Another letter, written in the following century by the Hittite king to the king of Ugarit, asks for a ship and crew to transport 2,000 measures of grain – estimated to be 450 metric tons – in one or, at most, two trips.

22 The representation of the Syrian ship which brought copper to Egypt is too poorly preserved for detailed study, but we possess a good copy of the representation of several Canaanite ships in the fourteenth-century Tomb of Kenamon at Thebes. The hulls are short and tubby, forerunners of the 'round' merchant ships of later periods; stems and stern posts are high and vertical. Above the gunwale is a wicker fence to keep out the waves (cf. *Odyssey* V. 256–7), and below this thwarts protrude through the hull. The broad square sail is attached to upper and lower yards, as on Minoan and Egyptian ships, and held on a mast stepped amidships; the lower yard is supported by lifts.

Some authorities believe the ships in the Tomb of Kenamon are too inaccurately painted for serious study, being only poor copies of Egyptian models by an ignorant Egyptian artist. Surely, however, the tub-like hulls are closer to those of the Minoans and are more worthy of a seafaring tradition than the long Egyptian ships, requiring hogging trusses and bound ends, which evolved on the Nile. And the artist has correctly interpreted Syrian trade goods and clothing in the scene.

The route westward from Syria, known from a Ugaritic document, passed by Alasia (Cyprus?), western Cilicia and Lycia to Kaphtor (Crete?). A Canaanite ship, with Cypriot cargo, was following this route when it sank in 100 feet of water near Cape Gelidonya in Lycia. 23 Peter Throckmorton learned of the wreck from Turkish sponge divers and, after verifying its date and position, returned in 1960 with me to begin its excavation.

The ship had sunk onto a rocky bottom, and the lack of protective sand and mud had allowed shipworms to destroy almost all traces of the wooden hull. Only brushwood dunnage, under the cargo, and fragments 1 of thin planks held together with wooden dowels remained. Nevertheless, the distribution of cargo, still stacked as it had been on board, allowed an estimate of about 30 feet for the ship's length.

The cargo consisted mostly of the materials necessary for an itinerant smith: 34 ingots of nearly pure copper, averaging 20 kg. in weight, were found with bun- 29 shaped bronze ingots and rectangular tin ingots; wicker baskets held bits of broken ingots as well as hundreds of fragments of scrap bronze in the form of broken 32 tools. At one end of the site were two smooth stone hammer-heads of the type used for metalworking, and nearby were a whetstone and numerous stone polishers for putting final touches to finished products; a large, hard, flattish stone in the centre of the ship may have served as an anvil, and elsewhere was found a bronze swage, much like those used today for making pins and 31 rivets.

Most of this material was encased in rock-hard con- cretion which had formed on the cargo over the mil- lennia. Much of our time, therefore, was devoted to chiselling large lumps of this cargo-filled concretion, 30 weighing several hundred pounds apiece, free of the sea bed; these were raised to the surface either with cable and winch or, more safely, with air-filled lifting balloons. The positions of the lumps on the sea bed had been carefully plotted by triangulation, and the cargo could thus be reassembled accurately on land and cleaned. Sand pockets under and around the cargo were inspected with a metal detector and cleared with two air lifts, or suction hoses. As on a land excavation, each stage of the operation was recorded by drawings and photographs.

From their shapes and inscriptions, we know that the ingots and tools were made on Cyprus about 1200 BC, a date confirmed by a radiocarbon analysis of the brush-wood dunnage. The nationality of the ship was shown by the personal possessions of the men on board: a Syrian cylinder seal, five scarabs made on the Syro-Palestinian coast, stone mortars and hammers from the same region, and a clay lamp of Syro-Palestinian type. Several sets of haematite balance-pan weights contained the standards which would have allowed the merchant-man to trade in Egypt, Syria, Cyprus, Asia Minor, and Crete.

A fifteenth-century BC ingot carrier, following the same route, sank while crossing the Bay of Antalya between Cilicia and Lycia. Another, of the same date, lies in the sea near Cymae on Euboea. Ingots from both were salvaged by divers earlier in this century, and still other ingots have been netted near Knidos in Asia Minor. The eventual location and excavation of these and other Bronze Age wrecks, now contemplated, will one day allow us to know not only how ships of the period were constructed but, more importantly, who manned them.

*23 From the distribution of cargo on the Cape Gelidonya shipwreck the length of the missing hull could be deduced. Personal possessions and remains of food (olive stones) were all found at the east end, indicating living quarters near the stern*

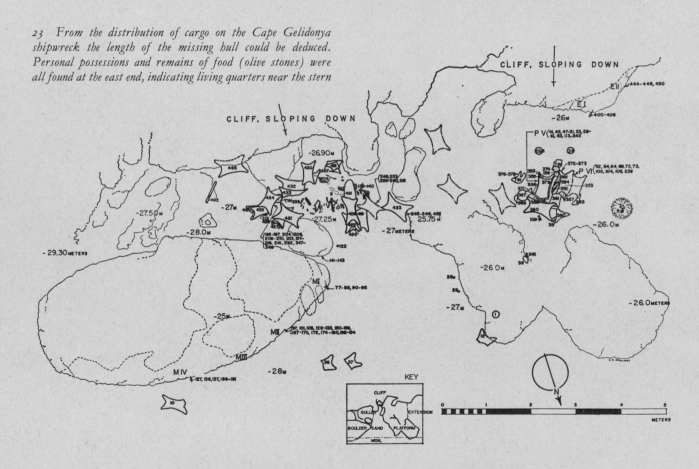

1 Odysseus's last task in building a boat was to 'spread over it a great deal of brushwood'. Its purpose was seldom understood by modern translators of Homer before the discovery of a ship which sank about the time of the Trojan War. Here an excavator from the University of Pennsylvania Museum cuts beneath the brushwood dunnage, with bark still preserved, which lined the hull of the Bronze Age ship found near Cape Gelidonya, Turkey. Most of the vessel had been destroyed by ship-worms, but fragmentary wooden members revealed that methods used in its construction were identical to those described by Homer: planks formed with an adze were fastened together by wooden pegs driven into holes bored to receive them. Cargo, implements, and personal possessions from the small merchant vessel are shown in illustrations 29 to 36.

24

3

4

2–5 The high swinging stem and stern of a clay model (2), a grave offering at Fara about 3000 BC, are characteristic of many Mesopotamian river boats of the fourth and third millennia. A model from Eridu, nearly a thousand years older, shows a second tradition with level gunwales (3); it resembles a model sailing vessel from *c.* 3500 at the same site.

By contrast, boats painted on Egyptian vases in the fourth millennium were low, sickle-shaped craft with a pair of cabins, numerous paddles, a curving branch at the bows, a mooring line just below, and a tall pole for an ensign. Mast and sail are rare but appear in at least one instance. Here an armed warrior stands on the forward cabin (4).

Both the high-ended Mesopotamian type and the lower Nilotic craft are shown in our earliest scene of naval warfare. Carved on an ivory knife handle (5) said to come from Gebel el-Arak, it is from the same Gerzean period as the vase (4).

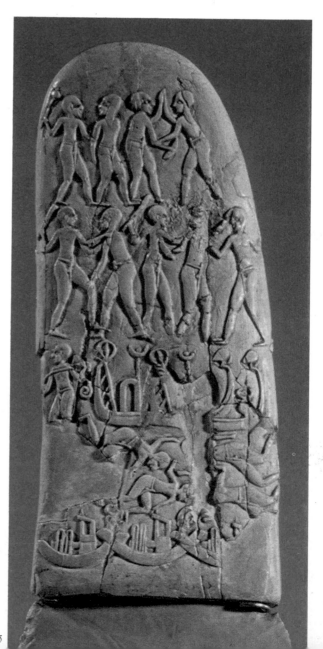

5

6–7   The two distinctive boat types of the naval battle on the Gebel el-Arak knife (5), which may be intended to represent an invasion of the Nile Valley by foreigners, appear together again at Hierakonpolis in Upper Egypt (6). A fleet of low, crescent-shaped Nile boats, similar except for an absence of paddles to those depicted on Gerzean vases (4), was painted on the plastered mud-brick walls of a tomb dating to the same period. Sailing among them is a boat with high straight stem, its darker colour obviously intended to emphasize its individuality. Whether or not this 'foreign vessel' represents an enemy is not certain, but this may well be the case since warriors are shown engaged in combat elsewhere in the frieze.

In the cemetery at El-Gebelein, not far downstream from Hierakonpolis, was found a tattered piece of linen with two more predynastic Nile boats painted on it (7). In this case the helmsmen and paddlers, all facing forward, are clearly shown, as are the usual double cabins situated amidships.

8–11

12–14

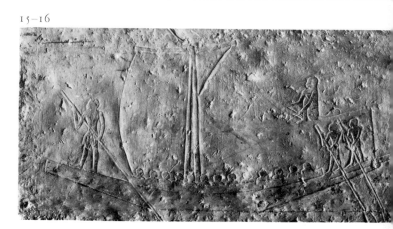

15–16

17–18

8–11 Two cylinder seal engravings, separated by about a thousand years, indicate the continuity of boats with high stem and stern in Mesopotamia. The earlier craft (8), from the Uruk period at the end of the fourth millennium, is steered by a kneeling helmsman, while a lookout with forked punting pole stands at the bows. The later Akkadian seal (9) presents the fanciful scene of a deity steering an anthropomorphic boat whose stem is a human leg. Boats of the distant Indus in the third millennium BC were sometimes similar to those of Mesopotamia, with high ends, but an Harappan terra-cotta amulet from Mohenjo-Daro (10) shows that a low, crescent-shaped form existed there as well. Contemporaneous sea-going vessels in the Aegean were characterized by high, raking stems, numerous oars or paddles, and straight 'fixed rudders', as seen inscribed on Early Cycladic pottery (11).

12–14 Third-millennium boat models were constructed in a variety of materials: a silver model from Ur in Mesopotamia, with paddles and forked punting pole (12); a lead model of an Early Cycladic boat, with typical high stem (13); and an Early Minoan clay model, with what may be two pairs of thole pins, from Mochlos on Crete (14).

15–16 'Give attention to the rope! The wind is behind thee again,' shouts the captain to a sailor handling the braces from the roof of a ship carved in the offering chamber of the tomb of Ka-pu-re (15). Both this ship and those from the pyramid of Sahu-re (16), returning to Egypt with Syrian prisoners, show the typical bipod mast used to support a tall, narrow sail in third-millennium Egypt; the rope 'hogging truss' on Sahu-re's ship is a feature which will continue until at least 1200 BC (another example appears in illustration 24).

17–18 The tomb of Meket-re, who was buried at Thebes about 2000 BC, contained a large number of boat models. Two papyrus-bundle skiffs drag a trawl net in a scene which has been incorrectly restored, with paddlers and net facing the wrong directions (17). One of the deceased's boats sails upstream against the Nile (18); other models of the same boat in the tomb show it being paddled in the opposite direction, with its mast unstepped.

19

20

19–20 Meket-re's fishing and fowling boat is paddled downstream against the prevailing wind, its mast un-stepped (19). The steering oar passes over the side of the boat, near the stern, and is lashed to a rudder post rather than rotating in a notch on top of the stern post, as on his travelling boat (18). A rug over a wicker frame provides shelter astern.

As long timbers were not to be found in the Nile Valley, Egyptian boats were characteristically built up with numerous small planks joined end to end and edge to edge. A fishing boat painted in the tomb chapel of the sculptor Ipuy during the thirteenth century BC was clearly made in this way (20).

21–22 Scenes carved in the Fifth Dynasty tomb of Ti represent stages in wooden boat construction, from trimming tree trunks and sawing planks to the place-ment of the final hull timbers. Here (21) boatwrights plane and trim with adzes, saw, and cut mortises with wooden-handled chisels. Compare the actual boat in illustration 27.

The ancient tradition of a strong Minoan navy around Bronze Age Crete is substantiated by numerous ship representations on seals. Three examples (22) from between 1600 and 1400 BC exhibit typical features: oars, masts with stays, forked 'figureheads', and structures variously identified as sails, cabins, or deck cargo.

21

22

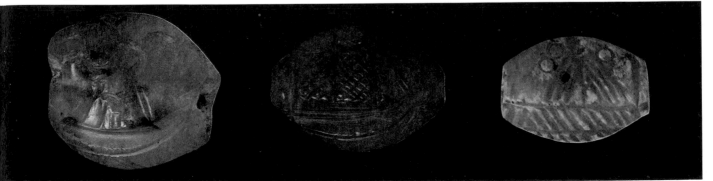

23 An Egyptian boatwright pulls hard on the binding at one end of a papyrus-bundle boat (twentieth
century BC).

24 A bas relief of Queen Hatshepsut's expedition to
Punt reveals that by 1500 BC the Egyptian sail had
become broader than it was high and had acquired a
standard lower yard since the time of the Old Kingdom
(see 15, 16). A rope truss still runs the length of each ship,
to prevent the bow and stern sections from sagging.

23

25 A Late Bronze Age anchor from Cyprus, pierced
to take a hawser and two stakes to dig into the sea bed.

26 A Nile boat's papyrus log, of 1239 BC, preserves
a daily tally of crew members and bread rations.

25

26

27 Two Nile boats were buried in the sand near the pyramid of Sesostris III (1878–1842 BC) at Dashur. Their planks were held together with wooden pegs, mortise-and-tenon joints, and dovetailed clamps.

27

29

28–30 More than a dozen Egyptian tomb paintings, of between 1500 and 1200 BC, depict copper ingots brought as tribute or merchandise to the Land of the Nile. They are usually, as in the fifteenth-century tomb of Rekh-mi-re (28), associated with Syria, in one case carried from a Syrian ship. Actual ingots of this type, however, excavated in Late Bronze Age sites throughout the Aegean, were mostly cast on Cyprus from native ores.

Still stacked as they had been in the hold of the ship which sank thirty-two centuries ago near Cape Gelidonya, Turkey, were 34 copper ingots of similar form. Compacted in large masses by layers of marine concretion, groups of the ingots were chiseled and prised free from the sea bed (30) after their positions had been recorded *in situ*. By fitting together the amorphous lumps on land and removing the concretion, it was possible to ascertain exactly how the ingots had been stowed in the ship (29); traces of matting indicate that they had been wrapped to avoid shifting. Tin ingots were also found.

31

31–32 With the raw metals for bronze-working on the Cape Gelidonya wreck (29–30) were baskets of scrap metal to be re-melted, unworked castings, and tools ready for use (32); the socket of the unfinished billhook would have been shaped by being hammered in the end of the bronze swage (31). The swage, stone hammers, and whetstones and polishers for sharpening finished implements, suggest the presence of a tinker on board the metal-carrying ship.

32

33–35

33–36 A merchant's cylinder seal (33), a number of Syro-Palestinian scarabs (34 and 35), and a lamp from the same region, confirm the evidence of Egyptian tomb paintings that copper was sometimes traded by Syrian, or Canaanite, ships. Sixty stone balance-pan weights (36) formed various sets of *shekels*, *neṣefs*, and *qedets* – Near Eastern weight standards found also in Cyprus and Crete during the Late Bronze Age.

36

# 2

# Greek, Etruscan and Phoenician ships and shipping

KEITH DeVRIES
MICHAEL L. KATZEV

# Greek, Etruscan and Phoenician ships and shipping

The period between the destruction of the Late Bronze Age states and the founding of the Hellenistic kingdoms saw extensive maritime activity in the Mediterranean. Once the countries at the eastern end of the Mediterranean had recovered from the upheavals that occurred around the end of the second millennium BC, urban civilization, with all the trade and need for communications that it involves, began spreading westward into the central and western Mediterranean. And as the distances over which mariners could now range increased, an unusually heavy reliance on seafaring alone seems to have developed with only a minimal use made of land travel and trade.

The principal seafaring peoples of the time were the Phoenicians, Greeks, and Etruscans, and it is to them that particular attention should be paid, though a number of minor peoples who also took to the sea should not be wholly ignored.

*1 Ropes, probably nautical, were found at ancient Ezion-Geber, once the port for King Solomon's merchant fleet*

The evidence for the seafaring of the period has until recently consisted mainly of ancient literary and historical references (luckily quite numerous for the Greeks) and of ship representations on extant ancient objects. In recent times, however, underwater excavations have begun to furnish some new and more direct data. A number of cargoes have been at least partially recovered, and in two instances parts of the ship and some of its equipment have been found as well. More than half the hull is preserved of a fourth-century ship excavated off Kyrenia, Cyprus; while a fifth-century wreck excavated at the Straits of Messina is much more fragmentary, the ship parts found are none the less valuable, and not least because of their earlier date.

1, 28, *18, 1*
24, 25

With this added source of information to corroborate the written and representational evidence, it is possible to present a clearer picture of the maritime activities, both peaceful and military, that were characteristic of the period and also of the kinds of ships that were involved, the way they were constructed, and the nature of their fittings.

## Maritime Activities

*Trade and colonization.* The first important sea-trading venture known from the period took place outside of the Mediterranean. The joint enterprise of the Hebrew King Solomon (ruled *c.* 965–925 BC) and the Phoenician ruler Hiram of Tyre caused the port of Ezion-Geber (or Elath) on the Gulf of Aqaba to be developed as a base for trade on the Red Sea, a trade that brought the famous cargoes of gold, jewels, and precious woods described in the Old Testament. The port then came to be controlled for a time solely by the Hebrews until it finally passed in the eighth century into the hands of the people living in the area, the Edomites.

The excavations under the late Nelson Glueck at this site in 1938–40 found evidence of maritime activities, but only for the later period, in levels dating from the eighth century to the fourth century BC. The excavators uncovered what seem to be the remains of stores of material used in ship construction. Besides a great quantity of large copper and iron nails and an assortment of ropes, they found chunks of pitch, used for caulking vessels in both the Levant and Greece.

*1*

In the Mediterranean itself, activity was first resumed in the eastern regions. Phoenicians were colonizing in Cyprus by the end of the ninth century BC, and they had re-established trade relations with the island long before. Greek merchants also entered the eastern Mediterranean quite early in the period: about 800 BC they founded a commercial emporium at what is now Al Mina on the north Syrian coast, just to the east of Cyprus. Greeks must inevitably have come into close contact with Phoenician merchants in the Levantine ports – a relationship to which a story in Homer of a Greek and a Phoenician entering into trade partnership lends support. Perhaps it was here that the adoption of the Phoenician alphabet by the Greeks took place. And it may be that the mariners on meeting exchanged information about the central and western Mediterranean – the expansion westward of both peoples seems to begin at about the same time, in the middle of the eighth century BC.

In this westward movement the Phoenicians were the more audacious; they were already settled in Spain by the beginning of the seventh century when the Greeks had advanced no farther than Sicily. And by c. 600 BC when the Greeks were just beginning to venture a short distance outside the Straits of Gibraltar on commercial voyages, the Phoenicians founded a small trading colony at modern Mogador (Essaouira) about 600 miles south of Gibraltar on the Atlantic coast of Morocco.

It is not particularly surprising that the Phoenicians should have surpassed the Greeks in reaching distant places for trade and colonization. There is much evidence that until the fifth century they were the better sailors. It was to the Phoenicians, for example, that Pharaoh Necho of Egypt entrusted the alleged circumnavigation of Africa around 600 BC, while he found the Greeks better fitted to be mercenary soldiers.

A certain amount of evidence suggests that Phoenician settlements were undertaken mainly for commercial reasons, while the Greeks as a whole were most interested in finding new, good agricultural lands. Whatever the original motives for settling a colony, however, its foundation would inevitably entail trade between it and both the homeland and the neighbouring regions. The wealth of Greek and Phoenician objects found around the Mediterranean attests the volume of commerce that did develop.

Eventually, the Etruscans came to rank with the Greeks and Phoenicians as prominent seafarers and traders. Under the stimulation of near-by Greek and Phoenician settlement, a group of Etruscans living in central Italy soon set about establishing a developed civilization. Their ships had probably long plied the Italian coast, but it is during the last decades of the seventh century BC and first half of the sixth that there is evidence for a widespread Etruscan seaborne commerce. At this particular time Etruscan pottery is found quite extensively in a belt running across the width of the Mediterranean from North Africa to Sicily and southern France. While scantier further to the east, it occurs at several sites in the Aegean area and has even been found at a Greek settlement on the Black Sea.

That much of this pottery may have travelled in Etruscan hulls is suggested by the abundance of Etruscan ship representations from this period. More direct evidence is presented by the cargo of a pillaged wreck excavated in the 1950s off Cap d'Antibes in southern France by G. Pruvot and V. Romanovsky. All the pottery recovered was Etruscan, and it is a lamp of western Phoenician type alone that introduces a slight element of doubt as to whether the ship was Etruscan. The pottery dates to the first quarter of the sixth century, thus within the period that seems to mark the high point of Etruscan commerce.

*Cargoes.* The Cap d'Antibes wreck is important because it not only appears to confirm an extensive Etruscan trade but provides, along with four other commercial cargoes that have been recovered, valuable clues to the mechanics of Mediterranean sea trade. These add considerably to what we can learn from literary sources. The Cap d'Antibes ship seems to have been heavily stocked with amphoras; about 150, comprising two different types, were raised from the sea bed. These surely were traded for their contents. Since, however, some Etruscan fine pottery of the same type as that encountered on land sites in southern France was also found, there was apparently a secondary, ceramic cargo on board as well.

On the Kyrenia merchant ship of the late fourth century (discussed below), the finds indicate a considerable diversity of cargo; represented are stone grinding mills, almonds, and a large number of amphoras, the majority assumed to have contained wine but with some divergent types perhaps once holding foodstuffs. (Similar mixtures of pottery and grinding stones continued into the late Byzantine period, as evidenced by a shipwreck at Pelagos in the Northern Sporades.)

The less completely recovered cargo of the fifth-century ship in the Straits of Messina likewise shows much variety. While the main load consisted of amphoras (of at least nine types), the ship was also carrying a minimum of two life-sized bronze statues as well as lead ingots and raw silver, some still in nugget form.

Taken all together, the Kyrenia, Messina, and Cap d'Antibes wrecks indicate either that several, independent merchants may have travelled in a single ship or, if there was just one trader (or more than one in partnership) on each of these two vessels, that merchants must have dealt in varied cargoes. That the latter could sometimes be the case is shown by a cargo cited in a fourth-century BC Athenian lawsuit in which two partners had accumulated one or two jars full of wool, a dozen pots of salted fish and a few bundles of goat hide along with their main load of wine.

It seems safe to regard two other deposits from the period as cargoes, though in neither case was any trace

*7, 8*

*27, 28,*

*25*

*24*

of a ship found. Both comprise metal objects, and both, if they really were on ships, were probably carried by peoples other than Phoenicians, Greeks, or Etruscans. The first was dredged up from a depth of 30 feet below the bed of the estuary of the River Huelva northwest of Gibraltar, which definitely suggests that it was part of the cargo of a sunken ship.

All objects recovered are of bronze. Weapons predominate, but there are also articles of personal adornment, helmets, and possibly fragments of bronze vessels. The latest objects date the hoard to the seventh century BC, but the many earlier objects it contained had at first led scholars to overestimate its age appreciably. The most probable reason for the inclusion of out-dated objects in the consignment was their value as bronze that could be melted down and reworked. The finds, which point to connections with Sardinia and Sicily on the one hand and the Atlantic regions on the other, confirm an important two-way metal trade stretching from the western Mediterranean through the Straits of Gibraltar and up along the Atlantic coast to Britain.

The other metal deposit, recovered by A. Bouscaras during excavations initiated in 1964, was found some 550 yards off Rochelongues near Agde in southern France and was lying at a sea depth of 20–26 feet. Again, the most likely explanation is that the objects were part of a ship's cargo. Dating to the sixth century, a hundred years or so later than the Huelva deposit, the finds give a clearer idea of the probable nature of what we abstractly term 'metal trade'. Like the Bronze Age Cape Gelidonya 22, 23 ship (chapter 1, pp. 23–24), the presumed Rochelongues vessel is likely to have had on board a tinker who was as willing to manufacture a new object on the spot as to trade already finished articles. A large number of copper ingots (800 kg. have been recovered) as well as tin ingots will have provided the tinker with the two necessary ingredients for making new bronze. More simply, he could just melt down scrap bronze objects, which were as well represented among the finds here as they were at Gelidonya and Huelva. Hammers and burins found on the site can be interpreted as his tools rather than trade items in their own right.

The hoard also contained large quantities of metal objects in good condition, ranging from belt buckles and decorative miniature chains to razors and arrowheads; these represented articles in current use and were undoubtedly being traded in the form they took. Order was apparently introduced into this varied assortment by the articles being divided up by types and stored separately.

We learn from literary sources that human cargoes were conveyed on ordinary merchant ships for journeys of any appreciable length, whereas for short, ferrying trips, small boats indistinguishable from fishing boats seem to have been the chief conveyers.

*Sailing speed.* Ancient literature contains few references to the speed of merchant and other ships under sail, and these are vague by modern standards. Thucydides, for example, comments that the trip around Sicily takes 'not much less than eight days' for a merchantman, and Herodotus says that ships generally cover 70,000 fathoms 'in a long day'. Such indications have allowed scholars to calculate a sailing speed under favourable conditions of about 4–6 knots for this period, as well as for later antiquity.

*Naval warfare.* The first sea battles, as portrayed in the first millennium BC, appear to have differed little from 3, 9 the encounter of the Egyptians and the Sea Peoples at the end of the Bronze Age (chapter 1, fig. 18). They seem little more than land battles staged at sea: warriors on opposing ships are missiles against each other, and one gets the impression of an attempt to board and occupy the enemy decks. There is, however, one important new feature of the Mediterranean ships that will eventually change naval warfare radically and that is the ram – the deadly projection at the bow that can pierce the 6–8 hull of an enemy ship and disable it. It looks to be an adaptation as offensive armament of the harmless timber that had continued the line of the keel beyond the stem of the Bronze Age Aegean ships.

With the ram, the ship itself became a weapon. The new possibilities of warfare that this opened up were perhaps not wholly realized until the sixth century BC, and they were most fully exploited during the fifth (well before a partial reversion to older ways that set in with the Hellenistic era). Fighting men came to have relatively little importance and on Greek ships, at any rate, were kept down to a minimum, as the main attention was now devoted to the contests, the ramming duels, between the ships themselves. The adroit manoeuvres that now came to be accepted practice – for example, rowing a line of ships quickly between the individual vessels in the opposing enemy line and following this by a rapid wheeling about and a ramming of the unprotected enemy sterns – demonstrate the impressive skill in rowing and steering acquired by the crews of the Classical age.

Historically, there are certain broad patterns discernible in the naval rivalries. Greek and Phoenician fleets found themselves in opposition time after time in the sixth and fifth centuries. In the colonial area of the central and western Mediterranean, the western Phoenicians (generally known as Punics) allied themselves with the Etruscans against the Greeks in a prolonged struggle for the domination of the seas. In the eastern Mediterranean, including the Aegean area, Greeks and Phoenicians likewise fought, but the Phoenicians were here sailing, as a subject people, in the service of the Persian empire. In both zones, the Greek forces emerged as decidedly the superior during the first half of the fifth century. Among the Greeks themselves, the most notable achievements were made by the Athenian navy. Supreme at sea in the fifth century, it was still a force to be reckoned with during the fourth.

*2   This vase painting of* c. *660 BC may depict Greek colonizers fighting peoples already established in the central Mediterranean. The left-hand ship is a normal Greek galley, the deep hull and angled ram of the other suggest an Etruscan ship*

## Ship Types

The sharpest contrasts between ship types are not between those of one area and another but between two classes of vessels: merchant ships and warships. In the case of merchant ships, what was wanted was a strong hull with plenty of space for the storage of goods; for the warships, the builders were simply after speed and manoeuvrability. The merchant ships accordingly tended to be broad and heavy, the warships slim and light; this, in turn, called for two distinct skills of seamanship. In their most extreme, tublike form, merchant ships had to rely almost exclusively on the sail and were rowed, ineffectively, only when absolutely necessary. Aristotle likened this type of merchantman being put under oars to a large insect with small, weak wings, trying to fly. Warships, too, probably travelled under sail in normal circumstances, but it was when they were rowed, most particularly in battle, that they showed their full potential. It was rowing alone that provided the precision needed in tactical manoeuvres and that gave the ships controlled speed and power.

Then, too, the lighter wood (fir) used in constructing warships was highly subject to rot, and it was therefore necessary to haul the ships up out of the water whenever they were in port for any length of time. In earlier times they were simply beached; but later, special buildings were constructed in the home ports to house them (chapter 4, pp. 90–92). The merchant ships, on the other hand, with their more durable timbers of pine, could be left in the water, either at anchor or brought up alongside quays. This led to still another distinction: since the merchantmen were not so subject as the warships to repeated hauling, they did not require such sturdy keels.

Conditions on board provided a contrast, too, because of the differences in dimensions. Merchant ships were roomy enough to take passengers as well as a profitable cargo, but conditions aboard the slim warships were extremely cramped. In Greek literature, the complaints of the galley rower are already recorded by Homer. The fifth-century comedy writer Aristophanes drew inspiration for a vivid joke or two from the close quarters aboard, and the fourth-century author Xenophon considered it highly exemplary that the men in a warship were able to keep order and not be constantly hindering each other's movements. It was difficult for the crew to find room to eat or sleep on board, and the possibility of having meals on the ship was even further limited by the lack of space for carrying provisions. Consequently the warships put in to shore at night and at the time of the midday meal. This meant in turn that the ships had to travel near land as much as possible.

In the more spacious cargo ships, it ought to have been possible for the ordinary routines of life to have been carried on in some comfort. From Greek literature, one gets the impression that it was not uncommon for the vessels to travel day and night and to undertake voyages across the open sea. A speech from a lawsuit, for example, tells of a direct sailing planned from Syracuse to the Piraeus; the ship was two or three days out from land when the voyage was interrupted by a contrived accident. On the Kyrenia ship, though, the absence of cooking equipment has suggested to the excavator, Michael Katzev, that the crew put into land at meal times (below, p. 50), and thus this merchant ship, at least, would have hugged land as tightly as any war galley.

*Warships.* From quite early in the period, warships nearly everywhere show the same essential features, many of which seem to derive directly and indirectly from late Mycenaean ships. This inheritance is one that, naturally, is most apparent in the Aegean. Here representations of ships began to appear in quantity in the eighth century BC, especially as painted on vases of the current Geometric style. Unfortunately, the degree of stylization gives rise to many ambiguities.

A basic ship type can be recognized through many artistic variants. Conspicuous are latticed fore and after platforms between which is a lower, more open railed   *3, 3, 4*

3  A ship with its sail up and mast firmly stepped appears on a Greek Geometric vase of c. 700 BC. The checkerboard pattern on the sail hints at individual pieces of cloth being sewn together to make up the broad expanse

4  This Greek vase painting of c. 750 BC shows rowers propelling a galley. The abstract circular ornament at the prow will become an eye, or oculus, on later Greek ships

5  The warship depicted on a Greek ivory plaque of c. 600 BC is much the same type as that of fig. 4, but the more realistic conventions allow for a more accurate representation, especially of the position of the rowers

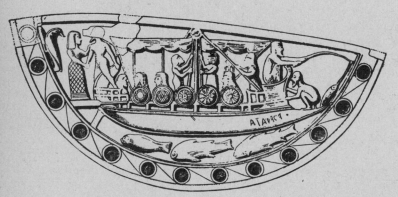

area – features that had appeared in representations from the end of the Greek Bronze Age (chapter 1, fig. 19). As mentioned above, the ram jutting out from the concave prow seems likely to be an extension for military purpose of the small projecting timber visible on the Bronze Age ships. The hornlike ornament often to be seen at the prow is another legacy from the Bronze Age, and the inward-curving stern, while not appearing on the particular late Mycenaean representations that otherwise seem so close, was a common enough feature on second-millennium Aegean ships (chapter 1, p. 22). The painted, usually circular ornament at the prow is a decorative device found in several variations; even it *3, 4* was anticipated in the Bronze Age. The thin projections beyond the stem and stern probably are somewhat misrepresented ends of wales.

Difficulties in interpretation come when one tries to understand the position of the rowers and of the fighting men. The most satisfactory solution is to interpret these arrangements in the light of more realistic representations by Greeks in the two centuries that followed and *6, 5* of a contemporary ship depiction from the Levant. Accordingly, we must visualize a raised platform for the fighting men running down the centre of the ship about at the level of the waist rail. The rail and central platform are often, understandably, conflated by the Geometric artist with the result that he paints a single thick rail. *4* The oars pass over the gunwale, and the rowers' bodies would have been partly visible above it behind the framework of posts and rail. The vase painters, in an attempt to show more of a complete picture of the rowers, sometimes lift them up to the height of the rail and platform.

A few representations, each to some extent ambiguous, seem to indicate that there were ships rowed on two levels, the lower-level oars issuing through ports in the *4 ,* side of the hull. Certainly, contemporary Phoenician *14* ships and later Greek ones could be rowed in just that manner.

Basically, this type of vessel continued to be the standard Greek warship up to the time of the introduction of the trireme in the late sixth century, but certain changes from the eighth to the sixth century can be traced. The after platform, the helmsman's station, becomes much less prominent; sometimes it completely *10* disappears from the representations, and in these cases it is likely that the helmsman has nothing more than a *2* thwart to sit on. The fore platform persists but is solidly *cf. 11* enclosed.

The curves of the prow ornament and of the stern extension become less pronounced by the end of the seventh century BC. In the sixth century the prow ornament loses its hornlike form and becomes a vertical post, while the stern extension splits into several timbers, which are sometimes carved to end in birds' heads. The painted circular device at the prow becomes an eye, and continuing from this, the Greeks eventually work the whole ram into the form of a boar's head.

There is no doubt that by the sixth century there were Greek biremes, that is, ships rowed on two levels. Entanglement of the oars was avoided by staggering the two banks of rowers so that no oarsman was directly above another.

The usual term for the Greek pre-trireme warship was *pentekonter*, or 'fifty rowed', and obviously referred to the number of oarsmen. When the ships designated by ancient sources as 'pentekonters' were biremes, as some must have been, the count of fifty will have included only the men on one bank.

The Levantine warships are close to the Greek and closest of all is the ship on the relief already cited. It was found at the North Syrian site of Karatepe (in modern Turkey), which is, significantly, not far from the early Greek commercial settlement at Al Mina. Dating from about 700 BC, the ship shares with the Greek galleys of the time the general form of a long drawn-out curve, a form imparted by the inward-arching stern and the projecting ram. More specifically, there are close resemblances in the latticed fore and after platforms and in lower central platform.

A correspondence between Greek and Near Eastern ships of the first millennium can be seen again in the fragmentary eighth-century painting of a sea battle from the Assyrian palace at Til Barsib. The bow of the ship, still visible on the painting, was fitted with a ram; the type of painted circular ornament that appears so often in the contemporary depictions on Greek vases seems to be absent. The Assyrians themselves were no sailors, and the ship is likely to be Phoenician.

A better look at Phoenician warships is afforded by a relief of about 700 BC found in the Assyrian palace at Nineveh. Again the basic line of the warships, with the inward-curving stern and the ram, is much like that of the Greek and Karatepe vessels. There is a striking difference, though, in the very high deck which extends across the full width of the ship and incorporates into one the fore, after, and central platforms of the Greek and North Syrian ships. The Phoenician ships are biremes, and just as on the sixth-century Greek representations, the oars are staggered.

Etruscan ships conform in many ways to the Mediterranean norms, while exhibiting some pronounced variations. Fore and after platforms appear on the earliest known Etruscan representation, incised on a vase dating to about 675 BC; other familiar elements, a hornlike prow ornament and an inward-curving stern, are also recognizable. At variance, however, with the usual practice elsewhere is the treatment of the ram. Instead of continuing the line of the keel, it is angled to it. A similar sort of positioning is evident on a vase painting of nearly 100 years later. The two portrayals are consistent also, in spite of the differing artistic conventions, in showing a deep, rounded hull. Clearly a heavy type of ship, it is in sharp contrast to the light and easily manoeuvrable vessel that already was preferred for warfare farther to the east.

*6  The after platform, the old position for the helmsman, has disappeared on a ship of Greek type incised onto a fourth-century metal vessel of Latin or Etruscan workmanship. The artist has been confused by the conventions for more elaborate ships with high, closed decks (cf. fig. 9).*

*7  An early version of an Etruscan ship as incised onto a vase from the first half of the seventh century BC*

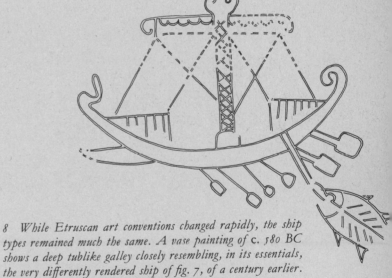

*8  While Etruscan art conventions changed rapidly, the ship types remained much the same. A vase painting of c. 580 BC shows a deep tublike galley closely resembling, in its essentials, the very differently rendered ship of fig. 7, of a century earlier.*

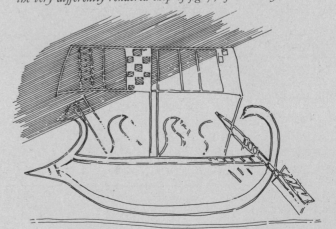

A vessel shown on a seventh-century vase, probably made and painted in one of the Greek colonies in Italy or Sicily, would seem to indicate how Etruscan ships appeared to Western Greeks. The vase painting shows *2* a battle between an obviously Greek ship and one that has the features, impressionistically exaggerated, of an Etruscan vessel – the great hulking mass and the angled ram.

In the fifth and fourth centuries BC, when skill at naval warfare became so highly developed, the standard ship was the trireme. It probably first appeared in the Medi- *9* terranean in the late sixth century. Already during the invasion of mainland Greece by the Persian king Xerxes in 480, it was the only kind of ship that counted in both Greek and Persian fleets (the latter being composed of, among others, subject Greeks and Phoenicians); soon afterwards, at least in the eastern Mediterranean and the Aegean, the trireme was practically the sole warship type in use. It was not until the second half of the fourth century that it began to be superseded.

Opinions still differ as to the exact form of the trireme, but some recent, thorough-going studies have securely established the most basic points. It was rowed on three levels; for the exact arrangement of these levels, we are, *5* as always, best informed about Greek vessels. It needed more than a simple adaptation from the old two-level ships by increasing the height of the hull until the new, third, bank was as high again as the second was above the lowest. If this had been done, rowers of the third bank would have had to work with oars so long as to be unwieldy. It seems that the Greeks did raise the free-board to some extent, as the oars of the middle bank (the old upper bank) issued now out of ports, but the most important change was the extension of a light outrigger construction beyond the sides of the hull, through which passed the third bank of oars. In this way the naval architects were able to set the uppermost rowers further outboard – though undoubtedly not in the outrigger *10* itself – and thus close enough to the water to avoid their oars having to exceed in length those of the lower banks. The topmost men did, however, have the most difficult stroke, since they rowed at the sharpest angle to the water. Thucydides mentions one occasion on which they were given extra pay, presumably to compensate for their added exertion. As on the two-banked ships, entanglement of the oars was avoided by a general staggering of oars. The rower in each bank sat slightly forward of the man below him; the rowers were thus disposed in oblique, not vertical lines.

In its general appearance a Greek trireme is more difficult to visualize than the earlier galleys, since not a single certain representation of a trireme shown in its entirety survives. Many of the more conspicuous features, however, can be determined from a few partial depictions and from written sources. The split timbers on the stern can still end in birds' heads or can even be decorated now with carved human heads. The post at the bow, which had initially curved inwards and then

*9  Painting of a Greek trireme of* c. 410 BC *showing two rows of oarports. The top oars would pass over the gunwale*

*10  The most satisfactory reconstruction of the rowing system of a trireme is by the English scholar J. S. Morrison*

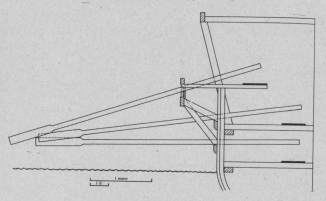

become straight in the sixth century BC, now continues its evolution and turns outward. The ram, unlike the stern, loses its ornamentation and is no longer given the appearance of a boar's head. The eye, though, continues to appear on the bow. On the Athenian triremes it was not painted but took the form of a separate attachment, and several handsome marble examples were found during the nineteenth century in the Piraeus. Above the ram the wales project in the traditional manner and may have been supplemented by other timbers. One reason for the attention given to the projections is that they may have helped to cushion the stem against the full impact of a ramming. There is evidence, too, to suggest that a subsidiary ram was fitted onto one of the upper timbers.

From literary sources we know that the deck was extended across the full width of the Athenian trireme in the second quarter of the fifth century BC. Previously there had been only a partial deck, probably much like the standard midship fighting platform to be seen or deduced on Greek galleys from the eighth to the sixth century. The Greeks to the east seem to have adopted the full deck somewhat earlier, at a time when they were under Persian domination.

Athenian inscriptions, among other evidence, show that the triremes carried an imposing number of men. The rowers numbered 170, with one man to an oar, and in addition there were on board 30 officers, specialized crew members, and marines. The oarsmen were divided up into three ranks, which correspond to the three levels on which the ships were rowed, the men on the lowest bank being termed in our sources the *thalamioi*, the middle the *zygitoi*, and the topmost the *thranitai*. The *thranitai* seem to have had the most prestige, and although, as mentioned above, they had the most difficult stroke they may have enjoyed the most tolerable conditions; they were at least assured of light and air. Each oarsman, we learn, was issued his particular oar, along with a seat cushion and a strap for securing the oar to the thole-pin.

As for the Phoenician triremes, one may well assume that they were not much different from the Greek. Indeed, it is altogether possible that as the most nautically proficient people in the Mediterranean in the sixth century BC, the Phoenicians were the first to develop the trireme and that the Greeks just copied and adapted their solutions. It is significant that a model of a Levantine merchantman from Cyprus, dating probably from the time when the design of the trireme was being worked out or from only slightly later, has an outrigger extending beyond the gunwale. Whether its real-life counterpart be taken as a prototype or a reflection of the trireme outrigger, it is clear that this structural feature was to be found on eastern Mediterranean vessels and on merchant ships as well as galleys.

It may be a Phoenician trireme, as the most important class of ship in the Persian fleet, that is represented on a number of seal impressions found in the palace of the Persian kings at Persepolis. Certainly Phoenician are the ships depicted on coins of the Phoenician cities dating to the fifth and early fourth centuries, though again, it is no more than a probability that the vessels are triremes. The seal and coin representations are too small to give much detail, but they correspond in showing most commonly a relatively low freeboard, a feature, which, if the ships really are triremes, suggests that the third bank was accommodated by an outrigger construction rather than by the upward building of the hull.

There is literary evidence that the Phoenician triremes, in the manner of the East Greek ships but in contrast to the Athenian, had full decks at the time of the Persian invasion of mainland Greece. Probably such a deck was traditional for the Phoenicians, since it can be seen on their eighth-century biremes.

The Phoenicians, like the Greeks, had a taste for ornamenting their ships with lively bits of art. One of the stern timbers of the Persepolis ship appears to end in a bird's head, just as on Greek vessels. More uniquely, the ships on Phoenician coins bear ornaments of animal protomes or full-figure warriors in the bow.

The Etruscans, in contrast to the other maritime peoples, seem not to have adopted the trireme to any large extent, if at all. Thucydides reports that they sent two ships to help the Athenians in the siege of Syracuse in 414 BC, but that these were pentekonters, the old 'fifties', ships that must have struck the Greeks as utterly out-dated. Moreover, a late fifth-century Etruscan grave relief shows a warship which has just one bank of oars

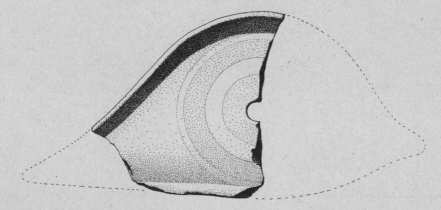

11 *A fragmentary marble eye, from Piraeus, possibly from the early fifth century BC, that must once have decorated a ship's prow. Eyes, a common feature on Greek ships, were probably most often painted onto the timbers*

12 *The bulky type of warship is still seen as late as the fifth century BC on a grave relief from Bologna, suggesting that the Etruscans had made little change in the rowing system. Clearly this is a major war vessel, and yet it is still rowed with oars on one level only. In contrast, triple-banked galleys were the rule among Phoenicians and Greeks by this time*

and which is clearly a continuation of the old Etruscan heavy, tublike vessel. It may be that the Etruscans considered their position at sea so hopeless after a decisive defeat by the western Greeks in the early fifth century that they took little interest in changing to the new ship type. Their worsening position on land in Italy, too, may have deprived them of the money needed for an ambitious naval construction programme.

In Greece and Phoenicia there were still further developments in the course of the fourth century BC: new warship types, the quadrireme (Greek, *tetreres*, 'four rowed') and the quinquereme (*penteres*, 'five rowed') appeared. The numbers must refer to some combination of the oarsmen, just as the three in 'tri-

reme' (*trieres*) refers to the three rowers who sat one above another in an oblique line. How the 'fours' and 'fives' were arranged, though, is highly problematic. One of the clearest things about the trireme is the number of banks it had; for the quadrireme and quinquireme even this is uncertain. That they had four and five banks is dubious, and it seems most likely that new combinations of rowers were devised for the old three-bank system, utilizing more than one man to an oar.

The date of their introduction also poses a problem. According to one report, they were invented at Syracuse in the early fourth century, but in that case it is odd that there is no reference to the quadrireme in what is extant of the naval records of nautically-minded Athens until

330, and to the quinquereme until 325 BC. Alexander is said to have encountered them in Phoenicia in 332, but in the light of the Athenian records, they are unlikely to have been adopted there more than a generation before Alexander. The new ships seem to mark, towards the end of Classical times, the first stage in the frantic multiplication of rowers that was to characterize the Hellenistic era and that indeed was well under way by 300. (Ship architects had worked up to at least an 'eleven' by then.)

It may be that we do possess a few representations of the 'fours' and 'fives'. The coins issued by the Phoenician city of Aradus in the period c. 350–325 BC show a ship type that differs from those hitherto seen on Phoenician coins (and that continue to appear on the issues of other cities). It does, however, closely correspond to a ship model from Egypt, in its general tall appearance and specifically in its two tiers of stanchions. The model, which on the basis of its find-spot can be dated to c. 350 BC or later, clearly shows three banks of oars but it has no outrigger; instead the topmost bank is set vertically above the middle bank (but with the oars staggered) and as far from it as this bank is from the one below. In such an arrangement the topmost oars would have to be longer than the others and have to be rowed at a much sharper angle, but these problems would be neutralized if the ship is in the 'four' or 'five' class and if in such a type there would indeed be more than one man at each of the oars of the top bank.

It is unfortunate that no actual warships of the fifth and fourth centuries have yet been found; no more characteristic a monument of that age can be imagined. In the case particularly of the triremes, though, the chances of ever discovering one are slender. They were so light that they were unlikely to sink after being wrecked in battle; if they were not salvaged by the victors they would drift to shore and break up there. The one hope would seem to be of finding part of an abandoned hull preserved in the mud of some harbour bed.

In lieu of the ships themselves, some of the slips used by Athenian galleys have been excavated (chapter 4, p. 92), and these give some indication of the ships' dimensions. Since these slips are no broader than some 20 feet, the width of the hulls they accommodated must have been slightly less; the length of the slips – not precisely determinable – is likely to have been around 130 feet.

*Merchant ships.* Among the merchant vessels, of which we do have an actual example in the Kyrenia ship (see below), there is less unity observable than among the warships. This is understandable, for there was not the same urgent necessity for each area to keep pace with, and to adopt the innovations of, others.

The trading ships *par excellence* were the kind called by the Greeks *holkades*. Deep, broad vessels, they deviated most from the warships and all but renounced the use of oars; it was these that Aristotle compared to large insects with tiny wings. Clearly it is to this class that the Kyrenia ship belongs—its dimensions, though not yet accurately determined, are in such marked contrast to the longer, narrower ones estimated for the Athenian triremes. Another probable *holkas* is the merchantman found at the Straits of Messina. The excavator, D. I. Owen, has estimated from the positions of the small finds, including nails from the hull, that this vessel had a length of some 82 feet; thus, while longer than the Kyrenia ship, it still would fall significantly short of the warships.

Among representations, the closest parallels between *holkades* are provided by a Greek vase painting of the late sixth century and by a more monumental Etruscan tomb painting of the mid-fifth century. In both depictions, the ships have a similarly shaped deep hull, and the prows have a like profile, which differs radically from that on contemporary warships. However, the fore platform, housing for the helmsman, and stern ornament, are rather dissimilar, and, most notably, the Etruscan ship carries a foresail, the only known ship of the period to do so.

A model of a roughly contemporary Cypriote *holkas* which may be close to the Phoenician type has about the same lines as the Greek and Etruscan ships, though the prow differs in bearing a rudimentary ram. This ship possesses two remarkable features. One is the platform that extends out beyond the hull in the form of a gallery, closely resembling the kind that became standard on Roman merchantmen (chapter 3, fig. 5). The other is the outrigger noted above in the discussion of the trireme; here it is unlikely to have been for any rowing purpose but, like the gallery, probably served as an outer passageway.

*13 Mid-fourth century BC coins from Aradus show much heavier-looking ships than those on earlier Phoenician coins (cf. ill 7); seemingly they represent new ship types, perhaps galleys with four- and five-man rowing units*

14  *An Assyrian relief* c. 700 BC *shows Phoenicians making their escape from a hostile army on early biremes. In this detail both ships have high decks, one has a ram*

14    Another, more varied class of merchantmen did rely considerably on oar power. On the Assyrian relief of *c.* 700 showing Phoenician vessels, the ramless ships conveying refugees seem suited for normal use as trading ships; not only are they being rowed but they look specifically designed for rowing, the oarsmen being disposed on two banks, as on the warships of the same relief.

11    In its proportions the rowed merchant ship portrayed on an Attic fifth-century vase seems a compromise between the long warship and the rounded *holkas*. Unlike the eighth-century Phoenician ships, it is equipped with a ram, a much more serviceable one than that on the Cypriote model. This, along with the precise movement that was possible with oars, gave the ship a military potential. Such vessels may have been popular among ship-owners whose concern was to fight off pirates; they may well have been favoured by pirates themselves.

*Small boats.* Small craft are occasionally represented and take much the same form from Italy to the Levant. Painted inscriptions show that the modest two-man boat depicted on a fifth-century Attic vase is being used for
17  fishing, while those that accompany a very similar craft on another Greek vase establish this as a ferry boat.
12  What is obviously a fishing boat in an Etruscan painting shows the same basic lines, as does, with modifications, a Cypriote model.

### Ship Fittings and Construction

*Rigging.* It has usually been supposed that the square sail was the only type in use throughout the period under consideration. However, the excavator of the Kyrenia ship, Michael Katzev, has suspected from the position of the mast step that a fore-and-aft rig was employed on this merchantman (p. 52). And still within the square-sail system, an interesting elaboration is seen in the
13  painting of the Etruscan merchant ship, where a foresail

appears in addition to the normal mainsail. Just as for the possible fore-and-aft rig, it is difficult to know how common such a feature was on ships of the period.

The sails in representations give the impression of considerable breadth. It is clear on some Greek examples that the long yard needed for this sort of sail was made by lashing two spars together, as had been the Egyptian custom for centuries (chapter 1, ill. 24). The lower yard seems to have gone out of use everywhere, and it has become standard for the sails to be fitted with brails.    10, 11, 13

Other rigging in use includes forestays, backstays, halyards, braces, and sheets. For the most part, shrouds are lacking in both representations and literary references, and other pieces of rigging may have doubled for them. In Homeric ships, for example, there were two forestays and these seem to have been secured in such a way as to give the needed lateral support to the mast. In some depictions the halyards appear to serve as shrouds, a practical enough arrangement since, at least on Greek ships, the mast was up only when the sail was. Lines to check excessive billowing are occasionally to be seen running across the front surface of the sail; that the sheets were secured to rings at the lower corners of the sail can also be observed.

*Steering oars.* The pilot continued to depend upon a pair of steering oars, as he had to do until well into the    2, 10 medieval period. A fragment of a sixth-century Greek vase painting clearly shows the upper part of these oars, along with the tiller with which the helmsman worked them and the pivot to which they were lashed.

*Anchors.* Of all the equipment used on ships of the period, the anchor is by now the best known, some actual examples having been recovered which considerably supplement the information available from the usual    21 pictorial and literary sources. The hook anchor makes    15, 16 its appearance at some time during the first part of the millennium and is adopted by Greeks, Etruscans, and at least the Western Phoenicians. That such anchors already have the basic form of the Roman examples from Lake Nemi (chapter 3, fig. 18) and, for that matter, of the modern anchor is a point of interest. Some scanty references in Greek written sources show that the anchor could be of iron, but anchors with wooden shanks and arms must have been more common. In the form in which these parts are shown in several depictions, they could only have been carved. A gem from the Phoenician colony of Tharros on Sardinia, in fact,    15 shows a carpenter at work on the flukes of an anchor.

There was a certain variety in the stocks fitted to these wooden anchors. A number of stone stocks have been found both on land and in the sea in Greek areas; two from the maritime island of Aegina can be securely dated to the fifth century on the basis of their inscriptions, and one from the early levels of Miletos must pre-date the    20 destruction of the Greek Ionian city by the Persians in    19 494. A stock of lead, later the standard material, is    17 apparently associated with the Etruscan wreck at Cap d'Antibes. Its short, stubby form contrasts with the elongated stocks of the Hellenistic and Roman periods and bears out that it is early. Two lead stocks, which bore either Greek or Phoenician inscriptions, seem certain enough to have fitted onto anchors of the ship in the Straits of Messina. Unfortunately, their precise description is not known, since they were looted from the site and destroyed before the wreck came to the attention of archaeologists.

The Messina anchors are known to have had other metal accessories as well. Bronze sheaths, three of which are extant, probably capped the flukes, and there was at least one lead collar (looted and now destroyed) that ran between the arms and enclosed the shank. The size of the various metal fittings indicates that the Messina anchors were very large, with, at least in one example, a total weight of wood and metal amounting to over a ton.

To judge from a rather crude fifth-century vase-painting, and a more reliable Roman relief, hook anchors did not always carry stocks. The seaman must sometimes have trusted the flukes to grip a sandy bottom firmly enough to hold his ship.

Weight anchors of stone continued to be used in the first millennium along with hook anchors. Some pyramidal and ovoid anchors found in the waters around the Phoenician island colony of Motya in Sicily are reminiscent of those dedicated in a Middle Bronze Age temple at Byblos and may represent a long-lived Phoenician type. It is possible, of course, that the anchors date from

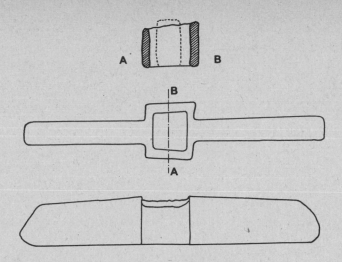

17 *The earliest anchor stock known, associated with an Etruscan wreck of the early sixth century BC, is composed of lead, later the standard material of Graeco-Roman times*

a later period, but there is good reason to believe that they were lost between the eighth and fifth centuries in the heyday of the colony, before it suffered severe destruction in 398 BC.

A more sophisticated type of pyramidal weight anchor, fitted with a lead shaft at the top, has been found in Greek waters, and three examples were raised in the 1965 excavation, directed by Peter Throckmorton, of an Early Hellenistic merchantman sunk near Taranto, Italy. The ship probably dates to the early third century BC, but it is difficult to say whether the anchors it carried could have been current any earlier.

*Construction.* The fragments of the Messina ship and the relatively well-preserved hull of the Kyrenia ship have made it clear that already in this period there was current the system of naval construction well known from Graeco-Roman wrecks: a system characterized, on the one hand, by the building of the shell first with a secondary insertion of the frames and, on the other hand, by an elaborate and thorough mortising and tenoning of the strakes. It had already been supposed that the construction technique went back into this era, in fact back to at least the eighth century; for, as Casson has ingeniously shown, the description of the building of Odysseus' boat in Homer's account could best be interpreted by assuming that Odysseus proceeded in the manner of a Graeco-Roman shipwright.

The Kyrenia and Messina wrecks have revealed that another well-known feature of ships of later antiquity, the sheathing of lead around the hull, also goes back to Classical times. While it is uncertain how extensive sheathing was (though present) on the Messina ship, lead covered all the extant parts of the hull of the Kyrenia merchantman.

This ship, the only example of a Greek merchant hull to have been found so far in an excellent state of preservation, was recently excavated by Michael Katzev, who adds a brief description of his operations and findings.

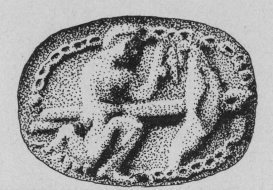

15,16 *The main body of the hook, or admiralty, anchor, an invention of the first millennium BC, was normally of wood. On a gem (15) of c. 500 BC from Sardinia, by then colonized by Phoenicians, we see a carpenter doing the final shaping on his anchor. Just how fine the working of the wood could be is indicated by the anchor on a coin (16) from Greek Apollonia of the fourth century BC. The arms flare out attractively over a broad expanse*

## The Kyrenia Ship

BY MICHAEL L. KATZEV

The wreck, lying less than a mile northeast of the town of Kyrenia, was first discovered by a Cypriote diver. In 1967 he led me and my team of archaeologists from the University of Pennsylvania Museum to the small pile of amphoras 100 feet down on the grassy sea bed. The mound of almost 100 stacked jars measured just 16½ by 10 feet. We were in doubt at first whether the small cargo that was visible indicated a full-scale merchant vessel. Staking out a cord grid, we probed the surrounding area with metal rods in search of more amphoras and found that wreckage lay concealed by the sand over a distance of 62 by 33 feet – the dimensions of a trading ship. Next a metal detector and a proton magnetometer picked up concentrations of iron and other metals and established their locations. By shape the amphoras were Rhodian and thought to date to the last third of the fourth century BC. The survey was a valuable guide for the excavation to come. For in addition to the date of the site, it showed not only that there was a large cargo here, but also just how the ship was oriented under the sand.

In the next two summers we were to uncover a 'time capsule' of Greek seafaring. Realizing the importance of the discovery, great pains were taken to ensure that no scrap of evidence would be lost. Over the site we set up interlocking grid frames of plastic pipe. These grids served both as orientation for the divers and as a fixed frame of reference from which the positions of small finds could be recorded. Stereo photography (photogrammetry) was used to plot the placement of amphoras, other large objects, and eventually the wooden hull. Twice a day a photographer would 'fly' over the wreck, firing two pictures simultaneously from cameras mounted at either end of a 2-metre bar. By means of these 'aerial' photo pairs, plans and sections of the excavations could be drawn to an accuracy of 2 cm.

Divers used 'air-lifts' as their main excavating tool. Seven of these, varying in size from 2 to 6 inches in diameter, were positioned around the wreck site. Each was equipped with a valve for regulating the suction so that they could be adjusted for heavy or light work. A diver would actually 'dig' with his hands or a knife, feeding unwanted debris into the air-lift mouth to be expelled at an angle some 60 to 100 feet away. Like their land colleagues, the aqualung archaeologists cleaned delicate areas, such as the hull, with brushes.

From the Kyrenia ship comes evidence that the merchant seamen of the period traded a variety of wares on the same voyage. The ship carried ten distinct styles of amphoras, each the key to a different port of call and perhaps a different commodity. Out of a total of 404, 343 jars are from Rhodes. They undoubtedly contained the wine of that island which was so widely marketed throughout the Greek and Roman worlds. Only one other shape can now be identified: it came from the island of Samos. Some of the amphoras bear stamps impressed on their handles, probably the mark of an official who certified that they met a standard capacity. It seems reasonable to assume that the other eight types of amphoras carried foodstuffs for the voyage or rare commodities, for they were only found in small numbers, and in several cases there was but one example.

Close to 10,000 almonds were found heaped in separate areas of the ship, lying directly against the inner hull. Originally they must have been stowed here in sacks, long since rotted away. Although the nuts have disintegrated, their shells still remain perfectly preserved after more than 2,200 years of burial.

Another form of cargo comprised stones for milling grain. Twenty-nine of them lay beneath the lowest level of amphoras. They were laden on a thin 'flooring' of interior planking in three trim rows parallel to and above the keel. Since these grain-mill blocks vary in size and finish, and do not match into usable pairs, it is believed that they were the remnants of an earlier cargo sold off at previous ports. At this stage in the voyage the odd number of blocks probably served simply as ballast. Thus, we have found that the Kyrenia ship carried three quite distinct products: wine, almonds, and millstones. And at least one or two of the other amphora types must have contained different commodities intended for sale.

Other finds allow us to reconstruct the daily life of these sailors, and possibly the events that led to the merchantman's sinking. Small pottery lay in two areas, forward and aft of the main cargo, indicating separate 'cabins' in the bow and stern. Since all the cups were found towards the bow, the ship's drinking water might have been kept here, as is the custom on modern caiques in the eastern Mediterranean. Cooking and dining utensils were concentrated in the stern: simple black-glazed plates and bowls, small pitchers and oil jugs, a copper cauldron, terracotta ladles, sieves and casseroles. A wooden bowl and four wooden spoons complete the list. This suggests that on the ill-fated last voyage there were at least four sailors, including the captain, since there are four identical cups, salt dishes, oil jugs and spoons. Unlike later Roman ships which carried portable braziers and the seventh-century Byzantine merchantman off Yassi Ada (see chapter 6, pp. 140–4) which was equipped with a galley containing a sizeable hearth, the Greek ship offers no evidence for cooking on board. Rather, we suspect that the crew prepared all hot meals ashore, suspending the cauldron over a fire on the beach. Lead weights from two nets tell us they fished for food during the day. Only one small fragment of a terracotta lamp was found. It is to be assumed from this, and from the absence of any cooking facilities, that this relatively small ship did not often run at night.

Why then would cautious mariners have lost their ship here, less than a mile east of the ancient anchorage at Kyrenia? There is no evidence of burning or violence from piracy; no submerged reef like that which caused the destruction of innumerable ships off Yassi Ada. This

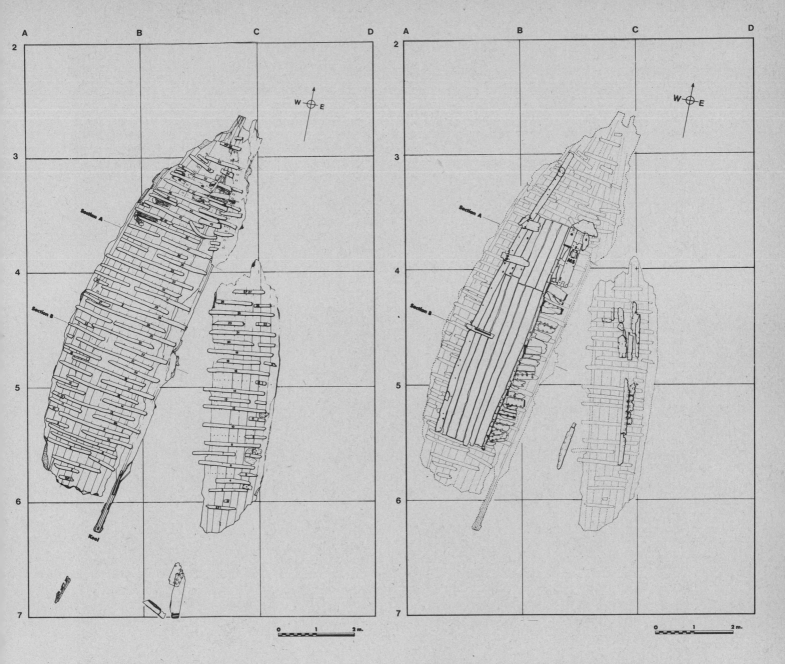

18 *The Kyrenia ship, fourth-century BC. Reconstruction plan of the vessel's outer hull, obtained with the aid of a grid frame and photogrammetry*

19 *Plan of the remaining inner planking of the Kyrenia ship, superimposed on the plan of the hull shown in the left-hand drawing*

stretch of the north coast of Cyprus is free of navigational hazards. Kyrenia does, however, lie unprotected from winds that drive down from the Taurus Mountains. In late summer and early autumn the island's north coast bears the brunt of many a sudden storm, of sufficient violence to cause a ship of this size to founder. Is this, then, the explanation? Lead rings of the kind used in ancient rigging lay in a confined area astern; they indicate that the sail had been taken down and stowed.

In the well preserved mast step no sign of the mast could be found; this suggests that it had been lowered before the merchantman sank. Though five small bronze coins were recovered amid the fishing nets, we did not find a cache of silver or gold denominations which would have been the earnings of what was clearly a long summer's voyage. And apart from the common pottery, no remains of personal belongings, except for eyelets and scraps of leather from a sailor's sandal, were found. The ship, probably overtaken by a storm, seems to have been abandoned by the crewmen, who gathered up their valuables and made for shore after trying in vain to save her.

The vessel seems to have come down on her keel, to rest on her port side in the soft sea-bed. In the course of time, marine borers and other sea creatures would have begun attacking the superstructure and the exposed starboard. As a result, it appears, this side soon collapsed outward, the hull having split open just to starboard of the keel. In breaking open, the cargo stowed along the starboard side splayed out, and the amphoras became randomly scattered. The port side, however, settled deeper into the silt; the amphoras remained neatly stacked as they were originally laden; and this part of the hull was sealed from further ravages by marine life. Preserved for a length of over 36 feet, the vessel may have once measured as much as 52 feet long. In all, due to the protective qualities of the sandy mud bottom off Kyrenia, more than 50 per cent of the hull is preserved, including much of its original curvature.

At the stern the ship was blunt-ended and appears to have carried a gallery. The bow, as preserved, is pointed and seems to project forward much more radically than in either the Greek or the Etruscan merchantmen. Her contours might be better compared to the Cypriote model; though there is no evidence for an outrigger over the gunwales, in other respects she may have been quite similar – concave pointed bow, two massive outer wales, and steered from a gallery aft.

The ship was built almost entirely of pine. Her shipwrights worked in the 'shell-first' tradition; that is, they laid the keel, and then over a temporary scaffold they built up the outer strakes, joining them edge to edge with closely spaced mortises and tenons, which were secured by wooden dowels. Next, into this shell they laid the frames, nailing them in place with copper spikes driven in from the outside. In contrast to the modern Western system, the frames were less a skeleton on which the vessel's structure depended than a simple method of internal buttressing.

Over the entire preserved hull the merchantman bore a sheathing of lead fixed on with copper tacks. Such a casing, designed to keep out marine borers, was common in the Roman world. The Kyrenia and Messina wrecks now show that this method was used by the Greeks as early as the fifth and fourth centuries BC. On board the Kyrenia ship also were extra rolls of lead sheet and carpenters' mallets for quick repairs to her 'armour'.

Less than one-third aft of the preserved hull's bow, the excavators found an intricately cut mast step, surrounded by supports for braces which once constituted the tabernacle. Because the mast was placed so far forward, it is very probable that the Kyrenia ship carried a fore-and-aft rig. This is a sail which runs the length of the vessel, rather than a square sail which spans the width. Lionel Casson has traced the use of fore-and-aft rigging in the Mediterranean back to the second century BC. The Kyrenia merchantman may indicate that this type of rigging was invented at least two centuries earlier.

Bronze coins discovered amid the wreckage were minted during the rule of two successors to the empire of Alexander the Great: Antigonus the 'One-Eyed' and Demetrius the 'Besieger'. They place the wreck no earlier than 306 BC. However, C14 analysis, which dates the almond cargo to 288 ± 62 BC, indicates that trees used for the ship's planking were cut in 389 ± 44 BC. Hence, we may conclude that the Kyrenia ship, having served merchants throughout most of the fourth century, was at least 80 years old when she sank – testimony enough to the skills of the Greek shipwright. Now some twenty-two centuries later the hull of this, the earliest sea-going vessel yet recovered, has been raised to stand as a monument unique in the historical study of Classical ships and seafaring.

---

1 The underwater archaeology that has in recent decades contributed so materially to our knowledge of early shipping is epitomized in this photograph of divers at work above the hull of a Greek merchant vessel which had foundered near the coast of Cyprus northeast of Kyrenia. The first intimation that here might lie a wreck from ancient Greek times was the discovery in 1967 by a Cypriote diver of a small mound of amphoras. During the next two summers Michael Katzev and other members of a team of archaeologists from the University of Pennsylvania Museum systematically explored the site, uncovering what has proved to be the earliest seagoing hull yet found, and excavating many interesting items of cargo and equipment.

The photograph clearly shows substantial portions of the hull lying *in situ* on the sea-bed beneath the grid made of plastic pipe set up as a frame of reference. The divers, equipped with aqualung breathing apparatus, hold the ends of 'air-lift' suction tubes used for clearing the finds of sand.

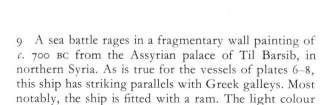

10 At the left of this Attic vase painting of the late sixth century BC appears the merchant ship *par excellence*: the great rounded *holkas*; of somewhat clumsy proportions, it could be rowed only with difficulty and relied

12 Shipping afloat on the Mediterranean in the first millennium BC was not confined to warships and cargo carriers. This late sixth-century Etruscan tomb painting shows boys fishing from a gaily decorated boat.

9 A sea battle rages in a fragmentary wall painting of *c.* 700 BC from the Assyrian palace of Til Barsib, in northern Syria. As is true for the vessels of plates 6–8, this ship has striking parallels with Greek galleys. Most notably, the ship is fitted with a ram. The light colour that the ram is painted hints that this presumably wooden projection is given a protective metal sheathing.

The oars issue from the hull through ports, a system which had already begun to be adopted by the Greek shipwrights of the time (4) and which was standard throughout the Mediterranean by the middle of the first millennium BC.

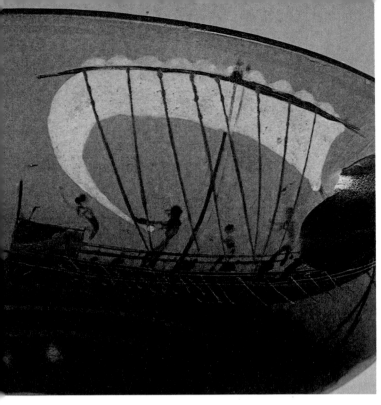

mainly on wind power. In contrast, the low, sleek war galleys like that at the right were specifically designed for the effective utilization of oars; as often, the oars are accommodated in two banks.

11 The ship carrying Odysseus in this Attic vase painting of the fifth century BC seems a compromise between a merchant vessel and warship: while short and steep, it is capable of being rowed and it bears a ram.

13 In its general lines, the *holkas* of this tomb painting of the mid-fifth century BC from Etruscan Tarquinia resembles the Greek representation of a half-century earlier (10); there is, however, one major difference. The

ship is seen to have two masts, the forward one bearing a small supplementary sail. The painting thus serves to show that two-masted ships existed before the Hellenistic period.

14

14 Model warship from Egypt dating to about the fourth century BC; it has three banks of oars but may be a type more complex than the true trireme. Since there is no outrigger housing for the topmost oars, they are positioned relatively high above the waterline, possibly requiring more than one man at each oar.

15 Five warriors, armed with shields, sit in a model warship made in Corinth, c. late sixth century BC. The men may be part of a regular force of marines.

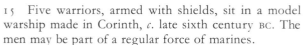

15

18 Weight anchors of stone continue into the first millennium BC. The two types below found near the Phoenician colony of Motya in Sicily are strikingly close to Bronze Age anchors found at Byblos in the Phoenician homeland.

19–20

18

16

17

16 Model of the Cypriote *holkas*, dating to *c.* 500 BC; it differs from its Greek and Etruscan counterparts (10, 13) in the timbers that extend beyond the gunwale in a manner recalling a trireme outrigger, and in the fenced walkway round the sternpost.

19,20 The hook, or admiralty, anchor appears during the first millennium BC. Stocks were normally of lead, like the example (19) from Syracuse harbour, but they could be of stone, like the one from Aegina (20); its fifth-century inscription reads, 'Don't move this'.

17 A boatman throws anchor as the rower manoeuvres the small craft in this Attic vase painting of *c.* 440 BC. The names painted in faint letters by the men – Halimos, 'old salt', and Komaris, a kind of fish – suggests that they are fishermen.

21 A hook anchor appears as a shield emblem in this Attic vase painting of the late sixth century. While the stocks of such anchors were stone or lead (19, 20), the finely curved and somewhat bulging shanks and arms suggest a wood construction.

21

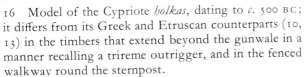

**22,23** A massive deposit of metal objects dating to the sixth century BC found in deep water off Rochelongues, in southern France, seems explicable only as the cargo of a wrecked ship. The variety in the load was considerable. Ingots of copper and tin, as well as a large amount of scrap metal represent the raw material from which purchasers (or perhaps a tinker on board the ship) would shape new artifacts. Many finely worked items of personal adornment, though, were carried as finished goods, exemplified by the two bronze pendants (22). Lamp bottoms, seen among the medley of objects on the sea-bed (23), suggest that there may have been a small non-metallic cargo, but perhaps the lamps were for use on the ship rather than being intended for trade.

22

23

24,25 Though badly pillaged, the cargo of a ship sunk *c.* 400 BC in the Straits of Messina proved to be of considerable importance. The ship was carrying at least two life-sized bronze statues (24) as part of a metal load that was otherwise characterized by lead ingots. The statues remain fragmentary, although the excavators conducted an intensive search of the sea bottom for additional parts that looters might have missed (25).

Other representative finds from the cargo include several types of amphoras, which presumably contained wine, olive oil, or perhaps other foodstuffs. While only a fraction of the original load, the material found gives a striking picture of the diversity of goods on a merchant ship of classical times.

24

25

26

26 A mound of amphoras, the gravestone for a watery tomb, marks the burial of a Greek ship. At a depth of 100 feet a diver surveys the site near Kyrenia, Cyprus. For two summers a team of marine archaeologists uncovered the remains of this merchantman. Then the timbers of its hull were raised for reconstruction.

27 The cargo of the Kyrenia ship consisted of over 400 amphoras. Some ten distinct amphora shapes were identified, each style representing a different port of call made by the merchantmen. Here a diver removes one example of the type manufactured on Rhodes during the last third of the fourth century BC.

28 Beneath the amphoras the excavators found blocks for mills. Two blocks made up each mill. Grain poured into the V-shaped upper blocks fell through the narrow slot. Working the upper blocks over the lower, the grain was ground. The blocks of volcanic stone were probably quarried on one of the Aegean islands.

27

28

29 From the Kyrenia ship came ladles, bowls of various sizes, plates of different types, four small oil jugs, pitchers of all kinds, four drinking cups, and an oddity possibly used as an inkwell. Their numbers suggest that the merchantman was crewed by four sailors, and their distribution indicates that there were cabin areas fore and aft in the ship. Such terracotta objects as these, when compared to similar vessels found in the Chatby cemetery of Alexandria or the excavations of the Athenian agora, permit the excavators to date the sinking of the merchantman close to the year 300 BC. We see that the crew of the Kyrenia ship ate off the glazed crockery so common to the Hellenic world in the decades just after the death of Alexander the Great. Thus, these vases provide us with a clearer picture of shipboard life in antiquity. Today the pottery and other finds from the excavation of this merchantman are exhibited in a new museum established in the Crusader castle at Kyrenia. They constitute a display intended to depict the contributions which underwater archaeology can make to our understanding of ancient man, and particularly to our knowledge of his maritime activity through the remains of this ship, her cargo and the implements used by her crew.

30 A sample of the almost 10,000 almonds found in the excavation reflects another aspect of the cargo carried aboard the Kyrenia ship. Allowed to dry, the almonds would have disintegrated. The waterlogged, wooden timbers of the hull would have similarly deteriorated. Therefore, a process of conservation was instituted, involving the immersion of the timbers in a bath of polyethylene glycol, a water-soluble, wax-like compound. During a treatment of over six months this compound diffuses into the wood and replaces the water. Upon drying, the polyethylene glycol solidifies rather than evaporating, thereby bulking the wood and preventing its disintegration. Using the original timbers after they have been reconstructed, the hull of the Kyrenia ship could be reconstructed, providing a material display of the oldest sea-going hull yet recovered.

# 3

# Romans on the sea

PETER THROCKMORTON

# Romans on the sea

## Overseas Expansion of Imperial Rome

There was little tradition of Roman seafaring when the Republic began to expand rapidly through Italy in the fourth and third centuries B C. It was the acquisition, and then administration, of new territories which turned Rome into a maritime power, more or less in spite of herself.

Unlike the British two millennia later, Rome had neither a large navy nor a merchant fleet ready to meet the demands of empire. Republican settlers along the coast between Ostia and Cosa, at such places as Pyrgi, Norba, Ardes Antium and Terracina, were mainly landsmen – ex-soldiers, merchants and administrators, oriented towards Rome a few miles away.

Yet their grandsons moved into Sicily and, starting in 264 B C, fought for Roman interests against the powerful Carthaginians throughout a hundred years of Punic wars. When Rome emerged victorious, she found herself both mistress and policeman of the Mediterranean.

Once Carthage was defeated, Rome had little competition. The Aegean held only small maritime states, more or less dependent on the sea, of which the most powerful was Rhodes. Rhodes found herself in the traditional role of a tiny state, playing the balance of power between the largest neighbouring sea powers, Ptolemaic Egypt and Macedonia. But before the turn of the third century B C, the Rhodians were begging the Roman Senate for help.

By the first century A D, the Romans were administering the whole Mediterranean, east and west. And until the empire split into two halves, four centuries later, Imperial Rome was the greatest maritime power the world would know until the Royal Navy imposed the Pax Britannica on international sea routes in the early nineteenth century.

As a result of colonial conquest, Roman tastes became very much more sophisticated. The change was slow, in modern terms, but none the less spectacular. Bread was baked with flour from Egypt and North Africa. Olive oil came from Spain. Wealthy Romans dressed their wives and mistresses in Chinese silk. Cosmetics were carried from Arabia for Roman ladies and – something new to the great city built by soldiers and statesmen – for a growing number of the menfolk themselves.

Spices came from South East Asia and India, wine from the Greek islands. Grain imports have been reasonably estimated at 150,000 tons a year, a third of it from Egypt. There are no statistics for oil or wine, but literary and archaeological evidence suggest that the quantity must have been immense.

Civic life became grander. Public buildings were constructed or faced or decorated with imported granite and marble, since local supplies were unable to meet the demand. The Carrara quarries were opened in 40 B C, but could produce nothing like the quantity demanded by the building programmes of Augustus and his successors. Buying marble from 'undeveloped' places – as we term them nowadays – and carrying it by sea cost Roman centres less than quarrying it with more expensive labour nearer at hand and transporting it overland.

The system was reorganized by the middle of the second century, when marble was obligatory not only for public building in Rome but also in her subject cities of any pretensions. Stone was quarried and stored in bulk wherever possible throughout the Empire. Red and grey granites came from Elephantine Island far up the Nile. Marble came from the Greek mainland and islands, Asia Minor, and the Sea of Marmara.

There was at the same time a redeployment of sculptors. The Roman aristocrat was frequently laid to rest in a sarcophagus of marble from Asia Minor, roughly hewn before shipment and finished with lions and rosettes carved upon it in Rome by Greek sculptors who had emigrated from one or another Anatolian Greek city. The wealthy Roman was never far from the fruits of empire.

By the first century B C, the economic facts of life had caught up with shipbuilders and, consequently, the port authorities. Larger ships were more economical to run than smaller ones, in terms of cost per unit of cargo handled.

Hitherto ships had proceeded up the Tiber from the sea, as far as the docks of Rome, before unloading. Bigger ships could no longer manage this. In consequence, a system of river barges was developed for carrying the cargoes piecemeal from coast to capital. Also harbour improvements to meet the requirements

*12*

of the larger ships were planned at Ostia; these were carried out in part by the emperor Claudius and later more extensively by the emperor Trajan, as described in the next chapter. Our concern with this port, and its smaller counterparts throughout the Empire, is to learn what we can of the ships and seamen which Ostia was built to contain.

3 *Life and society in Ostia, Rome's seaport.* The excavations give a clear picture of Ostia as a lively, brawling seaport, where plenty of money was continually changing hands, and with a comprehensive social and commercial system of organizations acting, obviously with government consent and support, to keep the cosmopolitan populace occupied and under control.

Most 'Ostians' were freedmen and foreigners. Numerous inscriptions have been found in Ostia and in the graveyards near the Imperial naval bases at Ravenna and Misenum. There are few aristocratic Roman names among them, but many from the Greek-speaking colonies; in the naval cemeteries in particular the names of Egyptians who left their villages to see the Imperial world figure prominently.

The layout of the city itself is depressingly familiar to anyone in the twentieth century who has had to do with public housing units built by the city or by private interests to hold a maximum number of tenants. The upper storeys formed a honeycomb of living quarters; on the ground floor were the shops, stews and taverns normally associated with a busy port. Again, judging from the quantity of inscriptions found in the city and in near-by cemeteries, including Portus, the lingua franca in the noisy streets was Greek, rather than Latin.

4 The large square behind the theatre held the offices of over seventy commercial associations. Mosaic pavements and inscriptions there show that most of them had to do with the sea. They depict workmen unloading amphoras from big ships into the Tiber barges, curious fish and sea animals, various ship types, and imported animals from the exotic Imperial world.

There were social organizations to cater for the needs of caulkers, river boatmen, bargemen, seamen, divers, stevedores, watchmen, and warehousemen, but we are not told what form their communal activities took.

## Naval Warfare

The Romans, not being a seafaring people, had little to contribute to warship design or naval military tactics. The earliest, fourth-century fleet consisted of only twenty ships, and all of these may well have been triremes of the old Greek type (see chapter 2, p. 44). Even when the first Punic war called for a rapid increase to 120 ships, the demand was met for the most part by the addition of Hellenistic quinqueremes; these were probably, as J. H. Thiel has suggested, neither built nor manned by Romans.

At this stage the relatively heavy and slow quinquereme was preferred to the more manoeuvrable trireme because it readily lent itself to a purely Roman innovation: the boarding bridge. If the Romans were no sailors, they remained excellent foot-soldiers, and by transforming sea battles into land battles as much as possible, they were able to exploit their strength successfully. The method by which the heavy boarding bridge was dropped onto an enemy deck and pinned in place, allowing marines to cross two abreast, has been described by Polybius and others, but it is still not perfectly understood. Less than two decades after its inception the boarding bridge was already being replaced by the simpler grapnel. Marines retained their important role, however, 120 being assigned to a quinquereme about to enter battle.

Still other Roman warship types were borrowed from alien peoples. Perhaps the most noteworthy was the Liburnian, a swift, single-banked raider used by pirates living on the Illyrian coast of Yugoslavia. The Romans adopted it in the first century BC, sometimes building it as a two-banked bireme.

Archaeological evidence concerning Roman warships is very scanty, though representations depict ships of one, two and three banks, with high, protective sides, 14 and the use of turrets (from literary evidence we know that the turrets were usually of wood and that rowers were protected by a deck over their heads).

## Merchant Ships

No actual warships or parts of warships having so far been found, we will limit the remainder of our discussion to the vast Roman merchant fleet, about which a considerable amount is known.

*Construction.* Ship carpentry and boat-building are perhaps the most traditional of all trades. Even today the techniques of building are a jealously guarded secret, to be handed down from father to son as a valuable legacy.

No treatise on ship carpentry has come down to us; the formulas used by ancient builders died with them. Yet a good deal can be deduced by searching the archaeological evidence and the surviving constants of this very ancient trade. Although one civilization succeeds another, the sea does not change, and nor do the shipbuilder's tools and materials and, until very recently, the uses to which ships are put.

Hull forms have evolved by a process of trial and error, often extending over dozens of generations. For example, some traditional Norwegian and Greek fishing boats are similar in shape not because of any shared nautical tradition, but because shipwrights have necessarily answered similar needs with similar solutions.

Not enough excavation has been done to allow us to reconstruct more than half a dozen ancient Mediterranean ships, including the earlier and later wrecks described in chapters 2 and 6, and the Torre Sgarrata shipwreck near Taranto in Italy is the only example 1, 11, 8 from Imperial Roman times. But these, together with parts of keel and floor timbers from wrecks at Mahdia, 2, 14

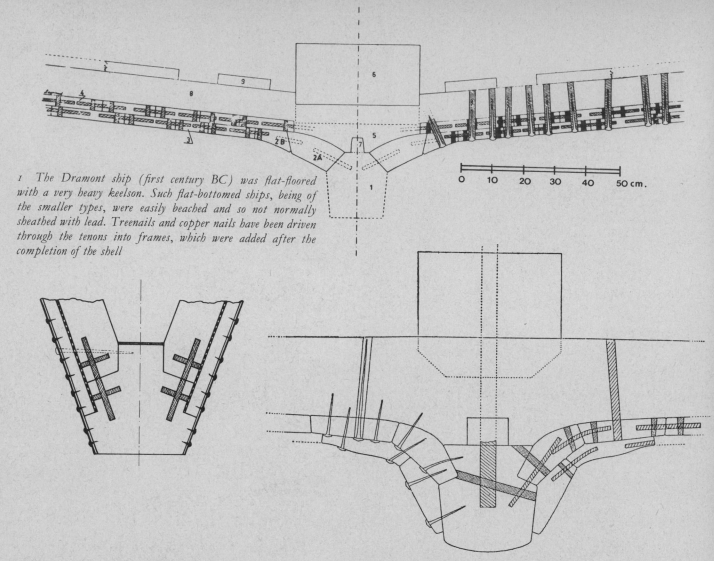

*1   The Dramont ship (first century BC) was flat-floored with a very heavy keelson. Such flat-bottomed ships, being of the smaller types, were easily beached and so not normally sheathed with lead. Treenails and copper nails have been driven through the tenons into frames, which were added after the completion of the shell*

*4   The Titan wreck (first century AD) was flat-floored and 'boxed'. The second layer of planking covers seams below*

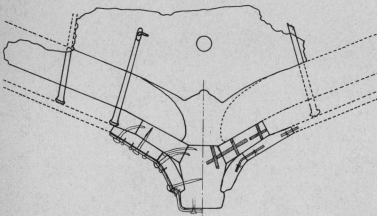

*2   The Mahdia ship, though of much the same date as the Dramont vessel, seems definitely to have been of a different kind, sharper and lead-sheathed*

*3   The Grand Congloué ship, though resembling the Mahdia vessel, is probably earlier. Bolts were inserted through the frames and floors after the first planking layer was fitted*

Dramont, Titan and La Chrétienne A, are sufficient to demonstrate continuity of the shipwright's traditional methods, in that these ships not only resemble one another but also, in the area just above the keel at least, have lines that are perpetuated in the modern Aegean *perama*.

For a ship to be genuinely seaworthy the design of its hull must fulfil certain essential requirements. First, it must have a good shape. As a hydrodynamic form it must slip through the water easily without creating a disturbance behind the stern which could cause following seas to break over it. It must be stable, both when light and when loaded. It must be able to carry sail safely. It must be shaped above the waterline so that waves are warded off, rather than being scooped up to break on the deck. While tough and resilient, it must

7, 8, 1, 4, 7

also be reasonably light. Building materials must be of good quality and of the right sort for their specific jobs.

The traditional shipwright, in ancient Rome as now, begins by laying the keel, the key to the other dimensions, and follows this by setting up the stem and sternposts. He then proceeds to construct the hull, either by setting up frames or ribs and fastening planks to them, or by building up a shell of planking from the keel with long planks which are attached to one end of the ship, bent to the necessary curve, and then attached to the other end. The hull now has its fair shape, and floors and frames can be fitted into it, giving it much of its strength.

The second, hull-first technique is typical of Scandinavia, where its development is well documented (see chapter 7). Called clench or clinker building, with each plank of the shell laid outside the plank beneath it and fastened to its neighbour with clenched nails, this technique spread all over northern Europe until it was partially supplanted in the late Middle Ages by the technique of carvel building on frames (see chapter 8, p. 192).

The Egyptian builder of Dynastic times, as we have seen (chapter 1), solved the problem of getting a fair hull shape in the same way, hull first and frames afterwards. Long planks being scarce in Egypt, he must have used a long flexible batten to get the shape, and then fitted small bits of planking together with mortises and tenons, or dovetail joints. A modified version of this technique still survives on the Upper Nile.

The only Greek ships to have been excavated (see chapter 2, the Kyrenia and Messina wrecks) followed the hull-first tradition, their planks being held together with mortises and tenons.

Tenons were used throughout the Roman world, even though there were adequate supplies of tall timber. Except for two of the three Roman period ships found in the Thames (see chapter 5), all known Roman shipwrecks were tenoned; the exceptions were probably due to the fact that they were locally built and belonged to different shipbuilding traditions.

Material evidence of the typical Roman method of ship construction came early to archaeologists, with the discovery of the first identified Roman cargo ship. Found in 1864 in a building excavation in Marseilles, she was misleadingly called 'Caesar's Galley' and left untouched for 90 years. Now that the ship is on display, the mortise-and-tenon construction is clearly revealed.

Another small merchant ship, found in London in 1910 (see chapter 5, p. 116), showed its excavators that the frames had been put in after the outer hull was set up, and planks were tenoned and fastened onto the frames with treenails.

The two Imperial pleasure barges uncovered by draining Lake Nemi in the 1930s, carefully studied and published by Guido Ucelli and others, were built in the same tradition. Although they were not sea-going vessels, they were undoubtedly built by shipwrights to

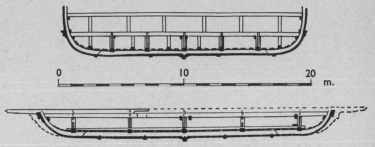

5 *The Nemi ships, one with projecting platforms, were barges, but their construction was to 'grain ship' standard*

the standard specifications of the largest sea-going ships of the day. The huge hulls, both over 200 feet long by about 60 feet wide, were tenoned, copper-fastened, and lead-sheathed.

The first Roman sea-going vessel to be examined by divers was a ship which sank during the first century BC off the island of Antikythera. Found in 1901 by Greek sponge divers, it attracted attention mainly by the tons of marble and bronze statuary it was carrying, much of which was recovered. Bits of the ship itself were found, but except for a comment by an archaeologist that the construction of the ship was unlike that seen today, no attempt was made to study the hull. A few years ago I examined these fragments in the storerooms of the National Museum in Athens. Although now powdery and fragile – the largest piece being only two feet long by six inches wide – it was obvious that the Antikythera ship had been built shell first and held together with tenons.

When diving became easier and more popular, following the invention of the aqualung in the 1940s, a number of other Roman shipwrecks were found in the Mediterranean. They include amphora carriers off Sparghi, Sardinia, and Albenga, Italy, both partially excavated by Professor Nino Lamboglia in the early 1950s, and several in the south of France; the most interesting of these were the first-century BC wrecks at Titan, Dramont, and La Chrétienne. All were tenoned, as was the hull of the Mahdia wreck now revisited and explored by aqualung divers.

The Mahdia ship had been discovered off the coast of Tunisia by Greek sponge divers in 1907 and, like the Antikythera ship, was principally noted for its cargo of sculpture and marble columns. Like the Antikythera ship, too, it had sunk in the first century BC. Pieces of the hull raised during the 1950s by the Club for Underwater Studies of Tunisia at Mahdia reveal the carefully cut mortises and tenons we might have expected.

The level of craftsmanship seen in the surviving remnants of tenoned hulls is extremely high. As Jacques-Yves Cousteau said of the woodwork techniques in the Grand Congloué ship near Marseilles, it is more akin to cabinet work than ship carpentry. Navy shipwrights in Italy who saw the remains of the Torre Sgarrata wreck were astonished at the fine quality of the work.

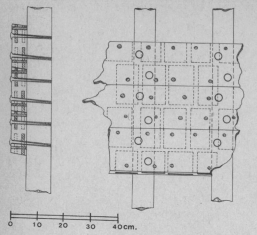

6  *The Antikythera wreck's planking was attached with treenails drilled through and then copper-nailed. These nails and treenails are driven through the tenons into the frames. Note that this reconstruction does not show the curve of the side.*

0  10  20  30  40cm.

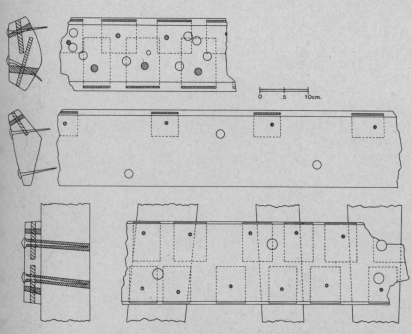

0  .5  10cm.

7   *These planks from the Titan wreck (see fig. 4) show the shell-first construction typical of this period*

8   *In the Torre Sgarrata ship the copper fastenings were driven in without treenails, apparently as a late repair*

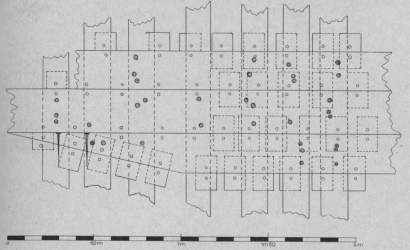

0  .50m  1m  1m50  2m

Planking up to 4 inches thick was adzed and planed so that it fitted together without any caulking. The natural swelling of the wood made a watertight seal.

In this technique tenons were used every few centimetres, but the practice began to die out towards the end of the Empire (see chapter 6), probably when the mould floor technique was evolved at some time, most likely after A D 500. (The mould-floor, or scrieve-board, method allows the shipwright to lay out the ship's lines with battens on the floor, a much simpler system than bending actual planks to the hull and then cutting out frames to fit.)

Tenoning is vestigial in the latest two ships which concern us here, the Pantano Longarini ship and the seventh-century ship at Yassi Ada (see chapter 6). Tenons were there used only as part of the process of getting the underwater lines straight during construction. In both ships the tenons were not fastened in with wooden treenails, and seem to have been used only for temporary strength.

The Roman shipwright, then, first set up his keel, stem and stern posts, and probably followed this by some sort of ceremony before starting the long process of shaping the first strakes (Greek island shipwrights of the last century – and even occasionally today – sacrificed a lamb on the keel, once the structure was upright). Next the master carpenter, with his batten, laid out the curves. When the outer shell had been completed, the frames and floors were shaped with an adze and fastened into place. Small 'packing pieces' of wood were sometimes wedged beneath the roughly shaped frames, against the outer planking; on a second-century merchantman sunk near Torre Sgarrata, Italy, we found these to be of ilex, a shrub most common in the East, and not indigenous to Italy.  1, 8

Evidence that the frames were put into place after the hull shell was made is plentiful: the presence of score lines on the inner side of the hull planking of the La Chrétienne A and Yassi Ada ships to mark the intended placement of frames; the location beneath frames of treenails driven from the inside of the hull through mortise-and-tenon joints (on the fourth-century Yassi Ada ship); and a copper fastening nail driven through a tenon in a plank raised at Antikythera. In the two late ships mentioned as having vestigial tenoning (at the Pantano Longarini and at Yassi Ada), the hull was built up only to the waterline before the frames were inserted, but hulls at Fiumicino, Yassi Ada, and Torre Sgarrata show that as late as the fourth century tenon construction was usually carried up to the gunwale, the wales or rubbing strakes being edge-joined to the planking in each case.  7

Wales always appear in Roman ship representations. Ends of beams protruding from the sides of the ships are often shown tucked over the edges of these wales, and this type of construction persists well into medieval times. Unfortunately the beams are not preserved in Mediterranean wrecks, as they lay above those parts of

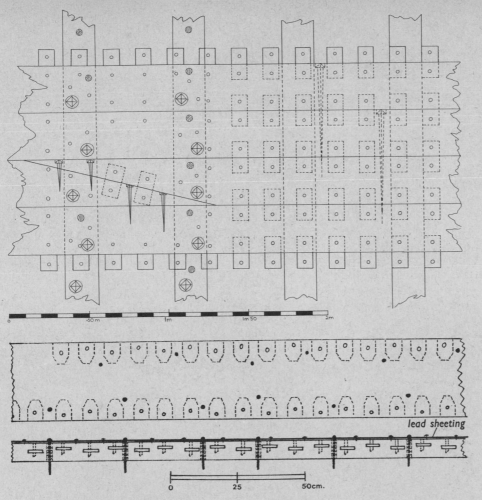

*9 Although never meant to go to sea, the first-century AD Nemi ships (see fig. 5) were built for a Roman emperor to the highest standard for seagoing ships: tenoned, lead-sheathed, copper-fastened, and treenailed*

*10 All the early tenoned ships had staggered tenons, for maximum strength, as this plank from the Grande Congloué wreck shows*

**lead sheeting**

the hull that were protected against shipworms by mud or sand. On the ship excavated on land at the Pantano Longarini (chapter 6, p. 144), however, we were able to learn how these had been cut and fitted into place. There we found one side of the stern of the ship from the line of the upper bulwark to just below the waterline. The planks below the lowest wale were tenoned together. Unlike the tenons in earlier ships, these were spaced about three feet apart. Just above the tenoned planking below the waterline was a massive wale, 16 inches in height and half rounded. Above this 'waterline' wale was a plank, then another wale, then a plank, and so forth up to what seemed to be the cap rail. The frames, spaced so close together that they formed nearly a solid mass of timbers, were hardwood logs roughly adzed to fit the inner shell of the tenoned planks. The whole structure, which was something like an enormous box girder, was held transversely together by beams which ran across the ship and tucked over the wales.

Such ships must have had enormous longitudinal strength. Their weak point was at the waterline wale, and it was here that the Pantano ship had broken in two lengthwise, after pounding on the offshore bar. Modern parallels provide an indication of the value of this type of construction. Writing about a Foochow pole junk, in *Junks and Sampans of the Yangtze* (Shanghai, 1947), G.R.C. Worcester notes 'Longitudinal strength is provided by three enormous hardwood wales which, lying close together and following the curve of the bilge throughout, also serve as bilge keels, as they are placed so low on the hull that, except at bow and stern, they are at or below the water line, according to whether the junk is light or loaded. Three lighter wales or strakes, are situated at and above deck level at varying intervals.' Worcester saw junks of this type for which the captains claimed 150 years of service. They were built of softwood with hardwood frames. He further describes a junk called *Keying*, which sailed from China in 1846, rounded the Cape, hit a gale, went to New York, finally got across the Atlantic in a series of storms, and throughout 'gave excellent proof of her seagoing qualities and, it was said, "never shipped a drop of water"'.

*Construction materials.* The materials used by Mediterranean shipwrights have changed little since Roman times. Hulls were most often of pine, cypress, or cedar, with the occasional use of elm below the waterline. Frames were most often of oak. Tenons and treenails were frequently made from different kinds of bog oak or hard fruitwood like pistachio or olive.

The ship nails used by the Roman shipwright were identical to the square, hand-forged, round-headed nails used by present-day traditional builders in the Mediterranean and elsewhere. Large, lead-sheathed cargo ships were usually copper-fastened, with the sheathing attached by lead-dipped copper nails. As in expensively built traditional Mediterranean ships, copper nails were used below the waterline, with iron perhaps more generally in the upper works. Later Roman ships were iron-fastened throughout, judging from the fourth- and seventh-century wrecks at Yassi Ada, the Pantano Longarini ship, the twelfth-century ship recently excavated at Pelago Nisos in the northern Sporades, and dozens of other Late Roman and Byzantine shipwreck sites I have examined in recent years.

Perhaps the Roman shipwright's technique shows to best advantage in his use of copper nails. They were often driven into a treenail of hardwood that had been fitted into a drilled hole and then drilled again.

Lead was more common throughout Roman ships than it is today. It was used for fastening ringbolts in place, for scupper pipes, for sheathing the hull below the waterline, and possibly for parts of the sails and in pumping systems. The Albenga, Titan, and Grand Congloué wrecks produced curious lead wheels which might have been parts of rope-spinning equipment or some sort of windlass.

Terracotta was used for roof tiles, and possibly for hearth tiles as well, although some hearths were undoubtedly of stone, as on the fourth-century ship at Yassi Ada (see chapter 6, pp. 137–9).

*Sizes and types.* There are many literary references to ancient ship types, as well as representations in mosaics, small sculptures, and frescoes. The eminent philologist Cecil Torr lists more than 30 Greek and Latin ship types mentioned in literary sources; yet no one has succeeded in clearly identifying a single known shipwreck with any of his classifications, and comparisons with pictorial evidence are scarcely more rewarding.

16    The best representation of what seems to be the most typical of Roman cargo ships is on the famous bas-relief from Portus, dating to the end of the first or beginning of the second century AD. It shows a medium-sized, double-ended sailing ship with two masts: one, amidships, carries a large square sail, with triangular topsail set above; the other, stepped forward, is evidently for a

cf. 17    small steering sail called the *artemon*. The ship has wales or rubbing strakes (heavy timbers running along the sides), and steering oars. Other reliefs depicting similar, but generally smaller ships of this type have also been found near Ostia.

Roman Imperial records generally refer to two categories of cargo ships, the smaller of which was able to make its way up the Tiber to unload in Rome. The Portus ship, and those like it, may be assumed to be of this smaller general type. The ship of standard size could carry 3,000 amphoras.

*11    First-century AD graffito found at Pompeii. Note the wales, the sharp stem, and the carefully drawn rigging. The Torre Sgarrata ship (see fig. 13) might have looked like this*

The second category is distinguished principally by its greater size, as well as by differences in design discussed below. The vessels employed by the Roman government, for instance, commonly had a capacity of 50,000 *modii* or about 340 tons. These big ships, able to carry 10,000 amphoras, had to be unloaded onto river barges at Ostia. There were also some exceptionally large ships of no less than 1,200 tons capacity built expressly for the transport of grain from Alexandria to Ostia.

A first-century AD graffito depicting this type was found at Pompeii. The ship is called the *Europa*. Her    11
bow is straight, unlike that of the Portus merchantman,    16
but otherwise the profiles and rigging are much the same.

The two types are seen together in a mosaic on the floor of what once were the offices of the shippers of Sullecthum (Tunisia) at Ostia. Another ship somewhat    4
like the *Europa*, with a yet more exaggerated bow extending like a ram, and eight wales along the sides, is seen in a mosaic from Themetra.

Yet, helpful as are the many extant wall paintings and mosaics of Roman provenance, in which ships and their rigging are depicted, one must make allowances for the fallibility of the artist. Many apparent variations in details may well be the result of imperfect observation or faulty execution. For more reliable information we must look to the ancient ships themselves, still available for scrutiny in the shape of shipwrecks or fragments of shipwrecks scattered throughout the Mediterranean and beyond. At the same time Aegean ships of the present day, based on long-established traditional designs, help us to fill out the picture.

Several examples of small ships from Roman times have been found. The first of these was 'Caesar's galley',    5
probably of the second or third century AD, mentioned earlier (p. 69). Although little of it survives today, remains of the hull more than 55 feet long and 23 feet broad were measured during its excavation.

The small merchant ship found in London in 1910, known as the County Hall ship (see chapter 5) was originally about 60 feet long with a beam of 15 or 16 feet.

8, 4, 7    The Titan wreck, when found, was a concreted mound of amphoras. The wreck had been looted before it was excavated by Philippe Tailliez, who raised 700 amphoras, leaving behind a few broken necks; it seems reasonable to assume that the ship carried well over 1,000 amphoras. Tailliez estimated the length of the original hull, without projections, at a little more than 80 feet.

1    The Dramont wreck had also been pillaged before it could be studied. 'About' 500 jars had been removed and 'several hundred' smashed before the remnants were raised by Siverine and Dumas, who salvaged an additional 180 jars, so here again the total must have been in the neighbourhood of 1,000. The wood was not well preserved, but enough remained for it to be compared with the Titan ship.

7    Frédéric Dumas, who has done a great deal of work on the La Chrétienne A wreck, has been able to reconstruct a section of it at the mast step, at which point the ship was 26 feet wide. It is reasonable to assume that this was the main mast step, since it differed from an *artemon* or foremast step which I found at Torre Sgarrata in southern Italy. Dumas' mast step was let into the strengthened keel, while that of the Torre Sgarrata was let into a huge block of timber cut to fit the curves of the inner stringers of the ship. The mainmast of the La Chrétienne A ship was probably stepped amidships or slightly forward of amidships, like that of vessels of the same type depicted in reliefs or mosaics, including the
16    bas-relief found at Portus.

## Roman Wrecks and Modern Parallels

The exact dimensions of the La Chrétienne and other comparable early Roman ships are not known, but they probably differed little from those of the most common Aegean type of today, the *trehandiri*. There are, of course, not sufficient data to prove that either the present-day *trehandiri* or the *perama*, another traditional type of sailing ship, is descended from any particular ancient ship type. Yet from many known details of design and construction, it seems reasonable to assume a relationship. Furthermore, ships built for identical conditions of wind and weather, out of identical materials, with similar tools, for the same purposes, would in all likelihood tend to resemble each other, whether or not a continuous tradition existed.

The ship on the Portus relief has much in common with both *trehandiris* and *peramas* (as well as with dozens of other traditional Mediterranean ship types with which I am not directly familiar). Like the latter, it is double-ended with the stern post carried up, and has a raked stem post, also carried up.

The basic difference between *peramas* and *trehandiris* is that the *perama* is narrower in relation to length, but deeper and shorter over-all, with flatter floors. A traditional *trehandiri* formula from the central Aegean calls for length over-all to equal length on keel plus one third; width to equal half the length of the keel, and depth in hold to equal one third width.

The earliest evidence for a *perama* is a late Byzantine jar in the Maritime Museum in Piraeus, which has a graffito showing such a vessel under sail. The protruding stern and stem posts are very plain. The type seems definitely Eastern in origin. The most extreme *perama* types are built today in Turkey and on Chios and Lesbos. One formula for *peramas* reads: LOA = LOK plus 25%; width = 1/3 LOA; depth = ½ the width.

Thus, if more like a *perama*, the over-all length of the La Chrétienne ship would be about 80 feet; if more like    7
a *trehandiri*, just under 70 feet. In the same way, the Titan    8, 4, 7
hull, whose keel was preserved to a length of 66 feet, would have been either 82½ feet long by 27½ feet wide by nearly 14 feet deep, or 88 feet by 33 feet by 10 feet. The proportions of the ship wrecked at Dramont were probably similar to this.

These dimensions compare well with those of one of the last surviving sailing *peramas* in the Aegean; *Evangelistria*. Built in 1938 in Syros, to a slightly varied    17
traditional formula, she is rigged as a gaff schooner. She earns part of her living in the wine trade, as did the Titan, Dramont and La Chrétienne ships in their day. She has a registered tonnage of 85, is 66 feet on the keel and 82½ feet over-all; her width is 20 feet and her depth in hold 6½. When carrying wine to the islands in the autumn, she is usually loaded with 60,000 *okas*, or about 77 metric tons of liquid, not counting the weight of the barrels in which the wine is shipped. The same amount of wine could be carried in about 2,500 Roman amphoras. It is difficult to calculate the exact weight of the barrels needed to carry her wine cargo, but certainly these are considerably more efficient than amphoras, and a wise captain would not load his ship as heavily for a voyage under sail from Italy to southern France as he could safely do for a short trip under power in the Cyclades. The weight of 1,500 full wine jars of the type found at Titan would be between 50 and 55 tons, the lading at which *Evangelistria* is at her best as a sailing ship.

The vessel's pine deck planking is 2¾ inches thick and her pine sides are 2 inches thick. Her average speed under sail is six knots, the same speed at which ships for which the *Periplus* (see below) was written seemed to have sailed. The dimensions of her keel and bottom cross section amidships must be much the same as were those of the Titan and Dramont ships. She is not copper-sheathed.

The late Professor Fernand Benoît distinguished two construction types of tenoned ships during the Roman period: 'single'- and 'double'-keeled ships. The 'double-keeled' ships all had keelsons, were flat-bottomed like the Titan and Dramont ships, were all of under 150 tons, and were not lead-sheathed. By 'double-keeled' Benoît meant ships with very heavy multiple keelsons.

*Evangelistra*'s 2 inch planking compares well with the $1\frac{4}{5}$ to $2\frac{2}{5}$ inch planking of the La Chrétienne A wreck. The Dramont wreck had $2\frac{3}{4}$ inch planking. One of the seven Roman hulls excavated on the bottom of Claudius' harbour at modern Fiumicino (see chapter 4, pp. 98,99) was also much heavier, with $2\frac{3}{4}$ inch planks; the second had 2 inch planking. *Archangel*, a modern heavily built traditional *perama* from Euboea, is 53 feet on deck by $16\frac{1}{2}$ feet amidships, carries 30 tons of cargo, and has $1\frac{3}{8}$ inch planking.

It seems possible that ships like *Evangelistria* or *Archangel* might be descended from the smaller merchant ships of the first centuries before and after Christ, or, more precisely, from a family of similar designs including the wrecks described above. These are the 'double-keeled' ships with comparatively flat floors, easy to beach, and therefore often not lead-sheathed.

It is certainly not possible to say definitely that all the ships mentioned above were like that in the Portus relief, but some of them must have been.

*Larger cargo ships.* These are the big 'single keel' ships of 150–200 tons, difficult to beach, often lead-sheathed, with steeper floors than those of the Portus (?*perama*)

12  *Map showing the wreck sites mentioned in this chapter. Note especially the clusters of stone-carriers at Sapienza, the gulf of Taranto, and southern Sicily. One sea route to Rome for big carriers from the east must have led past Antikythera, then to Sapienza, northwards up the coast to Corfu, across to a landfall near Gallipoli, and down to the straits of Messina*

type – so large that they would have been unloaded in Ostia rather than make the trip up the Tiber to Rome. Of the two lists below, the first includes wrecks which yielded structural wood that could be studied; the second, wrecks whose cargoes were sufficiently intact to enable the tonnage to be estimated, though nothing of the hull remains.

*6*  1. The Antikythera ship was never completely excavated, and it is difficult to estimate the tonnage of the cargo which covered an area of about 100 by 33 feet; but it was certainly well over 100 tons and quite possibly over 200.

2. The Mahdia ship carried at least 230 metric tons of *10, 12, 2, 14* cargo. Her keel was 86 feet long, close to the length of keel of a 300 ton *perama* recently built in Syros, which measures 80 feet on the keel and 100 feet over-all; her planks are $2\frac{2}{5}$ inches thick, similar to those of the Mahdia ship, which were 2 inches, but lighter than those of the Antikythera wreck, whose planks were $3\frac{3}{16}$ inches thick.

3. The Albenga ship, a large Roman amphora carrier, was found on the Italian Riviera in 1949. She sank, as did the Antikythera and Mahdia vessels, during the first century BC. The visible parts of the wreck measure about 100 feet by 26, and are still unexcavated.

The above-mentioned vessels were lead-sheathed and copper-fastened, and there is some evidence that all three could have been built in Italy.

4. The Torre Sgarrata ship, carrying about 170 tons of *11, 8, 13* marble from Asia Minor, sank near Taranto in southern Italy. Her construction is similar to that of the other large ships, except that there is less use of copper nails, which seem to have been used only when the time came for her to be renovated. Wood analysis suggests that she was built somewhere along the southern littoral of the Mediterranean. Patches on the hull showed us that she was old when she sank, sometime in the late second century AD.

In the case of the following wrecks the estimated tonnage is based solely on the cargo found at the site:

1. Torre Cianca, southern Italy: cargo of four monolithic columns each 9 × 1 metres, second century AD. 120 tons.

2. San Pietro, southern Italy: cargo of marble sarcophagi, second century AD. About 150 tons.

3. Isole Corrienti: cargo of marble blocks, perhaps second century AD. About 350 tons.

4. Marzamemi, Sicily: cargo of column drums, first or second century AD. 172 tons.

5. St Tropez: cargo of marble blocks and column drums, second century AD. Estimated at 200 tons.

6. Marzamemi, Sicily: prefabricated paleo-Christian church, sixth century AD. Over 100 tons. (See chapter 6, pp. 136–7.)

7. Sapienza island, off the Peloponnesus: cargo of granite columns weighing 121 metric tons. Either late Roman or medieval.

There exist several dozen other wrecks of Roman or late Roman merchant ships with similar cargoes, but they have not been sufficiently surveyed to allow reasonably accurate tonnage estimates. Most of these wrecks lie on the traditional trade routes from the East. There are several by the Tremiti islands, one off Taormina, another in Zakynthos, several others off the Peloponnesus and southern Sicily, and several more in the Sea of Marmara and off the Turkish coast.

Though they have not been surveyed, they seem to fall into the pattern of the wrecks listed above. From the cargoes, it is possible to conclude that the carrying

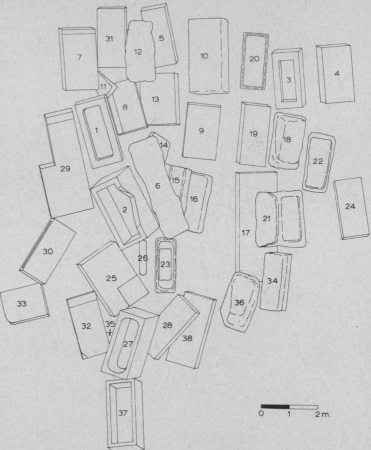

13 The ship wrecked off Torre Sgarrata, near Taranto, in the late second century AD was carrying more than 160 tons of rough-cut marble from Afrodisias. The appearance of the wreckage after the sand was cleared is shown in this plan

14 Sketch plan of the Mahdia wreck, showing the cargo as seen by Cousteau's divers in 1948

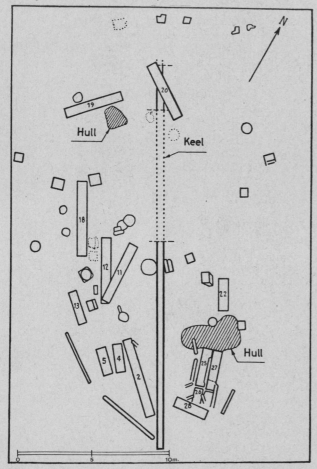

capacity of the class of large ships used for transporting marble building materials from the East was between 100 and 200 metric tons. Only one of the wrecks above carried more than 200 tons, the average cargo being between 150 and 170 tons.

Modern practice is never to load a ship with stone beyond about two-thirds of its gross tonnage, and this in the Aegean for short trips under power. The captain of a Roman sailing ship on a long voyage would presumably have been very much more cautious about not overloading his ship.

Cargo has been used as indication of the ship's size, rather than heaviness of construction, since the latter is not necessarily a criterion. One of the Fiumicino ships, for example, was certainly not more than 60 feet long but had $2\frac{3}{4}$ inch planking. The Albenga wreck, on the other hand, was undoubtedly a large ship but had planking of only half that thickness.

No one has yet found the wreck of any Roman seagoing ship which provides definite proof that it was larger than the 300-tonners mentioned above. But there are many references to such vessels, and the Lake Nemi ships show that this size of craft was built.

*Rigging*. The rig of Roman cargo ships in representations usually varies only in the size of the *artemon*, or steering sail, which sometimes reached considerable proportions, and the occasional use of a triangular topsail above the large, square mainsail. (In a study of over 500 ship representations in Roman mosaics and wall paintings, David Rupp of the University of Pennsylvania found only one three-masted ship, a large merchantman with ram-like bow.) Such cargo carriers, built double-ended, were designed to run with the sea behind them. No one has experimented with a Roman mainsail and *artemon* on a *perama* hull, but it seems clear that this was an efficient and practical rig; given the wind abaft the beam, a 'Roman'-rigged *perama* could undoubtedly outsail a schooner-rigged *perama* of similar lines.

These ships were probably not very effective to windward, yet one wonders whether there may not be more than meets the eye in many representations of Roman ships with the tack (that is, the forward lower part of the sail) hauled all the way forward and seemingly lashed near the stem post. The Roman square rig might well have been more effective to windward than it looks.

Its disadvantage was that it required a large crew. A Roman ship of *Evangelistria*'s dimensions needed at least ten men to handle its big square sail; properly rigged as a schooner, *Evangelistria* can be sailed by a crew of three. Rig is an indication of the availability of labour in the trade for which the ship was built, rather than a technological development. In the nineteenth century, for example, when sailors were to be had cheap, many *peramas* and *trehandiris* were square-rigged.

Fore-and-aft sails were known in Roman times, but they were not common. Lionel Casson has found at least four representations of spritsails between the second and fourth centuries AD, with an earlier example going back to the second century BC. He has noted also the appearance of an 'Arab' lateen on a second-century stele, and a triangular lateen in a fourth-century mosaic.

*Daily life on board.* Almost every Roman wreck so far found has produced terracotta tiles from its galley roof, and flat tiles on a few wrecks suggest the possibility of hearths like that in the galley of the seventh-century Byzantine ship at Yassi Ada (see chapter 6, p. 140); both point to the constant fear of cooking fires spreading. Also numerous brazier-like terracotta stoves, mostly of the second and first centuries BC, have been netted by Aegean fishermen who sometimes cook on modern counterparts, almost identical in form, made of empty oil tins.

Collections of cooking pots and tableware, often including fine ware presumably for the captain, have appeared on all Roman shipwrecks, along with jars for the storage of the provisions needed by the crew. Millstones and stone mortars aided in the preparation of food. After dark, light was provided by terracotta oil lamps, another common find in underwater excavations.

All Roman wrecks so far excavated have produced quantities of lead sinkers. Some of these may, however, be more recent than the wrecks, since wrecks attract quantities of fish.

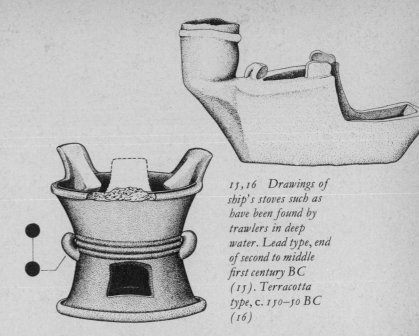

15,16 *Drawings of ship's stoves such as have been found by trawlers in deep water. Lead type, end of second to middle first century BC (15). Terracotta type, c. 150–50 BC (16)*

*Anchors.* Lead anchor stocks have been found by the hundreds throughout the Mediterranean, both in isolation and in association with shipwrecks. They range in weight from tiny dinghy anchors to large ones weighing well over a ton.

Big Roman ships carried many anchors. A ship that went ashore off Taranto in the late first or early second century AD let go five anchors, each weighing in the neighbourhood of 600 kg. The famous account of Paul's shipwreck in the New Testament (Acts 27) provides a good description of the use of anchors.

The stocks are often inscribed with names of gods, generally in Greek but sometimes in Latin, and often misspelt. Astragals, used for playing knucklebones, are also common; the practice of inscribing dice on an anchor with the seven or eleven throw visible, although not a part of modern nautical folklore, would seem perfectly natural to a modern seaman.

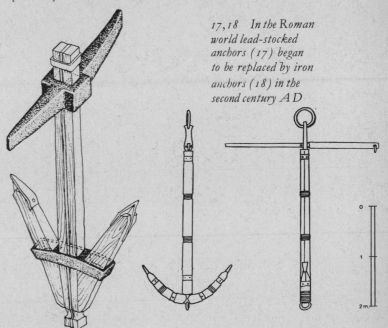

17,18 *In the Roman world lead-stocked anchors (17) began to be replaced by iron anchors (18) in the second century AD*

*17* The lead stocks and collars of these Roman composite anchors seem to have been cast around the hardwood shank and flukes of the anchor. The function of the lead stock is obvious. It made the stock part of the anchor fall to the bottom so that the flukes would dig in, and kept the anchor cable pulling at the correct angle to the fluke. The collar kept the wooden arms rigid. While heavier and harder to handle than an iron anchor, these composite anchors must have been very effective. Some even had folding stocks.

Iron anchors came into use early and were used along with composite anchors, as is shown by the pile of seven anchors – four of lead and wood, and three of iron – excavated by Nino Lamboglia on a mid-second-century BC shipwreck off the Italian island of Giannutri. Iron *18* anchors, usually sheathed in wood, seem to have come into more general use towards the end of the Empire, along with vestigial tenoning and a more general use of iron instead of copper for fastening.

*Navigation.* The Greek skippers of ancient Mediterranean cargo ships used much the same system of navigation as their modern descendants. The old-time caique sailors I have sailed with, those who learned their trade in sailing ships, still don't use a compass. They distrust compasses. They navigate solely by the stars, and very well too. The perama *Archangel*, mentioned above, was for years engaged in the business of carrying lemons to Thessalonika from Poros – a long passage, made mostly at night and in winter. Her compass, up to 40 degrees out on some headings when I bought the ship, was used only to keep to a course fixed on a star. Much use was made of stars to steer by at night in antiquity, and the average captain must have had a good practical knowledge of astronomy as it applied to navigating while out of sight of land without the use of a compass.

The great variability of winds in the Aegean, and in the Mediterranean in general, meant that skippers in pre-engine days had to know not only stars, but where and when the winds would blow at different times of day and at different times of year. Sailing instructions for traversing the Aegean go something like this: 'Wait at A in the month of June till you have a NW breeze. Leave at 0500. Sail to B, arriving at 1200. Anchor. Wait for NE breeze, then sail for C at 0300 the next day.' And so on. Each of the old-timers I know has a mental list of such instructions, and the good ones can sail right round an island in the *meltemi* (the Classical Etesian wind from the north) and never start a sheet because they know where the wind-slants off the mountains are to be expected.

Written instructions used by the Greek skippers of antiquity have survived from Roman times, either whole or in fragments. These vary between simple coastal descriptions, giving few distances or bearings, such as Arrian's second-century *Periplus of the Euxine* (literally 'Sailing-around' of the Black Sea), and the first-century *Periplus of the Erythraean Sea* (Indian Ocean), which is a comprehensive guide for merchants as much as a set of sailing directions for the Red Sea, the Persian Gulf and the way to the west of India. The third-century *Stadiasmus Maris Magni* differs from other guides by describing much of the Mediterranean coast with distances given in *stadia* rather than in the usual 'day's sail'.

Although no charts have survived, it seems likely that they existed. The captain thought of directions in terms of a system of eight personified winds, which were halved and halved again to give thirty-two points. He simply estimated his speed. There is, it is true, a single reference, by Vitruvius, to a device by which an outboard paddle-wheel caused a ball to drop into a receptacle every mile, but it is uncertain if the gadget was really used. Close to shore, there were lighthouses to assist the mariner (see chapter 4).

Growing interest in marine archaeology, coupled with improved techniques for locating, investigating and salvaging underwater wrecks, are likely to make available for study a great deal more material on Roman shipping in the next few decades.

---

1 The most solidly constructed, and probably the largest, sea-going ship from Imperial Roman times so far discovered is the vessel wrecked off Torre Sgaratta near Taranto on the 'foot' of Italy. A merchantman, she was carrying a cargo of marble from Asia Minor. Analysis of the surviving hull timbers indicated that she was built somewhere on the southern littoral of the Mediterranean Sea. The hull was patched in several places and refastened with copper nails, suggesting that the vessel had been in service for a considerable time before she was wrecked in the late second century AD.

Here a diver stands on the sea bed, making an underwater drawing of the planking. The remains of the ship's frames and strakes are clearly visible.

6

7

8

6 Two luxury barges from Imperial Roman times, known for many centuries to have lain on the bed of Lake Nemi, seventeen miles southeast of Rome, were uncovered when the lake was drained in the 1930s. Though presumably never intended for use on the open sea, these great vessels can compare with the largest sea-going ships of their day. Measuring more than 200 feet long by 60 feet wide, they were tenoned, copper-fastened and sheathed. Pictured here is one of the salvaged ships on display in a building beside the lake; it was set alight and destroyed by German soldiers in 1944.

7 Frédéric Dumas has been able to identify sufficient pieces of a first-century AD Roman ship wrecked off La Chrétienne on the French Mediterranean coast to ascertain that it will have differed little in size and specifications from vessels such as the *trehandiri* or *perama* plying the Aegean today. At the top of the photograph can be seen the mast-step; on the right the ends of the inner planking project from the sand.

8 Divers with air-lift tubes over the Roman ship wrecked off Titan, Ile du Levant. Even though the wreck had been looted earlier, Philippe Tailliez, who excavated the site, recovered 700 amphoras.

9 This second-century AD statue, of a priestess (?) in chiton and mantle, was found in the vicinity of the Lake Nemi wrecks (see 6 above).

10, 12 A Roman ship containing Hellenistic works of art was lost three miles from the Tunisian coast near Mahdia in the first half of the first century BC. Greek sponge divers located it in the opening decade of this century. Among a vast quantity of statuary recovered was the bronze figurine of a dancing dwarf shown left (10). Much of the Mahdia cargo remains beneath the waves. It comprised mainly architectural members such

as marble columns, bases and capitals, weighing in all well over 200 tons. One of the columns photographed under water during the 1955 operations is shown below (12). In 1948 Commanders Tailliez and Cousteau, using the newly invented aqualungs, were able to carry out systematic archaeological investigations which led, in 1954/55, to the first mapping of the site and study of the parts of the hull that were still intact.

11   A sarcophagus – one of many that made up the cargo of the Roman merchantman which was wrecked off Torre Sgaratta (see 1 above) – being raised with the aid of balloons. Having lain exposed to the waters on top of the wreck, it had suffered damage from sea creatures that had bored into the stone.

9

10

11

12

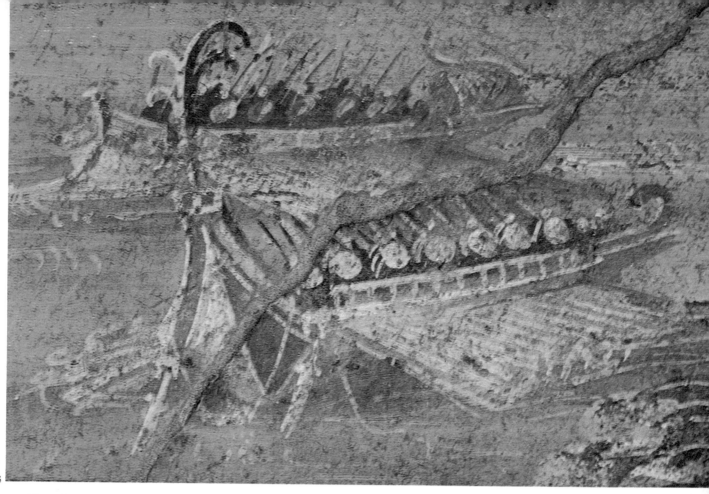

13

13 Four Roman warships engaged in a mimic battle (*naumachia*). Two are shown with tall 'plumed' stems, two with *oculi* painted on the prow, and all have the characteristic in-curving stern. Fresco in the Casa dei Vettii at Pompeii, dating from before AD 79.

14 Relief from the Temple of Fortuna Primigenia in Praeneste, showing a large Roman bireme. The rowers working the two banks of oars are wholly enclosed. Passing up beside the curving stem, behind which stands a fighting turret, is the mast for the *artemon*.

14

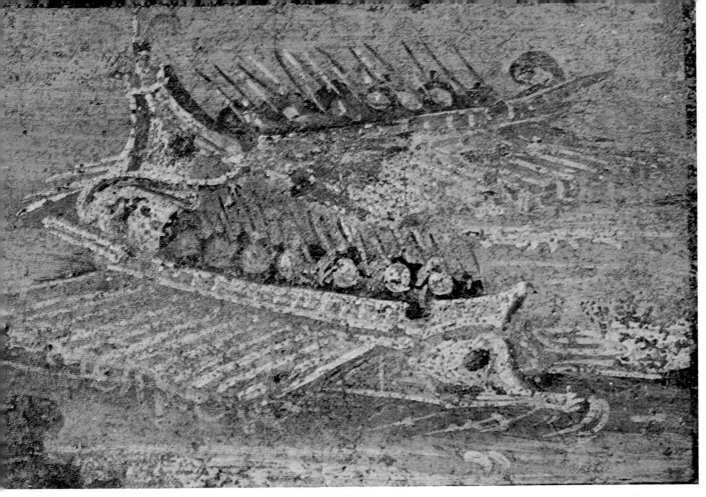

15 Ulysses and the Sirens. A third-century AD mosaic
from the House of Ulysses and Dionysius at Dougga,
Tunisia. The ship has a flat-ended stem and a tall
in-curving stern. Surmounting both the *artemon*-like
foresail and the mainsail are triangular topsails.

15

16

17

16 A merchantman has just docked in Portus, Rome's harbour, to unload. Note the flat-topped stem (cf. ill. 15) and the artemon mast (its end broken off), the wales, the long, heavy steering oars, the projecting cross-beams, and the large triangular topsail through which a forestay passes from mast to deck. Part of a second-century AD bas-relief from Portus.

17 The bow of *Evangelistria*, one of the last surviving sailing *peramas* used, as were the Roman ships of comparable size wrecked off Titan, Dramont and La Chrétienne in southern France, for carrying wine. If the king post at the inner end of the bowsprit were to be moved back a few feet and the timbers at the stem which hold the bowsprit were to be extended upwards, together with the stem post above which the sailor is sitting, the bowsprit's outboard end could be raised, thus forming a forward-raking mast, on which a square *artemon* could be rigged.

# 4

# Greek and Roman harbourworks

JOSEPH W. SHAW

# Greek and Roman harbourworks

## The Earliest Harbour Installations

The history of harbours begins when the first boatman searched for a safe, permanent moorage along the shore, where his ship would be secure from the currents of the river or the waves of the unpredictable sea. In such sheltered, easily accessible places his fellow-boatmen, fishermen, ferrymen, merchants or travellers might join him until the time came to move on. Gradually, small riverside communities were established in this manner.

Stable communities changed the random pattern of early boating into an enterprise from which the state profited and upon which the citizens depended for their very existence. For instance, farmers producing a surplus of grain needed to ship it up or down river in order to receive goods or credit in return. At the same time the military forces of certain states gradually came to depend upon water transport, first simply for ferrying soldiers

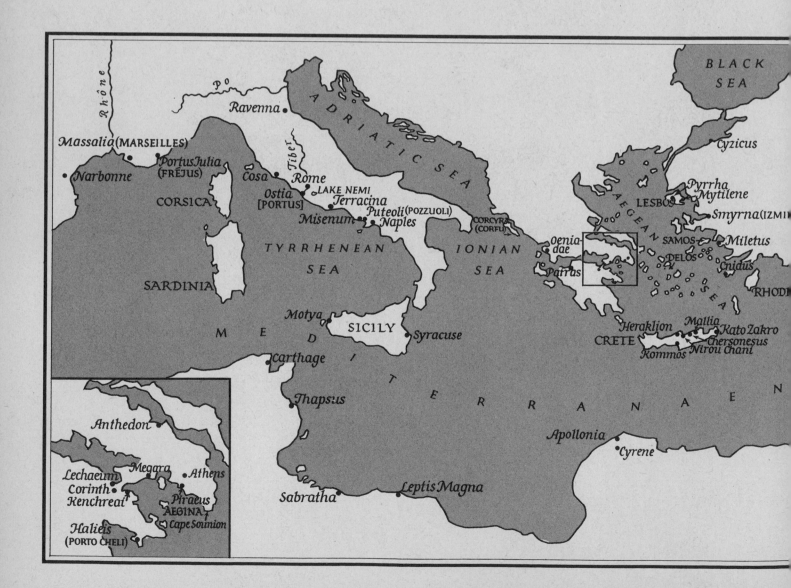

and supplies from one place to another and then, when the ship had become a tactical instrument and the seas were better known, as a platform from which to give battle.

In the Mediterranean, the first navies of the Egyptians, Minoans, Phoenicians and Greeks were probably composed of relatively small ships that could be run ashore and pulled up the beach; there they would be propped along the sides, as is still done today. During the non-sailing months in winter the ships might be covered over by coarse cloth or branches, or surrounded by stones, in order to protect them from seasonal rains and gales.

In these earliest phases of harbour development, a combination of economic advantage, shelter and, of course, defensibility determined the locations of harbours, whether they were on river banks, at deltas or along the sea coast itself. The archaeologist studying these early times knows of many such settlements, especially those along the rivers Tigris and Euphrates, where the water was used for irrigation as well as drinking. For a number of reasons, however, very few

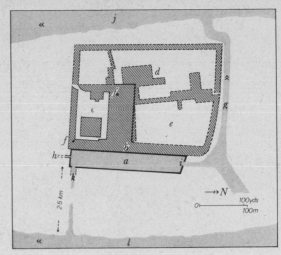

2 Lothal, India. Earliest known artificial harbour installation. Ships entered the dock basin (a) through a channel (i) from the mullah (g) until in 1970 BC this channel silted up, the river changed course and a new approach channel (k) was dug: j, l initial and later course of river; b wharf; c acropolis; d lower town; f wells; h spillway; e unexcavated area

*1 The Mediterranean, showing harbour sites discussed in the text. The sites are not all contemporaneous, nor of equal duration in their commercial or military roles. Some, like Motya, Terracina, Oeniadae, Delos, Mallia, Kommos, Kenchreai, Pyrrha, Cyzicus, and Leptis Magna, had a short life span; others like Marseilles, Patras, Piraeus, Heraklion, Izmir, Tyre, and Alexandria, have a history that can be reckoned in millennia. While the earliest harbourworks were probably made in the East, it is not until Greek and Roman times that we have securely dated examples (e.g. Piraeus, Portus, and Leptis Magna.)*

permanent harbour works were built then. The earliest harbours appear to have been located outside the Mediterranean area, though the existence of some of these is known to us only from ancient texts for no actual remains have been found.

In India, for example, recent excavations at Lothal, not far from the fertile Indus River Valley, have revealed an enormous rectangular basin of the third millennium BC, probably originally excavated in order to serve as a dock for ships entering the Gulf of Cambay. Constructed of thick, kiln-fired mud-brick walls with two openings construed as an entrance and an exit for ships, as well as what is believed to have been a sluice gate which controlled the water level within the basin, it is the earliest known example of an artificial enclosure built for ships.

In Mesopotamia, somewhat later, Babylonian records attest the existence of warehouses and other special harbour buildings placed along the river bank for storage of goods, mostly grain. A later Assyrian stone relief represents what has been interpreted as a dry-dock which served rafts and freighters. Such a presumed dock has been found, cut out of a river bank along the Euphrates at Til-Barsib. In Egypt, where ships were used from the earliest times, dockyards for their construction appear in the transactions of the Pharaoh Thutmosis III (1504–1450 BC). Even so, the best known ancient Egyptian quays were alongside monumental riverside entrances to funeral temples; and these quays were probably reserved for special occasions rather than for daily use.

Along the coasts and among the islands of the eastern Mediterranean, a number of so-called early harbour works have been traced. These take the form of anomalous walls in the water at Dor in Palestine; a deep rectangular trench cut from bedrock next to the modern shoreline at Nirou Chani, Crete; a long narrow cutting in bedrock perhaps for a wall's foundation at Mallia, also in Crete; a series of impressively large and well-constructed piers, jetties and breakwaters at Alexandria, Sidon and Tyre, assigned by various scholars to the Bronze Age or at least to a period anterior to the seventh century BC. For such early times, however, there is still no carefully documented archaeological evidence for a tradition of harbourworks in the Mediterranean. Indeed, such works as have been found are variously described as being Egyptian, Minoan, Phoenician or Roman and their dates cannot be firmly established either by means of stratigraphic study or through comparison with the methods of building in associated structures found on land. It seems best, therefore, to begin a sequential study of Mediterranean harbourworks with the better dated examples of the Greeks, for it was they who founded a tradition which the Romans later transformed into complex port plans and building construction, many features of which are reflected in present-day harbour designs.

## Greece

In Greece the sixth and fifth centuries BC may be regarded as the formative period for the construction of moles for breaking the force of water and wind, ship-sheds for the protection of the military fleet as well as ancillary harbour facilities. The historian Herodotus speaks with admiration of the construction by the Samian tyrant Polykrates (d. 522 BC) of an immense breakwater that projected into the harbour some 440 yards to a point where the sea was some 115 feet deep. Herodotus also mentions the use of ship-sheds at Samos about this time. The presence of heavy breakwaters, now below water level, bear out his statement; moreover, masonry blocks, presumably belonging to a tower foundation discovered on a smaller, second mole near by, were until fairly recently visible at the end of the longest breakwater at Samos.

The development of building techniques on land from the sixth to the third century BC is reflected in the maritime establishments found along the shore, and although a good deal of research on land and under water still remains to be done, our general picture of the harbour enclosures and the various types of buildings within them is fairly well established. Above all, one can see how various geographic situations were adapted for sheltering and servicing the ships. Mytilene on the island of Lesbos, Cyzicus which is on a trade route leading to and from the Black Sea, and Old Smyrna in western Turkey each had a citadel located on a point of land projecting into the sea, thus affording two natural harbours, one on either side of the headland; the low, flat land of the isthmus was probably cut by an existing lagoon or by an artificial channel that protected the acropolis from invasion by land and

allowed merchant vessels and warships to transfer from one harbour to another irrespective of weather conditions.

For the separate military and commercial harbours on the island of Aegina, impressive, thick walls of limestone blocks extended out from the shore and after a few minor bends turned at right angles toward each other. Where they ended rectangular towers probably stood, separated by a gap through which only a few ships could pass at a time. Elsewhere, as at Piraeus, the port of Athens, natural bays were simply closed off by means of extensions of fortification walls already surrounding the town, leaving gaps which could be closed in order to keep out intruders. In numerous cases, when inland cities established harbour towns along the neighbouring coast, port towns, separately fortified, were established at convenient points. For instance in early times Corinth, located astride an isthmus controlling east–west traffic by sea and north–south traffic by land, established the two ports of Lechaeum and Kenchreai, the former on *1* the Gulf of Corinth on the west, the latter in a convenient cove of the Saronic Gulf on the east. Elsewhere, as at Syracuse, Nisaea, or Cnidus, advantage was taken of the shelter of an offshore island or reef, or of a headland projecting into the sea. In some cases, such as those of Piraeus, Corinth, Patras, and Megara-Nisaea, parallel fortification walls linked the port to its inland city.

*Piraeus*. The inland city of Athens established the port *1, 3, 4* of Piraeus in the fifth century BC and may well have set the example for other Greek cities by its port planning and administration. Fortunately, because of the wealth of literary texts and inscriptions, the latter discovered both in Athens and in Piraeus itself, we are better informed about Piraeus than any contemporary harbour town.

Unlike port cities with longer histories, Piraeus was not always the chief harbour of Athens. With great foresight the famous Athenian statesman and admiral Themistocles in 493 transferred the naval establishment from the open, indefensible beaches of Phaleron to the rocky peninsula of Piraeus; this projects into the sea from the southwestern edge of the Attic plain, just to the east of the large island of Salamis, which had become Athenian territory in the sixth century BC. During the following 50 years an expanded Athenian fleet helped defeat the hordes of invading Persians and also tamed the rival naval powers of Corinth and Aegina, thus securing for itself naval supremacy in the western Aegean and establishing a base for its future political and economic expansion.

Fortification walls ringed the harbour areas, cutting across the peninsula's base on the land side and then skirting close to the exposed shore lines. The walls along the shore had square, rectangular, and round towers at different periods of their history, and at one time were extended into the harbour entrances on moles ending in towers. The walls were composed of heavy limestone

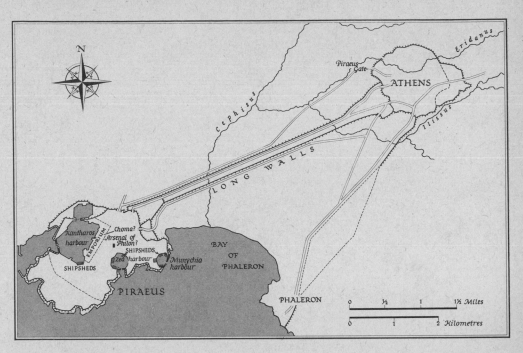

3 *As part of its growth as a major seapower, Athens moved its harbour installations in 493 BC from the open Bay of Phaleron to the more easily defended peninsula of Piraeus to the west. Piraeus was surrounded by walls, and its three natural harbours (Kantharos, Zea, Munychia) were enclosed, except for narrow entrance channels that could be blocked by chains. To preserve their lifeline to the sea, the Athenians built parallel fortification walls linking the inland city with its port. Traces of another fortification wall have been found to the east.*

blocks with the upper stone courses clamped together by metal, and were set upon rubble foundations. While commanding the short gaps left for friendly ships to pass through, the towers on the moles could have functioned as lighthouses as well. Between them were drawn protective chains. At Zea, moles narrowed the harbour entrance to only 120 feet.

The Athenians came to depend so heavily on Piraeus that, in order to develop their capacity to resist a siege from land as long as their vital link with the harbour remained unsevered, they built the 'Long Walls'. These were first two, and later three, immense fortification walls in between which supplies of food and weapons might pass from port to city, or vice-versa, regardless of enemy invasions. Also, in time of siege the country people could find shelter between the walls. Such an arrangement was repeated at Corinth, Megara, and elsewhere.

Hippodamus, the first city-planner known by name, is said to have designed much of Piraeus. It would seem that he determined the lay-out of civic areas and the orientation of streets, separating military and commercial areas from residential quarters and markets.

Descriptions in literature, inscribed boundary markers found in their original positions, and other discoveries made in the past have enabled us to gauge the outer limits of the commercial and military areas fairly accurately. The shore of the smallest enclosed harbour, Munychia (modern Tourkolimano) to the east, was occupied by sheds built for triremes; but the roomy central harbour of Zea (modern Pasalimani) provided the real base for military activities. Here most of the warships were stationed, sailors met at special assembly grounds, and distinctive buildings were provided for storing naval equipment. The even larger harbour of Kantharos to the west, today the central harbour of commercial Athens, was the great centre of trade, the 'emporium'. Merchants from all areas of the Mediterranean came here to buy and sell their goods. First, however, their cargoes would be inspected and they might have to pay both port and customs fees to the harbour officials. Having done this, they would either anchor out in deeper water within the harbour and then transfer their merchandise into smaller vessels, or lie up at quays that may have extended along the shore.

Voyagers approaching Piraeus from the sea will have been met by an impressive sight: five colonnaded porticoes, or stoas, with their white marble gleaming in the bright Attic sun against the blue sky. Indeed, the harbour works here were a great source of pride for the Athenians, to judge by their references to them. The stoas, of which significant remains have not yet been found, probably lined the northern and eastern shores of the largest harbour, Kantharos, some distance back from landing areas now obscured by modern filling operations. At least one of these porticoes, the so-called 'Long Stoa', served for the distribution of grain imported from the Black Sea and elsewhere; for, as happened in Rome at a later date, Athens relied on grain importation to supplement local production. The other stoa known to us by name is the 'Sample Market', or 'Deigma', where varieties of goods both from Greece and abroad were shown and where banking and exchange activities took place. Near by was a special quay called the 'Choma' where departure ceremonies took place on the eve of great military expeditions. The famous, ill-fated expedition to Syracuse in 415 BC, whose destruction was to cripple the Athenian navy, probably set sail from here.

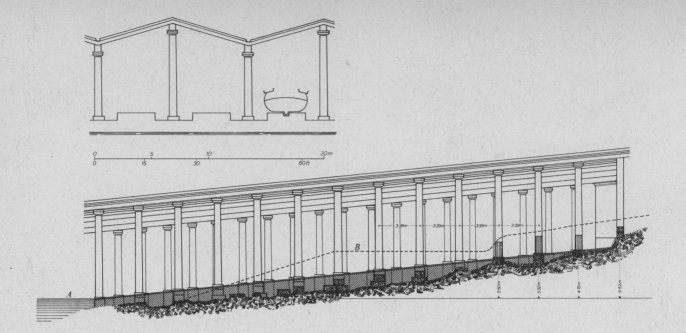

*Ship-sheds*. Ship-sheds, where the military vessels were stored, have been found on the mainland of Greece, on various islands, as well as on the coast of North Africa. The discovery toward the end of the last century of the sheds in Piraeus was particularly fortunate, however, for together with historical records and inscriptions they have furnished material for estimating the size of the Athenian fleet. They are also useful in the study of the maximum dimensions of the trireme, types of wood and rope gear carried aboard the ships, and the type of public administration necessary to keep the fleet fit for service. The Athenian ship-sheds differ from others discovered elsewhere in certain aspects of siting, interior arrangement, and architectural detail; but the typical long, garage-like spaces sloping down into the water are common to many Greek harbours. To these long, narrow buildings the triremes were brought for minor repairs, but mainly for stowage, especially during the winter, in order to prevent rot and damage by seaworms. The ends of the sheds were built in such a way as to project down into the water, so that ships could be hauled up easily, probably stern-first, by manual labour or by mechanical means such as the block and tackle, or perhaps the winch.

In Piraeus the ship-sheds, of which there were at least 372 in the fourth century BC, cost the equivalent of $1,000,000. In the harbour of Zea (Pasalimani) they were apparently arranged in units of four or eight parallel sheds, each slipway being separated from its neighbour by a row of columns, the bases of which became increasingly lower as they approached the sea. Pairs of slipways were covered by a single roof joined along their eaves with another roof sloping to meet it. Remains of these sheds can still be seen running into the now polluted water of the modern harbour.

Interesting remains of ship-sheds have also been found at Cape Sounion, near the famous sanctuary of Poseidon, at Oeniadae in western Greece, and at Apollonia in Cyrenaica. Elsewhere, for instance at Pyrrha in Lesbos, at Rhodes, at Chersonesus in Crete, or at Corcyra in the Adriatic, remains have also been reported, but they are so fragmentary as to be of very little help to us in our studies. Those at the island of Aegina, in shallow water, remain unexcavated. Of the three first-named, those at Sounion are among the smallest, being a single pair cut out of the cliff along the shore. Some 65 feet long, their inclination down to the sea (about 16 degrees) is the steepest known. They were approached from the west by a flight of stairs. Those found at Apollonia and Oeniadae were also cut out from the bed-rock along the shore. At Apollonia the ship-sheds were discovered only lately through underwater research, for they now lie submerged some $6\frac{1}{2}$ feet below the surface. The Apollonia sheds represent the only case in which the actual measurements are known (about 125 feet long, in one case 20 feet wide), so they are especially important in determining the length of the ships they could house. At Oeniadae there were six stalls, five equipped with grooves up which ships were pulled, and another separately roofed, flat space probably intended for equipment storage and assembly. As at Piraeus, the continuous roof at Oeniadae was supported by colonnades, but in this case there was probably a single gable over each shed, rather than over every pair.

*The Arsenal of Philon*. In Athens some of the equipment for the military vessels was stored aboard the ships or somewhere within the ship-sheds, but the majority of the extra sails, rudders, cordage, and anchors rested in storehouses built near the shore. The most famous of these buildings was the Arsenal of Philon, named after Philon of Eleusis, the most prominent architect of the mid-fourth century BC. The building was located behind the ship-sheds of the harbour of Zea, not far from the

*4 Restored cross-section (above) and longi-
tudinal cross-section (below) of covered, parallel
berths of ships ('ship-sheds') in Piraeus. The
ships were drawn up on raised platforms in
which a groove was sometimes cut for the keel.
The exact appearance of the seaward end of
such buildings, and their total length, is usually
not known*

*5 Schematic cross-section of the Arsenal of
Philon in Piraeus, where the gear used by the
military fleet was stored. While no trace of this
building, which was destroyed by Sulla, has
been found, a series of detailed inscriptions or
stone slabs set forth specifications for the
construction*

Hippodamian Agora. Though the remains of the building have not been found, numerous ancient writers
tell us that it was one of the most impressive monuments
in either Piraeus or Athens. Moreover, an inscription
supplies unique information about its composition,
construction, and size.

The walls and foundations were marble blocks quarried from the near-by hill of Akte. It was 405 Attic feet
long and 55 Attic feet wide. Around the sides were
openings for light, probably taking the form of large
windows far up on the high wall and small slits for light
and air lower down. Double doors at each end provided
access to the interior. Within, two rows of columns
divided the floor space into three great aisles. While the
centre aisle functioned mainly as a thoroughfare for the
cartloads of equipment, the keepers of the stored goods,
the sailors, and the ever-curious public, the side aisles
contained the gear itself. Here behind each pair of
columns was a separate enclosure with lofty rows of
shelves for ships' cables and girdles, the latter being
ropes which passed around the outside of the ship to
reinforce the hull. On the floor were large chests for
folded sails. Above, in a loft running along the wall,
was more storage space.

## Phoenician Harbours

Certain harbour constructions established by the Phoenician settlers and traders in the west were contemporary
with or, perhaps, even earlier than those developed by
the Greeks. The Phoenicians, for instance, probably
introduced the first artificially constructed harbours in
the Mediterranean – great basins scooped from the
shore-line. Such inner harbours, or 'cothons', were connected by one or more narrow channels with the sea and
were often bordered by stone quays. In later times, ship-
sheds and other establishments, commercial and military,
were associated with them. Curiously enough, no such

cothons have yet been found along the Syro-Palestinian
coast, so it is possible that the cothon was exclusively a
development of the western Phoenicians.

On the west-Sicilian island of Motya is the only well-
dated closed harbour of this earlier period. Since the
city was destroyed in 397 BC, and was never extensively
resettled, it is safe to assume that the small cothon there
was built sometime before this, probably in the sixth
century according to recent excavations. Elsewhere, for
example at Carthage which was destroyed and then
settled by the Romans, it has so far not been possible to
separate clearly the Phoenician from the later Roman
harbour remains.

*6,7*

*6*

*6 Motya, plan of inner harbour ('cothon'). The harbour,
built behind the town walls, may have sheltered ships during a
siege. Recent excavation has shown that the basin had a
somewhat different plan in its earliest phase*

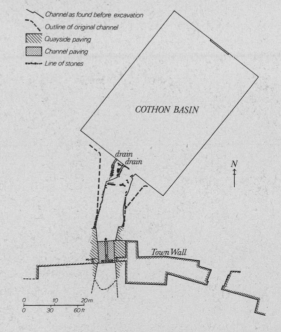

Channel as found before excavation
Outline of original channel
Quayside paving
Channel paving
Line of stones

COTHON BASIN

drain
drain

N

Town Wall

0    10    20m
0    30    60ft

7   *Entrance channel of the Motya cothon, looking seaward. The channel was bordered by quays. A central groove (for keels?) and a blocking wall were uncovered recently*

The entrance channel of the Motya cothon, some 16½
7   feet wide, was made for small ships with a maximum draft of about three feet. The bottom of the channel was paved with large blocks, and a wide groove running along the centre of the pavement may have been intended to furnish additional clearance for the ships' keels. The channel was bordered by massive quays composed of rectangular limestone blocks set with their long sides parallel to one another and their ends parallel to the quay walls. To protect the ships, the basin was placed within the encircling fortification wall of the town, and the entrance channel was probably closed by a gate. Perhaps as a further precaution the channel was constructed with a built-in angle, and the basin itself is at an angle with the shoreline.

The most recent excavations, by B. Isserlin and his associates, have shown that the entrance channel was blocked by a wall sometime before the town was destroyed. They also have suggested that the rectangular shape of the basin, which is about 105 by 167 feet, may have been different at the time that the entrance-way from the sea was being used. Further excavation will establish the facts of the matter, although the presence of an inner harbour contemporary with the entrance channel remains unquestioned.

## Hellenistic and Roman Harbourworks

From the fourth century BC, expanding state boundaries led to the growth of many ports and the creation of new ones. Up to this time, the Mediterranean countries were generally small; however, the conquests of Alexander the Great, the precarious unity his successors forced onto the mainland of Greece, and the subsequent rise of Rome's influence created much larger states whose great economic and political power increased the volume of both private and state-sponsored traffic. Henceforth,

although the small type of Greek harbour enclosed by a fortified perimeter did not disappear, it was gradually superseded by its larger descendants.

With more and larger ships being used for military and commercial purposes, new facilities for anchoring, mooring, docking, and storage were bound to develop. For instance, since large merchant vessels and warships could only with difficulty be pulled up on shore for storage, and direct loading and unloading from the shore was most economical, the crude shore-side quays of earlier times were often replaced by spacious platforms furnished with flights of steps and special mooring devices. Gradually such changes were developed and later incorporated by the Romans into their over-all harbour plan.

Although we have a clearer general picture of these later stages of harbour development, it is still not easy to disentangle the remains of different historical periods; to distinguish early harbour remains outside of Italy from those superimposed upon them by Roman engineers is particularly difficult. Complicating the matter are geological changes which have occurred in some areas since antiquity, such as the subsidence of entire coastal areas into the sea. Moreover, harbours situated on coasts subject to much sedimentary activity, or as at Ostia on estuaries, have become so silted up as to be unrecognizable as great emporia where international sea-trade once flourished. In other cases, however, ports lie preserved under mud or sand that, it is to be hoped, will some day be removed. Moreover, extensive remains lie visible under water, as for example at Apollonia in Cyrenaica, in North Africa, or at Kenchreai in Greece. Such semi-submerged sites can sometimes be easily surveyed by divers, and with the steady improvement of shallow-water excavation methods they can be explored and excavated by archaeologists to provide information on plan, construction and dating.

At a number of sites, walls, quays and pavements, clearly visible under water, run onto the land to disappear below accumulations of earth and rubble resulting from later habitation on the same site. Further excavation of such remains will help to date walls that now lie sandwiched between distinct cultural layers of this type. Unfortunately, as is the case with many inland sites located in areas which are, geographically, as strategic as they were in antiquity, ancient port sites are often so densely populated now that their study is difficult, if not impossible.

*Alexandria.* The great harbour of Alexandria has been    4, 5
used continually since the second millennium BC, through Egyptian, Greek, Roman, Byzantine and Arab times to the present day. Thus in order to date an object discovered there, it must be examined in its archaeological context, or in the light of its physical relationship to objects or structures that themselves can be reliably dated. In the case of Alexandria, there are huge, well-built quays now under water to the north of the island

of Pharos – an island named after the lighthouse which was built on the site. These monumental harbour remains, among the first underwater structures to be explored in the Mediterranean, have been variously attributed to the early Egyptians, to Minoans from Crete, to Phoenicians, as well as to the inhabitants of Hellenistic and even Roman times. It is better, perhaps, to regard them as Roman until they have been proven through underwater excavation to be earlier. A similar problem of dating holds true for the builders of the breakwaters to the east and west of the island, for although we know that Deinokrates, the architect of Alexander the Great, planned the Hellenistic city of Alexandria, these breakwaters might well be later additions to and improvements on his original scheme. Dating them might be possible through excavation under water or along the shores of the modern city; but at the moment, the exact history of many such Alexandrian monuments, still visible today or known through literature, remains obscure.

4 The base of the 'Pharos', the great lighthouse of Alexandria, erected by one of the early Ptolemies to guide sailors, can still be seen built into the modern Fort Kaidbey on the eastern tip of the island of Pharos. Pharos was once separated from the mainland (actually, itself another island) by a broad strip of water, though the two are now joined by the deposition of silt and the expansion of the modern town towards the sea. Even so, Pharos still overlooks much of the huge eastern harbour, now bordered by wide avenues and residential buildings but then lined with quays, the royal palace, the ship-sheds, storage facilities as well as the great market.

The lighthouse, little short of 430 feet high, was built in three stages, the first of which was certainly square and tapering. In time it became one of the Seven Wonders of the World, together with the Colossos of Rhodes which was set up at the entrance to the harbour there. But unlike the Colossos, which, after its collapse, was never re-erected in ancient times, the Alexandrian lighthouse became a symbol signifying security, to be imitated by the Romans who placed smaller versions of it at the entrances to their own monumental harbours.

Alexandria is said to have been one of the largest and busiest harbours in the Mediterranean. The island of Pharos and the mainland behind which lay Lake Mareotis were situated at a point of the Nile Delta where silt was washed away by the strong west–east current, and where access to the vast Nile Delta and the fertile river valley was convenient. To unite the island with the strip of mainland to the south, Alexander had constructed the Heptastadion, a causeway five-eighths of a mile long 5 pierced at two points in order to allow ships as well as the cleansing currents to pass through. Thus two inter-linked harbours were created, the one to the east being the haven for the Roman grain ships sailing in with ballast-laden hulls from Ostia or Puteoli – for Alexandria exported much of the grain needed by the people of Rome. However, it was not restricted to trade within the Mediterranean, for the old Pharaonic canal leading from the Nile into the Gulf of Suez, and thence to the Red Sea and Indian Ocean, was re-dredged. Also, a canal was cut through the strip of land on which Alexandria was built, enabling ships to pass farther inland or to work their way along and through the Delta to the Red Sea canal.

*Delos.* Quite different from the lasting prominence of 8 Alexandria as a port was the relatively ephemeral mercantile glory of the harbour of Delos, located in the centre of the Cycladic Islands, only one day's sailing from Piraeus, slightly more from Alexandria, and perhaps a week from Rome itself. During the development of Classical Greece, Delos was primarily a religious centre dedicated to the God Apollo, who is said to have been born on the island. With the eastward expansion of Rome's influence, however, the island suddenly acquired great commercial importance. In 167 BC Rome declared Delos a 'free port', open to trade without the usual customs duties levied elsewhere. Up to this time, most of the permanent residents on the island were associated with the religious sanctuaries there; but with the opening of the island as a free transfer point for goods and, especially, for slaves, traders from many points in the Mediterranean settled at Delos. Thus the island became a great centre of exchange not because of

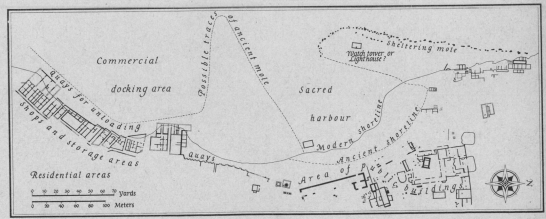

*8 Delos, plan of commercial area. Although originally a religious centre dedicated to the worship of Apollo, the port of the island was proclaimed in 167 BC to be duty-free. This encouraged settlement by merchants and the building of commercial structures. The existing moles were probably enlarged at this time and quays for unloading and harbour-side traffic were constructed. Mooring stones are still standing*

its unique geographical situation, for other near-by islands possessed natural harbours, but largely because of its recently conferred political status.

In this new situation the merchants from Italy built an agora, a large colonnaded court surrounded by shops where they could meet and transact business. The harbour itself, partially sheltered by offshore islands, was fitted out with quays 26 to 66 feet wide, supported on the sea side by retaining walls of rough stones first built out into the water and then filled in behind with rubble. At some points rough, pointed stones were set in vertically along the shore, to function as mooring posts.

The main harbour is now mostly filled by debris from the modern excavations of the town, but in antiquity it was some 10 to 13 feet deep, ample for almost any ship then in use. Facing west, it was partially enclosed by two moles, a smaller one to the south and a longer, hooked one to the north built of heavy stones and rubble dumped into the water. On the tip of the north mole are traces of a rectangular building, perhaps a watchtower or lighthouse. To the south was a small harbour where ships may have been beached for temporary repairs. In between the two harbours was a long series of paved quays interrupted by occasional building platforms projecting into the sea. Lines of shops and warehouses, some two storeys high, and enclosing a square, colonnaded court, faced the quays. Here material imported for transshipment was stored and bargaining no doubt went on, leading to plans for future voyages and the profits to be expected from them.

## Lechaeum and Carthage

Two of the most important but least known ancient Mediterranean ports are those at Lechaeum, which was the western port of Corinth, and at Carthage, founded by the Phoenicians near modern Tunis, on the coast of North Africa. Both harbours have long histories as bases for military and commercial sea-power, the one strategically located just to the southwest of the Isthmus of Corinth, and the other on land controlling the east–west passage between Africa and Sicily. Carthage was also a convenient point from which to export grain produced by the fertile province of North Africa.

Though Corinth probably never possessed the extensive influence or territory that Carthage was to acquire, both later developed along somewhat similar lines, for each opposed the gradual Roman take-over of the Mediterranean world. In the end, Roman armies razed both cities in 146 BC. Almost a century later both were refounded at the instigation of Julius Caesar. The similarity between the two ports becomes stronger if we note that each of them has an inner harbour, or 'cothon', excavated from the low-lying, sandy beach area or a pre-existing lagoon. During Roman times, perhaps earlier, both possessed 'outer harbours' formed by breakwaters and quays projecting into the sea.

9　　At Lechaeum, the perimeter of the inner harbour snakes for over 2¾ miles; much of it is marked by a wall

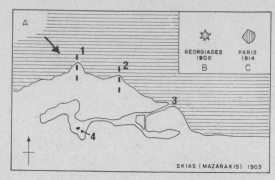

9　Plan of Lechaeum. Moles (1, 2) protected the outer harbour from the prevailing wind (arrow). Aligned with the channel to the inner harbour (3) is a monument base (4) of which two early plans are shown (inset)

of limestone blocks. The periphery behind the quay, however, has not been excavated, so that nothing is known of the surrounding buildings or of the possibly separate commercial and military zones which existed either here or at Carthage. The only monument now visible is a rectangular or square base of heavy limestone blocks on an islet in the centre of the western harbour. Perhaps a small lighthouse or a statue stood here. To the northeast, leading to the sea, is a canal lined by walls constructed of limestone blocks. Beyond the present shore-line three moles are still visible below water level; these extend onto the land to disappear beneath the accumulated sands, and are believed to be the remains of two major docking areas.

At Carthage, the shape of the inner harbour is somewhat clearer, although excavation has not yet established the exact size and position of the canal entrance(s). The first basin is long and rectangular, about 330 by 550 yards. It was probably a commercial area, used along with the one established on the sea-shore itself. Of the administrative buildings which once stood near by nothing is known archaeologically. From this basin a channel leads into a circular one about 360 yards in diameter. Here, according to the historian Appian, were ship-sheds with a capacity of 200 warships, as well as magazines in an upper storey for their rigging and tackle. In the middle of the harbour was a round island, still visible today, where the admiral's house may have stood. From here, he could have observed and managed the affairs of the port, and could have also maintained a look-out for hostile ships approaching the shore.

## Ports in Italy

When building ports in Italy itself, in some cases the Romans began with a slight disadvantage, for the coasts of the peninsula have few natural inlets and bays, nooks in the coastline where ships could be sheltered and harbour installations could be placed. Consequently, they often constructed partly artificial harbours by extending great moles out into the sea. In some cases they excavated immense basins from the land areas of river deltas, or enlarged lagoons somewhat in the manner of the western Phoenicians, though on a much grander scale. For building their port structures they often used hydraulic cement for underwater foundations.

14–18, 10 *Puteoli*. Puteoli (modern Pozzuoli) is some 150 miles southeast of Rome, and lies on the Bay of Naples. Here came the eagerly-awaited grain ships, sailing in from North Africa, Sicily or Alexandria to unload cargoes that would then be sent either overland, or by small ship up the coast and the River Tiber, to the city of Rome. Puteoli was one of the few natural harbours used by the Romans in Italy, and was Rome's chief harbour before the artificial Ostian ports were fully developed at the mouth of the Tiber, to the north. The harbour itself was sheltered from the strong south winds by a promontory behind which it and the city lay. Of the landing areas little has been found because of silting and subsidence, although traces of porticoes have been reported in the sea some 80 feet out from the curving beach.

In the water off the peninsula, however, could until comparatively recently be seen monumental quays and docking areas; near by was a great breakwater built some time during the early Empire. This magnificent structure is, unfortunately, now hidden by the modern breakwater laid over it; but from observations made during the past century we know that it consisted of a series of huge arches resting on masonry piers. The total breakwater length was some 407 yards, and since pierced mooring stones project from the piers we presume that ships not unloading at the quays either anchored offshore in the lee of the breakwater or were tied up along-side it. Their crews must have gathered above on the high promenade furnished for the city populace as well as for visitors. Depictions of this breakwater on ancient wall paintings and glass vessels show near its end an 14–17 imposing triumphal arch, two columns bearing statues of divinities, as well as a lighthouse.

In effect, this breakwater must have looked like a great aqueduct standing in the sea. The system of construction used may well have derived from the many Roman land aqueducts, just as the Greek walls built into the water to enclose harbour basins probably descended directly from the construction of city fortification walls. Here at Puteoli, it is believed, the builders first drove long oak pilings into the sand until a rectangular space was formed on the interior; the piles were then bound together, and once the loose sand below was cleared out, a thin layer of beams was probably laid down. Finally the concrete, composed of lime, rubble, and stone mixed with a hardening agent (a local volcanic earth called *pozzuolana*), was poured in and allowed to harden into an almost indestructible mass. Upon these platforms rested the arches, made of bricks, cut limestone blocks, and rubble filling, all bound together with *pozzuolana*.

South of the breakwater was a series of unusual basins protected from the sea by a double wall, sections of which were built separately using the method described. The outer part of the wall is composed of tall, rectangular pillars like those of the great breakwater. It also may have been topped by an arched promenade. On the inner part of the wall, centred between its openings, were blunted, triangular concrete pillars which broke the force of currents and waves penetrating the gaps between the arches. As a result, the silt that would otherwise collect on this side was presumably washed away, while the interior still remained calm enough to provide shelter for ships.

*Misenum and Ravenna*. While Puteoli was basically a commercial port, that of Misenum, according to A. Maiuri 'the finest natural port on the Campanian coast', was used as a military harbour from early times. During the rule of Augustus, his admiral Agrippa established this port as the centre for the naval forces of Italy. In fact, Misenum was intended to protect western Italy while Ravenna, on the Adriatic, was to defend the eastern coast; but gradually Misenum became the base for the most important Imperial fleet in the Mediterranean.

The siting of the two ports differs greatly, for the Ravenna harbour was an enlarged lagoon in the delta of the River Po, and was equipped with moles, a lighthouse, and military camps. Canals communicated with the sea and with the Po. In the case of Misenum, a natural bay was linked with a once land-locked lagoon by means of a channel perhaps spanned by a bridge. The outer bay, formerly the crater of a volcano, was protected by a series of moles similar to the one at Puteoli, and these were likewise equipped with pierced mooring stones. But at Misenum two parallel rows of

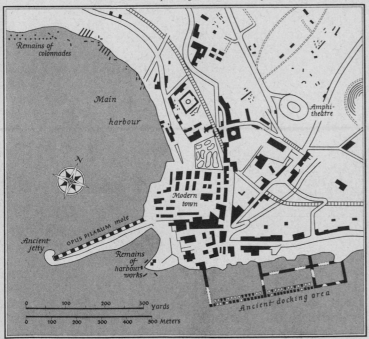

*10  Reconstruction plan of the harbour of Puteoli (Pozzuoli)*

pillars were set at alternating intervals in order to break the force of waves and currents. Along with these currents that passed through the moles, streams of water coming down two tunnels bored through headlands probably prevented silting within the outer harbour. On the southern side of this bay was the town centre for the fleet, while probably within the lagoon lay the dockyards, safe winter quarters for ships, as well as arsenals, and barracks for naval trainees. Their exact locations, however, are still unknown.

*Ostia.* While Puteoli was the port *par excellence* during the Roman Republican period, that of Ostia gained control of commerce during the Empire. The position of Ostia, just south of where the Tiber flows into the Tyrrhenian Sea, prevented marauders from approaching Rome from the west, and provided adequate landing and storage areas for supplies destined to be sent up-river to Rome. At the same time, it served as a base for Roman naval expeditions.

Before the development of artificial harbours in the delta area to the north, supply ships approaching Ostia unloaded off-shore into lighters. Some of the partially unloaded ships, riding much higher in the water than before, could pass over the shallows of the delta. The transfer of goods in the off-shore waters, however, was risky, for storms, problems in unloading, and possible delays endangered both ships and cargo. It is no surprise that Puteoli remained the preferred port, even though its greater distance from Rome caused inevitable delays in the shipment of goods.

The problem of furnishing shelter for ships approaching Rome by a direct route was considered by various Roman rulers. Among the projects proposed were canals linking Rome with Puteoli, or Rome with Terracina, the latter port about midway between Ostia and Puteoli. Julius Caesar and perhaps Augustus seem to have considered the Tiber mouth as a possible site for a major harbour, but work on it was not actually begun until AD 42 under the Emperor Claudius – against the advice of his engineers who claimed that its cost was prohibitive. Here, to the north of the Tiber's mouth, he cleared an area of some 2,700 sq. yards which he flooded after the construction of heavy moles built of concrete and cut stone, that curved out like gigantic pincers into the sea.

Recent excavations have partially clarified but not solved the topographic problems of the ancient port, which lies almost directly under the modern Fiumicino airport. With the gradual silting up of the delta, the ancient port became isolated from the sea and eventually filled with sand. It now lies about a mile from the sea. Ironically, ships wrecked or abandoned in Claudius's harbour in the first century AD have been discovered practically underneath the airport runways. Thus the first glimpse one has today on arriving by air is a view of the vast fertile delta lands, substantially unchanged since ancient times when passengers from abroad lined the railings of ships approaching Ostia or near-by 'Portus', the Claudian port itself.

Claudius embellished his harbour with a lighthouse, the base of which has been tentatively identified as overlying part of the north mole. In the event, he died before his project was completed, and the Emperor Nero dedicated the port and commemorated its opening with a series of coins minted for the occasion. The moles themselves were from 10 to 75 feet wide, composed of *pozzuolana* cement faced by limestone blocks and laced horizontally by heavy timbers for reinforcement. Part of the north mole was built of rectangular travertine limestone blocks set four or more courses high and fastened together by iron clamps and dowels secured by lead. In some cases the hulls of ships were used as forms into which the cement was poured. Elsewhere, vertical wooden pilings formed the sides of great caissons which were subsequently filled with concrete.

The Claudian harbour appears to have afforded ships ample space to anchor or tie up. They could unload alongside the moles or transfer their cargoes into lighters in the traditional way. For these lighters and some of the smaller ships, canals were excavated in order to provide access to the Tiber and hence to Rome. At the turn of the first century, however, the Emperor Trajan decided to add a harbour annex, in plan a monumental hexagon 413 yards on each side, excavated just inland from Claudius' work. Five of the sides were lined with long, deep warehouses and other buildings – some at least two storeys high. The sixth side was left partly open as an elaborate entrance-way from the old harbour, which still remained in partial use. Like the harbour of Claudius, it was also connected to the Tiber by a canal.

*11 Portus. The outer, Claudian harbour (a) had two curving moles (g, f) with a lighthouse (i) at the end of the latter. The inner basin (b) built by Trajan had a mole (h) protecting the entrance channel, dockyard (c), aqueduct (e), canal (d) and was equipped with warehouses, temples, and baths*

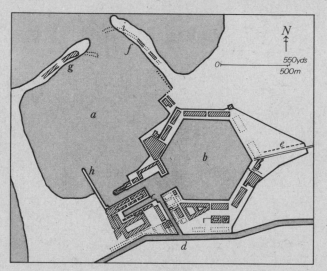

Perhaps Trajan's project was spurred by the sinking in the earlier harbour of 200 vessels during a storm and the need to provide better protection for the fleet, or perhaps by the simple necessity of providing warehouses to supplement those built by Claudius. However that may be, Trajan's harbour was an impressively organized complex featuring lines of symmetrically arranged warehouses, and in its final stages incorporating various structures, including an imperial palace, a lighthouse, an aqueduct, markets, baths, a hotel, as well as colossal statues of the emperors.

These quays would be crowded with merchants from many countries, inspectors of standard weights and measures, various shipowners and magistrates, sailors, porters, ballastmen, guards, all concerned with the unloading of cargoes and their storage at Portus or their immediate trans-shipment to Rome; in many cases goods would no doubt be carried there along the highway in carts. The quays themselves were faced with brick and paved with limestone blocks. Pierced travertine blocks lining the lowest of the two quay levels served as mooring rings for the 200 or so ships that could be accommodated here. One unusual quay facing onto Claudius's harbour rests on a brick arcade; elsewhere numbered columns indicate specific mooring stations, in a fashion similar to the berths at our own piers or indeed, at Fiumicino airport near by.

*The Tiber banks.* When ships carrying imported goods up the Tiber arrived at Rome, they pulled up alongside wide landing platforms that must have been equipped with hoisting machines for unloading. In some cases special wharves were used to land particular products, such as grain, marble, salt, lead, vegetables, etc. At one of the Augustan marble wharves, a jetty about 85 feet long jutted out into the river, pointing downstream. Here will have been unloaded bulky cargoes such as mammoth columns, building blocks, and other architectural marbles, as well as rough-cut sarcophagi, and cut marble blocks to be used for sculpture, all imported from various areas of the Mediterranean. Along the near-by river bank were quays partly faced with travertine laid over a concrete core. Traces of vertical wooden palisades, which once supported the quay in front, have been found.

Such palisades are among the most interesting achievements of the Romans, and in many places still survive. On the Tiber itself, square beams of oak 20 to 26 feet long were first driven into the river bottom, slightly out from the bank. They ended in four-pronged caps of iron. One piling was joined to another by means of a wooden mortise, and sheets of lead were nailed against the inner face of the palisade to protect it from rot. The space between the bank and the palisade was then filled with concrete. At intervals ramps led up to the normal ground level, and a variety of mooring rings were affixed to the sloping masonry walls of the banks and quays themselves.

## Leptis Magna

Away in North Africa, the Romans founded a number of fine cities; one such was Leptis Magna on the sea coast not far from modern Tripoli. Built mainly during the second and third centuries A D, it is a classic example of a late Roman harbour constructed on a monumental scale. The harbour was originally built at the mouth of a river, and later several offshore islands were united in the arc of its enclosure. To prevent silting, the river was later diverted by erecting a dam upstream. The enlarged shoreline was built up with exquisitely constructed quays equipped with platforms at different levels, all reached by interconnecting steps and stairs and backed by a continuous line of stoas. These stretched for some 1,300 yards.

## Marine Archaeology

In the early years of this century, work involving underwater investigation was begun by such pioneers as Negris and Georgiades in Greece, by Gunther in Italy, and by Jondet at Alexandria. Negris (1904) made a catalogue of submerged moles and piers throughout Greece, while Georgiades (1907) attempted to discuss and describe examples of ancient Greek ports which he personally surveyed. In Italy, Gunther (1903) was concerned with scattered submerged Roman constructions along the shores of the Bay of Naples. But the first large-scale interpretation and survey of harbour remains was published in 1916 by Gaston Jondet, who made plans of and observations about the so-called 'Prehistoric Harbour' at Alexandria, north of the island of Pharos (see pp. 94–5 above). The most systematic attempts to plan and investigate partly submerged port structures were published by Pierre Poidebard in his studies of Tyre (1931) and Sidon (1951). Poidebard's work is in many ways a model of systematic research combining air photography with underwater survey and excavation. Unfortunately, it is still difficult to date the structures that have been examined at Tyre and Sidon, and only further excavation and study will link them with their proper historical tradition.

Since the invention of the aqualung, happily, there has arisen a great deal of interest in exploring submerged offshore remains; this has in turn led to research dealing with harbour facilities now inland. Contemporary archaeological expeditions engaged primarily in excavation on land now find it practical to explore remains extending out from the shore. A recent survey under water at Apollonia in Cyrenaica by Nicolas Flemming has revealed the entire layout of the harbour basin, including towers and fortification walls, as well as unique docks and ship-sheds that invite further study. In Tripolitania and Tunisia a group of hardy divers from Cambridge University led by R. A. Yorke recently carried out a systematic survey of ancient remains in the shallow coastal waters. Along the coast of Palestine the Israel Underwater Exploration Society, headed by Elisha Linder, has spent much time and effort exploring the

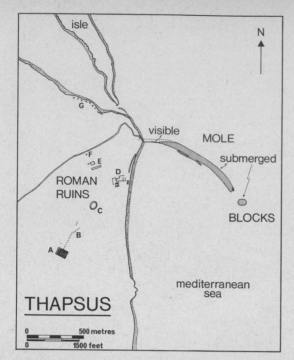

*12  Plan of Thapsus mole. The part of the mole visible above water near the shore had been studied earlier; recent excavation underwater has shown the mole to be much longer*

27  ancient moles of the great harbour town of Caesarea, and it is now engaged in surveying the harbour facilities (possibly Phoenician) at Akko. It is to be hoped that further work by this group will clarify the role played by the Phoenicians in the development of harbourworks. Similar survey work has recently been completed on Crete by John Leatham and Sinclair Hood, with their examination of the moles and offshore buildings of Roman Chersonesos, east of Heraklion. On the mainland of Greece experiments by Robert Scranton and myself with survey and excavation equipment at
8–13  Kenchreai on the Saronic Gulf have revealed a most interesting plan of the port as it was during Early Roman times, when warehouses lined the western and southern sides of the harbour basin, in a way reminiscent of the great warehouses along the quays of Trajan's harbour
26  at Ostia. At Porto Cheli (Ancient Halieis), south of

Kenchreai, a team led by Michael Jameson and Thomas Jacobsen has been surveying and excavating a possible inner harbour within the circuit of the city wall which now lies partly submerged. At both Kenchreai and Porto Cheli new types of dredges that will assist in shallow-water excavation are being developed.

In the process of such exploration, the chronology of specific harbour works is slowly being established on a more solid basis than has been the case in the past. At Anthedon in Greece, not far from ancient Thebes, for  3 instance, archaeologists (Schäfer, Schläger, and Blackman), after re-surveying the exposed remains, have re-dated parts of the harbour works to the sixth century A D, as opposed to the fourth century B C date originally proposed for them. Much the same thing applies to Kenchreai, where the construction and use of the moles were originally considered to be early Greek, but now upon investigation appear to be Roman, at least those parts that are visible. In general, the recent tendency is to credit Roman engineers with much of the visible harbour construction in Greece.

To the west, in Italy and France, promising work has been carried out in harbour areas, both exposed and submerged. Of the former type, M. Guy has made a valuable survey and interpretation of the visible remains at Narbonne; at Cosa Frank Brown, aided by John D. Lewis and Miss Anna Marguerite McCann, is excavating remains of piers offshore and, inland, what may be a small dock. In this area ample remains of the wooden forms used by the builders of the dock are preserved *in situ*. Elsewhere, conventional excavations initiated by the late Fernand Benoît and continued by Maurice Euzennat and François Salviat at Marseilles are revealing  24, 25 parts of the ancient shoreline, including well-preserved fortification walls and quays. In Italy, air photography instigated by Dino Adamasteanu has revealed at Portus Julia an entire harbour front with its shops, quays, and moles quite intact. By the same means the original layout of the city of Ravenna and the positioning of its harbours and canals is being pieced together. In Sicily, Gerhard Kapitän has spent much time in exploring the famous harbour of Syracuse, which has yielded many important artifacts lost during ancient times.

---

1  Piraeus, the port of ancient Athens established by Themistocles in 493 BC and said to have been designed by Hippodamus, still serves the Greek capital today. The rocky peninsula was chosen because it was easy to defend against attack from the sea, and three of its natural harbours offered ready protection to shipping. Supplies which passed between the port and the city were safeguarded by the strongly fortified 'Long Walls'. The harbours of Zea, present-day Pasalimani (just left of centre) and Munychia, present-day Tourko-limano (bottom right), are clearly visible, in this air photograph, as is the main harbour, the former Kan-

tharos (top centre), the largest ancient harbour and that used now for modern shipping. Here was the Choma, from which major military expeditions would depart. The famous Arsenal, where much of the ships' gear was stored, was in the Zea harbour area. Though the remains of the original harbourworks are still to be found in places, much of the area is now built over. We therefore have to rely largely on literary texts and inscriptions – of which a great many have been discovered both in Athens and in Piraeus itself – when attempting to form a picture of what the port looked like in Classical times.

2   This rare photograph shows the remains of ancient Greek ship-sheds in the harbour of Zea at Piraeus before they were partially covered by modern buildings and streets. Triremes would have pulled up between the rows of stone columns, which ran down to the shore.

3   Anthedon, the southern harbour of Boeotian Thebes. The findings of a recent land and underwater survey indicate that these installations of the 'south-western quay' date to the sixth century AD. The unique channels cut in the upper surfaces of the harbour wall may have housed timber to bind the stone courses together.

4   Reverse of a coin of Antoninus Pius (AD 86–161) depicting the Pharos at Alexandria. This great light-house set on the eastern tip of the island of Pharos was built between 299 and 279 BC. Its base can still be seen built into the modern Fort Kaidbey.

5   The features of ancient Alexandria depicted on this Roman lamp include the Heptastadion, a causeway nearly a mile long uniting the island of Pharos with the mainland. It was pierced at two points in order to allow ships, as well as scouring currents, to pass through.

6   Air view of Carthage, showing the horseshoe-shaped military port and, south of it, the commercial port. The dark shadow bordering the promontory to the east probably indicates the Roman breakwater, now below the surface.

7   Air view of Apollonia, the Hellenistic and Roman port for Cyrene in Cyrenaica. Recent underwater investigations have revealed extensive remains of an inner (closed) and an outer harbour (here visible beyond the present coastline), as well as ship-sheds and quays.

5

6

7

8

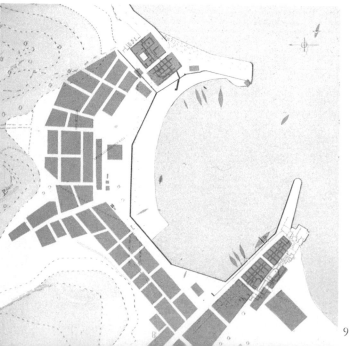

10

9

8–13 Kenchreai, on the Saronic Gulf, was one of the two ports of ancient Corinth, the other being Lechaeum on the Gulf of Corinth. With these two ports the city, astride the isthmus, was able to control east-west traffic by sea, as well as north-south traffic by land. As a result of surveys and excavations carried out by members of the universities of Chicago and Indiana, we now have a very good idea of what Kenchreai looked like in early Roman times.

8 Air view of Kenchreai, showing the present coastline and, beyond it, the ramifications of the ancient port, now under the sea.

9 The excavating team's tentative reconstruction. On the basis of extensive trenching in the areas back from the shore, the main blocks of buildings with their separating roads have been restored. Along the shore areas, where excavation was more complete, a number of buildings have been studied in their entirety. Top (i.e. to the east): the northeastern mole, directly south from a number of Roman buildings set on earlier remains. Centre: quay area separating shops and/or storehouses from the sea. Lower right: the southwestern pier, most of which is partially submerged in shallow water. At its southeastern tip a mole projected into the sea. In the angle formed by this mole and the body of the pier a group of fish tanks seem to have been installed. Between here and the land were a series of large warehouses for storage of exported and imported goods. South of the second warehouse from the end a partly submerged temple has been found.

10 Within the sunken apsidal temple was discovered a series of unique glass mosaics. Some of these carry representations of ancient harbours, of which a detail is illustrated here.

11 A Greek caïque, used as a base for diving on and excavating the submerged remains of the South Pier, anchored north of the easternmost warehouse.

12 The apse of the temple (10), with a marble fountain basin in the centre, as it looked when the water was let in again after the excavation.

13 Divers examine what is thought to be a Roman structure in shallow water near the northeast mole.

11

12

13

20

21

22

20–23 Leptis Magna in Libya, North Africa, is probably the best-preserved example of late Roman harbour development. The reconstruction (20) by Italian archaeologists shows the harbour as it probably was when its quays, warehouses, temple and lighthouse were built in the time of the native-born emperor, Septimius Severus, about AD 200. Remnants of the lighthouse on the northern promontory survive. The southern arm (23), seen across the long-dry harbour,

has been extensively excavated. On its inner side the mole is built on two levels, the lower one providing anchorage for shipping. Pierced mooring stones still project from the elaborately constructed upper quay (21, 22), and recurrent flights of steps connect the two levels. The massive ruin (23, slightly left of centre) was a large tower at the end of the southern arm, which may have acted as an extra signal station. A small temple lay to the southwest of the tower. West of these, facing the harbour, stood a range of warehouses fronted by a colonnaded portico, of which a few columns (re-erected) survive. Behind the warehouses lie traces of the sixth-century Byzantine town wall. The port was built at the mouth of a small river which then, as now, flowed seasonally. The solid and continuous construction of the quays undoubtedly contributed in large measure to the silting-up which soon rendered the harbour useless, while at the same time preserving it.

24, 25 At Marseilles, the late Fernand Benoît initiated on-shore excavation work in the area around the Bourse. The ancient shore-line has now been established, and well-preserved walls and quay foundations are being exposed. The air view (24) takes in the southern part of the excavation area, with the fresh-water fountain in the foreground; in the middle distance is the Vieux Port, the present inner harbour. A wall of the west quay (25) shows the solid construction of the ancient harbour walls. The original water level in the port is shown by the dark line, caused by marine organisms.

26 Recent excavations by a team of American archaeologists from the universities of Pennsylvania and Indiana have exposed extensive remains of the fifth- and fourth-century BC town of Halieis (present-day Porto Cheli) on the Saronic Gulf, some hours sailing distance south of Corinth. Divers and surveyors have been working for a number of seasons on the reconstruction of the port area that now lies submerged in the shallow bay waters. This remarkable photograph shows the base of a circular fortification tower, flanking what appears to be an entrance to a small inner harbour. Until this photograph, taken from a balloon trailed and triggered by a diver (centre) brought it so clearly to light, the existence of this tower was completely unsuspected.

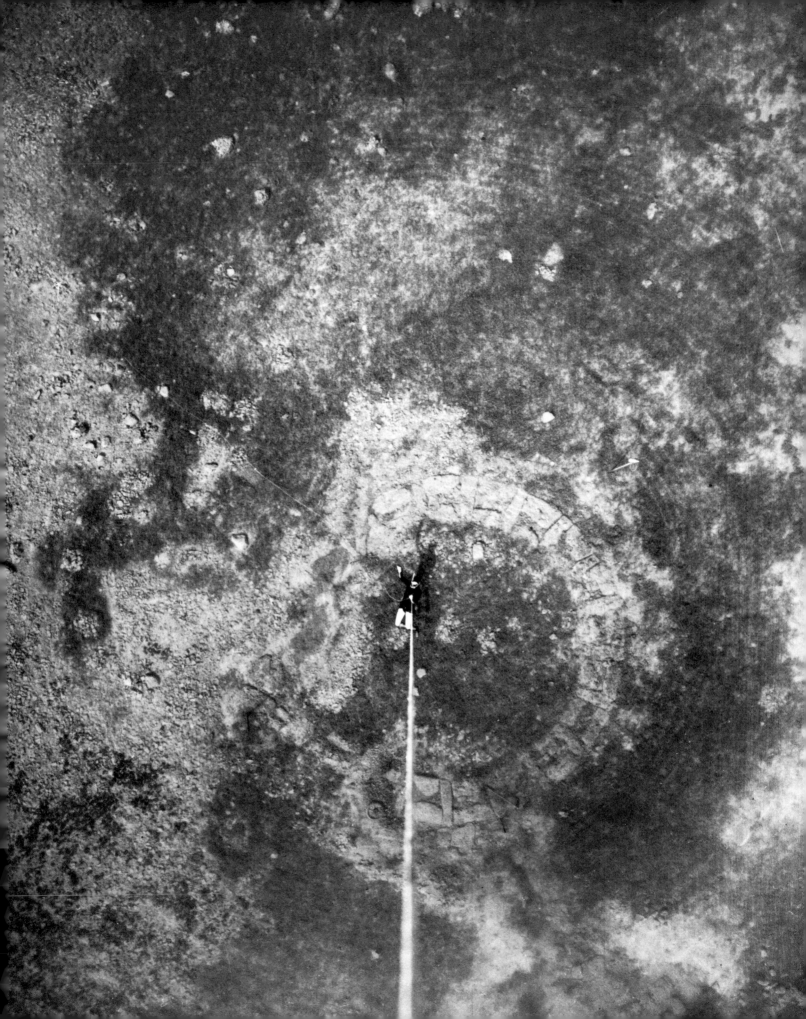

27 The vast harbour basin of Caesarea is now deserted; there is little to be seen on land today apart from the widespread ruins of the ancient city. Remains of the ancient moles (large dark areas above and below) can only be inspected under water, while most of the exposed moles (lower and upper right) are of more recent date. The historian Josephus described how, when Herod built the harbour structure, immense stones were lowered down from above to form foundations for a great jetty backed by arches. At the entrance to the harbour (near boat anchored on left) were set colossal statues. Underwater inspection has revealed that column drums were also used as filling material for the foundations and, at either side of the entrance channel, there are still huge blocks of stone which threaten to slide down the slopes. This picture shows Edwin Link's research vessel *Sea Diver* anchored at the site during his exploration in the 'sixties.

27

5

# Ships of the
# Roman period
# and after in Britain

PETER MARSDEN

# Ships of the Roman period and after in Britain

'Their ships were built and rigged in a different manner from ours.' Written twenty centuries ago by Julius Caesar, as a result of his encounters with the Celtic people of northwest Gaul, this is the opening sentence of one of the most provocative passages in Classical literature. Its significance is great for, although Caesar does not tell us how their ships were constructed, he does in effect say that the Celts had a shipbuilding tradition completely different from that of the Romans in the Mediterranean.

Part of this non-Roman tradition is becoming known through archaeological research in Britain. Through it we are building up a history of early ships and shipbuilding in these northern islands which, inevitably, have always been closely linked with the mainland of Europe. Britain's history is largely a story of the effects of successive waves of peoples who migrated from the continent and settled in her southern areas, often forcing the previous inhabitants to move farther north and west.

Caesar's detailed description of northern Europe is the earliest known, and, as there was no native literature, its importance cannot be overestimated. The numerous Celtic tribes had strong cultural affinities with each other, which archaeologists find reflected in their art, architecture and pottery styles. They settled in northern Gaul and the British Isles; farther east lay the Teutonic tribes of Germany and the Nordic peoples of the Baltic region. However, the situation was not as simple as this suggests and there was evidently a considerable overlapping of peoples and cultures. The Belgae, for example, were a group of mixed Celtic and Teutonic stock from the Low Countries, who had migrated across the English Channel and who by the time Caesar was campaigning in the north, had occupied nearly all of southeast England.

This basic cultural distribution of the first century BC must be understood before the history of ships and shipbuilding traditions can usefully be discussed, for all of these peoples were to have important parts to play in shaping the history and culture of Britain during the following millennium.

Nor does the story end there, for into this northern theatre was thrust the completely alien culture of Classical Rome. Caesar's conquest of Gaul during the middle of the first century BC brought the Gaulish Celts under Roman domination; less than a century later, in AD 43, the Emperor Claudius drove Roman rule into Britain and brought about profound modifications in native British culture.

Archaeologists must make some sense out of this extremely complex situation and must interpret the significance of man's buried remains correctly. A study of ancient ships and boats is just one aspect of this vast subject, but one that is of particular importance; for it gives us not only valuable information about the technical abilities of the different peoples and cultures, but also an insight into the character of water-borne trade and communications. It is believed that before the Roman conquest of northern Gaul and Britain, trading was on a limited scale. The Romans, however, brought their superior industrial and commercial skills to these new provinces of their empire and developed them with great success. In so doing they also inspired and helped develop much of the best in native British culture, which, we believe, embraced some forms of native shipbuilding.

## The Early History of Boatbuilding

The origin of naval architecture in Britain, as in the rest of the world, is unknown, but survivals used by existing primitive peoples can provide useful clues to the earliest types of craft. In Britain these probably took the form of logs, used either singly or in groups lashed together, and skin-covered boats. Such primitive craft soon gave way to vessels of more sophisticated design, though, surprisingly, dug-out canoes continued to be made and used in Scotland as late as the nineteenth century, and skin-covered boats are still to be found in the west of England and in Ireland. Because of their flimsy structure, traces of the latter are rarely found, and the many dug-outs exhibited in British museums are mostly undated – providing enormous scope for future research. A few, it is true, have been dated to the Roman period, but their importance to the economy of the country must have been very limited.

The most far-reaching innovation was the use of planks in ship construction, a method which ultimately led to the building of great wooden vessels like H.M.S.

*Victory*. At what date this type of boat was first built in Britain is not known, but presumably it was during the Bronze Age – about 3,500 years ago – when specialized tools could be made for the exacting task of cutting planks which, when fastened together, formed a watertight hull. It has long been clear, however, that at least some of the native peoples of northern Europe developed methods of shipbuilding peculiar to themselves and, as many of them had settled in Britain at various times, archaeologists have the problem of tracing the history of several methods of plank shipbuilding.

The three Bronze Age boats found at North Ferriby, in Yorkshire, are the earliest discovered plank-built boats in Britain; they date to *c.* 1500 BC according to a recent assessment. They were primitive craft without keel, built of broad planks sewn together edgeways. Two of the boats were found in 1946 and another in 1963 by a local amateur archaeologist, Mr E. V. Wright, who had been exploring the muddy bed of the River Humber at low tide. But because they are the sole dated examples of prehistoric boatbuilding using planks, it is impossible to judge how they fit into the over-all picture. Are they examples of a type of boatbuilding which was in general use in Britain? Does the fact that they had no keels, and that the planks were sewn together, suggest that they were evolved from skin boats? These are but two of the many questions posed by their discovery.

Parts of at least two other boats with planks sewn together have been found in the Baltic area, the most complete being the famous Hjortspring boat from Jutland, dating from about 300 BC

Since no pre-Roman Iron Age boats have been found in Britain, we have no means of telling when the sewing of planks was succeeded by the use of wood and metal nails fastening the planks to ribs.

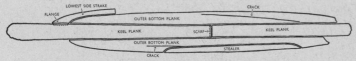

*1   Plan of the main surviving elements of the late Bronze Age carvel-built boat I, discovered at North Ferriby, Yorkshire*

### Skin Boats of the Roman Period

Although skin-covered boats represent a very primitive form of boatbuilding, they are still used in parts of the British Isles today. During the Iron Age (*c.* 400 BC–AD 43) skin boats were probably in common use in all parts of Britain, and certainly in south-east England. Julius Caesar saw them there during his British campaigns of 55–54 BC, and he described how his army made skin boats in Spain in 49 BC, modelled on those he had seen the Britons using: 'Caesar ordered his soldiers to make boats of the kind that his knowledge of Britain a few years before had taught him. First, the keels and ribs were made of light timber, then the rest of the hull of the boats was wrought in wickerwork, and covered over with hides.' The use of keels shows that these could not have been coracles, but were more like the Irish curragh in form.

Pliny, in the first century AD, referred to boats that 'are made in the British Ocean of wickerwork covered with hides'; in another passage he added that the hides were sewn together. During the third century AD another classical writer, Solinus, recorded that 'the sea which separates Hibernia (Ireland) from Britain, is rough and stormy throughout the year; it is navigable for a few days only; they voyage in small boats formed of pliant twigs, covered with skins of oxen. During the time they are at sea, the voyagers abstain from food.' Clearly skin boats were unknown in the Mediterranean at that time, and Solinus's description of hungry men sailing in boats made of twigs and ox-hides in the violent Atlantic must have caused surprise to his readers. The impression gained from these short descriptions is that skin boats, as far as the Romans were concerned, were peculiar to the British.

### Roman Warships in Britain

In AD 43 the Emperor Claudius invaded Britain, and although warships of the Roman Imperial Navy will have been seen off the south coast of England before then, these now became a common sight, remaining so until the end of the fourth century AD when Roman military strength was largely withdrawn from Britain. Unfortunately, Romano-British representations of warships are extremely rare, and it is difficult to determine the history of warship design. A few tentative conclusions may, however, be drawn from contemporary documentary evidence and representations on coins.

During his campaigns in northern Gaul and Britain, about the middle of the first century BC, Julius Caesar found that his Mediterranean type of warship was most unsuited to the more violent weather and tidal conditions of the north.

After the Claudian invasion of Britain, however, warships were constantly attendant upon the army, being particularly used to ferry men and supplies to the fighting front and to protect communications between Gaul and Britain in the English Channel. Before the end of the first century a new fleet was formally created, called the *Classis Britannica* or British Fleet, with major bases on both sides of the Channel.

In view of Julius Caesar's comments about the inadequacy of his warships, we naturally wonder what modifications were later introduced to make them more effective around Britain.

During the first and second centuries AD warships are represented as long sleek vessels, often with the *artemon*,

2 *Reproduction drawing of an early type of Roman warship on a coin of Hadrian, minted AD 132–4*

3 *Reproduction drawing of a late type of warship on a coin of Allectus, minted in Britain at the end of the third century AD*

2 or bowsprit, raking over the stem; but the mainmast is rarely shown in a raised position. The forms of these ships can be traced on coins, stone reliefs, and frescoes in the Mediterranean area, and presumably the warships used around Britain were of a similar type.

3 Later Roman coins show a different, and it would seem shorter, form of vessel, usually fitted with a straighter stem post, to the bottom of which was attached a simple ram. The rig of these later vessels is also different: there is normally no *artemon*, and the mainmast is almost invariably shown in the standing position. This suggests that it was a fixed feature, particularly since the sail is not seen to be hanging from the yard, and the crew is normally shown at the oars.

This change in the manner of representing warships may have been a result of the general decline in artistic aptitude which is known to have set in during the third and fourth centuries A D; or it may have been due to an actual change in warship design, probably as a result of the complete naval reorganization of the third century. In Britain as elsewhere, the great fleet was scrapped, and the naval force was apparently split into small squadrons based upon coastal forts.

The fourth-century Roman writer Vegetius mentions the use of Liburnian galleys in Britain. It seems likely that the late Roman Liburnian (see chapter 3, p. 67) was very different from the vessel developed in the Mediterranean several centuries earlier, but it probably retained the old name because of its similar purpose. This survival of names can be paralleled in our own time: a frigate of 1950, for example, is completely different from a frigate of a hundred years earlier.

21 An interesting group of warship representations occurs on a fourth-century mosaic in a villa at Low Ham in Somerset. Unfortunately they are very crudely executed, lacking both scale and perspective, and each is shown being propelled by sail and oars at the same time. Nevertheless, they give a good general impression of the form taken by late Roman warships.

A model bronze prow of a warship found in London about 1850 (the circumstances are no longer known) is to be seen in the British Museum. Inscribed AMMILLA AVG FELIX and decorated with the palm branch of victory, it is thought to have been made to commemorate a victory won by a warship called *Ammilla*. Apart from these, warship representations made in Britain are almost unknown.

## Roman Merchant Shipping in Britain

*The County Hall ship.* In 1910 a third-century ship was found in London which had been built in a shipyard somewhere in the northern part of the empire, but by the Roman method (see chapter 3, pp. 69, 70). This distinctive construction had been presumably introduced into Britain after the Roman invasion of A D 43, but it is doubtful whether it became popular in local shipyards.

The ship was discovered while the County Hall was being built on the south bank of the River Thames beside Westminster Bridge, by two senior members of the London County Council. They were supervising the building operations, when one of them 'noticed a dark, curving line in the face of the excavation immediately above the virgin soil' at a depth of 21 feet below street level. The great age of the wreck was immediately evident, as it was overlaid by fourteen feet of river-deposited silt, indicating that the site had once been part of the river bed.

Instructions were immediately issued to the contractor: he was to uncover the timbers carefully, and to collect whatever antiquities lay within the vessel. As a result four Roman coins were found, two actually wedged beneath ribs, with a quantity of pottery and portions of Roman leather shoes. The latest coin was minted between A D 295 and 296; the ship must therefore have foundered at the very end of the third, or early in the fourth century A D.

This is the first Roman vessel in the world to have been carefully excavated, accurately recorded and fully published. The London County Council published an extremely detailed report in 1911, and a revised edition in 1912, which even today is a model of technical reporting.

Its authors were, quite rightly, guarded about the significance of the find, calling it 'a ship of the Roman period' rather than 'a Roman ship'. As no other vessels of this period had been found, they allowed for the possibility that it was a native British type and not a true example of Roman ship construction.

It was not until about 1930 that archaeologists were able to examine undisputed examples of classical Roman shipbuilding. In that year, Lake Nemi, near Rome, was being drained, making it possible to recover the great ships which were known to be half buried in its muddy bottom (see chapter 3, p. 69, ill. 6). Although these ships had been designed for a completely different purpose, it was quite clear that their basic construction was almost identical to that of the ship found on the County Hall site, nine hundred miles away. The London vessel, then, was constructed on Roman lines, but a recent botanical examination of its timbers has shown that it must have been built in northern Gaul or Britain, as the species of oak used does not grow naturally in the Mediterranean area.

The ship was a small carvel-built merchantman of about sixty tons, probably engaged in coastal and river trade. It had an estimated length of 60–70 feet, with a

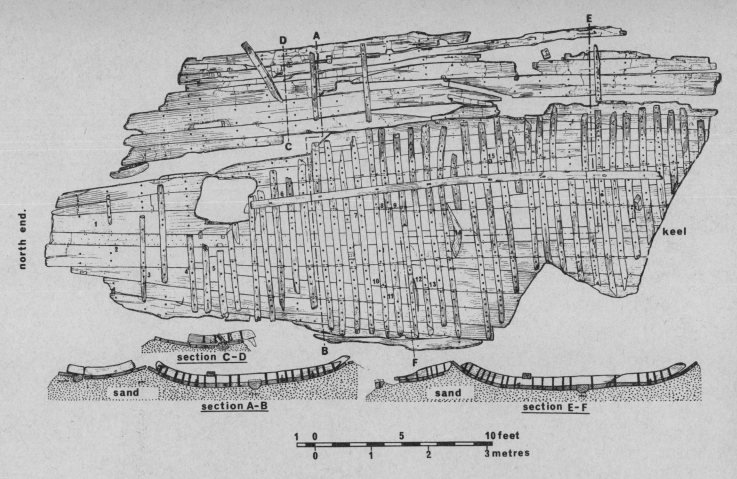

north end.

keel

section C–D

sand

section A–B

section E–F

sand

1 0       5       10 feet

0       1       2       3 metres

*4   Plan and cross sections of the third-century AD wreck found on the site of the County Hall,
London. This ship was built in northern Europe but according to the Mediterranean shipbuilding
tradition*

beam of 15–16 feet, and a depth amidships of about 6 feet. Once abandoned, it gradually broke up, the sides collapsed and finally it was entombed in silt deposited by the river. It must have been disappointing for excavators to find that all that had survived was a 38-foot length of its bottom, near the middle of the vessel, and part of a collapsed side; moreover, as both ends were missing, there was no way of telling which had been the bow and which the stern. By carefully recording the exact position of each timber, and by drawing sections across the collapsed remains, it has proved possible to reconstruct on paper an accurate cross-section of the vessel. Fortunately, the collapsed side yielded details of deck construction not preserved in any other excavated merchant ship of that period so far discovered.

It was made entirely of oak, unlike most Roman ships built in the Mediterranean, and the strakes were attached to each other and to the keel edgeways by the characteristically Roman mortise-and-tenon joints (draw-tongued joints). Next to the small keel the strakes were 3 inches thick, and away from this they gradually thinned down to 2 inches at the sides.

The fact that the ribs were not fastened to the keel at first puzzled the finders, but recent research has solved

this problem: in Roman shipbuilding, the planks were fitted together to form the complete hull before the ribs were attached. Thanks to the meticulous care taken in recording every detail during the investigations of 1910, it has subsequently proved possible to show that this was exactly how the County Hall ship was built. Not only was the keel not fastened to the ribs, but also many mortise-and-tenon joints in the strakes had been covered by ribs, showing that these were not an integral part of the hull but added later for strength.

The ribs were spaced about 1 foot 5 inches apart and measured about $4\frac{1}{2}$ inches broad and $6\frac{1}{2}$ inches deep. Only every other rib was carried up the side, and fortunately the upper end of one of these longer ribs had survived. At about 6 feet above the bottom it curved outwards through the planking and ended with a tenon, and it seems reasonable to suppose that it probably fitted into the missing gunwale.

Nearly 5 feet above the bottom of the vessel, a thick plank or wale had been fitted into the side of the ship, and at regular intervals of 3 feet there were slots in it to take the ends of the transverse deck beams, one of which had actually survived in position. The deck planks must have been fastened to the beams, but none of them had

3

117

been preserved. Originally there had been two keelsons, each lying parallel to and 3 feet 6 inches away from the keel, on either side of the ship's bottom. Only one of these had survived and in it, at intervals of 3 feet, were mortise holes to take the bottoms of a row of upright stanchions which supported the deck beams above. Unfortunately, none of the stanchions had survived.

There was no evidence to show how the ship was propelled, but the absence of any arrangements for rowing, together with the size and purpose of the vessel, indicates that it relied on sail. The vital area of the mast-step had been destroyed, but the excavators did find a pulley block and a length of timber, 10 inches in diameter, which they took to be part of the mast.

The subsequent history of this wreck deserves recording briefly. For about a year it remained on the site while experts tackled the problem of carefully drying it out in such a way as to preserve it. They tried soaking it with glycerine, but this was not successful, for as the timbers slowly dried they split, shrank and even twisted. The damage was, however, made good, and reconstruction work carried out.

In August 1911 the ship was offered to the then newly created London Museum – an offer which was gratefully accepted by Guy Laking, its director. The ship was encased in a giant box, 40 feet long and weighing 10 tons, and was hauled up to street level on two trucks pulled by twelve horses. At four o'clock in the morning, the procession began to move northwards across London to Kensington Palace, led by its director on horseback. This was indeed showmanship, for the journey took all day, severely disrupting metropolitan traffic, while for the benefit of curious Londoners the great tarpaulin covering the box proclaimed in large whitewashed letters 'Roman boat – London Museum'.

### Native British Plank-built Boats
It is mainly to the Roman occupation of northern Gaul and Britain that we owe our rather scanty knowledge about ships used by the Celts between the first century BC and about AD 400. For example, Vegetius recorded that 'to the heavier Liburnians were attached scouting pinnaces with about twenty rowers aside; the Britons called these *Pictae*'. They were camouflaged by being painted sea-green all over, including sails, rigging and even the sailors' clothes. There is little doubt that these were vessels copied from a type developed by the Picts of Scotland, and the number of rowers, as well as the nature of the mast and rigging, all points to their having been strong, plank-built, seaworthy craft.

In a developing economy such as existed in Britain during the Roman period one would expect to find a shipbuilding industry producing vessels particularly suited to specific purposes and local environments, and this is borne out by Vegetius's account.

Of particular importance is the first-century AD model of a double-ended sailing boat in beaten gold, found at Broighter in County Derry, Ireland. This is rightly a prized exhibit at the National Museum of Ireland, for it is the only good representation of native shipbuilding to have been found in the British Isles. It is a tub-shaped craft designed for nine oars on each side, and with thwarts for the rowers to sit upon, and a single steering oar at the stern. The mast supporting the yard from which a square sail probably once hung is situated nearly amidships. Not only does this model show that plank shipbuilding must have been well developed by the Celts before any Roman influence, but also that the sail was in general use.

### The Veneti
In 57 BC Julius Caesar's invasion force reached the north-west coasts of Gaul, and the Veneti were among the tribes who surrendered to Rome. The following year the Veneti rebelled, and Caesar was prevented from reconquering them for many months by their superior maritime strength. For this reason he took a considerable interest in their methods of warfare and defence – and particularly in their ships.

The Veneti were a Celtic people who had also settled in parts of southwest England, and they carried on trade between there and Gaul. Their settlements were built on the ends of headlands jutting out to sea, which the Romans found very difficult to attack. When the Roman soldiers succeeded in breaching the defences of such a settlement they would find it deserted. As Caesar soon discovered, what the Veneti did, when the situation looked hopeless, was to bring up some ships, 'of which they had an unlimited supply', into which they transferred all their property, and retire to a neighbouring stronghold equally well situated for defence.

Much to Caesar's annoyance this continued throughout the summer months and, as his warships were weatherbound most of the time, he could not attack the enemy at sea. The trading ships of the Veneti on the other hand were built to withstand the turbulent northern seas.

Caesar realized that the conquest of the Veneti depended upon his capturing or disabling their fleet, and the inevitable sea battle occurred in the late summer of 56 BC – the first large-scale naval action to take place in northern waters. The full complement of 220 Veneti ships faced the Roman force somewhere off north-west Gaul. The Roman warships tried ramming the enemy but failed as the hulls of the opposing vessels were too solid. They also tried throwing missiles and heaving up grappling-hooks to lock the ships together for boarding, but again without success owing to the greater height of the enemy ships. Eventually Caesar decided to exploit the Veneti's only apparent weakness: since their sole means of propulsion was by sail, if he could damage their rigging, they would be immobilized. Turrets were built on the Roman warships, and with the aid of pointed hooks on the end of long poles the halyards of the enemy vessels were snapped, thus bringing the yards down and leaving the ships at the mercy of the currents and the

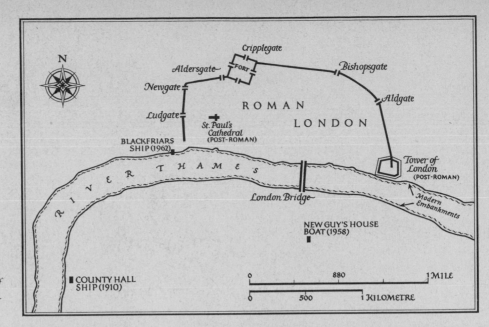

N

Cripplegate

Aldersgate

FORT

Bishopsgate

Newgate

R O M A N

Aldgate

Ludgate

St. Paul's
Cathedral
(POST-ROMAN)

L O N D O N

BLACKFRIARS
SHIP (1962)

R I V E R   T H A M E S

Tower of
London
(POST-ROMAN)

Modern
Embankments

London Bridge

NEW GUY'S HOUSE
BOAT (1958)

COUNTY HALL
SHIP (1910)

| 0 | 880 | 1 MILE |
| 0 | 500 | 1 KILOMETRE |

*5 Map to show the siting of Roman wrecks in London relative to the Roman city*

Romans. After the yards had collapsed, two or three Roman ships would pull alongside each stricken vessel and, in the words of Caesar, 'it was a soldier's battle, in which the Romans easily proved superior.'

Caesar must have examined some of the captured ships in person, for he left a detailed description of them. They differed from the Roman ships in their construction and rigging. They had flatter bottoms to help ride the shoals, and if stranded by an ebb tide there was no danger of their keeling over. They also had an exceptionally high stem and stern, the stern apparently being the taller. The hull planks were of oak and clearly of considerable thickness, as ramming by the Romans had no effect. They had cross timbers (? ribs) which were a foot wide and fastened with iron bolts as thick as a man's thumb. Caesar added that their anchors were secured with iron chains, and that the sails were made of raw hides or thin leather. It is clear to us that these heavy vessels were quite different from the comparatively fragile clinker-built craft being developed at this time by the peoples of the Baltic region.

The only fitting from a ship of the Veneti to have come to light is the iron anchor and chain discovered in 1881 in a prehistoric hill-fort called Bulbury Camp, at Lytchett Minster, in Dorset.

**Romano-British and Comparable Ships**

It was particularly exciting when the two ships of the Roman period described below were found in London, for they were constructed in a manner wholly different from that used for any contemporary vessels found in the Mediterranean. This has led to the conclusion that they were built by native shipwrights in accordance with a local native shipbuilding tradition. If this view is correct, then they serve as a valuable guide to the form and nature of some native shipbuilding in Britain before the Roman invasion. The vessels were found in 1958 and 1962 respectively, and by chance it fell to me to direct the investigation of both.

*The Blackfriars ship.* In September 1962 a mechanical grab ripped out portions of several massive old oak timbers buried in the bed of the River Thames at Blackfriars in the City of London. The grab was clearing obstructions to facilitate the construction of a temporary jetty beside the proposed line of a new riverside embankment wall. At the Guildhall Museum I was told of the discovery and visited the site on the same day.

The timbers were several feet long and were clearly portions of the ribs of a large ship. They were curved and pierced by long iron nails, the heads of which lay about two inches from the wood face – enough for the thickness of hull planking. It was difficult to estimate their age, but the smooth under-surface of the timber fragments suggested that the vessel was carvel-built, and therefore probably dated from either the Roman period or after AD 1500 when carvel construction was commonly used in Britain. At all events the blackened and waterlogged nature of the timbers showed that the wreck was at least several centuries old and worthy of further investigation.

The progress of the investigation is described in some detail to show how even the most insignificant scraps of timber can give us important information. The excavations were carried out in three stages, during which different parts of the vessel were exposed, and it was only after all the information had been collected that it was possible to draw conclusions about how and when the ship was built, and which end was the bow.

As a preliminary to further investigation it was necessary to dig a hole in the river bed in order to determine the depth at which the wreck lay, and its alignment. At high tide the site was beneath 20 feet of muddy water, but at low tide the river bed was exposed for about two hours. On the advice of the site contractor, the excavation was planned to coincide with the October low spring tides when the river bed would be exposed for an extra half-hour. We were given the use of the grab to dig the initial hole and the London Fire Brigade kindly agreed

119

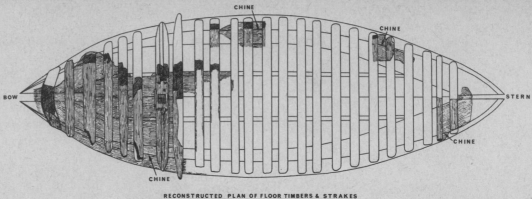

RECONSTRUCTED PLAN OF FLOOR TIMBERS & STRAKES

CHINE · CHINE · CHINE · CHINE · CHINE · BOW · STERN

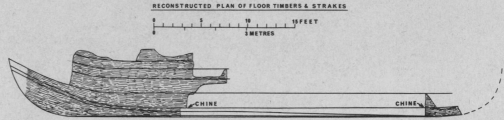

*6  Bottom and port side elevation of the second-century AD Romano-British ship from Blackfriars. The bow had been distorted owing to the weight of overlying river gravels, and in this drawing it has been given its probable original form*

RECONSTRUCTED ELEVATION OF PORT SIDE

CHINE · CHINE

to pump the water which would undoubtedly flood in. Several volunteers from a near-by theatre came down to the site to help.

The side of the wreck was located during the second low tide of digging, but we were confronted with an unexpected problem – the grab had so churned up the ground that the hole was nearly full of thick, grey, soupy mud which the pump was incapable of removing. Beneath this we could feel the ribs underfoot but could see nothing. The Fire Brigade worked extremely hard to clear the mud and on the fourth and last low tide of digging we saw the ends of two ribs and a small portion of planking.

Recording was very difficult as the shape of that part of the vessel could only be established by touch. Fortunately it was possible to check these findings later, but the difficulties of measuring under the mud were so formidable that some alternative method of excavating had to be found.

A second excavation was carried out on another part of the wreck during the low spring tides of November, on three consecutive mornings. This time the grab dug a large hole, 6 feet deep, to the level of the wreck and a deeper sump hole to one side. With a jet of water we washed mud and gravel into the sump which, in turn, was kept clear by the grab and a powerful sludge pump.

On the second low tide, a part of the wreck was exposed and it was soon established that we had found one end, which later proved to be the stern. No dating evidence was found but an important part of the ship's construction had been discovered.

Fortunately the new embankment wall was to be built across the site of the southern or forward half of the wreck, and when the 22-foot-wide coffer-dam was completed in July 1963, we were allowed three days to complete the archaeological work. This was a crucial

stage, and we sincerely hoped that we should be given longer, as it was clear that we could never accomplish the complete investigation of all that lay within the coffer-dam in so short a time. With the help of one or two volunteers the work of excavation was begun. It took all of three days to remove the 500 cubic yards of gravel overlying the wreck, but this left us no time to make vital records of what had been uncovered. Nevertheless, it was possible to establish that the wreck was Roman, for the gravel and silt within it contained hundreds of Roman pottery fragments, a coin, and parts of two dozen Roman leather shoes.

It so happened that the Lord Mayor of London, who wished to visit the wreck, was not free until the morning of the third day after we were supposed to finish. As a result, abandonment of work on the ship was delayed and we were able to complete the record of its construction. After the Lord Mayor's visit, the situation was taken completely out of our hands by one of the national newspapers which campaigned for the ship's preservation; literally one hour before it was to be destroyed the City Corporation decided that the timbers should be housed in the Guildhall Museum. This was indeed fortunate, since it meant that not only would the forward part of the ship be available for future study and display, but also that large-scale drawings of each rib in plan, elevation and section could be made, to supplement the general site record, before the timbers became distorted through drying.

When all the drawings were complete it was evident that the ship had a beam of about 22 feet and a probable length of approximately 55 feet. A large portion of the port side had collapsed outwards, but it was possible to make a reconstruction drawing of the cross section, from which it was established that the vessel was more than 7 feet deep amidships.

The hull was built entirely of oak, and comprised massive floor-timbers and comparatively slender side frames to the outside of which broad strakes had been nailed carvelwise. The bottom of the ship was nearly flat, enabling it to sit upright on the river or sea bed at low-tide. It had no keel but instead two central longitudinal planks, each 2 feet 2 inches broad and 3 inches thick, extending between the bottom ends of the stem and stern posts. The strakes averaged about 2 inches in thickness and the seams, which were caulked with hazel twigs, were often as much as a quarter of an inch wide. The strakes had been fastened to the massive floor timbers by specially made nails with hollow cone-shaped heads. Before each nail was used it seems that a hole about ¾ inch in diameter was first drilled vertically in the floor-timber, and an oak peg inserted. The iron nail was then driven through the strake and up the centre of the peg. The hollow head of the nail was driven slightly into the outer surface of the strake so that the nail gripped the strake tightly and made the fitting watertight. Several inches of the shank of the nail projected out of the upper surface of the floor-timber, and this was hammered down against the timber with the point embedded in the wood. The nails were especially large, the longest measuring 29 inches from head to point. The floor-timbers measured 12 inches wide and 8½ inches thick, but there were two exceptions; these were much wider, and overlay the stem post which they helped strengthen.

11

Each side of the ship met the nearly flat bottom to form an angle or chine of 30–35 degrees and on the strake just above the chine the lower ends of the side frames overlapped the ends of the floor timbers. These frames were about 5 inches thick and 7 inches wide, and the strakes were attached to them by iron nails similar to those used in the bottom of the ship.

10

In the central part of the ship, the floor-timbers and side frames were covered by a ceiling of oak planks one inch thick, which must have been the lining of the hold where the cargo lay. Forward of this, and more than two-thirds of the length of the vessel from the stern was the mast-step – a rectangular socket situated in a rather ornate floor-timber. No evidence of any other masts was found, and it is assumed that the ship was probably propelled by a single square sail.

12–14

The internal depth of the ship was so great that there must have been a deck, with a hatch in it over the hold abaft the mast, but none of the deck beams was found. The living quarters of the crew could not be identified, though the lack of any 'occupational debris' in the bottom of the ship forward of the mast-step, shows that this area was not so used. A cabin may have been situated on deck in the stern, but there was no confirmatory evidence.

When first discovered, the ship appeared to be much longer than it subsequently proved to be and it was only after the basic drawings had been completed that it became clear that the weight of the overlying gravel and water had flattened the timbers of the bow. It is probable that originally the strakes curved high upwards to meet the stem post, but that the stern was much flatter.

In the hold was a cargo of several tons of building stone, an analysis of which has shown that it was quarried beside the River Medway, near Maidstone in Kent. During the 350 years of Roman occupation thousands of tons of this stone were shipped to London, which contains no local building stone.

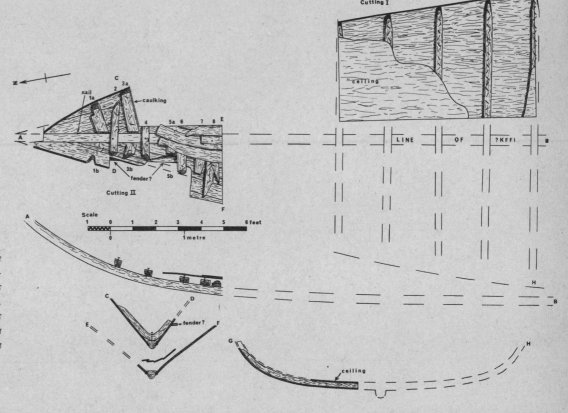

7 Plan and sections of the second-century AD Romano-British river boat found at Guy's Hospital near London Bridge. Like the ship from Blackfriars this is an example of a northern European shipbuilding tradition

The ships' last voyage, therefore, must have been up the River Medway, passing the city of Durobrivae (Rochester), and out into the estuary of the Thames. Here the heavily laden ship met salt water, and it was probably here too that on previous trips, the hull became infested with the dreaded *Teredo* (ship-worm). This salt-water mollusc lives in wood which it gradually eats away, and if it is not destroyed the safety of an infested wooden ship is endangered. When the hull planking was examined at the Museum, the characteristic *Teredo* borings were found, but the infestation seems not to have been dangerously advanced and it is unlikely to have caused the vessel to sink.

From the Thames estuary the ship probably depended upon the tides to help it upstream along the great meanders of the river to London. It passed beneath the Roman bridge and was within only 120 yards of the waterfront when it foundered. Though we shall never know the cause, the most likely explanation is a collision. From various sources we are fairly certain that the river was about 12 feet deep at the spot where the ship sank. We also know that something caused it to keel sharply over onto its port side, for the cargo had slid that way. Nevertheless, when the ship came to rest on the river bed, it lay on its flat bottom with a slight list to port.

*New Guy's House boat*. Once the Blackfriars ship had been satisfactorily dated, attention was immediately focused upon the second-century boat found at New Guy's House, the surgical wing of Guy's Hospital, London, in 1958.

The boat remains an enigma not only because it was found to have a unique construction, but also because very little of it could be examined. By chance I happened to be visiting the hospital building operations and saw workmen breaking up a group of curved oak timbers buried 16 feet below street level. The position, form and construction of these were hurriedly recorded and, as it seemed fairly certain that they were part of a boat of the Roman period, the hospital governors kindly consented to a small archaeological excavation being carried out in 1959 aimed at confirming these views. The trench coincided with one end of the vessel and there was sufficient pottery and coin evidence to date the abandonment of the boat to the end of the second century.

The extremities of the two trenches were 22 feet apart and sufficient of the in-curving sides had been found to show that the boat had a beam of about 14 feet. Its length is uncertain, but is estimated at about 40 feet. The vessel was an open boat with a shallow internal depth amidships probably not more than 4 feet, and it lay abandoned in a shallow stream or creek in the Thames-side marshes.

The boat seems to have been a small, flat-bottomed river barge; it was carvel-built and constructed of oak. The broad strakes were one inch thick and seemed to sweep up to the end of the vessel. They were covered with pitch outside and one seam was found caulked with

hazel twigs – exactly as was the case in the Blackfriars ship. Again, as with the Blackfriars ship, the strakes were not joined to each other edgeways; instead, they were kept in place by the iron nails which held them to the ribs. These nails had flat heads and square shanks unlike the comparable nails in the Blackfriars ship, but they had been used in almost exactly the same way, the pointed ends having been bent down against the inner faces of the ribs.

At the end of the boat there were no planks nailed to the top of the ribs, only a few loose boards. In the other trench nearer the middle of the boat the ribs were covered by a ceiling of oak planks $\frac{3}{4}$ inch thick, which had been nailed in place.

Unfortunately the boat cannot at present be fully excavated as it is covered by drains and two service roads in the hospital grounds; not until further excavation is carried out shall we be able to discover whether this was a sailing boat and whether it had a keel. Sufficient of the boat was found, however, for us to be certain that it was built according to the same tradition as the Blackfriars ship, even though its form is different.

When the Romans invaded Britain in AD 43, they probably found that native shipbuilding was based on several different traditions; the New Guy's House boat and the Blackfriars ship, however, show that more than one ship type could derive from a particular shipbuilding tradition. For lack of information regarding any others, we have to confine ourselves to this tradition. The Blackfriars ship was a barge-like freighter, probably capable of sea voyages, and the New Guy's House boat was almost certainly intended for river transport. The massive construction of the former, and the use of large iron nails, strongly recalls Julius Caesar's description of the Celtic ships of the Veneti.

*Continental counterparts to the Blackfriars ship?* The natives of southeast England were Belgic migrants from the Low Countries, and we might therefore expect vessels of similar age and construction to the Blackfriars ship to be found in that part of Europe. Such a vessel did in fact come to light many years ago at Bruges in Belgium, and the records describing the find, together with the surviving timbers, were recently studied by Mr Ole Crumlin-Pedersen. It has been estimated that the boat was some 45 feet long and 11 feet wide, but this seems very approximate. Fragments of ribs, a steering oar, and part of the stem or stern posts were recorded, but unfortunately none of the planking. As normally reconstructed, the boat has a clinker-built hull, but there is no actual evidence for this. It is clear that its skeleton comprised floor-timbers and side frames as in the Blackfriars ship, and the surviving floor-timber shows that it had a broad, flat bottom, an angle or chine being formed where the sides joined this. None of the characteristic notches to accommodate normal overlapping strakes were found in the side frames or in the floor-timber. The latter was severely damaged, and a 'notch' found in it which it has been suggested indicates a 'reverse' clinker construction (i.e. the lower strakes overlapping the one above) is slender evidence on which to base such an unlikely conjecture.

The most significant feature of its construction, however, is the preserved floor timber recently re-examined by Mr Crumlin-Pedersen, for it is an exact parallel to the comparable portion of the Blackfriars ship. Not only does it contain a rectangular mast-step socket, but the top of the timber also has the same medial ridge on each side of the step. In addition there are signs that the strakes were held to it by iron nails.

Unfortunately the Bruges boat has not been accurately dated; on very slender evidence it is believed to belong to the fifth or sixth century A D. In view of its similarity to the Blackfriars ship, however, it is probable that it is earlier than that.

A second discovery was made at Kapel Avezaath, in Holland, where the flat bottom of a ship at least 98 feet long was found a few years ago. I am most grateful to Mr G. D. van der Heide for kindly permitting me to mention this boat in advance of its full publication. The vessel had a double thickness of carvel-laid outside planks, which were fastened to massive floor timbers grouped in pairs by clenched nails similar to those used in the two London ships. Carbon 14 tests on the timbers make the ship date to the second century A D.

## Post-Roman Ships in Britain

When the Roman empire finally collapsed at the beginning of the fifth century, so did the Roman way of life in Britain. Trade dropped sharply, and we may infer that there was a great decline in shipbuilding and in the use of existing ships. Among the peoples who began settling in undefended England were Saxon migrants from the Low Countries of northern Europe. For a time the Britons continued to sustain some of the Roman culture though with diminishing success, and in due course the Saxons from whom the English are descended, came to dominate the former Roman province and apparently their shipbuilding tradition dominated England. Nevertheless, there was an appreciable Celtic population still living in Britain; they were in part absorbed by the newcomers, but many migrated westwards to comparative safety. Archaeologists would give much to know what happened to native British shipbuilding traditions under Saxon rule, but this period as a whole is poorly documented. The Saxons introduced clinker shipbuilding (see chapter 7, p. 164), most likely previously unknown to Britain; but there is no means of telling whether the native British carvel shipbuilding tradition continued to be used and developed even on a very limited scale, or whether it died out with so much else of Roman-dominated Britain.

No study of early ships in Britain would be complete without a mention of the famous Anglo-Saxon burial at Sutton Hoo, and a brief description of this remarkable find will, I feel, form a fitting conclusion to this chapter.

*The Sutton Hoo ship.* At the edge of a flat, sandy heath, 100 feet above the River Deben, and close to the small county town of Woodbridge in Suffolk, archaeologists unearthed the most wonderful treasure ever discovered in Britain, the most important feature of which from our point of view is the great ship in which it lay.

The discovery was made in 1939, near a place locally known as Sutton Hoo, a year after a landowner, Mrs E. M. Pretty, had started to investigate a group of ancient burial mounds on her estate. The archaeological investigation was carried out by Mr Basil Brown who worked under the general surveillance of the curator of the Ipswich Museum. In 1938, Mr Brown excavated three of the mounds and in one of these he found a sixth-century Anglo-Saxon burial, lying within a clinker-built boat. Unfortunately none of the timber had survived, and later robbing of the burial for possible treasure had destroyed almost all traces of the boat.

During 1939, Mr Brown turned his efforts to the largest mound of the group. A trench was dug through its short axis, and soon rows of corroded iron rivets were found, indicating that here was another vessel which, judging from the size of the mound, must have been much larger than the boat previously found. Everything pointed to a great Viking ship burial similar to those found in Scandinavia, and so Mr Brown stopped work pending consultation with the Ancient Monuments Branch of what is now the Department of the Environment and the British Museum. None of the wood planking of the ship had survived, all that remained in the sand filling of the burial pit being a thin, dark stain and rows of rusted iron rivets which once held the overlapping strakes. Not only was the find unprecedented, but clearly its excavation would require the help of very skilled archaeologists.

Mr C. W. Phillips, who first heard of the discovery in the middle of May 1939, visited the site in company with the curator of the Ipswich Museum. Little did they imagine what was in store for them. 'When it came the sight was a shock,' he wrote later, for the excavation had exposed more than half of a ship which seemed to be approaching 100 feet in length. 'In the event,' he added, 'its length proved to be 89 feet, but the first impact was staggering.' In mid-June he was invited to take over the direction of the excavation, and on July 10 digging was resumed.

The initial effort was directed towards uncovering the contents of the burial chamber situated in the middle of the ship. In it the excavators found an iron standard, a ceremonial whetstone or sceptre, a splendid helmet, sword and shield, spears, silver bowls, a stringed musical instrument, a set of two silver Byzantine spoons, drinking horns with silver mounts, a great gold buckle and a variety of other objects. Many of the finds were of gold and silver, marking the site as the grave of a Saxon king. The most important dating evidence was provided by a group of thirty-seven gold coins in a gold-framed purse, showing that the burial could not be earlier than

15–17

123

the first part of the seventh century AD. Though the precise date of the burial has not yet been established, it is thought to have taken place during the second quarter of that century.

18, 19 The ship, which was already old when used as a receptacle for the burial group, is generally considered to date from about AD 600 or earlier. By carefully removing all the sand and objects from the interior of the vessel down to the dark stain, the ghost-like form of the hull was revealed, together with the rivets. It was a remarkable achievement which demanded the greatest excavating skills on the part of the team of archaeologists engaged in the work. Fortunately the weather held, for any rain would have destroyed much of what had been uncovered.

The ship was a great, open vessel about 89 feet long and 14 feet broad. It was 4 feet 5 inches deep amidships, and its prow rose to a height of at least 12 feet 6 inches above the keel plank amidships. It was clinker-built, and the overlapping strakes and the keel plank were fastened together by iron rivets 7 inches apart. There were nine strakes, one inch thick, on either side of the keel-plank. Each of the strakes comprised several planks joined endways, presumably with an overlap scarf, and held by a few rivets. Sections were cut across the keel, which was found to be a plank 2½ inches thick with a rounded underside. The stem and stern posts had been scarfed onto the ends of the keel plank and held by iron bolts.

The hull was stiffened by twenty-six ribs. Since these frequently covered rivets which held the overlapping strakes together, it is evident that the ribs were put in place after the shell of the vessel had been built. The upper ends of two ribs in the stern on the starboard side were club-shaped and strengthened by being held to the strakes by several long iron rivets. This undoubtedly means that the steering oar was held in place here, but exactly how it was attached is unknown.

Unfortunately no clues were found to show how several important parts of the ship were constructed. For example, we would like to know whether the ribs had been fastened to the strakes by treenails or whether they were tied to wooden projections on the inner surface of the strakes. Even more to be regretted is the lack of any definite evidence for a deck or for a mast; the fact that the treasure lay in the bottom of the ship suggests

that, if present, both had been stripped out before the ship was buried. Nor was there any indication of a stern platform or deck for the steersman, and there was no sign of the steering-oar, though these must be presumed to have existed. The chamber containing the treasure lay amidships, roughly where a mast would be situated, and the fact that no sign of the mast or mast-step was found has given rise to doubts whether this ship was ever propelled by sail. The great size of the vessel, however, would suggest that it did have a mast and sail, even though the evidence for clinker-built vessels having been thus equipped at such an early date is inconclusive. Certainly the Sutton Hoo ship was capable of being rowed, for the tholes on the gunwale, to which the oars were lashed, were found. Even so, it is difficult to imagine that the Saxons had not used the sail, for their neighbours in northern Gaul and southern Britain had been doing so for many centuries before the Sutton Hoo ship was built (as witness the Bruges and Blackfriars boats).

The second World War started just after the Sutton Hoo investigation was ostensibly completed, and the treasure was given to the British nation by Mrs Pretty – perhaps the most generous act by an individual in the history of British archaeology. It now resides at the British Museum for all to see, magnificently restored and displayed. The ship-impression, however, was left in the ground, unprotected, and merely filled up with bracken and odd bits of chestnut paling to hold the bracken down.

In 1966 and 1967, Dr R. Bruce-Mitford of the British Museum re-excavated the ship (which had silted up to a depth of 5 feet amidships) in order to make an accurate plan of the vessel and to investigate the ground beneath. Unfortunately the upper parts of the ship's side had been destroyed by weather while it lay exposed during the intervening twenty-seven years, and much damage had occurred when tanks were driven through the partly filled-in excavation during the war. The excavators even found an unexploded bomb buried in the stern! Nevertheless, Dr Bruce-Mitford had the position of every surviving rivet and other feature of the ship precisely recorded in three dimensions. Finally a plaster mould of the ship's impression was prepared, from which a fibre-glass cast has been made as a permanent record of the ship as it was found.

---

1 This gold boat model, discovered at Broighter in Ireland, is one of the few known prehistoric or Roman representations of ships in Britain. It represents a rowing boat, pointed at both ends, which could be sailed. It was steered by an oar at the stern. The people who used boats like this about the time of Christ were the Celts, and it is reasonable to suppose that the shipbuilding tradition represented by this model continued in use during the period of Roman occupation in Britain from

AD 43 to about AD 400. As no boats dating from the century before the Roman invasion have yet been found in Britain our knowledge of their forms and construction is almost completely hypothetical. Nevertheless two of the Romano-British ships found in London presumably represent methods of native shipbuilding in Britain prior to the Roman invasion, although the evidence points to their having been built during the Roman period.

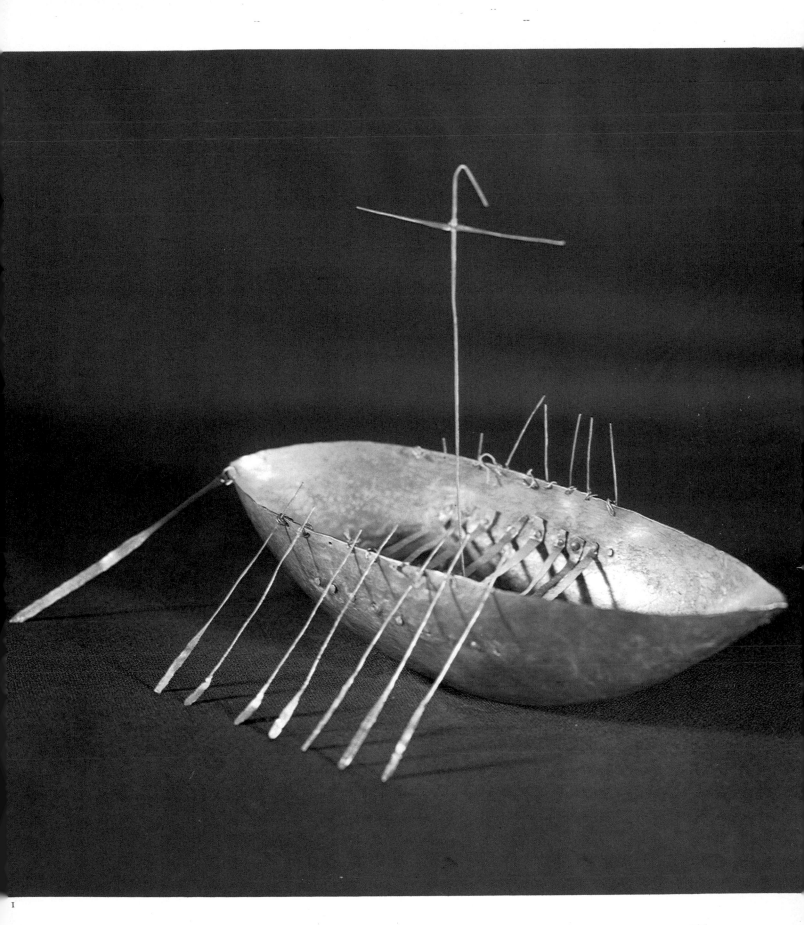

2–4 The type of timber used in the Roman ship found on the County Hall site, London, in 1910, showed that this vessel was built in Northern Europe. This is particularly interesting as the method of construction was developed by the Greeks, and was introduced into Northern Europe by the Romans. Only the centre section of this ship had survived (2), but enough remained to show that the deck beams (3) slotted into a wale on the side, and that these beams were supported by rows of stanchions. The remains of this ship, dated by coins and pottery to the third century AD, were carefully raised and transported to the then new London Museum. Crated up on site (4) the ship was dragged through the streets of London by a team of horses.

5, 6 Anchors are surprisingly difficult to date. One is clearly shown on an altar dredged up from the bed of the River Tyne, and probably came from a shrine to Oceanus and Neptune situated on a Roman bridge at this point (5). An Iron Age anchor and chain found in Dorset during the nineteenth century has recently been cleaned to show us a remarkably good example of a native British anchor of a type which probably continued in use into the Roman period (6). A particularly interesting feature is its moveable stock.

7, 8 The discovery of a second-century AD Roman river boat at Guy's Hospital, London, in 1959–60, with a construction unlike any vessels previously found in the Mediterranean, indicated that this boat had been built according to a native tradition during the Roman period. It is carvel-built, but unlike Classical ships, its planks had been nailed onto a pre-erected framework of ribs. Later ship discoveries indicate that this method of construction might have been brought to Britain from the Low Countries region before the Roman invasion in AD 43. A recent find, dated by Carbon 14 to the second century AD, at Kapel Avezaath in Holland, of a flat-bottomed ship nearly 100 feet long, shows a variation in the same building tradition. Here the ribs are grouped in pairs, and there is a double thickness of outer planks (8).

5

7

6

8

9–14 A second Roman ship was found in 1962, in the bed of the Thames at London, with a construction similar to that of the Guy's Hospital boat. Originally about 55 feet long, and 22 feet wide, this ship had been sunk during the second century AD while carrying a cargo of building stone to London. It had no keel, and a very flat bottom. The sides joined the bottom to form angles, and it was just above this point that they fractured when the ship began breaking up while on the river bed (10). About half of the wreck was excavated within a giant steel cofferdam (9) sunk deep into the bed of the River Thames for the construction of a new embankment wall. Massive floor-timbers (bottom ribs) were covered by inner planks amidships (11) to protect the hull from damage by the cargo of building stone. The mast was stepped just forward of amidships (12) into a special mast-step socket cut into a floor-timber. Though the mast was missing, a bronze coin was found in a small recess at the bottom of the mast-step, and had clearly been put there by the Roman shipwright to

128

buy good luck for the vessel – similar to the custom which exists in parts of Britain today. The wear on the coin showed that it had been in circulation for a long time and had evidently been specially chosen. It was a coin of the Roman Emperor Domitian (14), and had been minted in Rome in AD 88–89. Significantly its reverse lay uppermost showing the figure of Fortuna, goddess of Luck, holding a ship's steering oar (13).

11

13

14

129

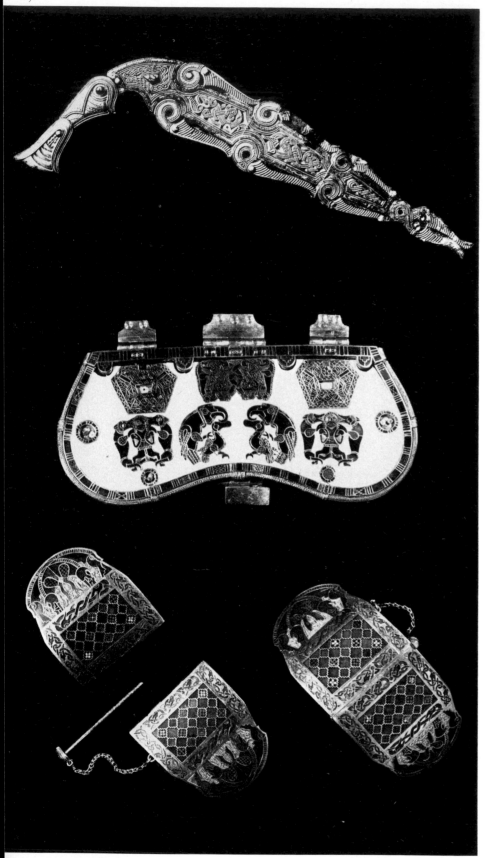

## 16

15–19  The great seventh-century Saxon ship found in 1939 in a burial mound at Sutton Hoo, Suffolk, (18, 19) belongs to a shipbuilding tradition developed in the Baltic region, and apparently ushered into Britain during the Saxon migrations of the fifth and sixth centuries, following the collapse of the Roman Empire.

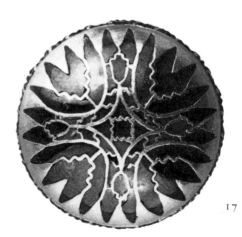

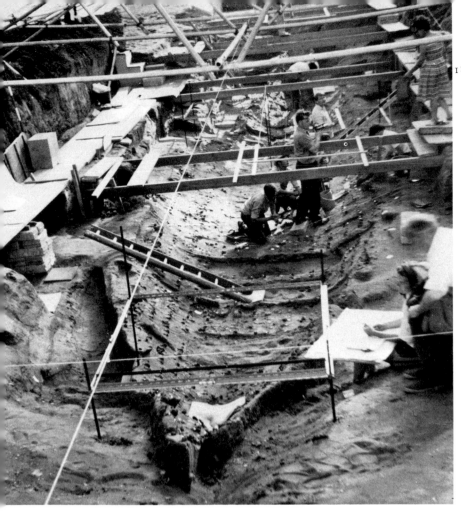

Characterized by its clinker construction of overlapping planks, this newly introduced method of shipbuilding originated before the time of Christ; and it was the foundation of medieval shipbuilding in Northern Europe. But what happened to the carvel, or edge-to-edge planking, traditions of Roman Britain during the Saxon period? This is an unsolved mystery the answer to which might be found in ship remains in those quiet backwaters of native life in Saxon Britain. A few items from the fabulous treasure found in this royal grave are illustrated here (15–17) including a decorative piece from a shield in the form of a winged dragon in gilt-bronze (top left); the gold lid of a purse decorated with garnets and enamel (centre left); a pair of gold shoulder-clasps decorated with garnet and enamel (bottom left); a pair of silver spoons inscribed in Greek with the names Saul and Paul (16); and the gold pommel of a sword, encrusted with garnets (17).

## 19

20, 21   One of the best representations of a Roman ship so far recovered in Britain is on a fourth-century Roman mosaic with scenes from the Aeneid, found at Low Ham, England (20). It shows a curious late Roman warship of a type which may have had a fixed mast. Similar representations of warships on late Romano-British coins underlines the theory that warships of that time were different in form from the earlier vessels.

Vessels of this kind were guided into the late Roman naval base at Dover, where there still stands a considerable part of a Roman lighthouse (21). Built at the time when the *Classis Britannica* (British Fleet) was based at Dover in the second century AD, the lighthouse was evidently retained in use when the *Classis Britannica* was apparently disbanded, probably during the third century, and a new naval organization, not bearing the old name, took its place.

# 6

# Byzantium, mistress of the sea: 330–641

FREDERICK VAN DOORNINCK

# Byzantium, mistress of the sea: 330–641

## Historical Summary

When the continental provinces of the West went into a severe decline following the disorders which beset the Roman Empire during the third century of our era, the Empire's economic and political centre of gravity shifted eastward and towards those regions which looked out upon her inland seas. In response to this shift, Constantine the Great (306–337) founded a new capital closer to the Empire's new focal area than was Rome. The site chosen, a hilly promontory on the European shore of the Bosphorus where the Greek city of Byzantium had stood, controlled both the land bridge between Europe and Asia and the waterway linking the Black Sea with the Aegean. The new capital was thus destined to become the crossroads for commerce between Europe and Asia. It was, moreover, exceptionally secure as long as control of the narrow sea approaches was maintained. Its dedication on May 11, 330, was to mark the starting-point for Byzantine history, in which, from the beginning, the sea played a central role.

Curiously enough, however, the reformed Empire was virtually without a navy until the end of the fifth century, a deficiency which contributed in no small way to her loss of dominion over the western Mediterranean in the wake of the Germanic invasions at the beginning of that century. Spain and southern France were occupied by the Visigoths, and soon after the demise of the Empire in the West (476), the great Ostrogothic leader Theodoric established a kingdom in Italy. More serious still, in 439 the Vandals captured Carthage, created a powerful navy, and carved out a naval kingdom which included North Africa, the Balearics, Sardinia, and Corsica. Vandal piratical expeditions terrorized the western Mediterranean and southern Greece with little opposition. Without a fleet, Majorian, then Emperor of the West, was reduced to the extremity of planning an *overland* expedition against North Africa via Spain, a plan abandoned after his death (461). In 468, Byzantium finally mustered a large naval expedition against Carthage. Ill-equipped to face the Vandal fleet on the high seas, this armada was destroyed at anchor a few miles from its goal while attempting to avoid a naval battle. The lesson was not wasted. By the beginning of the sixth century, Byzantium (and the Ostrogothic kingdom as well) was forming a palpable naval force.

Taking advantage of a general decline among the Germanic kingdoms, the Emperor Justinian I (527–565) undertook to restore the western Mediterranean to the Empire. Realizing that control of the seas would be the key to success, he began by dispatching an armada against the Vandal naval kingdom in 533. The Vandal fleet, still to be avoided at all costs, had been decoyed to Sardinia where Justinian had fomented a revolt. The Byzantine forces were able to capture Carthage without opposition from the sea, and the Vandal kingdom collapsed. Now the dominant power on the seas, Byzantium next moved against the Ostrogoths, and by 540 most of Italy including the Ostrogothic capital at Ravenna was in Byzantine hands. Persia, seeking among other things control over the eastern Black Sea, chose this moment to attack the Empire, but Byzantium emerged from this conflict in firm control of the entire Black Sea. In the meantime, the Ostrogoths moved to recover their kingdom. After building a large fleet, they won control of the seas, cut off the Byzantine armies from reinforcements and supplies, and reclaimed most of Italy. Then, in 551, Byzantium won an important naval battle near Ancona and partially broke the blockade. It was the turning point in the war. The Ostrogothic kingdom soon passed from history. Even as these events took place, a small Byzantine naval force landed in a Visigothic Spain beset by civil war and quickly took over the south-eastern corner of the peninsula and the African coast opposite. The coastline between Italy and southern Spain was to remain in Germanic hands, but as long as Byzantium occupied the Balearics, Corsica, and Sardinia, she indirectly controlled this coastline as well. The Mediterranean had again become a Roman lake. *1*

## Warships and Naval Warfare

The dromon (runner), a new type of light, swift warship, makes its appearance during this period. Earliest mention of it occurs at the end of the fifth century in letters of Theodoric. Dromons escorting the Byzantine armada of 533 were single-banked, had protective decking above the rowers, and may have had only one working mast. A passage in Procopius's *The Vandalic War* (i. 17), often cited as indicating that they had two masts, merely speaks of replacing large sails with small ones called *dolones*, in order to reduce speed. Another passage in *The Vandalic War* (i. 13) stating that the sails carried by the three command ships had a third of the upper angle painted red suggests that they were lateen sails. Until recently this interpretation of the passage presented an historical difficulty, as the earliest known examples of a definite lateen sail dated to the ninth century. We now have evidence, however, that the quadrilateral 'Arab' lateen and the triangular lateen sail were both in use in the Mediterranean by the fourth century of our era (see chapter 3, p. 77). It is quite possible, then, that the lateen-rig by permitting greater manoeuvrability was one of the features that set the dromon apart from the earlier liburnian (see chapter 5, p. 116).

The dromon placed a relatively great reliance on the ram as an offensive weapon. In the naval engagement near Ancona, for example, there was heavy hand-to-hand combat at first, but the ram largely decided the battle after the Ostrogoths had failed to maintain their formation. Warships were often manned by the best available troops, but each ship's contingent was relatively small and had to rely almost exclusively on light weapons: swords, spears, and arrows. Occasionally,

incendiaries were used. For example, a squadron of empty warships converted into fireships was launched by the Vandals against the Byzantine armada anchored near Carthage in 468. Many vessels caught fire, and in the resultant confusion, the Vandals followed up with a ramming attack, after which they captured the ships still afloat. In 516, a chemical compound invented by Proclus the Athenian and apparently very similar to the later Greek Fire, was used to burn a fleet led by Vitalian, a Byzantine general in revolt against Anastasius I, as it approached Constantinople. Vitalian failed to attain his objective but succeeded in demonstrating the capital's vulnerability to a combined land and sea attack.

Armies and consequently naval fleets were fairly small at this time. The Byzantine aramada in 533 consisted of 500 transports and 92 dromons. The transports, merchant vessels of from 120 to 200 tons burden impressed into service, were manned by 30,000 sailors and carried 10,000 infantry and 6,000 cavalry. The opposing Vandals apparently had only 120 warships in their fleet. During the last years of the Ostrogothic War, the Ostrogoths possessed 400 dromons. How many Byzantium had in action at any one time is not known, but it was well over

*1 The shaded area shows the extent of the Byzantine Empire at the end of Justinian's reign. Wreck sites and other places mentioned in this chapter are indicated*

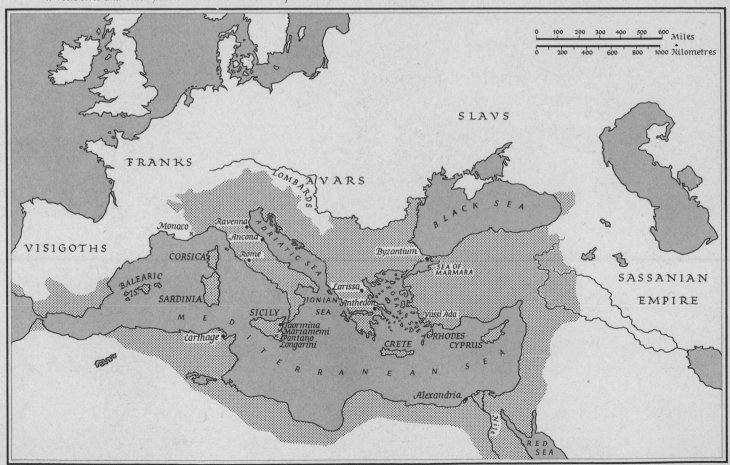

200. Yet in the important naval battle near Ancona, the Byzantine and Ostrogothic fleets numbered only 50 and 47 warships respectively. After the Germanic wars, squadrons patrolling the Empire's sea-lanes were seemingly modest in size. The squadron protecting the capital itself numbered only 70 vessels during the reign of Heraclius (610–641), even though the Slavs were threatening the capital both by land and sea. Not until the Arabs launched a Mediterranean fleet in 645 did Byzantium feel a need for larger warships and fleets.

## Justinian's Naval Empire

The Empire as restored by Justinian depended even more than heretofore on the sea for cohesion and unity. Indeed, the only real link between some of the more remote provinces and the capital was the network of sea-lanes stretching from the Caucasus to beyond the Pillars of Hercules and from the Crimea to the Red Sea. Strategically stationed all along this network were the small naval squadrons providing security for merchant ships and enforcing maritime law. Moreover, when danger threatened anywhere along the imperial borders, defended by a fortress chain chiefly manned by local militia, central army units were rushed in by ship. One might suppose that military disembarkation ports would have been developed at key points to facilitate this strategy, and indeed harbourworks recently excavated at Anthedon in central Greece by the German Archaeological Institute in Athens seem to represent just such a port built during the reign of Justinian. This system worked well except in the relatively few regions situated some distance from the sea: northern Italy, the Balkan interior, and the Persian frontier. At the end of the sixth century, both Lombards and Slavs attempted to challenge Byzantium's naval power but without success. Until the Arab invasions, the Empire remained undisputed mistress of her inland seas.

Justinian's building activities in the provinces were not limited to the construction of a defensive system of border fortresses and port installations. He also embarked on an empire-wide programme of church building designed in part to increase political stability within the restored Empire through the promotion of religious unity. To this end, Justinian built churches which everywhere exhibited a high degree of uniformity both in design and architectural adornment. To achieve this uniformity, architects and church plans were dispatched from Byzantium to all parts of the Empire, while the carved marble elements to be employed in the construction and furnishing of the churches often were hewn from quarries located near the capital and given a rough finish by Byzantine stonecutters, and then transported by ship to the building site.

## The Marzamemi Church Wreck

A consignment of church marbles, probably shipped from Byzantium during the second quarter of the sixth century perhaps to the province of North Africa not

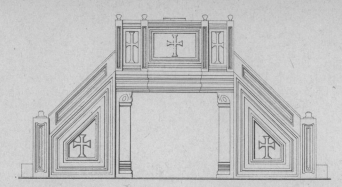

2 *Since its prefabricated elements of 'antico verde' had not yet been trimmed for final fitting, the ambo salvaged from the Marzamemi 'church wreck' can only be reconstructed on paper. Steps for the stairways were to have been made of local stone*

long after it was recovered from the Vandals in 533, came to grief when the ship carrying it ran aground on submerged rocks off Marzamemi, a small port near the southeastern tip of Sicily, and sank in only 30 feet of water. An investigation of this wreck was initiated in 1960 and 1961 by Gerhard Kapitän and P. N. Gargallo. Further excavation work was carried out between the years 1964 and 1967 by a German expedition under the direction of Kapitän in collaboration with Dr H. Wilms-Posen.

It was found that, owing to the shallow depth of water and a rocky bottom at the wreck site, the ship's timbers had been entirely broken up and dispersed. Only a few slivers of wood had survived, as well as some concretions which revealed that iron nails had been used in the ship's construction. However, the size of the area covered by the remains of the wreck suggests that the ship must have been at least 80 feet long, and it has been estimated that her cargo weighed from 200 to 300 tons.

The ship had been equipped with a galley or cookhouse which apparently had had a tile roof and/or a tile hearth. Objects from the galley so far found include a small square bronze weight for a steelyard used in weighing out merchandise, a terracotta 'wine-thief' for drawing water or wine, and numerous pottery fragments belonging to kitchen and table ware, pantry amphoras, and what was probably a large water storage jar.

The cargo of architectural elements included at least 28 columns accompanied by separate bases and capitals, all (with the exception of one column shaft) of white Proconnesian marble extracted from quarries located near Byzantium on the island of Marmara in the Sea of Marmara. The number of columns suggests that the church was to have been a large one of the rectangular, basilica type. Other elements of white Proconnesian marble in the shipment belonged to an altar, a *ciborium* or baldacchino providing an architectural canopy over the altar, and a low balustrade or choir screen which was to separate the sanctuary from the main part of the church. The screen was made up of panels carved in relief set between pillars which were topped by small

11

10

15

12–14

columns. In addition to the architectural elements of white marble, there were others of a greenish porphyry known as 'verte antico', derived from quarries located near Larissa in Greece. These elements belonged to an *ambo*, or pulpit, which had two staircases and lecterns. It would probably have been centrally placed on the basilica's longitudinal axis so that during Divine Service the preacher could be heard equally well by the men who occupied one side of the nave and the women who occupied the other.

The Marzamemi 'church wreck' has proved to be an archaeological document of unusual interest and importance. It has provided new insight into how a high degree of standardization in church architecture was attained throughout the Empire during the reign of Justinian and reveals the role played by ships in this process. Its cargo of prefabricated architectural elements also gives us our first opportunity of viewing an almost complete assemblage of interior marble adornments for a basilica of this period in their original, unaltered state.

## The Fourth-Century Ship at Yassi Ada

Although the merchant ships of Byzantium played an important role in the life of the Empire, we actually know very little about them, and such information as we have, gleaned from literary passages and representations in art, is for the most part of a very general nature. During the past decade, however, a University of Pennsylvania archaeological expedition led by Professor George Bass has acquired more knowledge of Byzantine merchantmen through excavation of the wrecks of two small coastal freighters first investigated by Peter Throckmorton and Honor Frost in 1958. The ships had been the victims of a treacherous reef lying just off the small coastal island of Yassi Ada located between the

Turkish mainland and the Dodecanese island of Pserimos.

One of these merchantmen had sunk in 140 feet of water during the second half of the fourth century while carrying a cargo of approximately 1,100 amphoras. Excavation of the undisturbed remains of ship and cargo, begun in the summer of 1967, was all but completed during the summer of 1969. The application of new techniques of deep-water excavation, many of them developed at Yassi Ada since 1961, permitted the making of a highly accurate and detailed plan of almost all the wreck remains within this short period of time. The resultant data have yielded a substantial body of information, particularly in regard to the ship's hull and galley.

Substantial portions of the hull on the port side had survived up to about deck level throughout most of the ship's length; only the foremost 10 feet of hull had entirely disappeared. Preliminary reconstruction essays based on these remains indicate that the ship had been very close to 62 feet long and had had a maximum width of about 21 ft 8 in. The resultant length/beam ratio was roughly 3:1. The hull appears to have been fairly symmetrical, for it attained its maximum width at or very near midships, the stern post, keel and stem contributing in almost equal proportions to the over-all length. Four pairs of wales girdled the sides of the hull between waterline and deck level. The lower two apparently ran in an essentially horizontal line throughout, while the upper two curved upward at stem and stern.

Mediterranean cypress (*Cupressus sempervirens*) was used throughout most of the hull. Only two exceptions have as yet been noted: the keel was of white oak, and treenails used in fastening frames to outer hull planking were of live oak.

*3 On the fourth-century Yassi Ada shipwreck, objects from the ship's galley lay concentrated in a small, well-defined area immediately forward of the stern post. Within this area were found some twenty slabs of stone (shaded), remnants of the galley hearth. The seven objects just to the right of the scale belong to a neighbouring seventeenth-century wreck*

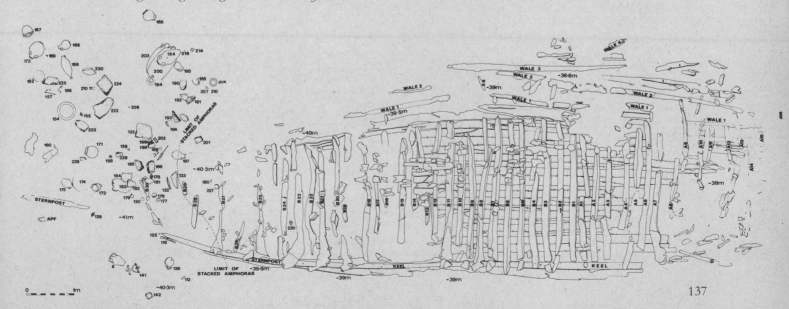

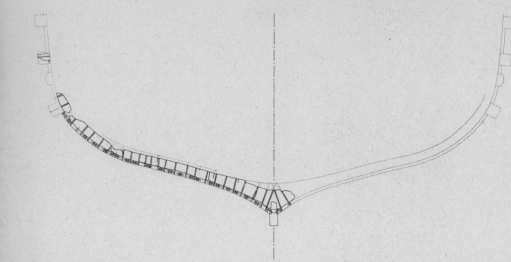

4    A tentatively reconstructed hull section amidships records most of the basic elements of the hull structure up to deck level. The keel had a maximum width of 12.2 cm. and was 22 cm. high. The outer hull planking had a thickness of 4.2 cm., and the wales tended to be about 16 cm. square in cross section. The frames throughout most of their length were 12.5 cm. high, and they normally had a width of 12 cm. The inner lining of the hull consisted of planking 3.8 cm. thick.

Traditional Graeco-Roman shipbuilding techniques were for the most part employed in the construction of the hull. Thus, the outer shell had been carried up at least as far as the second pair of wales and probably to completion before the insertion of frames was begun, which appears to have been customary in Graeco-Roman ship construction. The strakes of the outer shell, including the keel and the wales, were edge-joined together with mortise-and-tenon joints in which the mortises were 7–9 cm. wide and 5.0–5.5 cm. deep. The tenons were permanently fastened in place by pairs of treenails. Frames with floors alternating with frames without floors were then inserted throughout the length of the hull at regular intervals of about 24 cm. from centre to centre. Lines scored on the shell's inner surface were used to indicate where each frame was to be set. Treenails were used to fasten the frames to the outer hull planking; long iron nails driven from the inside, in fastening frames to wales. As was the general rule in Graeco-Roman hull construction, the frames strengthened and stiffened the hull but did not form an independently strong skeletal framework: the sections of each frame were not scarfed or fastened together in any way, and roughly four out of every five frames were not fastened to the spine of stern post, keel and stem.

Some features found in the hull, however, can almost certainly be attributed to new developments in Graeco-Roman hull construction occurring in the Roman Imperial period. The normal interval between neighbouring mortise-and-tenon joints was about 17 cm. (the normal centre-to-centre distance being about 25 cm.) throughout the outer shell, whereas the interval between joints in all known *sea-going* vessels of earlier centuries rarely exceeds 10 cm. Furthermore, the tenons were not as wide as the mortises in which they were set and were strongly tapered as well, thereby giving the shipwright plenty of 'play' while joining the strakes together. Tenons in the extant hulls of earlier centuries, on the other hand, are tight-fitting; at least this is so in all cases where the joints have been adequately described and illustrated. Iron bolts were employed in the fourth-century Yassi Ada hull to fasten the wale extremities to stem and stern post, and others which normally passed through every second or third frame floor were used in binding the spine to a keelson which unfortunately did not survive. Copper bolts were used in a ship uncovered at Monaco dating to the third or fourth century and possibly in a ship of roughly Hadrianic date which sank off Cape Taormina in Sicily, but metal bolts have not been found in any other extant Graeco-Roman merchantmen, nor were they used in the mammoth Lake Nemi barges (see chapter 3, p. 69, ill. 6). As the seventh-century ship at Yassi Ada has revealed (see below), a further lessening of the structural role of mortise-and-tenon joints coupled with an increasing use of metal bolts was eventually to lead to a more economical method of hull construction in which a greater reliance was placed on the skeletal framework of spine, frames and wales in imparting structural integrity to hulls.

The ship possessed a rather spacious but simply appointed galley set down within the hull at the very stern, its forward wall located about 10 feet forward of the stern post. The roof was not tiled, the hearth within

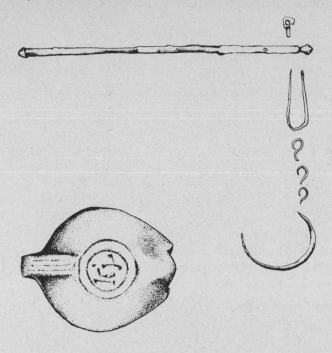

was constructed of rough stone, and judging from the
relatively small number of galley objects recovered, the
equipment inventory was modest. Terracotta objects
included six storage containers for food and water, a
funnel, four cooking pots, eleven pitchers, one cup, one
bowl, two large plates, a smaller dish, and four lamps.
Five glass vessels, a copper jug, an iron pickaxe, some
lead weights apparently for a hand-cast fish net, a small
and medium-size steelyard, and a relatively heavy lead
weight possibly belonging to a large steelyard not yet
located, round out the list of noteworthy equipment
found in the galley area.

Eight coins were also found on the wreck, all but one
from the galley area, but none was preserved well
enough to identify. The last half of the fourth century
as the date for the shipwreck is based instead on the
pottery, including a lamp signed K Y, which was almost
certainly made in a specific Athenian workshop at that
time.

No parts of the ship's rigging have as yet been traced,
nor have any anchors been found. Perhaps these were
all cast in an effort to keep the ship off the reef.

**The Size of Merchant Ships**
Small merchant vessels like the fourth-century Yassi
Ada ship have always played an important role in
Mediterranean maritime commerce, but this applied
particularly to the Byzantine period. When the huge
annual shipments of Egyptian grain to Rome were
diverted to Constantine's new capital, the 1200-ton
leviathans of the Roman grain fleet were no longer
required for the much shorter and easier Alexandria-to-
Byzantium run. The Palestinian monk John Moschus
(d. 620) describes a ship of 300 tons burden, the largest
ship recorded in the literature of this period, as having
unusually large proportions. Presumably, the Marzamemi ship, which had a similar capacity, would also
have been regarded as an exceptionally large vessel in
its day. Yet ships of this size had not been uncommon
several centuries earlier. John also tells us of a shipper
who, after building an 'unusually large' ship of 230 tons
burden, was unable to launch it despite the assistance of
300 men. The 500 vessels with capacities ranging from
120 to 200 tons in the Byzantine armada of 533 were
probably representative of large merchantmen at that
time.

Other factors besides the discontinuance of the
Alexandria-to-Rome grain traffic contributed to a
general reduction in merchant vessel size. While maritime commerce played an increasingly important role in
the Empire's economic life, the volume of goods involved was much diminished. War and plague had
severely reduced population levels within a shrinking
Empire, and the army, a major user of maritime transport, became smaller, especially under Justinian and his
successors. Furthermore, intermittent insecurity on the
seas fostered the building of swifter, slimmer merchant
ships able to outrun and outmanoeuvre hostile vessels.
We now hear of the *dorkon*, or gazelle, seemingly an
exceptionally fast and agile ship, and the lateen sail may
already have begun to replace the square sail as the
dominant rig on Mediterranean merchantmen.

There had gradually come into being during Roman
times a state merchant fleet financed by *navicularii*,
wealthy owners of lands whose rents were set aside for
this purpose. The shipper's guilds to which the *navicularii*
belonged were able to build and operate large merchantmen for the state's use. Since guild membership was
normally regarded as a burdensome civic duty to be
avoided if at all possible, the state found the system
difficult and perhaps increasingly impractical to maintain as the need for large merchantmen diminished. In
any event, by the end of the sixth century the policy of
maintaining a state merchant fleet had by and large given
way to a policy of chartering from independent ship-
owners merchant vessels which tended to be more
modest in size. At the same time, more economical
methods of ship construction were being developed
which enabled increasing numbers of middle-class citizens to become independent owners of small merchantmen.

Since they now played so indispensable a role in the
economy of the Empire, these independent shipowners
(*naukleroi*) became an important and influential class in
Byzantine society during the seventh century. They
codified the customary practices under which they
operated in the *Nomos Nautikos* or *Rhodian Sea-law*,
which most probably goes back to the seventh century,
and their importance also is clearly indicated by the
central position they occupy in contemporaneous religious literature. Even so, these sources reveal that they
were frequently men of relatively moderate means who
simultaneously played the roles of shipowner, captain,
and merchant.

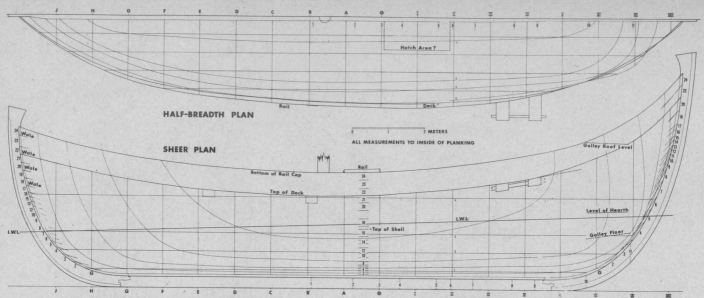

HALF-BREADTH PLAN

SHEER PLAN

0    1    2 METERS
ALL MEASUREMENTS TO INSIDE OF PLANKING

*7, 8   These line plans of the seventh-century Yassi Ada ship were developed after a series of scale models had been built based on the surviving hull remains, their final positions on the sea bed, and various topographical features on the wreck site, such as rock outcroppings on which the hull had come to rest and a depression made in the sand by the port-quarter bilge. It is*

### The Seventh-Century Ship at Yassi Ada

One such *naukleros* by the name of Georgios, who lived during the reign of Heraclius, owned or had some interest in a ship of some 40 tons burden. Although, as we shall see, the methods employed in its construction were more economical than those applied to earlier known Graeco-Roman hulls, the ship nevertheless represented a substantial investment. At a time when the annual wage of the ordinary working man was about 7 solidi, it had probably cost some 300 solidi to build, for according to the *Rhodian Sea-law*, the average assessment of a new ship was 50 solidi per 6.5 tons of capacity. Georgios' investment was unfortunately lost through shipwreck. While carrying about 900 amphoras of wine southward along the west coast of Asia Minor, the ship struck the reef off Yassi Ada and sank in 120 feet of water.

Although Georgios lost his ship, posterity did not. During four summer campaigns from 1961 to 1964, the undisturbed remains of this vessel and its cargo were also excavated by the University of Pennsylvania archaeological expedition. The resultant data, including a complete and accurate mapping of the wreck remains have yielded a more comprehensive picture of shipboard life than we presently possess for any other merchantman that sailed the Mediterranean in antiquity.

The hull, just about 62 feet long, was particularly elongated and streamlined in design, having a beam of only 17 feet and a resultant length/beam ratio of roughly 3.6:1. The mainmast seems to have been braced against the back of a through-beam which protruded on either side of the hull just forward of midships, and there is evidence to suggest that there were two other closely spaced through-beams near the ship's stern, their projecting ends probably forming the sides of box-like

mountings for the steering oars. Three ships with such mountings appear in a mosaic depicting Classis, the port of Ravenna, during the time of Theodoric. The Classis ships carry square sails. Was the seventh-century Yassi Ada ship so rigged? We cannot be sure, for nothing remains of the mast or rigging.

There were eleven iron anchors on board when the ship sank. Seven were compactly stacked on the deck 11½ feet forward of midships. The remaining four were stowed close by on the gunwales ready for use, two on each side. None had been cast at the time of the disaster. The anchors had movable stocks which were stowed with the anchors on the deck. Three iron stocks were recovered from the wreck. When in use, the stocks were seated in an elliptical aperture located just below the head of each anchor shank. It should be pointed out that anchors, stocks, and all other iron objects on the shipwreck, had long since been reduced to an iron oxide mush. However, thick layers of oxide-cemented concretion had built up around these objects forming an often perfect mould of the original. These moulds can be used in making replicas of the original objects and also make it possible to closely estimate their original weights. It has been calculated that six of the anchors had weighed about 73.5 kg. each; three, about 129 kg. each; and the other two were of some unknown intermediate weight. The three heaviest anchors lay at the bottom of the anchor stack, evidently to be used only as a last resort during a storm. It also proved possible to closely estimate the original weights of two of the anchor stocks. The calculated weight of one stock proved to be 14.5 kg.; of the other, 31.4 kg. Interestingly enough, the ship was carrying a set of weights based on a 'light' Roman pound of 0.29 kg. It may be that the stocks and anchors had specified weights just as anchors

18

26–29

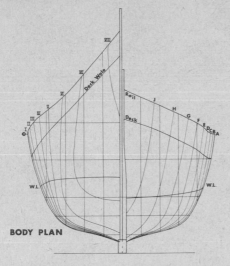

BODY PLAN

*doubtful whether a complete general reconstruction of the hull would have been possible had a thorough topographical map of the wreck site not been made*

did in the medieval period. If so, the light iron stock, the heavy iron stock, the six light anchors, and the three heavy anchors probably weighed 50, 100, 250, and 450 'light' Roman pounds, respectively. A comparison of the number and weight of these anchors with the number and weight of anchors on Mediterranean merchantmen of known size in the thirteenth century suggests that the trend towards fewer but heavier iron anchors on ships of any particular size, which can be documented from the thirteenth century on, had already made a modest start prior to this time. The method of stowing anchors on the ship also gives some indication of how as many as 28 anchors could be accommodated on large medieval Mediterranean vessels.

As had also been the case with the fourth-century Yassi Ada ship, there was a galley set down within the hull at the very stern. This galley, although smaller, was much more elaborate however. We now know that galley structures were not at all uncommon on Mediterranean merchantmen from the late Hellenistic period until at least the seventh century, but only this wreck has so far provided direct evidence of what such a galley was like.

It was unusually well designed, particularly for a vessel of only some 40 tons burden. The galley floor was set at as low a level as possible within the hull, and a transverse wooden wall, located 8 feet forward of the stern post and running the entire width of the ship, served as a partition between the galley and the hold. The superstructure rose only some 2.3 feet above deck level and was roofed over with tiles. One of the pantiles had a hole through which smoke from the galley could escape. Cooking was done on a large tile hearth fitted into the port half of the galley's interior. The hearth tiles, suspended above the floor by a system of iron bars

10

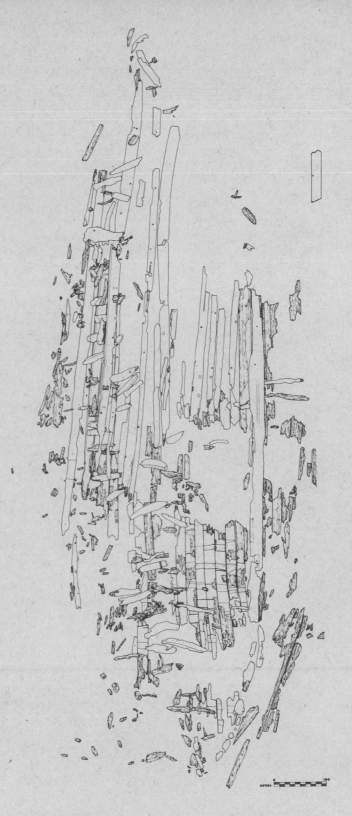

9  *Although the hull bottom of the seventh-century Yassi Ada ship was well preserved only in the area of the port quarter, substantial portions of the hull side and inner lining to port survived between the quarter and midships*

141

embedded in clay, were well insulated from surrounding wooden structures. The tile roof and insulated hearth minimized the possibility of accidental fire, one of the chief causes of disaster at sea in all periods. As a fire-prevention measure, the *Rhodian Sea-law* stipulates that a passenger is not to prepare his own cooking fire and 'is not to fry fish; the captain must not allow him'.

The galley was well furnished with utensils for the preparation, cooking, and storing of food. These included a mortar and pestle, more than twenty cooking pots of various shapes and sizes, two copper cauldrons, and a copper tray with a raised rim. Most of the cooking ware was kept in the immediate vicinity of the hearth, while perhaps as many as ten food storage jars were stowed in front of the hearth on the galley's starboard side. The ship's water jar stood within a small storage area between the galley proper and the stern post where in the main heavy, bulky articles including the two copper cauldrons were kept. There was a 'wine-thief'

for drawing water or wine, almost identical to the one found on the Marzamemi 'church wreck'.

The ship also boasted a fine service of tableware. There were perhaps three table settings, each consisting of red ware plates in two sizes, a one-handled cup, more than a dozen coarse ware jugs and pitchers, several glazed ware bowls, some often quite elegant copper and glass vessels, and a bronze censer customarily used to provide perfumed incense at the close of a meal. The fragile and costly tableware was kept in a locked cupboard within the partition wall on the galley's starboard side, while the coarse ware jugs and pitchers were stowed in the after storage area.

Set meals were undoubtedly taken on deck between the galley and the main hatch, perhaps within a light structure with open sides which could be canvassed-in during inclement weather and with a flat roof which could serve as a platform for the helmsman. A number of small stacks of mussel shells (the valves invariably

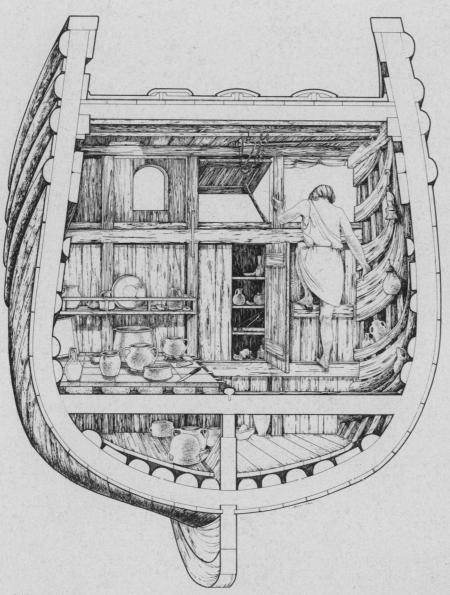

*10   The very stern end of the seventh-century Yassi Ada ship has been cut away to permit this general view of the reconstructed galley. The galley's forward wall rose some 2.3 ft above deck level thereby allowing for lighting, ventilation and access. The precise nature of these arrangements must, however, remain conjectural. The galley roof was tiled, and portions of all the tiles, including one with a round smoke hole, were recovered. All objects of terracotta, metal, glass or stone appearing in the reconstruction were actually found in the galley area. The distribution patterns of these objects on the wreck revealed the general layout of the galley interior. The large steelyard suspended from the ceiling bears the inscribed name of the 'naukleros' Georgios. The galley hearth is here reconstructed as a flat, tiled surface. Further detailed study of the hearth remains now indicates, however, that it more probably took the form of a tiled firebox covered over by an iron grill. The hearth structure was in any case suspended on a system of clay-embedded iron bars so as to reduce the chances of accidental fire*

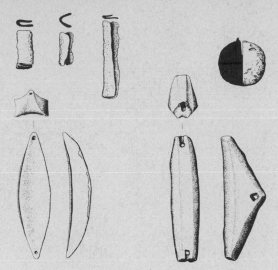

11  *Fishing weights found on the seventh-century shipwreck were used both on nets (upper left) and for bottom (lower left) and deep water (right) trolling with a line*

from the same side of the mussel) found only in this area of the wreck may have been remains of one of the last shipboard meals.

The ship's carpenter, who kept his tools on the starboard side of the deck just forward of the galley, was well equipped to make shipboard repairs. The iron concretions recovered from the wreck were found to include several bags of nails and almost fifty of the carpenter's tools. A sheet of lead and lead casting wastes further reveal that fittings and weights of this metal were cast on board.

Most of the other equipment was stowed within the galley. Here Georgios kept a large steelyard bearing his name. Another, smaller steelyard, a box of silver inlaid weights, and some twenty lamps, were kept in the galley cupboard. All of the sixteen gold and more than fifty copper coins found on the wreck also seem to have been in this cupboard for safekeeping when the ship went down. We are reminded of a chapter in the *Rhodian Sealaw*: 'If a passenger comes on board and has gold, let him deposit it with the captain. If he does not deposit it and says "I have lost gold or silver", no effect is to be given to what he says. . . .' The minting date still legible on many of the copper coins permits one to conclude that the ship had sunk either in the year 625 or shortly thereafter.

A grapnel for the ship's boat, and tools (two axes, a pickaxe, two bill-hooks, and a shovel) used by the crew while foraging for water and firewood on land, were stowed in the after storage area. Here too were kept needles and spare lead weights for repairing fish nets and a rather interesting assortment of lead weights for line fishing.

The earlier Graeco-Roman practice of completing or nearly completing the outer shell of the hull before inserting the frames was not followed in the construction of the seventh-century Yassi Ada ship. Instead, the edge-joined planking of the outer shell had only been carried up to waterline level before the frames were inserted. Here again, score lines showed where each frame was to be set. Nails driven from the outside secured the frames to the outer shell. Next, four pairs of half-timber wales girdling the upper sides of the hull were bolted to the frames, to which the remaining planking was then nailed. All fastenings were of iron. Full and half timbers were cypress; the frames, elm; the planking, pine; and the tenons used in edge-joining the hull planking below the waterline, white oak.

The degree to which the hull relied on the outer shell planking for strength and structural integrity cannot be precisely stated. The frames were so poorly preserved that we cannot say with any certainty where frame joints occurred or if frame sections were fastened together in any way. Even so, it is clear that the hull depended for strength and structural integrity considerably more on the skeletal framework of spine, frames and wales and considerably less on the outer shell of planking than had earlier Graeco-Roman hulls. Most of the frames, 14 cm. square in section and normally set at intervals of about 21 cm. from centre to centre, had floors which were securely fastened to a large-sized keel 22 cm. wide and 35.5 cm. high. About one-quarter of them were bolted to the keel; the rest were nailed. Bolted frames tended to occur where particularly sturdy frames were required. Frames were also set more closely together than usual in those areas where it was desirable to make the hull exceptionally strong. The wales, roughly 20 cm. in diameter, were bolted on the average to every fourth frame, and only one of the wales was bolted to each frame. The bolts passed through both wale and frame and then through an inner lining strake comparable in size to the wale itself. The bolt heads formed a rather regular and pleasing pattern along the sides of the hull. Hanging knees were used to support deck beams. For the most part, then, the skeletal framework possessed great strength and firmness. The outer shell planking, on the other hand, was only 3.5 cm. thick and had little structural integrity of its own. The mortise-and-tenon joints used in edge-joining the planking below the waterline were set at from centre-to-centre intervals of from 30 to 40 cm. in the stern area and at somewhat wider intervals not normally exceeding 90 cm. in the middle body of the hull. The mortises were normally only 5 cm. wide and 3.5 cm. deep. The tenons set within them had a maximum width of barely 3 cm., tapered strongly toward the ends, and did not exceed 0.5 cm. in thickness. Designed to facilitate as much as possible the fitting together of the planking and the shaping of the hull bottom, the tenons had considerable freedom of movement within their mortises, nor were they fastened in place with treenails. Their contribution to hull strength and integrity was both slight and incidental, and they were often dispensed with. They were not used, for

30, 31

25

19

29

11

example, in fastening the garboards to the keel. By minimizing the structural role of the mortise-and-tenon joints, Mediterranean shipwrights were laying the groundwork for the eventual emergence of the skeleton-first or carvel system of hull construction, the most widely followed method of wooden hull construction in the world today; indeed, it now appears quite likely that the first extensive application of carvel-building had occurred within the Mediterranean area by the twelfth century (see below), and by the fifteenth century the practice had spread to Northern Europe. Considerations of economy would seem to have been the main factor behind the new constructional methods. Reducing the number and size of joints and dispensing with the fastening of tenons meant that fewer man-hours were required to build a hull of any given size, and a further economy was effected in building the seventh-century Yassi Ada ship by lining most of the hull interior with rough, untrimmed half-timbers rather than with planking.

## The Pantano Longarini Ship

32-37

Such constructional economies also occur in the hull of a Byzantine ship of uncertain date recently excavated in the Pantano Longarini, a marshy coastal plain just west of the south-eastern tip of Sicily. The ship had apparently run aground and broken up on a reef just outside the ancient port of Edissa, and the upper part of her starboard side had subsequently been washed ashore and covered over with sand. These remains were brought to light again in the winter of 1963–64 while one of a series of land reclamation drainage channels was being dug in the area. Unfortunately, the forward and middle third of what remained of the hull was torn out by a bulldozer and used for firewood before the importance of the find was recognized. The destroyed timbers included the stem post and a hardwood plaque bearing both the ship's name written in Greek letters (the workmen's descriptions indicate that the name had five or six letters including a four-bar sigma, a phi, pi, omicron and perhaps a lunate sigma) and a horse's head carved in low relief above it. At the request of Professor Luigi Bernabò Brea, the Director of Antiquities in Syracuse, Gerhard Kapitän and Peter Throckmorton in 1965 undertook excavation of the still surviving stern section. After making a general plan of the remains, the timbers were dismantled, individually drawn in detail, and placed in fresh water to await future preservation, reassembly and exhibition.

The excavators estimate that the ship had a keel not less than 100 feet long, an over-all length of about 130 feet, and a capacity which certainly exceeded 200 and possibly even 300 tons burden. The outer shell and inner lining strakes of the hull were of cypress; the frames, of oak; and tenons used in edge-joining the outer hull planking below the waterline were of pistachio wood. This choice of woods suggests that the ship was probably built in southern Italy or in the Aegean area.

In construction, the ship was quite close to the seventh-century Yassi Ada ship. The outer shell was first carried up to waterline level with the aid of small, unfastened tenons which here again had no real structural function. The frames were then inserted, score lines being used to mark their positions, and finally the sides including massive half-timber wales were fastened to the frames. Deck beams were at least in some instances carried right across and through the sides of the hull, and these whole-timber beams as well as many of the half-timber inner lining strakes were left for the most part in a rough, untrimmed state.

In certain respects, however, the Pantano ship differed from the Yassi Ada ship in construction. Frames with floors alternated with frames without floors, and although all of the frames were apparently fastened to the keel, bolts do not seem to have been employed here nor in fastening the wales to frames. Instead, iron nails appear to have been almost the only metal fastenings used throughout the hull. The tenons were even more widely spaced than in the Yassi Ada ship, their normal distance apart being about 99 cm.

The most noteworthy feature of the hull revealed by the plan of the existing remains is an ostensible transom stern. If this proves to have been a transom designed for a stern-rudder, then a secure date for the ship will be of crucial importance, for it is generally held that the stern-rudder was first used in Northern Europe in the twelfth or thirteenth century and was then introduced from there to the Mediterranean area at the beginning of the fourteenth. At present, the only pointers to the age of the ship are a single radiocarbon date for some outer hull planking, some very small pottery fragments, and the hull construction methods employed. The planking has yielded a C 14 date of AD 500 ± 150 years, the pottery could conceivably date to as late as the medieval period, and one might argue with equal conviction that the ship was built either a bit earlier (fastenings) or somewhat later (spacing of tenons) than the seventh-century Yassi Ada ship. A scale model of the Pantano Longarini ship is presently under construction, and the excavators also hope to have a whole series of C 14 dates made on carefully selected samples from various hull timbers. The combined results of these undertakings would certainly be of great value and interest.

## Sequel (641–1100)

Some twenty years after Georgios's ship met with disaster at Yassi Ada, the forces of Islam reached the Mediterranean shores of Syria and Egypt. Alexandria fell in 641, and when a Byzantine naval expedition temporarily recaptured it in 645, the Arabs reluctantly set about building their own fleets, realizing that they would have to become a naval power if they were to maintain their conquests. Their first important naval victory, the 'Battle of the Masts', took place off the Syrian coast of Asia Minor in 655 when with 200 ships they destroyed a Byzantine force of 700 to 1,000 vessels through the unusual tactic of chaining their ships together so that their battle line could not be penetrated. In 673, an Arab armada appeared in the Bosphorus itself and besieged Byzantium. The city was saved only by the timely invention of Greek fire by a Syrian named Callinicus. Armed with this terrible new incendiary weapon (which may have been a kind of napalm, if its secret ingredient was in fact gasoline as has been recently suggested), Byzantium was finally able to re-establish her naval supremacy in the Mediterranean midway through the eighth century after a prolonged struggle. During the interim, however, the Arabs had with the assistance of their fleets added North Africa and Spain to their dominions and were in possession of all but the northern shores of the Mediterranean.

Unable to win back her lost provinces through force of arms, Byzantium had by the beginning of the eighth century embarked on a policy of waging economic warfare against her new adversaries. Taking advantage of her re-emerging naval strength, she blockaded Arab coastlines and restricted the great bulk of East–West maritime trade to the Black Sea and to the sea-lanes connecting Byzantium with her possessions in Italy. Maritime trade in Arab waters dwindled away, and the Arab fleets disappeared soon after.

The land-oriented Iconoclast emperors of the eighth century, however, tended to allow more and more of Byzantium's maritime commerce to be taken over by non-Greek middlemen: Armenian and Arab merchants in the Black Sea and Italian merchants in the West. Byzantium's naval power consequently declined, and Arab fleets once again ventured forth. In 826, an Arab force with only 40 ships succeeded in capturing Crete. With Crete an Arab naval base, Byzantium could no longer adequately defend her possessions in the West. By the beginning of the tenth century, the Balearics, Sicily, portions of southern Italy, and most of the Mediterranean Sea were in Moslem hands. Maritime commerce once again flowed freely in southern Mediterranean waters, inaugurating for North Africa, Spain and Sicily a new period of great prosperity shared by Italian maritime cities now less subject to Byzantine domination.

Byzantium's naval reaction to this state of affairs was vigorous but largely ineffective until 960 when she launched a vast armada of 2,000 warships and 1,360 supply ships, the largest fleet she ever built, against Crete and regained possession of the island. She then went on to re-establish her authority in southern Italy and even briefly regained control of eastern Sicily in 1038.

But the Latin West was now stirring to life. When in the mid-eleventh century the political fragmentation of North Africa, Sicily and Spain brought on a new decline in Moslem naval power in the western Mediterranean, the newly emerging Italian maritime cities of Genoa and Pisa, as well as Norman freebooters, were quick to seize their opportunity. During the last half of the eleventh century, Genoa and Pisa became the leading naval powers in the western Mediterranean, and the Norman conquerors of Sicily and southern Italy threatened to wrest from Byzantium and her client, Venice, control of the Adriatic and Ionian Seas. Byzantium, severely weakened by the Seljuk occupation of her Asia Minor heartland in 1071, had to rely heavily on Venice for naval support in meeting the Norman threat and in return was forced to grant Venetian merchants what amounted to a maritime trade monopoly within her waters. By 1100, the Italian maritime states controlled maritime trade in the western Mediterranean, in Byzantine waters, and, thanks to the First Crusade, along the Palestine–Syrian coast as well. A new chapter in Western naval and maritime history had begun.

The period just summarized saw many new developments in naval warfare. With the advent of the land-lubber Arabs who sought whenever possible to turn sea fights into land battles, fleets once again relied heavily on grappling and boarding tactics and on larger warships carrying greater numbers of fighting men. By the tenth century, Byzantine ships of the line were two-banked vessels with from 50 to 60 oars in each bank and ranged in length from about 120 to 135 feet; they were classified into three types, primarily according to beam measurement and resultant crew capacity. The smallest, the *ousiakoi*, were manned by a single company or *ousia* of 100 to 110 rowers with one man to each oar. The ram was their primary weapon, the upper-bank rowers alone being charged with any unavoidable close-quarter fighting. The largest, on the other hand, were designed expressly for fighting at close quarters. Known simply as dromons, they were manned by from 50 to 80 marines and by two companies of rowers with one man at each lower and two men at each upper oar. An intermediate type, the *pamphyloi*, had crews of from 120 to 160 men. All three types were lateen-rigged. Some of the largest dromons had three masts, while the *ousiakoi* and *pam-*

*12 Early medieval Mediterranean warships carried a gruesome assortment of missiles. These included jars containing Greek fire, two of which are shown in this drawing*

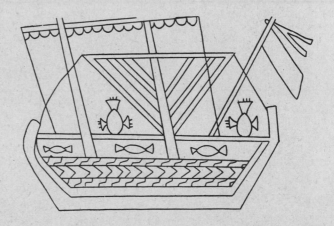

*phyloi* were probably in both cases two-masters. Some specially constructed warships in the 960 armada against Crete were able to land on beaches and disembark heavy cavalry down a sliding ramp. The standard dispatch and scouting ship was the *galéa*, a single-banked vessel.

The dromon of this later period possessed an ingenious and terrifying assortment of offensive weaponry. During a battle's initial stages, the ram and a large flame-thrower armed with Greek fire and mounted in the bow were the principal weapons. Larger dromons also carried two other large flame-throwers, one amidships and one astern, as well as some bolt-firing and missile-hurling catapults. Once an enemy ship had been grappled, marines protected by a coat of mail, helmet and shield swung into action with swords, spears, pikes, bows and crossbows. Hand-held flame-throwers and hand-thrown missiles were also used.

3, 4   We know practically nothing about the Byzantine merchantmen of the Iconoclast period (723–843) when the production of representational art was sharply curtailed. The earliest known post-Iconoclasm pictures of Byzantine ships are manuscript illuminations dating to about 880. In these representations we see for the first time the triangular, as opposed to the quadrilateral, lateen sail. It is quite likely, however, that the triangular lateen had already been in general use for some time, for manuscript illuminators worked with sterotyped traditional forms and rarely allowed innovative features to intrude into their art. The ships are depicted in a miniaturist style which does not permit any close estimate of actual size, but they seem to be fairly small one-

masters, and a general trend toward reverting to larger-sized merchantmen does not appear to have really begun until the twelfth century. Some of the foremost Mediterranean naval powers, however, were already building naval transports of very great size in the tenth and eleventh centuries. Some transports used in the Fatimid conquest of Egypt in 969 were said to have been 275 feet long and 110 feet wide, and in 1084, Venice launched against the Normans a fleet which included nine castellated ships carrying about 13,000 men in all.

With the possible exception of the Pantano Longarini ship, we do not as yet possess the actual remains of a Byzantine vessel dating from after the seventh century. At the time of writing, however, Peter Throckmorton has begun the excavation on behalf of the Greek government of a twelfth-century ship lost in the Northern Sporades. A cargo of marvellously decorated Byzantine plates and parts of a hull have already come to light. Throckmorton reports that the construction is more like that of a modern caique than that of the ancient ships excavated to date. The frames, of pine, are massive – $16 \times 18$ cm. thick. The planks, also of pine, are only $3\frac{1}{2}$ cm. thick, and are fastened to the frames with square forged iron nails. There is no evidence, so far, of tenoning, and it seems almost certain that the ship was a 'modern' construction.

It is beginning to look, therefore, as if we shall not have long to wait before enough is learned about shipping of the later Byzantine period to warrant a chapter of its own.

---

1   This reconstruction painting by Pierre Mion, showing work in progress on the site of the seventh-century Byzantine amphora-carrying ship wrecked at Yassi Ada off the west coast of Turkey (see also ills. 19–31) exemplifies the various underwater techniques employed in the development of marine archaeology. A narghile (hookah) diver guides an inflated cloth balloon which carries a lifting basket containing amphoras to the surface. The 'air-lift' sucks silt up from the sea-bed to a wire sieve fixed to the top of a tube anchored by two rock-filled oil drums and held upright by an air-filled buoyant drum a little way below the sieve; attached to the sieve is a bag that reclaims potsherds accidentally sucked into the tube. The diver on the right prepares to

raise the bag to the surface for inspection of its contents. The diver beneath the scaffolding controls the bottom end of the air-lift tube. The cameraman, bottom left, is taking pictures through the grid at the base of one of the two iron-framework photo-towers. Beside the other photo-tower at the far end an artist sketches anchors on a sheet of frosted plastic. Near the surface, an aqualung diver is undergoing decompression before returning to the anchored barge seen at the top of the picture. Large quantities of amphoras have already been moved to the sides of the shipwreck, revealing timbers of the vessel's hull beneath the scaffolding.

This painting and ill. 9 are reproduced by special permission of the National Geographical Society.

Preliminary surveys were undertaken in 1960–61 on a wreck located off the fishing-village of Marzamemi in Sicily after a local fisherman had seen blocks of marble on the sea bed. It soon transpired that here was a most unusual and interesting find. It has come to be known as the 'church wreck', for work on the site has shown that the ship was carrying pre-fabricated building parts for the interior architecture of a basilica of the early Byzantine period. Underwater excavation by German and Italian teams over the next ten years has yielded more than 500 pieces of marble, though the largest and heaviest elements have had to be left on the sea bottom. Little of the ship itself remained, though some of the fittings and equipment were recovered.

10 Among the potsherds salvaged from the wreck was this *terra sigillata* fragment from the base of a plate or bowl, perhaps of North African provenance. The incised design shows Christ blessing.

11 Part of the ship's gear, a 'wine-thief' for drawing water or wine.

15

12–14 Fragments of the marble choir screen intended for the Byzantine basilica. From the various pieces of marble recovered, it has been possible to reconstruct the symmetrical decorated pattern on the front of the screen. Two of the fragments (12, 14) bear portions of the relief design of balanced crosses on either side of the central medallion – a six-armed incised cross in a circle, part of which is visible on another badly eroded fragment (13).

15 Corinthian capital, probably intended for one of the nave columns. Note the identifying mason's marks, the Greek letters pi and omicron, incised near the top.

16 Part of the underside of an *ambo* (pulpit) destined for the basilica; it bears an eight-armed cross incised in a hollowed-out circle.

17 Diver with sandstone disk, probably a piece of ship's gear, of uncertain use.

12–14

16

17

18

18 Sixth-century mosaic from the church of Sant' Apollinare Nuovo, Ravenna, depicting three ships in Classis, the town's ancient port. No little interest to us of these rather crude representations of contemporary ships lies in the box-like mountings near the stern for the steering oars; for there is material evidence to suggest that the seventh-century Byzantine ship wrecked at Yassi Ada had just such a structure attached to two closely-spaced through beams.

19 Six of the sixteen gold coins found at the site of the seventh-century Yassi Ada wreck. They show, on the obverse, the emperor Heraclius (610–641), and a globe and cross on the reverse.

20–25 A few of the many galley-objects recovered from the seventh-century Yassi Ada wreck: a spouted jug and lid (22); a broad-based pitcher coated inside with resin (21); storage amphoras of diverse shapes and sizes (24); a stone mortar (23); terracotta lamps (25); a plate and a cup (20).

19

154

20

21

22

23

24

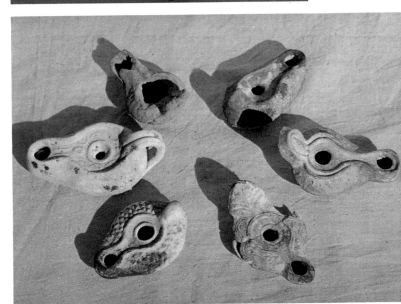

25

155

26

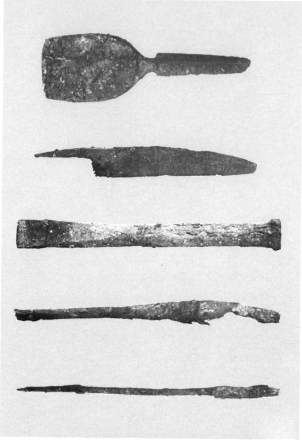

30

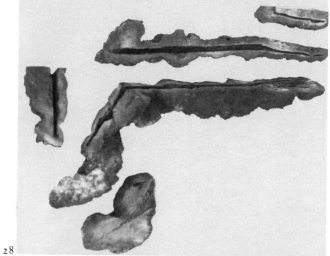

27

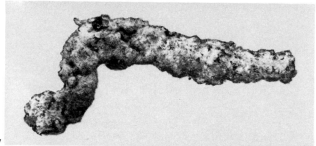

28

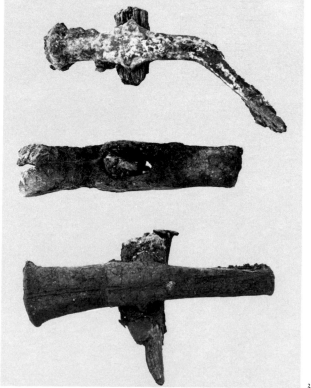

31

29

156

26–29 The excavators of the seventh-century Yassi Ada wreck, working at depths of about 120 feet, brought up more than 150 'concretions' of iron objects. In most cases, the iron had completely corroded away leaving concrete-like shells. Opened up and cleaned, these could be used like moulds in casting, a special quick-hardening rubber being poured into them to form the replica of the original object. The process is illustrated in the photographs on the far side of the opposite page. Michael Katzev uses a lapidary saw (26) to open up one of the concretions (27); the same concretion after several cuttings (28); rubber cast taken from the concreted mould, showing the object to have been a billhook with handle partially preserved (29).

30, 31 Rubber casts of a variety of tools found at the site of the seventh-century Yassi Ada wreck, obtained by the same method as the billhook (26–29).
30 (from top to bottom) adze, file, chisel, gouge with wooden handle, wood-boring bit.
31 (from top to bottom) hammer-adze, claw hammer, metalworker's hammer with nail driven through the handle to secure the head.

A Byzantine wreck, possibly fourth- or fifth-century AD, was recently excavated in the Pantano Longarini, a marshy littoral in south-eastern Sicily. Though otherwise like the seventh-century Yassi Ada ship, she had a transom stern. A scale model of the vessel was begun in 1966 but is not yet completed.

32 Inside view of the model, facing aft.
33 The port side based on the preserved portion of the wreck. The starboard side is a mirror image of this.
34 The model seen from below. Note the massive waterline wales coming to a point at the stern. The uppermost wale was similar in size; pending the construction of an accurate replica for the model, a batten has been put in place.
35 The model seen from the port side aft. Note the rows of wales, of which the uppermost is the batten referred to above. Note also the beginning of a skeg, which has been reconstructed, while the planks around it are copies of the tenoned planks on the wreck.

32

33

34

35

36, 37 The Pantano Longarini wreck. The upper photograph shows the area around the stern transom, of which only the starboard side is preserved. The port side, apparently left exposed for some time after the ship was wrecked, was partially destroyed in antiquity. The lower photograph, taken from above, clearly shows the uppermost surviving wale; the splits in it were no doubt caused by firewood collectors a long time ago. This wale rests on the through beam (left) whose inboard end was found to be missing, also probably through the depredations of firewood gatherers. The inner stringer that locked the through beam can be seen running at right angles beneath it. The worker is scrubbing the lowermost (waterline) wale, which was smashed and driven inside the surviving frames when the ship pounded on the beach. The forward end of the ship lies to the right in the photograph, the preserved starboard side of the wreck being the one facing the viewer.

# 7

# Scandinavian ships from earliest times to the Vikings

ARNE EMIL CHRISTENSEN

# Scandinavian ships from earliest times to the Vikings

It is not known whether, when the first settlers reached Scandinavia at the close of the last Ice Age, they came from Russia, by way of Finland, to occupy the harsh northern coast of Finnmark facing the Arctic Ocean, or whether they spread northwards from Germany in the wake of the retreating ice. Be that as it may, all the settlements of the stone-age hunters were closely associated with water. Most of them have been found on the coast or on islands; if some of the oldest of these sites now lie far above and some way from the present shoreline, this is only because the land had by then not yet had time to rise after having been pressed down by the enormous weight of the ice.

A site by the coast does not necessarily prove that people had boats, but settlements on islands do, and so does the large amount of fish bones found on some sites, including those of fish like ling and Norway haddock which can only be caught in deep water. It is therefore safe to say that from the first moment man appeared in Scandinavia, the boat must have been one of his most important tools. Opinion is divided as to what kind of boat he used, and it must be stressed that none of the different theories advanced by archaeologists can be definitely proved.

## The Origins of Plank-Built Boats

Primitive man has utilized many materials for making boats, but in Scandinavia most of these can be discounted on botanical or geographical grounds. Floating on gourds or using open rafts would be impracticable in the inclement northern climate, and in Scandinavia the long pliant reeds used for boatbuilding on the Nile, or Lake Titicaca in Peru, are not available. This reduces to three the choice of probable solutions to the problem of what kind of boat the early Scandinavians used. It may have taken the form of a 'dug-out'; it may have been made of bark; or again, it may have consisted of skins stretched over a wooden framework. Of these three, the second is the least probable, as Scandinavian trees seldom yield the large pieces of faultless bark that are needed.

The hollowed log, in one form or another, is the most widespread type of primitive craft in the world, and most early antiquaries took it for granted that this was the boat used by early man in Scandinavia. When, however, N. Nicolaysen published the Gokstad ship in 1881,

he suggested that there might be a connection between the Viking ships with their remarkably thin clenched strakes and the Arctic boats, where skins are stretched over a slender wooden framework. More recently, this hypothesis has been endorsed by G. Gjessing, as well as by A. W. Brøgger and H. Shetelig in their book on Viking ships, where it is given considerable space. Its most recent supporter is S. Marstrander, in a large treatise on east Norwegian rock carvings; when discussing the numerous ship representations on the carvings, he goes into the problems of early ships in detail. [1] Marstrander has also assembled a large amount of material concerning the use of skin boats in western Europe. His main conclusion is that the many ships depicted on the Scandinavian rock carvings must be skin boats. The principal arguments of the skin-boat school are that the planks of Scandinavian craft are thin, that they overlap, and that they are sewn together, in some of the early finds, as are skins of the Arctic boats. Moreover, the planking of a boat is still known as the 'skin' in many Scandinavian dialects. In addition to this, Brøgger saw similarities between the rib system of the oldest Scandinavian plank boat, the Hjortspring boat, [2,3] and the skeleton of the Arctic skin boats. According to him, the only uncertain stage in the evolution of Scandinavian craft is the transition from skins to thin wood used for covering the framework. Brøgger has drawn attention to a group of north Norwegian rock carvings depicting ships, where profiles of the boats show a striking resemblance to those of Arctic umiaks.

On the other hand, those who maintain that the log-boat was the ancestor of Scandinavian plank-built craft have stressed the technical parallels between these two types. The most ardent advocate for this hypothesis was Ph. Humbla, in his book on the Galtabäck boat. He is supported by A. Nilsson Eskeröd and Olof Hasslöf. Hasslöf's evidence in a recent paper is so strong that I am tempted to regard it as conclusive.

The main point is that clinker-built boats are what might be called shell constructions, with the outer plank shell constituting the main structural element. The plank shell is first built, and the ribs are inserted afterwards to strengthen the shell further. This principle has been applied to the log boat also; though it often consists of the shell alone, in many cases supporting timbers are

20

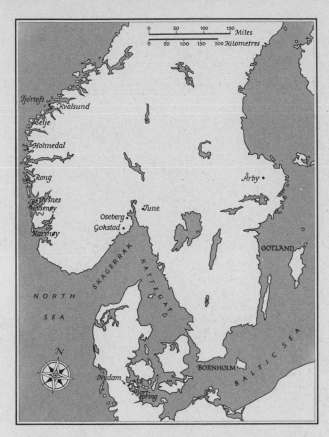

*1   Map of southern and central Scandinavia, giving location of the ship finds mentioned in this chapter*

inserted after it has been hollowed out, either as simple crossbeams or as ribs proper. The ribs may even be lashed to cleats left projecting from the shell when it is hewn to shape, giving the nicest parallel one might wish to the early boats of Scandinavia, where the ribs are lashed to cleats on the planks.

In skin boats, the strength lies in the skeleton, the wooden framework, the skins just serving to keep the water out. The latter may be taken off the skeleton for maintenance or storage, whereas the log or plank boat is a single unit once it is finished. The main strength of the skeleton of the open umiak lies in the longitudinal stringers. Usually, there is one substantial stringer along the middle of the bottom, one along the hard chine where the sides meet the flat bottom, one along each gunwale and one halfway between the bottom and the gunwale. The stringers are connected by short transverse laths across the bottom and sides. Unlike in wooden boats, the umiak has no proper ribs running from gunwale to gunwale in one piece; instead, the laths connecting the stringers are separate bottom- and side-pieces, and they are often staggered. Thus, when Brøgger comments on the similarities between the Hjortspring rib system and the umiak skeleton, he is basing his argument on an insufficient analysis of the material and his conclusions are not valid.

Even if we accept that the boatbuilding of Scandinavia is most probably derived from log-boat building, and represents a continuous woodworking tradition, there are still many questions which remain unanswered. We may postulate that log boats were enlarged by adding side planks and stem-pieces to the hollowed-out log, but we do not know when this was first done, or in which northern region. Quite a lot of log boats have been found all over Scandinavia, but nearly all are just plain 'dug-outs' and offer little help in explaining the transition from a one-piece boat to one fashioned from many pieces of wood.

In Finland, Estonia and the adjacent parts of Russia a particular variation of the log boat is used. Usually hewn from poplar or aspen, it is made with very thin sides, and after the initial shaping is considerably broadened by expanding the shell by means of fire or hot water. There are a few finds of expanded log boats among the archaeological material, but their age is uncertain, and so is the place of this technique in the history of Scandinavian boatbuilding.

## The Evidence of Rock Carvings

The Bronze Age of Northern Europe was a period of far-flung trade, and the ship evidently played an important role in people's lives, including the religious side of it. The most fascinating ancient monuments of the Bronze Age are the rock carvings, pictures incised in the sloping sandstone or granite cliffs near good grazing or farming land. Whereas these carvings are clearly associated with the religious cult of a farming and stock-breeding community, the most frequent motif is the ship. We find large and small ships, some plain, some elaborately carved, with human figures aboard and stems terminating in animal heads. These representations have been interpreted in a number of ways, some of them fanciful, ranging from two-storeyed rafts to elaborate skin boats, or log boats with different outrigger systems. In the light of recent research, we have reason to believe that the ships depicted on the carvings are log boats or plank-built craft, possibly both. There are, however, no traces in the Scandinavian archaeological material of the use of outriggers of the type used in the Pacific. The few examples of woodworking which have survived from the Bronze Age, mostly in Denmark, show a stage of woodworking technology quite advanced enough to allow composite wooden boats to be built.

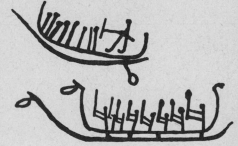

*2   Bronze Age ships on a rock carving from Gjerpen, South Norway. The type of ship here represented may be seen, with small variations, on hundreds of rock carvings in Norway, Sweden and parts of Denmark*

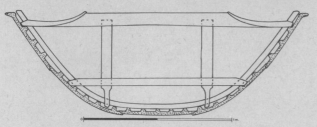

*3 Cross section of the Hjortspring boat, c. 350 BC. The lashings securing the hazel rib to the cleats of the planking have been omitted in the drawing*

## Early Plank-Built Boats

*The Hjortspring boat.* Though early Iron Age in date the Hjortspring boat may exemplify plank-built vessels of the late Bronze Age. This vessel, fragmentary but possible to reconstruct, was excavated in 1921 on the island of Als in southern Denmark. The boat had been deposited in a bog, together with a large number of spears, swords and other equipment. The shape of the weapons enables us to date this votive offering to the war gods to *c.* 350–300 BC. At that time, iron had been in use in the north for a couple of centuries, but the Hjortspring boat shows a high degree of workmanship and a sound constructional system which must have taken many generations to develop. That this boat is not an isolated specimen is shown by a number of rock carvings from the late Bronze Age and the early Iron Age, where boats of the Hjortspring type are clearly depicted. The boat itself shows many features which are common to Scandinavian boatbuilding up to the Viking Age – some of them still in use today.

The backbone of the 52½-foot-long vessel is the broad bottom plank, slightly curved from stem to stern. In the middle the plank has a shallow transverse curve, while towards the ends it gets narrower and the hollowing-out is pronounced. Fore and aft, specially hollowed 'end-pieces' are placed on top of the bottom plank and sewn to it. Two side-planks and two garboards finish the shell, only seven pieces of wood in all. The bottom plank and garboard continue as long 'beaks' outside the end-pieces. The lime-wood shell is entirely sewn together, and no iron is used. The inner supports are thin hazel branches, bent in a curve from gunwale to gunwale and lashed to rows of cleats left projecting from the planks. The seats for the rowers and the struts supporting them at the same time form part of the rib system. The boat, obviously a war canoe, had paddles for twenty men; a larger steering oar at each end enabled it to be paddled in either direction.

Between the Hjortspring boat and the next accurately dated Scandinavian vessel, the Nydam ship, there is a gap of nearly seven centuries. How shipbuilding evolved in the intervening period can only be surmised, with a few indications supplied by fragmentary finds. On the Danish island of Bornholm, graves from the first two centuries AD have yielded traces of boats. Owing to decay, no wood is left, so all we have to go by are discolorations in the soil, which of course are extremely difficult to interpret. It can be seen that the boats were sewn like the Hjortspring boat, but without the 'beaks' at stem and stern.

From about the same date comes a Norwegian find, from Halsenøy, south of Bergen. Here fragments of planking, one rib and a rowlock were found in a bog, and indicate a small sewn boat. It shows an advance on the Hjortspring boat in that the rib is a sturdy piece of naturally curved wood instead of the former's thin hazel branch. Another improvement is the permanent rowlock, allowing the boat to be rowed instead of paddled. For the rowlock, part of a tree trunk was used with the stub of a branch left on, a type still to be found in western Norway. While no part of the vessel's stem or stern was preserved, the plank ends indicate that the stems were not of the Hjortspring type, but more probably like the stems of the Nydam ship.

*The Nydam ship.* The big vessel from Nydam in Schleswig, excavated in 1864, is part of an offering of war equipment, like the Hjortspring boat. It can be dated fairly accurately to AD 350–400. Built entirely of oak, the shell of the ship consists of only fifteen pieces of wood: bottom plank, stem, stern and five strakes on either side. All timbers are unscarfed, except the gunwale. This use of unscarfed wood is a primitive feature, but it indicates an excellent technique of woodworking. It must have taken many trained men working in concert to split the enormous logs necessary to produce planks 82 feet long and 20 inches broad, hew them to shape and handle them while they were fitted to the hull. Unlike the older vessels, the Nydam ship is not sewn. The planks are fastened with iron nails, clenched on the inside of the hull over square iron roves. Ribs cut from sturdy curved branches are lashed to cleats on the planking, and rowlocks for thirty oars are lashed to the gunwale. A large steering oar was found close to one end of the ship during excavation; it is uncertain, however, in what way it was fastened to the hull. There are no indications that the ship carried a mast and sail, but the rather narrow hull shape makes this unlikely.

The ship is definitely a war vessel, to judge from the context in which it was found, but there is reason to believe that the type was in general use during the period in question. At that time, the beginning of the Migration Period in Europe, trade in the north was still rather primitive and undeveloped, so there is no reason to think that special merchant vessels were built; a ship was regarded as being equally well suited for warfare or trade. It is impossible to say exactly where the Nydam ship was built, but the equipment found with it indicates that the army which lost the battle at Nydam and had its equipment offered up to the gods could not have come from far away. We may therefore take the vessel to be representative for southern Scandinavia around the fourth–fifth century AD. Fragmentary finds from

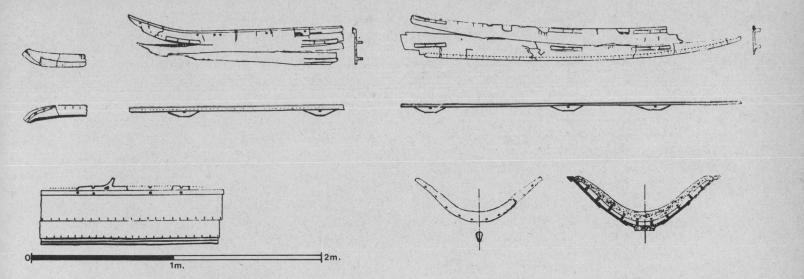

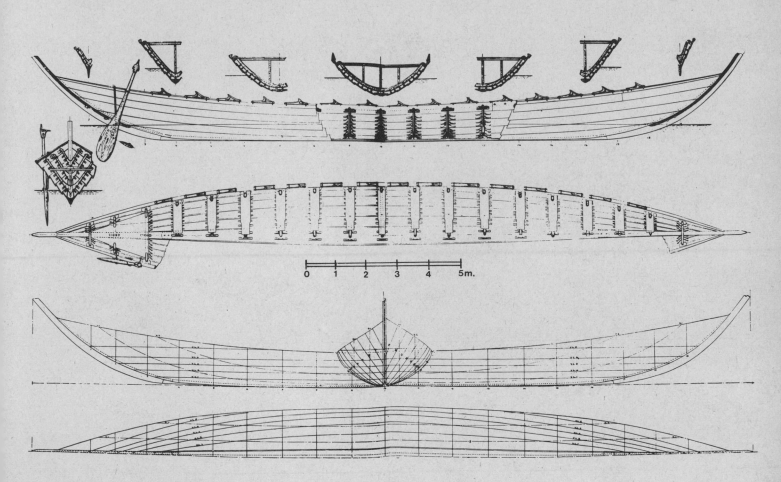

4  Boat remains found at Halsenoy. The top row shows, from left to right, the small plank that abutted the stem or stern, a strake with holes for the rowlock (reconstructed bottom left), and another strake with a row of holes for sewing. The end-on views show where the cleats were attached. Bottom right, rib fragment, as found and as reconstructed by the draftsman

5  The Nydam ship was the first ancient vessel to be properly excavated and reconstructed by an archaeologist. The magnificent vessel is now housed in the Schleswig-Holsteinisches Landesmuseum at Schloss Gottorf, Schleswig, Germany. This scale drawing, with some reconstruction, was done by H. Shetelig and Fr. Johannessen in 1930

western and northern Norway indicate that ships there were built on the same lines, but the sewing of boats continued for a long time in northern Norway. Finds of boat rivets in fifth- and sixth-century graves all over Scandinavia do, however, indicate that the new method of plank fastening was widely accepted.

It must have been in ships of the Nydam type that the Anglo-Saxons reached Britain, and in fact the next link in the evolutionary chain of ship finds comes from England, from the famous grave at Sutton Hoo in East Anglia. The find, treated more fully in chapter 5, seems to indicate that shipbuilding in Scandinavia and Anglo-Saxon England developed along parallel lines. Compared to the Nydam ship, the vessel from Sutton Hoo was broader and more seaworthy, with a more sturdy bottom plank. More and narrower strakes, made from several joined lengths, show that the shipwrights had gained experience in scarfing timber and no longer

insisted on having as much as possible in one piece. We see in the Sutton Hoo ship for the first time traces of a permanent rudder, placed on the right side of the hull aft. This is the side of the ship which is still called starboard, after the old Norse word *styri*, meaning rudder.

*The Kvalsund ship.* The Sutton Hoo ship can be dated to the first half of the seventh century A D. From Kvalsund, Herøy, western Norway, comes a bog find which must be slightly later. Like the Danish finds, it is an offering, but in this case only the ship and a small boat were left in the bog, together with a number of pointed sticks which probably symbolize the spears and other weapons that could not be spared for the gods. In the Kvalsund ship we see for the first time a rudimentary keel, instead of merely the bottom plank of the older finds. The plank is still there, but strengthened with a fillet on the under-

6

6  *The large Kvalsund boat, probably built around AD 700, is here shown in a reconstruction drawing by Fr. Johannessen. The fragments of the vessel may be seen in Bergens Sjøfartsmuseum, on loan from the University of Bergen, Norway*

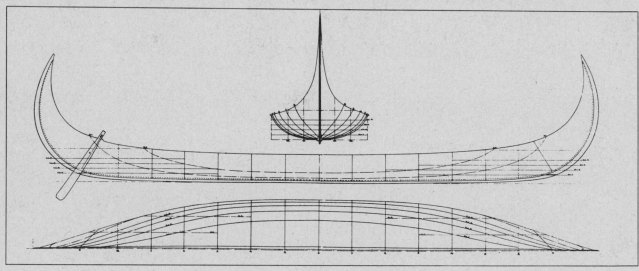

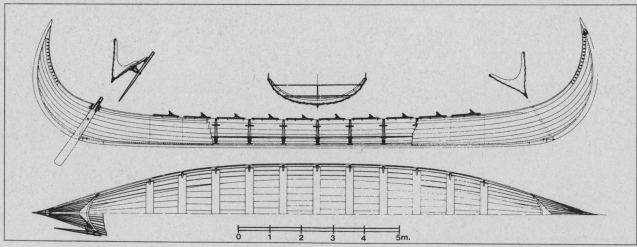

side, cut in one with it. This makes the boat much more resistant to 'hogging', enabling the hull to be broader and so more stable without loss of strength.

8    The big Kvalsund vessel, nearly 60 feet long, has oak planking, but the ribs are of pine. This combination indicates that it was built in western Norway, where this mixture of timber is still used in shipbuilding. It is an open ship, with no deck of any kind, but the deep steering oar or rudder and the fairly broad hull seem to indicate a combined sailing-rowing vessel, although no traces of any rigging were found. Most of the planking-rib connections still take the form of lashings with cleats on the planks, but on the keel the lashings are done away with, and the upper strakes are fastened with treenails. A specially shaped rib supports the rudder, with a corresponding bulkhead forward. The rudder rib is a triangular bulkhead with extra strengthening on the starboard side. The rudder rests against an oak boss nailed to the outside of the planking and is fastened by a withy. At the end of this withy is a lump of wood, which rests against the outside of the rudder. The withy is pulled through corresponding holes in the rudder, the boss and the ship's side, and made fast to the rudder rib. In this way the rudder is securely fastened to the ship, while the elasticity of the withy permits it to turn on its own longitudinal axis. A band round the rudder stock at gunwale height gives the rudder additional support. Unlike the other ribs, the rudder rib and forward bulkhead are notched to take the planks and fastened by nailing. The small four-oared boat deposited with the ship is constructed on the same general lines, but here all the rib fastenings are treenails. Evidently the elaborate system of lashing the ribs was considered unnecessary in a small boat at this time. However, the treenails still run through cleats left on the planks when they were cut to shape.

9

## The Introduction of Sail

Strangely enough, sailing vessels do not seem to have come into use in Scandinavia until the seventh century. By then the sail was long established in the Mediterranean and it must have been known for centuries in those parts of Western Europe which had seen Roman occupation. It is not easy to find the reason for this, but it probably lies in the ships themselves. The essence of Scandinavian lap-strake or clinker building is lightness and flexibility, and as long as the light vessels relied on a bottom plank instead of on a true keel, the hulls were not strong enough to stand the pressure of mast and sail. Moreover, until the eighth century the activity of Scandinavian sailors was mainly restricted to their own coastal waters, in which oars are often more efficient than sails as a means of propulsion.

Once accepted, the sail must have been a tremendous step forward in technology, while at the same time giving the shipwrights a lot of new problems to cope with. The evolution of shipbuilding in Scandinavia seems to have proceeded slowly but surely from the

stage represented by the Hjortspring boat to the one we see in the Kvalsund ship, without any foreign influences apart from the introduction of the sail. In the latter vessel the bottom plank is on the verge of becoming a true keel, sewing is discarded for the more solid iron nails, and a permanent rudder has been evolved. However, the main characteristics of both boats are the same: a light elastic shell with an inner support of widely spaced ribs, a gunwale with an external fillet to add strength to the hull, and a low freeboard which gives the oars a comfortable height above water. Fragmentary finds from other parts of Scandinavia show that the big rowing ship of the Kvalsund type was widely used. At Fjørtoft in western Norway and Bårset, far to the north on the Norwegian coast, bogs have yielded similar ships; and in Sweden they survive as rows of rivets in the rich graves of Vendel and Valsgärde.

We must assume that the first people who set sail in ships of the Sutton Hoo/Kvalsund type had some very nasty experiences. The freeboard was low enough to allow the North Sea to run freely over the gunwale when the ship heeled over only moderately, and the loose or temporarily fixed thwarts for the rowers must have given insufficient transverse support to the elastic hulls. Nevertheless, the superiority of sail as compared to oars for ocean travelling must have been evident.

## The Vikings

The Viking Age, when Scandinavian sailors explored known and unknown waters, does not start until *c.* AD 800. Before that time few Scandinavians can have had much experience in navigating outside their own coastal waters. However, there are indications that Norwegian colonization on the Atlantic islands started during the eighth century, and that the Swedes had carried on regular trade across the Baltic at the same time. As a Swedish archaeologist has put it: after adopting the sail, the Scandinavians spent a century perfecting their seamanship, and then they were ready for the Viking raids.

The background to Scandinavian expansion in the Viking Age is complex and not fully explained. Pressure of population at home was considerable, and it is widely accepted that it was chiefly on this account that the Vikings set out on their voyages. A fact that is often overlooked is that a large percentage of the Vikings were peaceful settlers in search of land. The reason for the tactical superiority of those who preferred plunder to tillage, however, is still not clear. Most of the bands were small and often loosely organized. When they met regular Frankish or Anglo-Saxon troops in battle they frequently lost the contest. Nevertheless, the Vikings managed to harass the coasts of Europe profitably for two centuries. Their main assets were the ships and the 'commando' tactics these enabled them to use. Appearing 'out of the blue', the shallow-draft vessels would land their crews on any suitable beach to carry out a quick raid and be away before any proper defence could be organized.

Their frequent voyages must have greatly increased the Vikings' knowledge of navigation, and at the same time the experience they gained led to the improvement of their ships. We can imagine the sailors coming home with praise or blame for the shipwright, and the behaviour of the vessels would be discussed again and again during the long northern winter. The shipwrights would naturally strive to improve the qualities of their ships, without straying too far from the well-known traditional solutions. The evidence seems to indicate that Scandinavian shipbuilding evolved more rapidly between c. AD 750 and 1000 than at any other time.

The period between c. AD 800 and 850 saw the first big expansion of Viking activities. Nearly every year ships went 'west over the sea' to plunder or seek new lands, in England, Scotland, Ireland, the North Sea Islands, Iceland and finally North America. Others went south along the German and French coasts or east from the Baltic, up the Russian rivers. No matter where the ships went, we may be certain that the two generations of Vikings active between 800 and 850 gained experience in sailing the open seas such as no Scandinavians had before.

## Viking Ships

*Oseberg, Gokstad, Tune.* These three Norwegian ships, which derive their names from the places where they were found, are all of the same type, but differ in details. The Oseberg ship can be dated fairly accurately by the carving on stem and stern to around AD 800. The Gokstad and Tune ships, on the other hand, must have been built c. AD 850–900. In the building of all three ships, which served as part of the grave goods for royal funerals, great care was taken and excellent materials were used, testifying to the high social status of the owners. They are also wonderful examples of the high technical standard of shipbuilding as a whole during the Viking Age. The good state of preservation in which the ships were found is due to the particular soil conditions of the outer Oslo Fjord area. Here the subsoil is a marine sediment of blue clay which preserves both wood and iron in a truly remarkable way. At Oseberg the burial mound was built from turf sods, which, by sealing the mound hermetically, helped to conserve practically every piece of wood in it; at Tune and Gokstad, where the loose earth of the mound allowed the air to enter, the upper part of the ships has rotted away.

The persons buried in the Oseberg and Gokstad ships have been tentatively identified as members of the 'Ynglinge' family, rulers of Viking Age Vestfold and the dynasty which later united Norway; the identity of the chieftain buried in the Tune ship remains unknown.

The Oseberg burial is a female one, and this considered in conjunction with the ship's rich carvings has led to the conclusion that the vessel was a pleasure craft, intended mainly for short trips along the coast. It has a low freeboard and must have been definitely less seaworthy than the Gokstad ship. However, the difference in date between the Oseberg ship on the one hand and the Gokstad and Tune ships on the other may account for most of the disparities.

Even though the sail gave the Norsemen new possibilities for open-sea travel, our sources indicate that on the whole they still preferred coastal waters. Cooking aboard Viking ships was scarcely feasible, so on the high seas the crews would have had to be content with cold food – dried fish and meat probably being the staples. Nights were spent in leather sleeping bags, two men to a bag. From information contained in the sagas we learn that as late as the twelfth century, not only did they do the cooking ashore, but also, whenever circumstances permitted, slept ashore in tents pitched for this purpose. 'Camping equipment' for shore use was found in the Oseberg and Gokstad ships; it included cauldrons of bronze or iron, with iron tripods or chains for suspending them over fires, wooden frameworks for tents, and even collapsible beds.

Viking navigation has long been a matter of debate among historians and archaeologists. Some authorities credit the Vikings with a knowledge of astronomy sufficient to allow latitude observations, and with the use of a kind of compass. Although individual mariners may have used navigation of a more sophisticated nature, most sailors would have managed with a sound knowledge of the coastline where they expected to make landfalls, and by telling the points of the compass from the position of the sun or the Pole Star.

Practical sailing instructions were, of course, passed by word of mouth from sailor to sailor; moreover, Icelandic records of the twelfth and thirteenth centuries contain such information as the following, extracted from *The Vinland Saga*: 'According to learned men, it is seven days' sail from Stad in Norway to Horn in the east of Iceland; and from Snaefellsness (on the west coast of Iceland) it is four days' sail to Cape Farewell in Greenland. From Hern Island, off Norway, one can sail due west to Cape Farewell, passing north of Shetland close enough to see it clearly in good visiblity, and south of the Faroes half sunk below the horizon, and a day's sail to the south of Iceland.'

As we have seen, the introduction of the sail came late in the north, and the Oseberg ship is actually the earliest find in Scandinavia of a vessel that can be shown to have carried both a mast and sail. The mast is stepped in a short keelson spanning two ribs and is given additional support from a 'mast partner' resting on four cross-beams. The beam in front of the mast has more sturdy scantlings than the rest of the beams, and the mast partner is partly let into it. Thus the latter gets some support sideways. Otherwise it is only fastened with treenails fore and aft.

That this construction was not sufficiently strong to take the pressure of the sail in all weathers, the Oseberg ship clearly demonstrated. The mast partner had cracked and was repaired by two iron bands nailed on. Unpleasant experiences like this, and instances when the

10–19

20–28

12

27

166

ship took water over the gunwale, must have led to the changes we can see in the Gokstad and Tune ships. The Tune ship is a shallow-draft vessel, extremely light and with a rather low freeboard, but the hull shape makes it a much more seaworthy craft than the Oseberg ship. The two upper strakes rake strongly outward, giving extra buoyancy when the ship heeled over, and keeping spray out effectively. Even greater improvement is seen in the mast support. The keelson straddles four ribs, and is supported sideways by knees nailed to the ribs. The mast partner spans five cross-beams and is recessed on the underside for each beam, a great improvement on the Oseberg mast partner which practically rests loose on the cross-beams.

In the Gokstad ship, the freeboard is increased by two strakes above the one with the oar-holes, and the latter can be closed by means of covers on the inside. The mast support is of the same type as in the Tune ship, but the scantlings are proportionately larger. With its fine, serviceable lines, the Gokstad ship is indeed a marvellous example of early shipbuilding. That a ship of this type is really seaworthy was proved in 1893, when an exact replica was sailed across the Atlantic to the World Fair in Chicago. Eighty feet long, and designed to be rowed by 32 men when the wind was not fair, the Gokstad ship must have been a very large vessel for its time.

When we examine the Viking ships, it is evident that they are based on the type of vessel evolved during the Iron Age, with a few important additions. Most significant is that a true keel has been developed, clearly derived from the reinforced bottom plank of the ships of the Nydam/Sutton Hoo/Kvalsund type. The ribs are still lashed to cleats on the planking, but the lashing cleats have been omitted on the keel, garboard and planking above the waterline. Where the ribs of the Iron Age boats ended on the gunwale, with its external strengthening fillet, the ribs of the Viking ships end on an extra thick plank in the water-line, which in the Oseberg ship still retains the inverted L-shape of the older finds. The Old Norse name of this strake was 'meginhufr', meaning literally 'the strong plank'. Placed in the water-line, it is the main longitudinal timber excluding the keel. The other way, from 'strong plank' to

'strong plank', run the cross-beams, one for each rib. Nailed to the cross-beams are knees, supporting the upper strakes. All scantlings are reduced to a minimum; the main strength of the hull still lies in the light flexible outer shell, and the lashings between ribs and planking in the underwater section add to its elasticity.

These three well-preserved ships give us an excellent opportunity to study construction and craftsmanship down to the smallest detail, but we are left with the question as to whether they are typical examples of Scandinavian shipbuilding of the ninth century, or whether they represent a type of ship associated only with the Oslo Fjord area or with a certain social group. It is also a moot point whether the ships are random examples surviving from a variety of types built at this time, or whether all ships looked more or less alike in the early Viking Age.

There are other ship finds from roughly the same period, all of them less well preserved than the east Norwegian ships. From western Norway come fragments of ships from boat graves at Karmøy and Holmedal in Sunnfjord; and from west Norwegian sites fragments of wreckage or possible bog offerings. A mast partner, found with a few other fragments at Rong near Bergen, comes from a ship which must have been close to the Tune ship in type, but somewhat smaller, while fragments of a stem from Selje are practically identical with the corresponding pieces in the Tune ship.

From the grave finds, on the other hand, it is possible to ascertain that the boats concerned do differ in certain respects from the east Norwegian ships, but the finds are too few and too fragmentary to show whether these differences apply only to details of construction or whether there are differences in hull shape as well. A couple of finds from northern Norway indicate that there boats were still being sewn, sometimes with a few iron nails used at keel, stem and stern. A Viking Age grave excavated toward the end of the last century by O. Nicolaissen on behalf of Tromsø Museum provides an example. All the wood had decayed completely, but the iron nails lay in place, a lump at stem and stern, and two rows along the keel. To use Nicolaissen's own words: 'The garboard was riveted to the keel and the

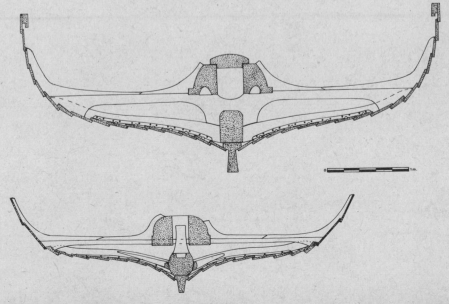

7 Cross section of the Gokstad and Tune ships, taken amidships, just behind the mast. Both ships were built between c. AD 850 and 900 and are of the same general type. The bottom strakes, six in the Tune and eight in the Gokstad ship, are lashed to the ribs, while the topsides are treenailed. On the underside of the Gokstad 'mast partner' two deep grooves have been cut in the wood to reduce weight

ends of the planks were nailed to the stem and stern, while the rest of the boat must have been tree-nailed or sewn.'

In addition to the big ship, the Gokstad mound contained three small boats which had been smashed as part of the burial rites. Two of them were reconstructed by Fr. Johannessen, but the third is still in fragments. The boats are graceful, light craft showing the same choice materials and excellent workmanship as the ships. We must suppose that the ordinary farmer or fisherman along the coast had a simpler vessel for his daily toil, but we know that the shape of the little Gokstad boats is typical of the smaller vessels of the Viking Age. In boat graves, where the wood has rotted but the rivets lie undisturbed, their rows show the same slender, elegant lines. That the coastal and inland waters required different boats, then as now, will be seen by comparing the Gokstad examples with the small boat found in a grave in Uppland, Sweden. This little elegant boat shows us the shallow-draft light hull of a typical inland vessel, excellent for rowing or punting on shallow lakes and rivers, but not suited for the open sea.

## The Survival of Boatbuilding Traditions

The Oseberg, Gokstad and Tune finds have acquainted us with the details of ships and boats of the early Viking Age, and we can obtain a fairly good idea of what medieval ships looked like from archaeological finds, representations and written sources. Changes took place in the hull shape, rigging and construction of ships as time went by and the historical situation altered. However, among the coastal population of Scandinavia life did not change much. The economy was based on a mixture of farming and fishing where the women often took care of the croft while the men went off to fish. As might be expected, the small boats these people used preserved many of the characteristics of their Viking prototypes, especially in western Norway, where boats built today still in the traditional manner differ surprisingly little in details from those of the Viking Age. This can be readily seen by comparing the Viking Age boat built for the Gokstad chieftain with a boat constructed in 1960 by a seventy-year-old boatbuilder. The similarity in the midship bends is especially illuminating. It should be stressed that the twentieth-century boatbuilder did not in any way try to copy the Viking boat; all he did was to build a four-oared boat of the type native to his district, and in all probability he did not even know of the existence of the other vessel.

It would be possible to assemble, in a more comprehensive survey, a mass of details which have remained unchanged, in the use of materials and tools, in terminology and building practice. In the Viking ships, for instance, there is a decorative moulding – obtained by scraping – along the visible edges of all the different pieces of wood used in their construction. The tool used is known from half a dozen Viking graves, together with other woodworking tools. A few boatbuilders continue to give their boats this finishing touch; most of them use a moulding plane, but the scraping-tool of the Vikings was still in use at the turn of the century. Treenails with conical heads and wedges are used to this day in western Norway to connect ribs and planking. If we compare nails cut in a boatshed in recent years with Viking Age ones, they will be found to be identical down to the way the grain of the wood is made to run in the wedges. These two examples will serve to illustrate the conservative nature of Norse boatbuilding.

Seen as a whole, this survival of tradition for more than 1,000 years might seem astonishing, but it can be explained by the fact that neither the natural environment nor the economic situation of the fishermen-farmers changed appreciably between the time of the Vikings and 1850. Once the combined rowing and sailing boat had been perfected, as happened in the Viking Age, there was no need to alter it. It was not until the beginning of this century, when the introduction of engines made the traditional hull shape less serviceable, that the first radical changes were made. Moreover, the coastal waters of northern and western Norway are dangerous enough to make the population extremely 'boat-conscious'. The status of the boatbuilder was high, he made a fair living in a community that was not well-to-do, and he carefully guarded his trade secrets. These were, however, passed on to his apprentices, and this largely explains why tradition is so strong. Up till 1949 no instruction manual in boatbuilding was written in Norwegian, and all teaching was based on the principle of the master instructing his assistants until the work became second nature to them in turn. Thus this specialized knowledge was passed on from one generation to the next.

---

1 Boats frequently appear in still extant rock carvings from the Bronze Age in Scandinavia. While these carvings almost certainly served a ritual purpose, the objects depicted are not only clearly recognizable for what they are, but the details are rendered with a fair degree of accuracy. Thus the boats carved in the rock face at Kalnes, Tune, in southeast Norway, here reproduced, bear a distinct resemblance to the Hjortspring boat of the fourth/third century BC, the oldest Scandinavian plank-built boat yet found (see ill. 2, 3). They also underline the remarkable continuity in Scandinavian boat and ship design down the ages, for not only do the vessels of the Vikings possess many features in common with these earliest boats, but even present-day boatbuilders can be seen to perpetuate the basic traditional shapes. (See also fig. 2)

2

3

4

5

2–5 Excavated in 1921 from a bog on the island of Als in southern Denmark, where it had been deposited as a votive offering to the war gods, the Hjortspring boat is thought to typify a war canoe of early Iron Age Scandinavia. Though in a somewhat fragmentary state when found, it was possible to piece this boat together with the aid of new planking (2). A reconstruction model was then made (3). The seats for the twenty men who operated the paddles form, with their supporting struts, part of the rib system of the boat, which had a large steering oar at each end, enabling it to be paddled in either direction. Many weapons and other equipment had been deposited in the bog with the boat. Reproduced on the left are a wooden sheath for a sword, an iron spear and an antler spear-head attached to a wooden shaft (4), and a wooden shield with a cut-out boss (5).

6, 7 The Nydam ship, the next accurately dated Scandinavian vessel after the Hjortspring boat, was also part of a votive offering and had likewise been deposited in a bog, together with several others. It belongs, however, to the Roman Iron Age, having been built some seven centuries later than its predecessor. A sea-going vessel, it is some 70 feet long, and only fifteen pieces of stout oak went into the making of its shell. Unlike older boats, the Nydam ship is not sewn, the planks being fastened with iron nails. There are fifteen rowlocks on either side, indicating a crew of at least thirty-one if we take into account the large steering oar found in the bog close to the ship. Instead of paddles oars were used, which helped to conserve the energy of the crew. The Nydam ship, too, is almost certainly a war vessel, and it is craft of this kind that must have brought the Anglo-Saxons to Britain. The tall stem post, the massive five-a-side strakes and the iron nails holding them together are clearly visible in the end-on view (6). Though the clinker-built Nydam ship is larger and more sturdily constructed, it has many features in common with the Hjortspring boat, as the reconstructed model (7) shows. Each relied on manpower for its propulsion, neither being fitted with mast or sail. Both are long and narrow, have upturned bow and stern, and no proper keel.

6

7

8, 9 Reconstruction models of a late seventh- or early eighth-century ship and accompanying small boat found in a bog at Kvalsund, western Norway. The bottom plank of the ship is strengthened with a fillet on the underside, forming a rudimentary keel; the planks are of oak, the ribs of pine. Both have steering oars.

8–9

Dated to about AD 800, the Oseberg ship is the oldest of three Viking vessels found in southern Norway, and now housed in the Viking Ship Museum in Oslo. All three were used in ship-burials of high-ranking persons. Like the other two ships, from Gokstad and Tune respectively, the Oseberg ship was found in a badly damaged state, but has been restored to its former splendour. In the process 90% of the original wood was used, as well as 60% of the original rivets.

11

10

10 A post elaborately carved in the form of an animal head, found in the Oseberg ship-burial. It is a striking example of the skill of the Viking craftsman in working wood.

11 The handsome stem of the Oseberg ship with its frieze of animals and 'dragon's head' at the top.

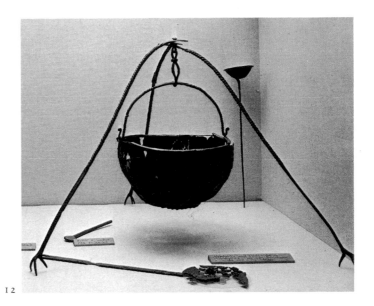
12

12–15 The burial customs of the Viking Age were based on the notion that the deceased should be suitably equipped to continue after death the kind of existence he or she had led on earth. Among the numerous objects large and small found in the Oseberg ship-burial were three sledges and a wooden wagon which was probably intended for ceremonial rather than for practical use. There were also iron-bound chests (13), which could have been put to use both as strong-boxes and as benches. Domestic articles included a cauldron with a collapsible tripod (12), which may have formed part of the ship's equipment, and two pairs of shoes, of which the better preserved pair is shown below (14). Of considerable interest is a 'rattle' with two ornamental handles, seen here (15) with several mounts from a bridle.

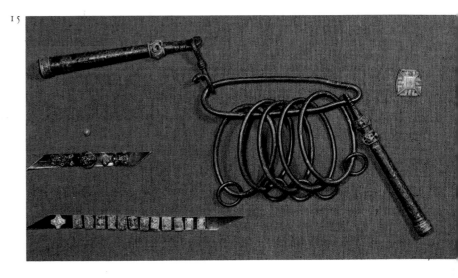
13

14

15

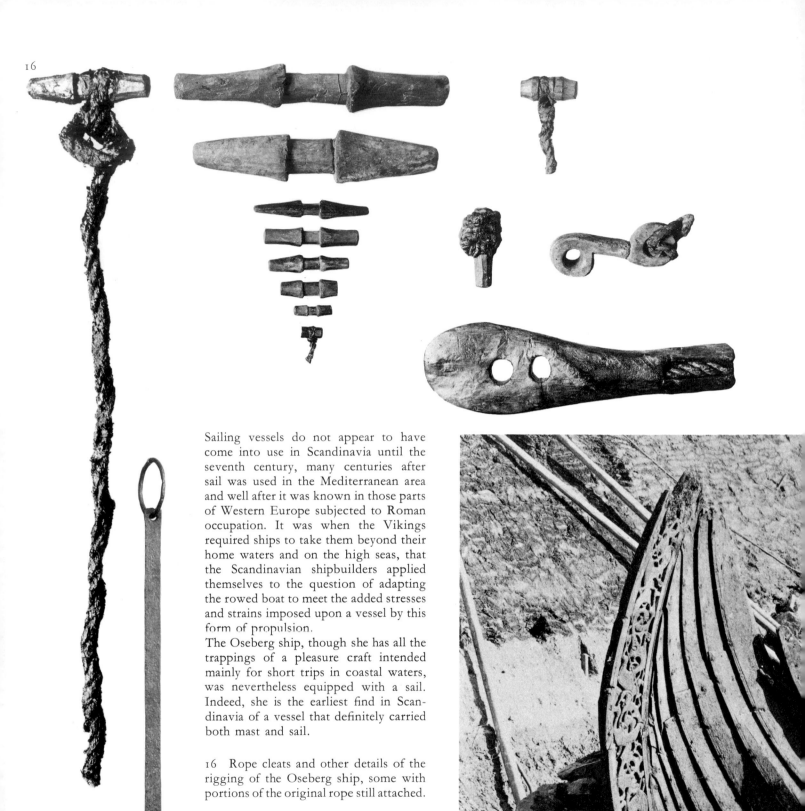

## 16

Sailing vessels do not appear to have come into use in Scandinavia until the seventh century, many centuries after sail was used in the Mediterranean area and well after it was known in those parts of Western Europe subjected to Roman occupation. It was when the Vikings required ships to take them beyond their home waters and on the high seas, that the Scandinavian shipbuilders applied themselves to the question of adapting the rowed boat to meet the added stresses and strains imposed upon a vessel by this form of propulsion.

The Oseberg ship, though she has all the trappings of a pleasure craft intended mainly for short trips in coastal waters, was nevertheless equipped with a sail. Indeed, she is the earliest find in Scandinavia of a vessel that definitely carried both mast and sail.

16 Rope cleats and other details of the rigging of the Oseberg ship, some with portions of the original rope still attached.

17 This long, slender anchor from the Oseberg ship was found, after cleaning, to be in an excellent state of preservation.

## 17

18

18 The reconstructed Oseberg ship as set up in the Viking Ship Museum in Oslo. The graceful lines of the hull with its tall, curving stem and stern, and its very low freeboard, are strikingly apparent. The Oseberg burial having been a female one, it seems appropriate that this particular ship should have been chosen as a final tribute to a lady of high rank.

19 This highly interesting contemporary photograph shows the Oseberg ship still *in situ* after excavation. As can be seen, the vessel was in a very badly damaged state, though it had retained its basic shape and nearly every piece of wood used in its construction was preserved owing to the burial mound having been built of turf sods which hermetically sealed its contents. The position of the mast approximately amidships can be clearly seen; the steering oar is still attached to the relatively intact stern.

19

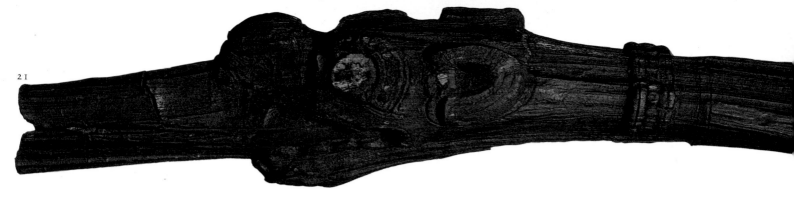

20 The second of the reconstructed Viking burial-ships to be seen in the Viking Ship Museum, the Gokstad ship, has a more businesslike appearance and less decoration than, but possesses the same graceful lines as, the Oseberg ship. Built about AD 850, it is close on 80 feet long and sturdier, having two more strakes above the one pierced by oar holes. These holes were protected by covers on the inside (see ill. 25). The keel, developed from the reinforced bottom plank of earlier ships of the Nydam/Sutton Hoo/Kvalsund type, is more pronounced. Fitted with a square sail in addition to 32 oars, the Gokstad ship was clearly intended for use on the high seas.

21 The tiller of the Gokstad ship, perhaps in order to make up for the lack of decoration on the vessel itself, is elaborately carved with a 'dragon's head' – yet one more example of the Viking woodcarver's skill.

22 No attempt has been made to reconstruct the third of the Norwegian Viking ships now in the Viking Ship Museum. The Tune ship appears to have been a handsome little vessel, finely constructed from first-class materials. Besides the remains of the ship little was found in the burial mound; since it lay on the opposite side of Oslo Fjord from the other two, however, it probably related to a different dynasty of chieftains.

23 The last phase of the Gokstad ship excavation. Clearly visible is the 'mast partner' (26), a solid piece of oak nearly 16 feet long, fixed to the cross-beams.

26

24 Decorated rowlock from one of the small boats found with the Gokstad ship.

25 Oar hole of the Gokstad ship, with the cover in the open position.

26, 27 Mast partners were devised in order to provide added support for the mast, when vessels were adapted for sail in the Viking period. The one fitted to the Oseberg ship had cracked and been repaired by nailing iron bands over the crack. The mast partners of the Gokstad (26) and the Rong ship (27) – a smaller version of the Tune ship – were more solidly constructed, and recessed to receive the beams to which they were fastened.

27

28 In addition to the large ship, the Gokstad burial mound contained three small boats that had been smashed as part of the funerary ritual. Two of these graceful light craft have been reconstructed, and their clean lines and fine workmanship are apparent.

29 These two west-Norwegian boats of a kind that is still being built today have the same generic hull shape as the Gokstad boats (28) of eleven centuries earlier. Even the fibreglass boat in the background has inherited the basic attributes of shipbuilding in the Viking Age. West-Norwegian boatbuilders even use the terminology known from Old Norse sources when talking about their boats.

30 A small boat of the late Viking Age found in a grave at Årby in the Uppland region of Sweden. It has the shallow-draft, lightweight hull of inland craft well adapted to rowing or punting on shallow lakes and rivers. Numerous boat and ship graves are known all over Viking Age Scandinavia, but usually all the wood has rotted away, and only the iron rivets remain to show what was there.

## 29

31, 32 Bronze gilt weather vanes from the late Viking Age. In more recent times the eleventh-century example (31) graced a church tower, but contemporary pictures prove that it was originally set up on the stem of a Viking ship. Its date tempts one to believe that this vane saw the conquest of England by King Canute. The custom of carrying such gilded vanes on ships continued into Christian times, as the twelfth-century example (32) shows.

33 Carved animal head on a fragmentary ship's stem found at Tysnes, Norway. Though early medieval in date, it demonstrates that the influence of Viking woodcarvers continued into the second millennium AD.

33

# The Vikings and the Hanseatic merchants: 900–1450

OLE CRUMLIN-PEDERSEN

# The Vikings and
# the Hanseatic merchants: 900–1450

### The History of the Single-Masted Ship

The period 900–1450 has been called the great age of the single-master, and rightly so. Wherever we encounter the North European ship of the period, the pattern is the same: a fairly straightforward hull, usually identical fore and aft, and one mast with a single square sail, the simplest possible canvas spread. At first sight there seems to be little variation from country to country and from century to century. And yet, literary sources of the period distinguish between a bewildering number of named ship types, and in fact a knowledge of the characteristic features of each can provide answers to several questions of major interest to the political and economic history of the period.

In the early part of this period North European shipping was dominated by the Scandinavian Vikings (see also chapter 7). They were seaborne traders and warriors, who travelled all along the North European coasts and by Russian rivers as far as Byzantium, and who, after colonizing Iceland, went on to Greenland and afterwards 'Vinland', and so were the first Europeans to set foot in North America. What is the explanation of this maritime supremacy? How did their ships, built for raiding and trading, differ from other North European ships? What indeed became of Scandinavian shipbuilding tradition after the close of the Viking period around 1050?

In literary sources the *cog* emerges about 1200 as the major ship of the Hanseatic League, soon to overshadow every other type, until eventually superseded by the *hulk*. But we hardly know the basic structural difference between the cog and the hulk, and moreover the pattern continually changed until towards the period's close the single-master had to yield place. Demands on cargo capacity and consequent need for spaciousness and strength had so increased, that the long-tried clinker building proved inadequate and the single sail finally became so large and unwieldy that it had to be split up. Then the situation was ripe for North European shipbuilders to adopt the carvel technique and the use of several masts. It now became possible to build ships that could be lived in under foreign skies for months on end – and the way was clear for European expansion across the oceans in the sixteenth century. But the early stages in this development still remain obscure for us.

Answers to some of the questions posed are to be found by making a careful survey of the source material which is at hand today: literary sources, contemporary pictures, and wrecks.

From about the beginning of the tenth century, literary sources concern themselves increasingly with maritime matters; at first these are only occasional and haphazard references, but in time rather fuller material appears in the form of saga texts, by-laws, customs regulations, and the like, mentioning contemporary ships. We thus learn the names of major ship types of the period and gain an insight into their relative sizes and frequency, but detailed facts about shipbuilding conditions appear only exceptionally.

Historians have, however, found the richest and most important source material in the many contemporary depictions of ships in town seals, miniatures, mural paintings, etc. In these it has been possible to study the general appearance and many details of the ships which are not to be found in literary sources. Representations of ships of the thirteenth and fourteenth centuries in miniatures and murals are often executed with no little care and skill. Seals of maritime trading towns in particular contain many reproductions of high quality especially in those two centuries; at that time the art of engraving seals stood high, and towns not infrequently introduced new, up-to-date pictures when the existing seals had to be replaced. They seem to have striven to provide the best possible pictorial record of the latest line in contemporary ships, the foundation of their urban wealth. In later centuries seal pictures lost the direct connection with their subjects, resulting in a stylization and schematization which, from the fifteenth century, render seals useless as a source of elucidation. Ship models and drawings from this period are unkown.

The scientific investigation of sunken ships is a comparatively recent development. Apart from the Viking ship excavations described in the previous chapter the first real archaeological investigations of medieval wrecks took place in Sweden about 1930. The excavation of a wreck at Galtabäck in Halland, begun in 1928, was followed in 1930–34 by excavations of wrecks in the Riddarholms Canal in Stockholm, at Falsterbo in Scania, at Äskekärr, and in the medieval harbour of Kalmar. 2, 3

1 *Map of Scandinavian and Hanseatic areas showing medieval wreck sites*

Medieval ships and parts of ships have also been found during excavations in Norway: in Bergen in 1948 and around 1960, and at Asker near Oslo in 1963. In the harbour at Hedeby in Schleswig, Germany, which dates from Viking times, divers in 1953 located the wreck of a Viking ship; and at Danzig-Ohra, on the southern coast of the Baltic, in the 1930s, three wrecks were excavated, providing, together with some vessels excavated earlier in the region of the Frisches Haff, in the Danziger Bucht and on Lake Leba, a good impression of local ship types in the eleventh–thirteenth centuries. This material has now been supplemented by two finds made at Stettin and at Ralswiek on the island of Rügen, thus enabling us to trace the development of Slav shipbuilding back to the ninth century.

In Holland, an exceptional contribution has been made during recent years in systematic archaeological studies of wrecks in the former Zuider Zee. When draining the 200 square miles of the Northeast Polder, 156 wrecks were located, most of them dating from the sixteenth to nineteenth centuries, a few of them earlier. The oldest wrecks so far examined appear to date from the twelfth century, when the sea broke through and created the Zuider Zee.

In Denmark, investigations of medieval wrecks have been made – or at least begun – under water. As early as 1847, a diver examined a fifteenth-century wreck off the island of Anholt in the Kattegat, and in 1943 the National Museum carried out a diving exploration of a medieval wreck in Kolding Fjord. The most important Danish ship find, however, was made in Roskilde Fjord, where five Viking ships, sunk in a channel as blockships, were charted by the National Museum in 1957–59, the

ships themselves being excavated and raised in connection with drainage in 1962. The same year the very well-preserved wreck of a medieval Hanseatic cog was found during the deepening of Bremen harbour in Germany. It took all of three years to raise the vessel.

An analysis of North European ship types in the period 900–1450 must obviously take these many finds of medieval wrecks into consideration. Unfortunately, descriptions of the various finds are very scattered and are of varying, often poor, quality – assuming they have been described at all. However, it is now imperative to let the finds speak for themselves, and to try, through them, to establish the separate identities of the various types and follow them in the ups and downs of history. Only thus can the archaeology of ships be built up and in turn contribute materially to the elucidation of social history in the Middle Ages.

The Skuldelev find, the name by which the five ships discovered in Roskilde Fjord are known, has been dated to the final phase of the Viking period and may thus be taken as representing a broad cross-section of Scandinavian ship types of about the year 1000. It thus makes a natural starting point for this discussion.

## Scandinavian Ships: 900–1200

In 1956 two amateur divers called at the Danish National Museum with pieces of a wrecked ship they had found in Roskilde Fjord opposite the village of Skuldelev. Locally, this wreck was known as 'Queen Margrethe's Ship', after a Danish queen who in about 1400 formed a union of the Scandinavian countries. Other pieces of timber had previously been brought up from the wreck, and it could now be established from these components that the ship was not a mere 400–500 years old but was more likely to have sunk at this point during the final phase of the Viking period, in the tenth–eleventh centuries. The wreck lay filled with stones to block a narrow channel, Peberrenden, leading into the cathedral town of Roskilde. The water at this point was very shallow ($1\frac{1}{2}$–10 feet), the fairway so sheltered that the site offered ideal conditions for training archaeologists to work under water. In view of this, Dr Olaf Olsen and I began an exploration, which at first was envisaged as a small practice exercise but which gradually grew in scale as, in diving operations during three summer seasons (1957–59), we charted the barrier and established that it comprised not one but several ships.

After the first two summers of exploration we realized that archaeological technique was still insufficiently developed for full excavation and salvage of the wrecks so far located, crumbling and crushed as they were under the weight of stones. It was therefore decided to construct a cofferdam round the ships, so that the area of the barrier could be pumped empty and the final excavation carried out in this drained compartment. Before this could be put into effect, however, the extent of the barrier was accurately demarcated in the course of the final diving season in 1959.

The draining and final excavation was financed by a number of Danish firms and foundations, which defrayed all the costs of erecting a sheet piling round the excavation area of 17,000 square feet, pumping plant, electricity supply, telephone, and wages of the excavating team.

23

Measuring the exposed parts of the wrecks by traditional means would have delayed the work quite considerably and probably rendered it impossible to complete the operation in the course of a single summer. Instead, the job was done with a special double camera capable of 'measuring' a wreck in all its details in under an hour. When the timber was exposed, measured, marked and described, the separate pieces were raised, packed and conveyed to the National Museum's ship preservation plant. It was a difficult task to safeguard the soft timber against further disintegration, but we succeeded in doing this by placing a sheet of hardboard under each plank and lashing them together with hessian before putting them into an airtight plastic bag.

24, 25

Further work on the wood was started in the preservation shop as soon as excavation was complete. The many fragments had to be washed, fitted together like a jigsaw puzzle for measuring and then packed and subjected to preservative treatment in large vessels containing a solution of polyethylene-glycol 4000, where they remained for from six months to two years. While this was taking place, the building, in which the ships were ultimately to be displayed, was erected in Roskilde.

The five ships, comprising two warships, two merchant ships and a smaller vessel of more uncertain character, perhaps a ferry or fishing boat, show a marked variety of construction and shape. Through this find, the broad range of Scandinavian shipbuilding design about a thousand years ago can be studied. Whereas before we could trace only one line of development, it is now possible to distinguish quite clearly both functional and regional differences in the types. Functionally, the merchant ship differs from the warship in having accommodation for cargo amidships. It has a half-deck fore and aft, and rowing facilities are confined to a few oars near the bow and stern. Sail is the principal means of propelling this type of vessel. The merchant ship's hull is short, squat and relatively tall when compared to the long, narrow and low hull of the warship, which has a continuous deck. Throughout the warship's length there are holes in the top plank through which the oars would be thrust when required. The warship was designed primarily to give the best combination of speed and manoeuvrability in battle, when the sail was not used.

But even within the categories of merchant ships and warships there are considerable variations. Take, for example, the two warships. One of these is about 60 feet long and 8 feet wide and had twelve pairs of oars; it is thus the typical Danish Viking ship as we know it from a tenth-century ship grave excavated in 1935 at Ladby on the island of Funen, and from the Norman 5 ships of 1066 in the Bayeux Tapestry. In this tapestry 11 we can follow the building of William the Conqueror's fleet; we can see too how well adapted this ship is to beaching on a sandy shore, for it was only necessary to wade ashore with the anchor or with goods and tackle. Horses could jump the low gunwale and thus be landed with ease. It is characteristic of this ship that the three uppermost strakes are of ash, which tallies with the fact that the type of vessel used by Danish Vikings to raid England in the ninth and tenth centuries is called in English sources *æsc* (a word denoting timber from the ash tree), the Vikings themselves being called *æscmen* by the English. There can be little doubt that the origins of this ship type lie centuries further back, and that generally speaking it was in craft such as this Skuldelev warship that the Vikings made their first long-distance expeditions from Denmark; a type which remained in use as a warship in Danish waters in the centuries to follow.

Towards the end of the Viking period there was a growing demand for larger vessels, and the longship took form. Among the Skuldelev ships there was one such, having a length of about 90 feet. The width cannot be determined, because only about a quarter of the ship has survived, owing to its exposed position uppermost in the barrier. A longship could carry 30–60 oars, perhaps even more, and its speed and the large number of warriors on board often struck fear into the enemy. In this case we cannot exactly determine the number of oars, but there seem to have been between 20 and 26 pairs, disposed along the ship's side at intervals of little more than two feet. There is reason to think that the Danish maritime defence order, the *leding*, was based on ships of this size and design, and that it was these ships which formed the fleets with which the Danish king Sweyn Forkbeard harried England around the year

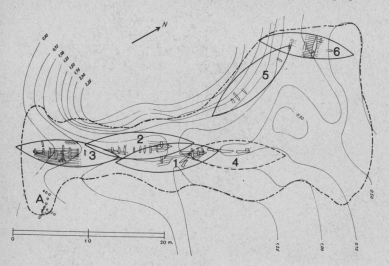

2   *The five Viking ships sunk near Skuldelev to block the approach to Roskilde, as mapped during underwater investigations 1957–59. 2 and 4 mark separate parts of the longship*

1000, subjugating increasingly larger areas until in 1013 the English were forced to accept him as their king.

There are also obvious differences between the two merchant ships in the Skuldelev find. The smaller one, the stem of which has survived in its entirety, is of oak, 45 feet long and 10½ feet across, with a half-deck forward and aft, and with an open hold amidships where the mast stood firmly in its socket in the keelson, without the large mast partner we are familiar with from Norwegian Viking ships. This ship is presumably a Viking coaster, the smaller merchant ship intended for service in the Baltic and on the North Sea. It is so lightly constructed that it could for short distances have been hauled over land, and could sail far up rivers.

The larger merchant ship is about 54 feet long and about 15 feet wide and is built from pine planks, the keel and lower parts of the ribs being of oak, the rest of lime wood. It is designed on entirely different lines from the other vessels. Whereas in them every effort is made in each unit to restrict the weight of material, so as to make it as easy as possible to haul the craft ashore, this ship is primarily meant to weather really rough seas. So by Scandinavian standards it is heavily built with stout ribs, which in the excavation showed up in the ship's surviving port side. The vessel was most probably built in southern Norway, and its peculiar design enables us to connect it with the only route in Viking waterways where the essential requirement was not a lightly built hull but an ability to stand up to really hard weather: the North Atlantic route from Norway to Scotland, Iceland, Greenland and 'Vinland'. The ship used on these voyages was known as the *knarr*, and its ample stem, which can also be observed in this Skuldelev find, was so characteristic that two Icelandic women in the sagas are nicknamed *knarr-bringa* (having a bosom like a *knarr*).

Here, then, for the first time we can study the structure of the vessel which took the Norsemen across the North Atlantic. It was with ships of this type that Erik the Red colonized Greenland in about 982 and his son, Leif the Lucky, sailed on to 'Vinland' in the year 1000 as the first European to reach North America. The journey cannot have been a pleasant one, the ship being just a big open boat offering no protection to crew or passengers in these stormy latitudes.

The last of the Skuldelev ships is also built of pine. It was 39 feet long and 8 feet wide and had carried a mast and sail, probably oars as well. The vessel was without a deck but had broad thwarts, which were situated so low down that they cannot have served as a seat during rowing. We interpret it tentatively as a ferry or fishing vessel.

The copious material recovered in the Skuldelev excavations enabled us to compare its details with other ship finds, thus confirming the first dating to the final phase of the Viking period. Series of radiocarbon tests indicated that the ships had been built in the latter half of the tenth century or about the year 1000, and that the barrier was set in place in the first half of the eleventh

3   *The small Skuldelev merchant ship: reconstruction drawing*

century at a time when Norwegian Vikings repeatedly raided the Danish coast.

Though differing widely in their proportions, materials and details, indicating that they are of different type and provenance, the five Skuldelev ships have a number of features in common. They are all clinker-built, and the hull has an elegantly curved double-pointed shape, the two ends being almost identical. They thereby reveal their Norse origin, their kinship with other Scandinavian ships not only of the Viking period but from the whole period of *c.* 300–1300 so far discovered. They belong to an evolution that can be traced in detail through archaeological finds of this period, and to this day there are boatbuilders in Scandinavia who practise their craft in that same tradition handed down for more than thirty generations.

All this points to a basic Scandinavian shipbuilding type, both for warships and merchantmen: a vessel whose main feature is the handsomely swung line which forms the double-pointed hull, built up round the keel, stem and stern. The warship seems to undergo few changes of design as we follow representations of it from the Gotland picture stones of the eighth century via the Bayeux Tapestry to the *leding* ships in wall paintings in Danish churches, where we get a final representation of the type before it is definitively superseded about 1300. Its speed and manoeuvrability, i.e. its battleworthiness, is chiefly determined by the number of rowers, and as the Scandinavians never built ships with more than one row of oarsmen on either side – the Mediterranean biremes and triremes had two and three, respectively – there was no call for any great change of type during those five centuries.

It is different with the merchant ship. The Skuldelev find shows us for the first time the distinctive cargo vessel that originated in Scandinavia before 1000. In the eleventh–thirteenth centuries the Scandinavian merchantman is known in England as the *keel*, perhaps because the keel was the characteristic feature of the Norse as distinct from the Frisian ship. A number of ship finds from *c.* 1000–1250 show that this particular type underwent a series of changes. Important among these finds is the ship from Ellingaa in Denmark, excavated in 1968. In 1922 near Frederikshavn in north Jutland an old wreck was found which then lay about half a mile inland, at a place that had formerly been a lagoon having the character of a natural harbour. The ship was clearly very old, but there was nothing datable in the wreck. Very sensibly it was covered up again and left for full excavation later, when better means of dating and preserving would be available. The opportunity came when wrecks from the twelfth and thirteenth centuries were found and excavated in various parts of Scandinavia between 1928 and 1964. Thanks to these finds, the Ellingaa ship could now be dated in the twelfth century.

In 1968 Frederikshavn celebrated its 250th anniversary and the occasion was used to provide funds for excavating and preserving the Ellingaa ship. Of this vessel, about 50 feet long, nearly the whole of the starboard side has been preserved, together with the rudder attachment and some cross-beams which show that the ship had a half-deck and an open cargo space amidships. Structurally, the Ellingaa ship is related to the two merchant ships in the Skuldelev find, but the frame spacing is reduced, the design generally indicating that 100–200 years had intervened.

While the Skuldelev find gives us a broad view of Norse ships in about the year 1000, there may well have been other types. We frequently encounter a strange shape of stem in Viking pictures of ships; a ram stem, which is reminiscent of the stem of classical Mediterranean vessels, both warships designed to ram and sink enemy craft, and more pacific merchantmen. In depictions of Scandinavian ships, however, both stem and stern are shaped in this manner, and this construction has never yet appeared in any find. It is possible that these vessels derive from the beak-shaped Scandinavian ships of the Bronze Age as we know them from rock carvings, but, if so, they represent a type which in essential respects lies outside the otherwise familiar Scandinavian basic type.

## Other North European Ships: 900–1200
To determine the pattern of the various North European ships of the Middle Ages is not easy. In general, the literary sources name only the types, without exactly stating their respective characteristics, and pictures seldom tell directly which type they represent. Confusion of the type names is also met with. Around 1400, a ship would often be called a hulk in one harbour and a cog in the next, although in the previous centuries these two types were kept quite distinct. Moreover, their relative sizes vary greatly according to period. In English harbour tariffs of about 1000, keels and hulks are both listed at a groundage of fourpence, smaller ships at a penny and very small vessels at a halfpenny. Here then, keel and hulk seem to be types of equal size. From about

1130 there are rules governing the prisage the Crown was entitled to charge in customs duty on wine ships coming to London from Lorraine. In these the keel is charged a good deal more than the hulk: 'And if it is a keel, they shall take two tuns below the mast and one before. . . . And if it is a hulk or other ship, one tun before and another behind. . . .' In the fourteenth century the pattern has changed again; now the hulk is larger than the keel.

Understandably, this source material has led to opposing conceptions of what in fact characterized the various types. We shall therefore endeavour to approach the question from another angle: by examining the archaeological material in the light of what we have learned from the Skuldelev find about the basic structural features of Scandinavian ship types. Unfortunately, ship finds from the period up to 1200 are far fewer in Western Europe than in the North; there is enough evidence, however, to suggest that here we are concerned with vessels differing basically from the Scandinavian ships.

*Frisian ships.* In 1930, at Utrecht in Holland, the wreck of a remarkable old vessel was found. It lay embedded in mud at a point which proved to be the sealed and overgrown bed of the Rhine where, up to AD 866, it had entered Lake Flevo, a freshwater lake which later became the salt Zuider Zee. After excavation the wreck was reassembled at the Central Museum in Utrecht.

The ship is shaped almost like a hollowed-out banana, curved both longitudinally and transversely, keel-less and stem-less, constructed from stout planks converging fore and aft. The strongly-built hull is $56\frac{1}{2}$ feet long and 12 feet wide with a rounded oak bottom plank $6\frac{1}{2}$ feet broad in place of a keel and a mast-step 16 feet from the forward end. The wreck has been dated by C 14 analysis at AD 790±45, which tallies with its having been sunk on the site before this arm of the river was closed about 866.

In its entire structure, feature by feature, the Utrecht ship reveals that it belongs to a type basically different from the Scandinavian Viking ships. The curved, keelless form and the siting of the mast well forward recur in two clay models of boats which, along with Pingsdorf ceramics of the tenth century, were found during peat-cutting near the Paterswolde lake in Holland, and are now preserved in the Rijksmuseum at Leyden. The advanced position of the mast has a natural explanation, provided by representations of, for example, Roman river ships. These show tow ropes leading from a short mast forward to bargemen on land. This suggests that the Utrecht ship is a river vessel. That is not to say that this type of hull could not be fitted out as a sea-going ship with a centrally placed sail-bearing mast. Indeed, we find this version of it with board planks all converging at the ends, on denarii struck at Dorestadt and Quentovic for Charlemagne and Louis the Pious (814–840), as well as on the font in Winchester Cathedral dating from about 1180.

*4 Votive ship with rope lashing around the bow end. Reproduction drawing of detail from a stained glass window, Malvern Priory church, Worcestershire, c. 1450*

This type is often met with again in later centuries, chiefly as the principal motif in the seals of maritime towns. A lucky chance has, moreover, enabled us to identify its name. The town seal of New Shoreham, formerly 'Hūlkesmouth', dating from 1295 and bearing a distinct picture of this ship type, has the legend *hoc hulci signo vocor o's sic nomine digno* – 'by this picture of a hulk I am called Mouth which is a worthy name.'

In the Utrecht ship, then, we have an archaeological specimen of the hulk, and have established certain of its constructional features. The name 'hulk' is an ancient one, which derives from the Greek ὁλκάς ('towed cargo ship'), and this ties up very well with the Utrecht ship being a river vessel. We still lack archaeological finds to show details in the development of the hulk type from the basic features indicated in the Utrecht ship; but there can be little doubt that its characteristic feature is the strongly curved shape with the hull constructed from stout boards, all converging at the ends of the vessel without any actual stern post, but in some cases held together in the fore part by a coil of rope, as shown in several pictures. Where and when the hulk developed from a river vessel into a sea-going ship we do not know for certain, but there is a strong indication that this development had its centre in the Frisian area on the lower reaches of the Rhine and in areas bordering the Channel, and that the first stages in this development are earlier than 800.

In the Frisian region, however, ships of quite a different kind have been found. The earliest of the wrecks excavated by van der Heide in the Zuider Zee (Wreck Q 75) was sunk in the twelfth century, in the fresh-water period before the sea broke through. Only the bottom part of the ship has survived, but in it we find the combination of clinker-built sides and a flat plank bottom. The floor timbers extend over the flat bottom and run up the clinker-laid board on either side alternately.

The flat bottom of the Zuider Zee wreck is an important constructional feature, which distinguishes this ship from the Scandinavian ships as well as the hulk. Another characteristic of this flat-bottomed type, the straight stem, manifested itself in 1943 in Kolding Fjord in Denmark, when a fisherman found a large side-rudder, $13\frac{1}{2}$ feet high, of the twelfth or thirteenth century. This led to a search for the vessel from which the rudder

came, and a wreck was located nearby in $11\frac{1}{2}$–13 feet of water. This wreck was clearly very old, and being protected by fjord mud invited archaeological investigation, which was carried out by the Danish National Museum with the assistance of a salvage firm. Divers established that the ship was about 60 feet long and some 20 feet wide, with a strong mast step about $6\frac{1}{2}$ feet in front of midships. In the fore-part were a number of potsherds, a large lump of clay, charred pieces of wood and split beech firewood, probably remains of a primitive galley. The ship's bottom was flat, constructed from planks laid edge to edge, the sides being clinker-laid. Enough survived of the stems to indicate that they had been straight, and that they met the bottom line at an acute angle. On the stern post were traces of rust from rudder braces, showing that the rudder found earlier did *not* belong to it. The position of its rudder indicates that the Kolding wreck can date from no earlier than the end of the twelfth century, and the construction in general suggests that it is from the thirteenth or fourteenth century.

The ship type we have here encountered appears again and again in town seals of the thirteenth and fourteenth centuries, especially those of the Hanseatic towns of northern Germany. The German historian Paul Heinsius has demonstrated that this 'edged' type with a straight bottom line and straight stem is the cog, the famous large ship of the Hanseatic towns which dominated the maritime trade of northern Europe from the beginning of the thirteenth century till about 1400, when the hulk came into prominence. It had long been generally assumed that the type came from the Frisian region, as the word *cog-sculd* occurs in the statement of revenues in the diocese of Utrecht in the tenth century, the supposition being that this referred to a tax imposed on local fishing vessels named cogs. Heinsius did not share this view. He believed that the cog was a Hanseatic type with keel and straight stem and stern, developed by German carpenters at the end of the twelfth century without foreign prototypes.

Since the archaeological evidence is insufficient to solve the question of the age and origin of the cog, it is worth following up another line of enquiry – namely, the possible connection between the type's form and local coastal conditions. And here we find a natural explanation for the flat bottom of the cog in the tidal areas of the Frisian Wadden Zee. There loading and unloading could take place when the ship was high and dry at low tide; to be refloated at next high tide.

Before the Viking raids began in earnest in the coastal areas of the North Sea about 800, causing an interruption in Frisian maritime commerce, sea-going merchants from the lower reaches of the Rhine had established a network of trade routes to England, France and Scandinavia. Clear evidence has been found of commerce with the Frisians as far northeast as the Viking trading town of Birka, near to present-day Stockholm. Scandinavian historians and archaeologists have debated whether it was the Frisians or the Scandinavians themselves who carried these wares so far north. Almost the entire route of ships sailing from the Frisian region to Birka or *vice versa* was confined to sheltered waters, from the Wadden Zee through the Limfjord and up through the Baltic. So it could be navigated both by shallow-draught Scandinavian ships and by Frisian ships of Wadden Zee type. It is thus of great interest that part of the harbour area of Birka, which vanished about A D 1000, is called Kugghamn, meaning 'cog harbour'. This strongly indicates that Frisian merchants did take part in voyages to Birka, and that the type of ship they used on this route was the flat-bottomed, straight-stemmed cog, the Wadden Zee vessel which, around 1200, was developed by Hanseatic craftsmen into the typical large ship of the Middle Ages.

*English warships.* In 897 Alfred the Great ordered the building of a fleet of warships that could oppose the steadily growing numbers of Viking ships that were raiding the English coasts. The Anglo-Saxon Chronicle tells us that 'they were full twice as long as the others; some had sixty oars and some had more; they were both swifter and steadier and also higher than others; they were shaped neither like the Frisian nor the Danish, but so as it seemed to him they would be most efficient.'

This decision to build up an English naval defence force has given King Alfred the reputation of being the father of the English navy. Unfortunately, we have no means of telling whether on this occasion an altogether new type of vessel was introduced, or whether an existing type of warship was modified. The Bayeux Tapestry reproduces the character of Danish–Norman warships of the eleventh century very aptly in the scenes showing William's invasion fleet, and the few English ships that appear in it do not look very different from the Norman ones. They differ from typical Viking ships only by having a break in the row of oar-holes, and perhaps a raised deck amidships.

After several centuries of intensive immigration to the British Isles by Danes, Norwegians and Swedes, who as Vikings had Scandinavian shipbuilding and sea-going navigation in their blood, it is scarcely surprising that the English ships in the Bayeux Tapestry should resemble actual Viking ships. But we cannot help noting that the large ships attributed to King Alfred after less than two hundred years have either vanished or been merged in Scandinavian traditions of building. The latter is the more probable. The English ships no doubt helped to promote the development of the Viking longship through the interaction that characterizes every arms race, but they did not survive as an independent type.

British record offices contain unrivalled material to illustrate English warship construction about 1300, in the form of the accounts for a number of galleys, long ships fitted with oars and sail that were built by private builders to royal order. Careful account had to be kept of the expenditures, in order that the builders might receive advance payments from the Treasury. Entries relating to the construction of eight galleys in 1294–96 are full of interesting details; in particular, Master William's accounts for one vessel built in this period in Newcastle provides a wealth of information. The accounts are in Latin; but as there was no Latin terminology for this clinker-built ship, English terms had to be used for the various parts. Most of these are derived from Old Norse words, and the terminology as a whole clearly indicates that the English galley of about 1300 is closely related to the Scandinavian longship. This is true of the hull, as shown in the terms *bord* (=plank, Old Norse *borð*), *underloute* (=keel element situated between keel and stem, O N *undirhlutr*), *brand* (=upper part of stem, O N *brandr*), as also of the rigging, where terms occur such as *betas* (=spinnaker, O N *beitiass*), and *rakke* (=yard shackle, O N *rakki*).

The English galleys were large ships with castle fore and aft and with a topcastle in the mast. They carried 80–100 oars, 40–50 a side, at intervals of only about 2 feet, so that the rowers must either have sat very closely behind one another or have been staggered in some pattern unknown. Each galley had as tender a barge of 30–40 oars, likewise set very close together. Most of the known Viking ships have a space of about 3 feet between the oar-holes, but the longship in the Skuldelev find has a considerably shorter distance, about 28 inches, between the frames. Apparently the longship type introduced a special arrangement of rowers, or a special rowing technique, which made it possible to provide room for a pair of oars for each 2 feet of keel, and probably the longship was a true North Sea vessel, developed in a cross-fertilization of English, Danish and Norwegian; a type of warship which seems in its principal features to have survived with an astonishing degree of consistency during the long period from about 900 to 1300.

*Slav ship types.* In the centuries preceding the Viking period Slav tribes from central and eastern Europe pushed north and northwest into the areas which now form East Germany and Poland, and which then lay deserted following the westward movement of Germanic tribes in the era of the Great Migrations. The Slavs penetrated to the southern shore of the Baltic along its whole length from the River Vistula in the east to the base of the Jutland peninsula in the west, and in the course of the centuries developed shipbuilding activities which enabled them to carry on maritime trade and to cross the Baltic with whole fleets of warships.

In the eleventh and twelfth centuries the Wends, as the Slavs were called by the Scandinavians, were strong enough to constitute a real threat to the population in the southern areas of Denmark. In order to protect the exposed Danish coasts, great barriers made of poles were erected at estuaries and across channels, so that the only points where Wendish armies could make landings were on the open coast far from any inhabited place. Some of these barriers along the Danish shores of the Baltic have been charted in recent years and exploratory work has been initiated at several points on the sea bed.

6, 7 Wendish warship types are known from several finds in the Slav zone, from Danzig in the east to Rügen in the west. In 1930, three early-medieval vessels were excavated near the city of Danzig. One of these, a warship 42 feet long, was fitted out for nine pairs of oars and clinker-built with keel and stern, ribs and thwarts as in Scandinavian ships, but with minor features – such as treenails in place of iron rivets between the boards – which suggest local make.

Similar vessels were recently found at Ralswiek on the island of Rügen, and their construction confirms that the Wendish warship would seem to have been a direct copy of the Danish warship, the narrow, low-built landing vessel of the Ladby and Skuldelev finds. Danish builders probably acted as teachers to the Wends, a more local individuality only gradually developing in Slav building of sea-going warships.

If for sea-going the Slavs had recourse to a borrowed tradition, on rivers they were at home. The transport of timber, grain, hemp and other goods was along the big rivers, partly on rafts and partly in large flat-bottomed river vessels, to ports of shipment at the river mouths. Large barges were used for trans-shipment and as ferries, and their Danish name, *pram* (=barge, Old Norse *prámr*), is of Slav origin (Old Slav *pramu*). It is still used as a name for flat-bottomed small boats and lighters, in Scandinavia, Germany and Poland alike.

The pram was an indispensable part of the transport system, among other places at the Skanør-Falsterbo market, the great medieval herring market in the Sound, where merchants from most of Northern Europe met and traded together and with Danish fishermen. At market time there was a teeming life in booths on land and on the merchant ships which lay at anchor in the roads. There was no real harbour here, only a broad, flat, sandy shore, which rendered contact between ship and shore difficult. When a cargo was to be brought ashore it had first to be trans-shipped into barges, which were rowed and punted into shallow water, where horse-drawn carts were waiting to convey the wares to the booths. The shore belonged to the king, and what touched it was regarded as royal flotsam. Consequently,

if a barge capsized or a cart broke down under its load, the goods would be immediately confiscated and taken to the royal warehouses. At Falsterbo and Skanør, castles were built for the Crown officers, and when the rampart was constructed round Falsterbohus, the most southerly of these, in about 1300, it had to be sited on the seaward side in order to secure it against landslip at high tide. For this they chose to use six barges, 45–60 feet long – found lying in a long row during excavations of the site in 1911 and 1934–35. The barges, one of which was taken to the museum in Lund, Sweden, are 5 quite flat-bottomed, pointed fore and cut rather short aft. The smooth, level bottom with a large number of close-fitting floor timbers survives in all the barges, most of the sides being lost. A characteristic feature of the barges is the shape of the plank which effects the transition from bottom to side. The section is cut like an L, the plank constituting both the edge plank of the bottom and the bottom plank of the side, and the very same detail has been noted in two or three other finds of medieval barges in the Baltic area, thus demonstrating this as a characteristic clue to the pram-tradition.

## North European Ships: 1200–1450

The terms of seafaring have always been dependent on economic and political factors as well as on the level of shipbuilding technique and navigation skill. Difficulties that seafarers hardly note today could in earlier times be almost insurmountable, with far-reaching consequences to contemporary society.

Take the important North European sea-trading route between the North Sea and the Baltic. Nowadays navigation goes on independently of wind and weather round the Skaw and through the Sound or Great Belt, eased by good navigational aids; in sailing-ship days it was very different. Long, dangerous shoals, then imperfectly charted and marked, made the passage through the Kattegat a hazard for large sailing ships, which needed plenty of room to manoeuvre and which were dependent on wind and weather. Numerous ships, indeed, never got through, but either foundered or became stranded in this area. On the small island of Anholt in the Kattegat alone 125 ships ran aground in the period 1858–81, even though the fairway there at that time was well marked.

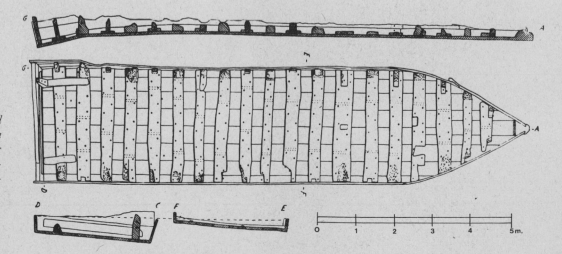

*5 Pram from around 1300. Reconstruction drawing of one of six barges found at Falsterbo, Sweden, and excavated 1934–35*

In the Viking period this dangerous waterway was avoided by sailing through the Limfjord or conveying goods overland the short distance across the base of the Jutland peninsula from Hollingsted to Hedeby. In the twelfth century, however, the Limfjord ceased to function as a through channel, probably because the western approach was closed by sand, and trade had now to rely entirely on trans-shipment and overland transport between Baltic and North Sea harbours.

This resulted in the expansion of a number of German towns on the southern Baltic shores, particularly Lübeck, which was founded in 1143. Hamburg and Lübeck were the new terminals of the east–west transit route, and realizing their common interests, they formed in 1227 an alliance designed to secure the route. The association was extended to other towns, and in time a whole chain of them, from the Zuider Zee in the west to the Gulf of Finland in the east, combined to form the politically and economically powerful Hanseatic League, which controlled the economic life of northern Europe through investments in silver mines in the Harz Mountains, salt from Lüneburg and iron and copper from Sweden, and which also had big interests in cod fishing in Norway and herring fishing and curing in the Sound.

The Scanean market on the Sound attracted not only Hanseatic herring buyers but merchants from the greater part of Northern Europe, who found there a central mart for the exchange of wares from distant parts. It soon became clear that West European merchants were not content to accept Baltic goods from Hanseatic middlemen, but preferred to make the uncertain voyage round the Skaw in order to get a share of their own in the Scanean market, where we first hear of them in 1251. Of course, this traffic was a threat to Hanseatic dominance, and the Hansa towns tried to check it. In 1384 the Dutch towns, which did not belong to the League, were excluded from the Scanean market, though with no other result than to make West European ships go directly to Baltic ports for their goods.

In this economic power game the financially strong Hanseatic 'shipping lines' prevailed over Scandinavian shipping, which was based on a looser and more decentralized economic structure. The Hanseatic cog, able to outstrip the Scandinavian ship in competition, has been given some of the credit for this development. We have seen how the Scandinavian merchant ship in its development during the period 1000–1200 grew progressively broader and deeper; there was nothing to suggest stagnation or decline. On the other hand, the ships from that period known through the finds are modest in size. All this might suggest that the cog's dominance over the Scandinavian ship was that it alone could be built sufficiently large and powerful to cope with the contemporary demand for mass transport of grain, herrings and timber.

A recent discovery in Norway refutes this argument. During Asbjørn Herteig's extensive excavations of Bryggen, the old harbour quarter of Bergen, he found,

about 1960, nearly 25 different parts of a large ship. The timber had been used in a wharf, which had been constructed soon after a fire in 1248, and thus the ship must date from the first half or the middle of the thirteenth century. It was built from the local shipbuilding material, pine, and in a manner that clearly proclaimed its Scandinavian descent. The dimensions, however, were without precedent in Scandinavian finds; nearly 30 feet wide and 85 feet long, it was a truly large ship. With this find the Scandinavian shipbuilders are acquitted. It was not their fault that the trade slipped from the hands of Scandinavian merchants. They knew their craft, and knew how to build large up-to-date ships in conformity with Scandinavian tradition. Moreover, they were alive to new trends and adopted, for example, the straight stern and stern rudder from the cog, as shown by the oldest of the ships which in 1933–34 were found in the medieval harbour of Kalmar, and which H. Åkerlund, who excavated them, dated in the thirteenth century. 3

The cog grew in the course of the thirteenth century into the leading merchant ship of Northern Europe, and the type spread as far as the Mediterranean. The Florentine chronicler Giovanni Villani noted in the year 1304: 'At this time people came from Bayonne in Gascony in their ships, which in Bayonnese they call cogs, through the straits of Gibraltar on buccaneering expeditions in the Mediterranean, where they inflicted much damage. After that time also people from Genoa, Venice and Catalonia began to employ cogs for their seafaring and abandoned the use of their own large ships owing to the seaworthiness and lower cost of cogs. Thus great changes were wrought in the ship forms of our fleet.'

The literary sources of the Middle Ages are far from precise when it comes to the measurements of the cog. Ships of a hundred 'loads' are not infrequently mentioned, but the term can be ambiguous; not only does it vary by giving weight and capacity measures alternately, but it also changes in size from one commodity to another and from one town to the next. A better idea of the maximum dimensions of ships is given in the limitation which had to be observed in harbour building. While Viking ships could use any natural harbour so long as the depth of water was at least 5 feet, the large cogs needed some 10 feet. In building a bridge at Riga at the close of the thirteenth century the passage bay in the middle was given a width of 33 feet for the passage of large vessels.

The freeboard, the height of the ship's side above the waterline, is stated only indirectly in literary sources. In 1214, during an engagement in the Baltic between a strong German and an Esthonian fleet of many large and small ships, the crew of the cargo ship, probably a cog, succeeded in destroying one of the ships and capturing another; the attack was beaten off, the cog being able to continue its voyage. With its high sides the cog was as impregnable as a fortress to the rowed warships. By exploiting the tactical advantage of the lofty deck, the crossbows could keep the greater part of the enemy 34

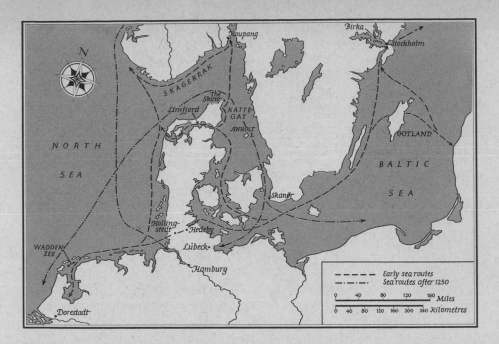

6 Map showing the sea trade routes between the North Sea and Baltic areas, following the coast during the Viking period and keeping clear of land after 1250

at a distance, and the few ships which ventured into close combat could be held by anchors and grappling irons until the crew was neutralized. It was soon evident that when two cogs sailed together, no warships of the longship type dared to approach them. At the same time, the cog was so slow that it could not take the initiative in fighting warships of longship type, except by manning any smaller accompanying ships and allowing these to operate in collaboration with the cog.

The Scandinavian longship, however, would not at this stage acknowledge defeat. Provided that, without impairing its good speed and manoeuvrability, its bowmen could be raised to the deck level of the cog, it could recover its position. The method of achieving this was quite simply to build castles – raised platforms forward and aft, and perhaps at the top of the mast – so that longships could launch their attack from there. The newly won superiority was, however, short-lived. The cog, as a merchant ship, was solely concerned with defence. Masters had no intention of sacrificing the impregnability afforded by their high freeboard. They therefore followed the longship example and furnished their cogs with castles. And so the battle was lost for the longship; the admired and dreaded warship of centuries was at one stroke made obsolete. Danish naval defence organization, the *leding*, which in the thirteenth century comprised a fleet of about 1,100 longships with 30,000–40,000 men, was in 1304 converted to the cog. Zealand, previously called upon to equip about 120 longships spread over the whole island, now had to finance the equipping of 5–10 cogs.

It was not until 1962 that, thanks to a lucky archaeological find, the precise character and appearance of the cog could be determined. In that year, while deepening Bremen harbour on the River Weser, the side of a large clinker-built ship came to light. It was constructed with straight stern and stem, a castle aft and other features which gave it a striking resemblance to the cogs illustrated on town seals of the thirteenth and fourteenth centuries. That October, the Focke Museum at Bremen hastily organized the careful salvage of the ship under the direction of Dr Siegfried Fliedner, and in the face of great difficulties succeeded in recovering nearly the whole of the hull, before icing on the river stopped work. The raising of the rest of the ship's timbers was continued by divers in the summer of 1963, and finally, in 1965, the archaeologists minutely examined the mud of the river bed at the site down to a depth of about 25 feet, operating from a bell-diving ship.

The result of the combined salvage operations was that the ship's timbers and planks were nearly all saved. For a start, the pieces were measured, in order to determine the ship's construction and principal dimensions. The length was 77 feet, the maximum width and height 24½ feet, so that with its cargo capacity of over 65 'loads' (of 2 metric tons) the ship was rather more than average size for cogs. The after castle was built up on stout supports, looking markedly 'stuck on', as it also appears in seals, where in the early ship representations the castles are clearly 'platforms on stilts'.

Above the castle aft a capstan with a vertical axis had been fitted, and below this a winch with a horizontal axis for hauling in the anchor cable, but neither of these showed any signs of wear. Certain features suggested that a forecastle was planned but not constructed. The planks of the main deck were missing, and apparently they had never been put in place. The mast, too, did not seem to have been fitted to the hull. On the other hand, a tar barrel and some shipwrights' tools were found on board. All this points to the ship's having been sunk before it was completed, and the excavators believe that it was swept from the building slip during a flood, and afterwards sank a few miles away, probably in the latter half of the fourteenth century.

As we learn more about the Bremen cog, we shall doubtless have to revise certain of our ideas concerning

27–30

31–33

191

the structure and fitting-out of medieval ships, for which archaeological evidence has previously been lacking.

A special exhibition building is being prepared in the new Maritime Museum in Bremerhaven where the ship can be reconstructed and conservation completed under conditions that will enable the public to watch the work in progress. Thus the old Hanseatic town of Bremen will ultimately have a medieval cog in a unique state of preservation, a worthy monument to ship archaeology in line with the Norwegian Viking ships of Gokstad and Oseberg, the Danish Skuldelev ships and the seventeenth-century Swedish warship, the *Vasa*.

With the Bremen cog we approach the close of the long period in which the principal ships of North European seafaring were single-masted, clinker-built vessels. In the course of the fifteenth century the pattern changed; one large square sail was supplemented by smaller square sails at the top of the mainmast and small sail-bearing masts developed fore and aft: the three-master was born. Great changes also took place in the method of building the hull. Two Dutch chroniclers relate that shipbuilders in 1459 and 1460 for the first time built *cravelschepen* in the provinces of Zeeland and Holland. The carvel technique of building, in which the planks were laid edge to edge, leaving the ship's sides smooth, and which rendered it possible to work with far heavier planks than in clinker-building, quickly gained a foothold in Northern Europe. It formed one of the principal preconditions of the progressively larger dimensions that could be given to ships, so enabling European powers in the sixteenth and seventeenth centuries to cross all the oceans and colonize continents thousands of miles away.

It has been claimed that the Bremen cog initiated this carvel-building period, as in this ship the three lowermost planks in the bottom lay flush, i.e. carvel-planked. But we have seen that it was a basic characteristic of the cog type that the bottom was flat, with the planks laid edge to edge. In the Bremen vessel we meet with this flat bottom as a rudimentary feature, and a new element has entered the picture: the keel. Among the North European ships that have been referred to above, it is only in the Scandinavian type that the keel occurs as a

basic feature. We know that the cog, once it had entered the large-ship category, borrowed constructive features from the hulk and itself influenced the latter's development so that by about 1400 it was often difficult to tell whether a certain ship belonged to one type or the other. Similarly, the cog may have adopted the keel from the Scandinavian merchant ship.

It might be supposed that the Bremen cog with its broad, heavy planks, represents the outside limit of clinker-building technique. A limit there must have been, for when the carvel technique established itself, clinker-building was soon abandoned in bigger ships. It is recorded in an English State paper of August 5, 1545, that 'clenchers' were 'both feeble, olde and out of fashion'. But the Bremen cog, with a keel length of 50 feet and a maximum breadth of $24\frac{1}{2}$ feet, was far outstripped in size by an English ship of that time with a keel some 130 feet long and a beam of about 50 feet, dwarfing even the *Vasa* of 1628 (see chapter 10).

The term 'carvel' derives from 'caravel'. This name is first mentioned in the 'Charter of Alfonso III' (1255) as a type of fishing vessel operating off the Portuguese coast. Later the name came to be applied to merchant ships of a particular type, and it achieved world fame thanks to Columbus's voyages. When constructing a carvel-built ship today it is customary to put together a skeleton with keel, stem and stern as the backbone, and with ribs cut to size and shape in accordance with an accurate scale drawing. This drawing tradition, however, is relatively recent, having been developed since the seventeenth century, with a few precursors in the sixteenth. It may thus be assumed that the *Vasa* was built without use of actual drawings. How this problem was mastered – and what the procedure generally was of building the first carvel-constructed ships in North Europe – remains to be determined. Ship archaeology has now procured for us a rich source of material for elucidating the history of the clinker-built ship down to about 1400. The future will show whether underwater archaeology can solve some of the many problems presented by the intensive development of shipbuilding in the period 1400–1600 ultimately leading up to the full-rigged ship common to the whole of Europe.

---

1 When a ship from some past age has been located under water, it is necessary to apply a combination of 'wet' and 'dry' archaeology if the remains are to yield the maximum amount of information. This work ranges from the piecemeal excavation of every piece of wreckage that may lie buried in the mud and sand of the sea bed by means of modern underwater techniques, to the reconstructing of an entire ship on land.

The excavation of five Viking vessels which had been used to block the passage through Roskilde Fjord, in Denmark, was a case in point. The site was mapped

under water in 1957–59, but not until a cofferdam was constructed around it in 1962, could the water be pumped out, and the ships extricated from the stones and accumulated mud and sand. Then followed the meticulous work of identification, preservation, and reassembly of various parts.

The complete stem portion of one of the ships was found to be more or less intact, and is shown *in situ* on the page opposite. The sturdy planks of the clinker-built vessel, sweeping in an elegant curve to the pointed prow, are a characteristic feature of all Viking ships.

2–7 In Northern Europe a number of medieval ships have been discovered at various times during this century. Often these were chance finds, but in recent years the majority have resulted from systematic archaeological investigation of areas that formerly constituted the sea bed.

2 The remains of a Viking ship from about AD 800 were found at Askekärr on the River Göta near Gothenburg, Sweden, in 1933. Unfortunately conservation methods adopted at the time were inadequate, and the ship was never restored.

3 During 1933–34 the medieval harbour of Kalmar, Sweden, was cleared of mud that had accumulated through the centuries, and several wrecks were uncovered. One of these turned out to be a small thirteenth-century coastal trader.

4 Excavation work by means of a cofferdam at Asker, near Oslo, in 1964 revealed the remains of a derelict merchant ship, 50–60 feet long, dating to about AD 1200.

5 A tenth-century Danish ship was found in a chieftain's grave at Ladby, on the island of Funen, Denmark, in 1935. Though the iron nails and the impression in the ground was all that remained of this 67-foot-long Viking warship, the resemblance to Norman ships in the Bayeux tapestry was marked.

6, 7 In recent years, Polish archaeologists have brought to light Slavic craftsmen's versions of Scandinavian boat types, as exemplified by the Charbrow boat (6) found in 1931 and raised in 1960, and the eleventh-century Szczecin boat (7) found in 1962 during archaeological investigations in the former German town of Stettin.

6

9

7

10

8

8 Underwater operations in the Viking harbour of Hedeby near Schleswig, Germany, in 1953 brought to light what appears to be a harbour defence system. Here a diver is seen with pieces of timber recovered from the remains of a 60-foot-long Viking ship which lay at the narrow entrance to the basin.

9, 10 G.D. van der Heide has developed an excellent technique for recording ship finds, by means of which he is able to supplement the evidence provided by the mere bones of an old hull (9) with the stratigraphical evidence derived from scientific excavation (10). He has applied it to many wrecks in the area of the former Zuider Zee.

11

12

13

11–14 The vast fleets of Viking ships that crossed the North Sea a thousand years ago have vanished like the Spanish Armada and other great invasion fleets of history. Of the ships themselves only a few scattered remains have been left to posterity, but representations of vessels descended from those the Vikings built are found in medieval iconography, ranging from the carved wooden stick to the illustrative tapestry, and from the illuminated manuscript to the large-scale mural painting.

11 Among the scenes woven into the Bayeux tapestry is one which shows the building of the fleet of William of Normandy in preparation for the conquest of England in 1066. In the detail here reproduced we see, on the left, trees being felled and planks cut to meet the specific requirements of the shipwrights, who are busily at work on two of the vessels. On the right, men are untying the cables in preparation for the launching, while the ships are lined up in readiness to cross the Channel.

12, 13 The Viking ship tradition was carried on for several centuries after the end of the Viking era about AD 1050. Representations of ship types descending directly from the merchant vessels or warships of the Vikings appear in manuscripts of the twelfth and thirteenth centuries.

14 Such craft are also depicted in murals in Danish churches. In Skamstrup church, an artist working at the end of the fourteenth century has illustrated the legend of the holy king Olaf. In this dramatic painting, the ship which is carrying the king across a stormy sea has, with its curving stem and stern post carved in the shape of a dragon's head, every appearance of being a Viking longship.

HIC TRAHUNT NAVES AD MARE

14

15–19 Remains of early medieval ships are scarce on both sides of the English Channel, but in 1930 the wreck of a remarkable old banana-shaped vessel of *c.* AD 800 was found in the bed of a former arm of the Rhine near Utrecht, Holland. After excavation (15), the parts were conveyed to the Central Museum in Utrecht and reassembled (16); whereupon the ship was found to bear a striking resemblance to those depicted on coins struck in the nearby town of Dorestadt in 814–840 (17). This type of vessel, without stem and stern posts and with all the planks running right up to the ship's ends, is to be seen also on the font in Winchester Cathedral, dating to *c.* 1180 (18), the earliest known representation of a ship with a rudder. The type reappears on the seal of New Shoreham, Sussex, England (19) dated 1295. The inscription 'hoc hulci . . .' accurately defines the ship type – the famous medieval cargo-carrying *hulk*.

20, 21 The contemporary English warship type can be seen in a detail from the Bayeux Tapestry (21); it is similar in design to the Norman ships except for the break amidships in the sheerline, a feature not to be found in the vessel depicted on a seal of Faversham, Kent (20) of *c.* 1300. This is a 'Viking-type' vessel with castles added forward and aft to provide fighting platforms for the soldiers on board.

17

18

19

20

21

22–25 Some pieces of wreckage raised by amateur divers operating in Roskilde Fjord, near Skuldelev, in 1956 ultimately led to the discovery of no fewer than five Viking ships; they had been filled with stones and sunk so as to block one of the channels giving access to the town of Roskilde from the sea. When the true nature of the find was realized, a coffer-dam was built round the site (22), in which archaeologists, using long wooden-cat-walks (23), could carry on their work. By a happy chance, all five ships turned out to be of different types: a deep-sea trader, a longship, a coaster, a smaller warship, and a fishing-boat or ferry. In 1969 they were taken to the Viking Ship Museum in Roskilde (24, 25), where the public can observe the intricate work of restoration, in which thousands of treated fragments are fitted together in such a way as to re-construct the originals in every detail, the missing parts being reproduced by slender metal strips to complete the exact profile of the hulls.

26 A parallel to the Skuldelev merchant ships was found at Ellingaa, Denmark, in 1922. This ship was not excavated until 1968, when divers built a 'cage' around it, so that it could be raised in one piece for conservation and restoration.

27

28

31

29

30

27–30 In the harbour at Bremen a late fourteenth-century wreck was found in 1962 (27). A dredger was at work enlarging the river harbour, when part of the side of a large clinker-built ship unexpectedly appeared at low tide. Although it had clearly lain there for a considerable time, the ship was in a sufficiently good state of preservation (29, 30) for it to be recognized as a cog. The Focke Museum in Bremen had the hull raised in sections after a preliminary numbering of the parts (28), a difficult operation that turned into a race against the tides and the coming of the winter's ice. In 1965, with the aid of a diving-bell, additional pieces of the ship were recovered, and now the greater part of the hull is available for detailed examination. It soon transpired that neither the superstructure (forecastle) nor the main deck had been completed, while a number of shipwright's tools were found on board. There seems little doubt, therefore, that the 77-foot-long, broad-beamed ship, of some 130 tons, was under construction further up the river when it was carried away from the slip by flood waters – to vanish from sight for almost 600 years.

31–33 Between the twelfth and fourteenth centuries the town seals of many European ports exhibited the ship types that were of especial importance to them. Though the representations are stylized and constricted by the circular shape of the seal, one recurrent type of ship can readily be recognized. It is single-masted and characterized by a straight stem and stern post set at an acute angle to the keel. The vessel in question is the *cog*, the famous Hanseatic merchant ship of the period. The seals here reproduced are dated 1242 (31), 1329 (32) and 1350 (33). The second of these belongs to Stralsund, the other two to Elbing.

32

33

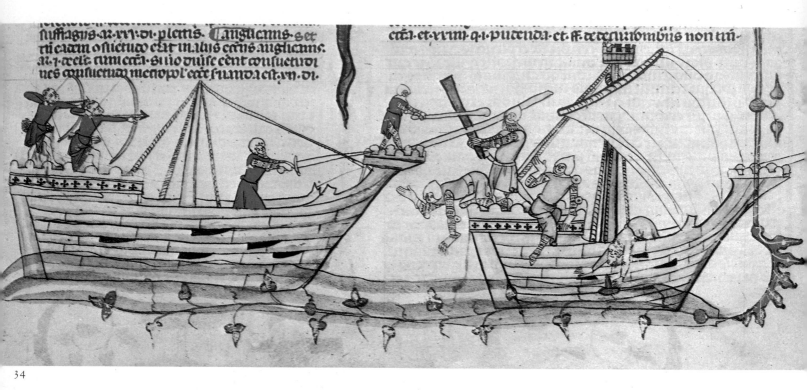

## 34

35

34 While the Viking chieftain demanded speed and manoeuvrability for his men-of-war, a trend which led to the famous Viking longships, the medieval crusader preferred a broad and slow cog. The cogs were by nature cargo ships, but they turned out to be suitable troop carriers, and for fighting at sea they were provided with fore- and stern-castles which served as platforms for hand-to-hand fighting, as portrayed in this early fourteenth-century manuscript.

35 The cargo ships of the turn of the fourteenth century in Northern Europe varied in type and size, but the largest were huge vessels equipped with a single mast and a very large single square sail, in which the clinker-building technique reached its limits. The application of the smooth-skinned carvel technique for building the hull, and the use of additional masts at the fore- and stern-castles, were steps needed to bring the North European ships into a new era. This miniature of a fifteenth-century manuscript in the Bodleian Museum in Oxford is meant to illustrate the equipping of the *Argo*, but the ship itself is a striking example of current changes in design and the first appearance of small masts fore and aft.

# The Maritime Republics: Medieval and Renaissance ships in Italy

ENRICO SCANDURRA

# The Maritime Republics:
# Medieval and Renaissance ships in Italy

## The Historical Background

At the beginning of the fifth century, the Roman Empire was foundering. The split between Rome and Constantinople was a *fait accompli*. And now, in 401, the first attacks launched by fierce tribes from the northern and eastern reaches of Europe heralded the twilight of the Empire in the West. Less than a decade later, in 410, a powerful army led by Alaric, King of the Goths, swooped down from the Alps and entered Rome. The Eternal City was sacked. Organized resistance was, for all practical purposes, at an end.

The destruction of the Western Roman Empire signalled the end of a refined civilization, with highly developed arts and sciences. More important for our history of seafaring, it also marked the loss of all that the Romans had learnt in the field of naval construction and navigation during the centuries they had ruled the Mediterranean.

Nevertheless, a new maritime tradition would eventually arise among the Italian people who managed to escape the carnage of these and later invasions. Many of them sought safety in the lagoon islets off the Venetian littoral, hoping to preserve their Roman values, their freedom and independence. By so doing, they placed themselves beyond the reach of the invader who lacked not only ships but knowledge of the sea. It was from these early refugee settlements that Venice was to grow. Other fugitives found safety in coastal places, such as Amalfi and Genoa, protected from the interior by mountains.

In the course of time, the integration of refugees and the indigenous populations – whose origins were purely maritime – resulted in the formation of city states which soon built up a flourishing trade with powers oversea. For the geographical setting provided a special incentive for such activity, the open sea being the only route unimperilled by the barbarians.

Other factors contributed to the growth of maritime commerce in these new republics. From the beginning, they were careful to maintain the closest relations with the last legitimate representatives of the Roman Empire – the Byzantine emperors of distant Constantinople. In later centuries, they were no less assiduous in cultivating close ties with Islam, which, after rapidly establishing its dominion along the entire North African coast-line and throughout Spain, was to gain undisputed mastery over the whole Mediterranean.

Also important to the development of the Maritime Republics were the Crusades, whose Christian princes turned again and again to Italian ships for transport to the Holy Land. The Republics, for their part, took an active role in the expeditions from the end of the eleventh century, thereby advancing their own power and prestige.

During the ensuing centuries, their merchant fleets played a major role in furthering the lucrative commerce between East and West, thus enabling the Maritime Republics to expand their sea-power by taking advantage of ports throughout the Mediterranean. But in the end, their increasing wealth and power led to internecine strife; one republic would get the upper hand and temporarily eclipse its neighbours, and so encompass their downfall.

Such was the case when the Republic of Amalfi was sacked by the Pisan fleet in 1135. In turn, the Republic of Pisa was defeated by Genoa in the decisive naval battle in the Meloria in 1284. And such was to be the end of Genoa, too, eclipsed both militarily and commercially by the greatest of the Maritime Republics – Venice.

Today, in memory of the glory of the Italian Maritime Republics, the flag of the Italian Navy bears in the centre of the national tricolour a coat of arms made up of four others: those of Amalfi (white cross on an azure ground), of Pisa (white cross on a red ground), of Genoa (red cross on a white ground), and of Venice (the Golden Lion on a white ground).

## Warships

In the Middle Ages, warships were called 'long' or 'slender' to distinguish them from the 'round' vessels used solely for commerce, and to define their shape and essentially military function more clearly. At that time a warship, propelled by oars, had to be fast, manoeuvrable in battle, and therefore light in design.

22, 23

*The galley*. As an answer to these requirements the Italian Maritime Republics introduced a new type of ship, the galley, at the end of the ninth century. With oars as its main means of propulsion, the galley was a natural product of the Mediterranean, where uncertain winds did not favour vessels relying solely on sail. It was unrivalled as a warship and became the basic unit for every Mediterranean fleet; from it were derived the other long and slender ships which formed the main body and strike-force of all medieval navies. It retained its role for well over six centuries, until the great voyages of exploration finally established sail as the major means of naval propulsion.

The galley might be considered the last derivative of the Roman Liburnian, the speedy and manoeuvrable ship which had its beginnings as a pirate raider (chapter 3, p. 67). But it was also influenced in its final form by another ship which had appeared in the intervening years – the Byzantine dromon (chapter 6, p. 134). By the ninth century this was most probably between 130 and 165 feet in length, and was propelled by two tiers of oars; we do not know what types of sails it carried, but there is good evidence that in the following century dromons were lateen-rigged, and perhaps the ninth-century versions were as well. There was also a Byzantine galley, but this was only a small scouting vessel.

The new galley surpassed the dromon, just as the Maritime Republics' navies were to eclipse the Byzantine navy long before the fall of Constantinople in 1543. By the thirteenth century the Italian galleys which protected merchant fleets of 'round' sailing ships on their journeys to the East and back, had developed into something quite different. Still slender, they differed from the earlier ships largely in the arrangement of their oars.

The rowers sat in one tier, but two or three (and later up to five) oars were pulled from a single bench. To make this possible, the benches, from twenty to thirty on each side of the ship, were set at an angle oblique to the keel so that each could accommodate three oarsmen

*1  Drawing of a twelfth-century galley with two tiers of oars, based on a contemporary manuscript*

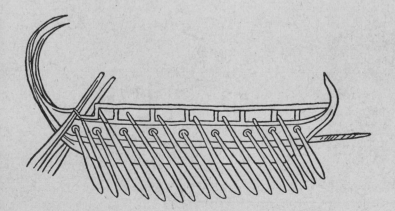

rowing independently with separate oars. The oars were, correspondingly, bunched in groups of two or three, with the tholes on which they pivoted grouped close together. This arrangement, like the galley itself, was called *a terzaruolo*.

We know the dimensions of some thirteenth-century galleys from a document, dated February 17, 1275, with which Charles I of Anjou ordered the construction of a number of such vessels of Provençal type: they were to have a keel 28.20 metres long, and an over-all length of 39.50 metres; a beam of 3.70 metres; and a depth of 2.08 metres. There were to be 108 oars ranging from 6.85 to 7.90 metres long. The foremast was to be 11 metres high, with a circumference of 0.79 metres, and the mainmast 18 metres high with a circumference of 0.79 metres; their respective lateen-yards were to measure 26.80 and 17 metres in length. Thirteenth-century Genoese galleys were somewhat smaller than those built in Venice, but by the beginning of the fourteenth century, according to the Genoa City Records, they were about the same size except for a slightly wider beam. Venetian galleys of the fifteenth and sixteenth centuries remained about the same length, but they grew broader.

Although the galley naturally underwent changes, particularly after the appearance of fire-arms, it retained its essential characteristics, which are especially well documented after the fourteenth century. In order to provide the rowers with oars sufficiently long to increase the ship's power, it was necessary to set the rowlocks away from the hull. This brought back the *posticcio* (*apostis*), or outrigger, of Classical Greek times (chapter 2, p. 44). The oars, instead of pivoting on the gunwale or in oar ports piercing the hull, were now tied to tholes on the outrigger. This outrigger consisted of a large wooden frame which went round the entire hull and projected beyond the sides of the vessel, itself often 130 to 165 feet long and 18 to 23 feet broad, by more than 5 feet. It was particularly strong, since it was subjected to the greatest stress and strain both during normal navigation and in battle; not only did it carry the weight of the oars and resist the full impact of the enemy's ramming, but it also had to sustain two gangways on which combatants fought, steel against steel. The shorter sides of the outrigger frame, the yokes, were about 33 feet in length, and the longer sides, or *correnti*, were about 130 feet long; the *correnti* were supported by nearly forty wooden brackets fastened to the hull.

Along the upper part of the outrigger, at intervals where the oars permitted, ran a parapet designed to protect both soldiers and oarsmen. Although this was reinforced with large, thick planks which came up to the soldiers' chests, it retained the name of *impavesate*, from the time when it was formed by the *pavesi*, or shields, of the warriors.

Running from bow to stern, about $3\frac{1}{4}$ feet above deck level, was the main gangway which interrupted only at the point where the mast was stepped. Its upper planking, about 6½ feet wide, was either removable or hinged, providing access to a long coffer-shaped locker beneath; here were stored such things as the spare mast and other cumbersome gear, including tarpaulins used for covering the oarsmen.

The bow yoke was the foundation for a covered platform in the forepart of the galley called the *rembata*, similar to a 'castle' and divided into two sections. Here the militia could be drawn up with a certain degree of protection before boarding an enemy ship, or for defence against attackers. The *rembata* also housed the galley's principal ballistic weapon which, before the general acceptance of fire-arms, was usually a mangonel, a mechanical contraption capable of hurling huge stones and other projectiles; the mangonel was fixed to the deck, so that the only way of aiming it was to steer the galley in the right direction. Other weapons of this kind were the *litoboli* (literally, 'shore-busters'), catapults, ballistae, and scorpions (all of which could hurl not only rocks but also inflammable mixtures enclosed in clay containers), javelins tipped with fire, and many more devices. As a protection against the terrifyingly inflammable mixture known as 'Greek Fire', ships were covered with raw hides, woollen fibres (perhaps dipped in vinegar), or iron hurdles.

To the fore of the *rembata* was the ram, which came to serve as a bowsprit or as a boarding deck when the use of artillery led to an abandonment of crash tactics.

At the stern, above the officers' quarters and the Council Chamber, was wont to flutter a luxurious awning bearing coats of arms and allegorical or decorative emblems.

The rowers' quarters took up the centre of the galley from the quarter-deck to the *rembata*, except for a gap left on the starboard side for the crew's kitchen, and another on the port side for the ship's boat. Below deck the galley was divided into six compartments, including pantries, storage lockers, and a room for the sick and wounded.

Some of the earlier galleys had only one mast, stepped at a point a third of the way down the gangway from the bow; there was usually a top for the crossbowmen (and later arquebusiers), which was also used by the

look-out when the ship was under way. The lateen-yard, made of two pieces of wood and about twice as long as the mast itself, was especially strong since it served also as a gangway in assaults on castle walls. It was nearly always trimmed with a triangular sail called *alla trina* (to distinguish it from the square sail called *alla quadra*), a term corrupted into *vela latina* or 'lateen', our current term. Depending on the force of the wind, different sizes of sail were hoisted; these included the *lupo*, a black sail used for camouflage at night or for mourning.

Other galleys had two masts: a mainmast stepped amidships and a foremast in the bow. Again, the size of sails used depended on the weather, but they included small square sails placed above the lateen sails in fine weather for sailing before the wind. Occasionally a small mizzenmast was placed in the farther end of the stern, but it was not used often because of lack of space.

Sails were used only on voyages from one port to another when the wind was favourable. When it was not, or when the galley was engaged in combat, the ship relied on its rowing-power. Even then, not all the oars were used at the same time; this happened only during parades or when the galley had to accomplish an urgent mission in a calm sea. Generally, the oarsmen rowed in shifts, a third of the full complement at a time.

In early times the galley, like every other Mediterranean ship, was steered by means of two large-bladed oars, one on either side of the stern. It was not until the end of the thirteenth century, after Marco Polo had seen it in China and made it known in the West, and after northern cogs had introduced it through the Straits of Gibraltar, that the rudder, as we know it today, became generally adopted.

The galley was usually equipped with four anchors: two at the bow, one near the ship's boat, and another by the crew's kitchen.

By the seventeenth century, Mediterranean fleets used galleys with an over-all length of 180 feet, a beam of 20¼ feet, and a stanchion of 7½ feet. The oars reached a maximum length of 40 feet, with five rowers for each; for by now the *a terzaruolo* system had given way to that known as *a scaloccio*, with only one oar but several men to each bench.

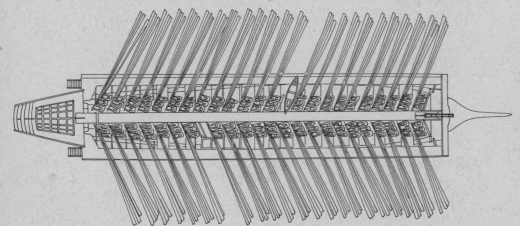

2 *Exact details of galleys rowed 'a terzaruolo' are not certain, but the late nineteenth-century reconstruction of a Venetian galley by Admiral Luigi Fincati is accepted as being essentially correct. The rowers pull individual oars, grouped in threes, which pivot against tholes set in the outrigger ('posticcio'). Benches set obliquely to the keel allow the men to sit side by side without interfering with one another as they row*

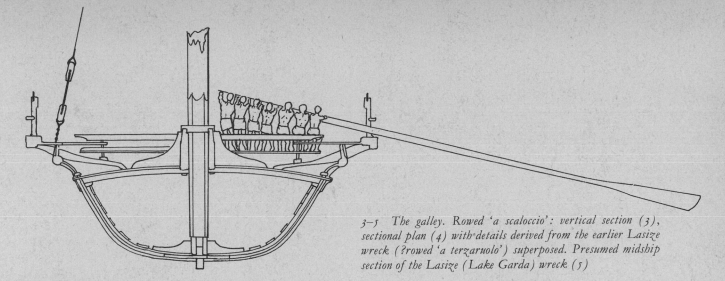

*3–5  The galley. Rowed 'a scaloccio': vertical section (3), sectional plan (4) with details derived from the earlier Lasize wreck (?rowed 'a terzaruolo') superposed. Presumed midship section of the Lasize (Lake Garda) wreck (5)*

## The Galley in Lake Garda

10–18  The only known extant Venetian galley was discovered recently at the bottom of Lake Garda by divers of the Malcesine Castle Museum working under my direction.

The ship was involved in an historical event of some importance, being one of a fleet of galleys transported from Venice to Lake Garda during the war waged between the Republic of Venice and the Duchy of Milan for possession of the lake and surrounding land. Venice had failed to furnish the lake with a strong fleet when she had had the chance, and now the southern route, up the Rivers Po and Minico, was blocked by the Milanese who were besieging the city of Brescia.

Sorbolo Candioto, a Greek seaman with many years in the service of the Republic, thereupon put forward a fantastic proposal: he offered to transport an entire fleet over land to the lake, via the mountains to the north. At first the Venetian Senate considered the proposition absurd, but finally they accepted the fact that they had no other choice. Sorbolo was given command of a fleet which, according to varying accounts, probably comprised two galleys, four *fuste* (small galleys), 25 *copani* (skiffs), and numerous other small boats (some historians hold that there were six outright galleys).

The incredible journey which followed began in mid-winter – January, 1439. The fleet moved up the River Adige to Verona, where equipment and men – both mariners and carpenters – were assembled, along with 2,000 oxen for towing the vessels. Using various documents as a guide, I have traced the route of this astonishing but little-known feat, only to marvel at the superhuman efforts required to overcome the obstacles encountered: the 'S' curve at the end of the Gorge of Cerano, where only an ingenious combination of oars, oxen and sails was able to move the ships against the current; the point near the village of Marco where a landslide had blocked the gorge, forcing the fleet over land; the bed of the little Rio di Cameras which was filled with earth and stones and then covered with logs as a road over which the fleet could be slid; and, finally, the pass 1,050 feet above sea level from which the ships were lowered down 35° slopes with winches and cables to Torbole, on the edge of the lake, some 800 feet below.

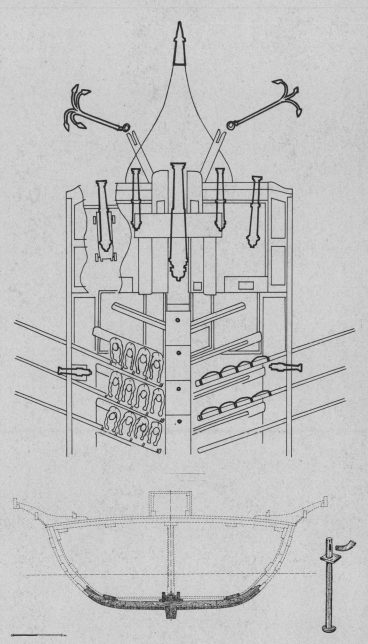

The Venetian fleet managed to afford Brescia some relief, but soon suffered a severe reverse at the hands of Milan's more powerful naval force already established on the lake. Only cartloads of timber, rushed over the mountains for the construction of still more ships at Torbole, enabled the Venetians to turn the tide of battle, liberate Brescia, and recover the contested territory. The victorious fleet was dismantled and the ships placed in the arsenal at Lazise, on the eastern shore of the lake.

At the beginning of the sixteenth century Venice faced a new threat. The major powers of Europe, united in the League of Cambrai, launched a violent attack against the Republic. The remnants of the Garda fleet, one large and two small galleys, were immediately prepared and placed under the command of Zaccaria Loredani. But this time events proved too much for the Venetians. Loredani was forced to scuttle his little fleet. In June, 1509, he sailed out of Lazise and ordered the galley, heavily weighted with stones, to be set on fire, and one of the two *fuste* to be sunk. The other *fusta*, or small galley, carried the captain to the near-by port of Garda whence, with his men, he rode to the safety of Verona.

In 1962 I began a search for the remains of these ships at the request of Professor Francesco Zorzi, former director of the Museo di Storia Naturale di Verona. Three years earlier we had collaborated on the study of a Turkish galley sunk off the Tremiti Islands in 1575, but there only bronze cannon and other metal finds were preserved; now, under the mud of a freshwater lake, we hoped to find an actual ship.

Exploratory dives, for which we had to rely on the hearsay of local fishermen, produced only negative results. Discouraged but determined, we began a search through the libraries of Verona, Venice and even some of the lakeside villages, and this was to prove more fruitful. For we discovered reference points for the locations of the two wrecks, recorded towards the end of the seventeenth century by one Francesco Fontana, chemist and natural scientist of Lazise: the galley was said to lie at a depth of 56 feet where two sightings intersect. It was most difficult to reconstruct Fontana's vectors, for the houses and other points along which he took his sightings had been largely lost in the course of time, but finally I was able to triangulate the positions of the galley and the *fusta* on an old map of the area.

When at last we discovered the disjointed pieces of a wreck, their depth proved to be 88½ feet and not 56 as stated by Fontana; only after the removal of masses of mud with a plastic suction tube were we sure that they did not belong to a more modern ship. The work was especially difficult in the murky water because the huge stones with which the Venetians had loaded the galley to ensure its sinking weighed more than 200 pounds a piece. But after two summers we had removed the stones and dug an enormous hole, more than 120 feet long by 36 feet wide, and from 3 feet to 5 feet deep. Wood and iron, as we had expected, were found in an excellent state of preservation.

By the summer of 1965 we were in a position to clean the wooden remains gently with water from a garden hose and make a complete photo montage to reveal the ship as we could never have seen it on the lake bed. The hull was nearly 100 feet long, indicating that the overall length of the ship was about 130 feet. Planking was $1\frac{1}{8}$ in. thick, the frames $3\frac{1}{2}$ in. deep and $2\frac{3}{4}$ in. wide (spaced approximately 10 in. apart), and the keelson $4\frac{3}{4}$ in. wide and $3\frac{7}{8}$ in. thick; ceiling planks and the mast step were still in place. We are still hoping to recover the entire hull and find its complete armament, but already the authenticity of the galley has been proven by the discovery of its cathead for the slipping of the anchor, four typical iron fastenings for the sail, and three typical anchors.

*Smaller warships.* Though remaining the same in essentials during its absolute supremacy in the Mediterranean, the typical war-galley went through a series of lesser variations in design. It was used mainly to effect the rapid transport of men or messages, for reconnaissance, or for coastal defence. The different versions included the *panfilo*, a tenth-century derivative of the dromon which in later centuries was transformed into a one-decked merchantman with its oars, each pulled by two rowers, in one tier; the *galeotta*, or galliot, a small galley with 16 to 20 oars, each rowed by a single man, on either side of the hull, and one or two lateen sails; the even smaller and faster *bergantino* or *brigantino* (brigantine), a fast, undecked ship widely used in the fourteenth century, but gradually increasing in size and later used even in the Atlantic on voyages of exploration; the *saettia*, or 'arrow', with long oars and great speed; the *fusta*, an undecked ship with a *posticcio*, very similar to the galley but smaller, more slender, and faster; and the *baleniero*, or whaler, a three-masted ship with seventy oars, adopted and modified by the Venetians, Genoese, and Catalans from a Basque prototype for trade, transport and war.

The *fregata*, or frigate, was the galley's service-boat from the thirteenth to the sixteenth century. Rowed by eight to ten men, and having one lateen sail, it was usually towed by the galleys' flagship. Only at the beginning of the sixteenth century did it become a sailing ship used for exploration.

The *feluca* (felucca) was at first nothing but a large, decked service-boat which the galleys took with them for minor tasks such as maintaining contact with land or between the galleys themselves at sea; it had six or ten oars, a single lateen sail and a bowsprit. Soon, however, it became a small coasting vessel, with deck and up to three lateen sails.

The *tarida* must also be mentioned among the slender ships used by medieval oar-propelled fleets, although it made far greater use of sail than of oars. Of Byzantine origin, it was used by the Genoese and Venetians mostly as a military transport, but on rare occasions it saw duty as a warship.

15

16, 17

6  *A great galley of the sixteenth century. Illustration from a contemporary manuscript*

**The 'galea bastarda'.** The galley also inspired a number of ships much bigger than itself. The so-called 'galea bastarda' was a slightly larger variation of the normal galley, having a more spacious stern and longer hull. Generally, it was the flagship of a fleet commander.

**The great galley.** From the fourteenth century, Venice and Genoa made great use of galleys designed and built specifically for trade, and carrying little or no armament except where there was risk of pirates. Although larger and broader (with a beam-to-length ratio of 1:6 rather than 1:8) than the fighting galleys, they were still faster than the 'round' sailing ships – and they were more reliable. Until the first half of the sixteenth century these vessels were common, especially for carrying passengers (often pilgrims to the Holy Land) and valuable cargoes; the heavier and cheaper commodities went by the slower sailing ships which were dependent on the winds.

Unlike the war-galley, the great galley could make better headway under sail than when powered by oars,

which were reduced in number to create greater cargo-space. As essentially a sailing vessel, it underwent numerous changes during experiments to find a rig best suited to it. Around 1400 it seems to have had two masts, the foremast being larger than the mainmast; in the middle of the fifteenth century, a still smaller mizzen-mast, also lateen-rigged, was added; but by 1480, the mainmast had become the larger – as we know from descriptions of pilgrims – just as in the contemporaneous 'round' sailing ships.

**The galliass.** The sixteenth-century *galeazza*, or galliass, was the last in a long line of descendants from the rowed warships of antiquity – a final attempt to give the old galley added strength in order that it might still oppose the growing supremacy of the sailing ship. It was, simply, the best response to the nautical revolution which followed the advent of fire-arms.

In fact, the galliass was nothing more than a large galley, with certain improvements and better armament: the oarsmen rowed beneath a deck on which missile-launching weapons and cannon could be manoeuvred with ease. The first galliasses carried three masts for lateen sails and a total of over 400 men, besides a formidable array of artillery. The men rowed *a scaloccio*, that is several men to an oar; the benches were now at right angles to the keel, and the oars no longer bunched in groups of two or three.

So much importance was attached to the galliass that only a member of one of the great patrician families could command one. The ship was given the name of its commander's House: *Foscarina*, *Contarina*, *Malipiero*, etc. Nor was that all: the commander of a galliass, on taking command of his ship, had to swear that he would fight single-handed, if necessary, as many as five galleys.

Pietro Martire d'Anghirera, who travelled on a galliass at the beginning of the sixteenth century, wrote that on board there were 150 oarsmen seated at 25 banks on each side of the ship. He goes on to say that there were 50 sailors assigned to the handling of the sails, besides 12 special seamen who not only climbed up the masts

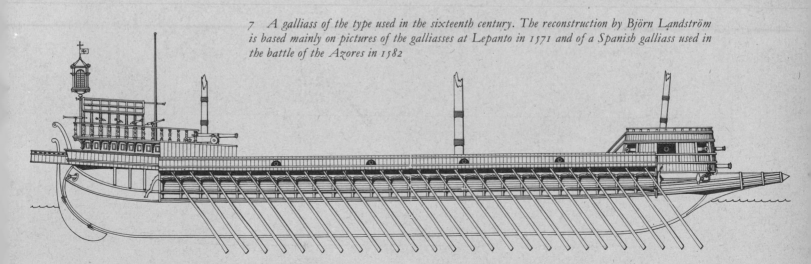

7  *A galliass of the type used in the sixteenth century. The reconstruction by Björn Landström is based mainly on pictures of the galliasses at Lepanto in 1571 and of a Spanish galliass used in the battle of the Azores in 1582*

and along the lateen yards to take in sail when necessary, but were also in charge of the rudder. Besides these, there were the bombardiers, soldiers and skilled hands.

In 1530, a decree of the Venetian Senate established that every galliass must have a length of 47 metres, a beam of 8 metres and a stanchion of 3.20 metres. It had a crew of 700 men: 1 master, 2 pilots, 4 subalterns, 1 boatswain, 1 boatswain's mate, 1 chaplain, 62 helmsmen and sailors, 3 second mates, 7 workmen, 268 oarsmen, 4 officers of the militia, 254 soldiers and 1 bombardier.

Six galliasses fought with distinction on the Christian side at the Battle of Lepanto, when the combined fleets of Spain, Venice and the Papal States met and defeated the Ottoman Turkish fleet off Greece in 1571. This fierce contest between 400 or more ships – 'The greatest occa-sion that past or present ages have seen or that future ones can hope to see,' according to Cervantes, who lost an arm there – was the last major encounter between fleets of oared warships. No longer would most of the fighting be hand-to-hand between boarding parties. Even the galliass with artillery was no match for the high, heavily armed sailing ship of the day, which could keep lower, oared ships at a distance.

Nevertheless, in 1588, galleys and galliasses formed part of the Spanish Armada; because of their manoeu-vrability they were still valued as auxiliary vessels. Eighteenth-century engravings by John Pine, copied from tapestries woven by Francis Spiernig about 1589, show the galliasses as large three-masted ships with 14 to 18 oars on either side. One such was the *Girona*.

*8    The Christian and Turkish fleets drawn up for battle near Lepanto on October 7, 1571. Their six galliasses contributed largely to the victory of the Christians*

*The 'Girona'.* We do not have the remains of any galliass built by the Maritime Republics, but Robert Stenuit has discovered the wreck of the *Girona* which was built in Naples, then under Spanish rule. She had sailed from Lisbon with 121 officers and men, and 244 oarsmen (161 convicts, 15 slaves and 63 volunteers). Armament comprised 50 artillery pieces with over 8,000 cannon balls of iron and stone, and provisions consisted of 750 pieces of hard tack, 100 casks of wine, 62.5 cwt. of lard, as much cheese, 60 casks of tunny fish and 40 of sardines, 15 cwt. of rice, dried beans and pulse, raisins, oil and vinegar, sugar, salt, and semolina. By the time she broke up on Lacada Point, near the Giant's Causeway in Northern Ireland, however, the *Girona* seems to have jettisoned most of her guns in order to take on board hundreds of crewmen from five other Armada ships which had already sunk along the Irish coast.

Relying more on local tradition than the vague and sometimes deliberately misleading Spanish and English documents which he had consulted, Stenuit located the remains of the *Girona* between 20 and 33 feet deep in 1967. Of the hull, which had probably been about 150 feet long and 23 feet broad, nothing was preserved, but Stenuit's team found part of its lead sheathing and copper nails – showing continuation of a practice going back to the earliest known sea-going vessel – and the only two surviving Spanish cannon from the Armada.

More important, perhaps, the objects mapped and raised in 1968 and 1969 give a vivid picture of life on board a sixteenth-century galliass: 2 astrolabes, 5 dividers, and 3 sounding-leads for navigation; 3 inkpots (?), 36 candlesticks and a candle snuffer of silver; dozens of silver forks, spoons, plates, bowls and silver bottles; tin and brass wares; cooking vessels of copper and terracotta; hundreds of gold, silver and copper coins, as well as seals, medals, buckles, and other objects in a variety of materials. Some of the numerous pieces of jewellery have been assigned by Stenuit to individual owners, including a cross which belonged to the master of the *Girona*, Captain Fabricio Spinola.

## 'Round' or Merchant Ships

Besides the great fleets of sleek galleys, there were always fleets of slower, tubby ships, propelled almost exclusively by sail. Carrying in their spacious holds bulkier and cheaper cargoes than did the faster and more reliable merchant galleys, these ships were ultimately derived from the round Roman *oneraria*, through the various types of Byzantine merchantmen from which they had acquired up to three lateen-rigged masts; there were usually two masts, with the foremast the taller. At some time after the seventh century (see chapter 6, pp. 143–4) they had become carvel-built, without mortise-and-tenon joints. They were steered, in the ancient Mediterranean fashion, by one or two great oars mounted near the stern. And, according to a Venetian Maritime Statute of 1255, they carried from 7 to 20 anchors, depending on their capacity.

There were many variations of 'round' ships, most of whose details are lost to us today. Among the more noteworthy was the *usciere*, or 'usher', one of a number of types of transport derived from the *hippago romani*, or Roman horse-carrier. Its name was based on the two openings, enabling horses to be loaded and unloaded at the stern, which was made up of three keel-posts. Such ships usually had two decks and were able to carry up to 100 horses, but for the most part only one deck was put to this use, the other serving to transport carriages and engines of war. Often the *usciere* was used to land infantry for assaults on Saracen coastal fortresses.

During the Ninth Crusade, Louis IX of France ordered a powerful navy from the arsenals of Venice and Genoa; included in the order of 1268 were some 120 *uscieri*,

9 *Plan, longitudinal section and midship section of an 'usciere' (horse carrier). Modern reconstruction drawing*

whose measurements were to be: over-all length 25.76 metres and keel-length 17.37, beam 6.10 metres, and height of sides 6.25 metres for the Venetian ships, the Genoese being slightly smaller. They were to have two masts for lateen sails, two complete decks, one spacious forecastle and an equally spacious quarter-deck, both built in such a way as to provide ample space for the cabins of the officers and crew.

*The cog in the Mediterranean.* At least as early as 1304, when Giovanni Villani recorded their appearance from Bayonne, northern cogs had entered the Mediterranean (see chapter 8, p. 190); even earlier appearances of northern ships, probably including cogs, date back to the twelfth century. Clinker-built, and with a stern rudder and prominent fore- and after-castles, the cog, with its single square sail, offered ease of handling and thus required a smaller crew than a lateen-rigged ship of the same size, whose yards were sometimes longer than the ship itself.

From this meeting of seamen from north and south, and from their exchange of ideas and experiences, came a cog which was carvel-built, but which had a stern rudder and a single square sail; its castles were no longer raised so high above the hull. Similar ships were subsequently seen, from the Baltic to the Mediterranean, throughout the fourteenth and fifteenth centuries. Some of those in the Mediterranean added a mizzenmast for a lateen sail.

6 *The carrack.* The square sail and the lateen sail each offered its own peculiar advantages, the latter being better for coasting but the former for heading across the open sea with a following wind. Both were combined in the middle of the fifteenth century on the 9 carrack, the largest merchant ship of the time. The exact origin of the carrack is unknown, but almost certainly it developed from the same combination of northern and southern influences that we have just seen at work on the cog. It had three, then four, and sometimes even five masts: the mainmast and the smaller foremast each carried a square sail, with a smaller topsail on the mainmast, but the mizzenmasts, whether one or two, were lateen-rigged. This arrangement made it easier to sail the ship into the wind or to tack. By using topsails, which meant setting a number of smaller sails in combination rather than one huge sail, the expanse of canvas could readily be varied, making the ship easier to handle.

The hull of the carrack bulged at its sides, providing 'tumble home' or 'fall home' (the inboard curve at the top of the hull), and there were castles, fore and aft. Its tonnage increased from around 400 tons at the beginning of the fifteenth century to more than 1,000 tons at the beginning of the sixteenth. We know of one carrack from this period that was 125 feet long with a keel-length of 85 feet and a beam of 34 feet.

Ships of this type could undertake long voyages even outside the Mediterranean, and that they could do so was largely owing to two revolutions in the art of navigating.

## Navigation

The only navigating instrument of the most ancient seafarers in the Mediterranean was the sounding-lead and line, used for measuring depth of water and for picking up sea-bottom samples in the lead's wax core. Otherwise, the sailor depended only on his knowledge of wind and stars; even Greek and Roman pilot books relied mainly on landmarks, and seem to have indicated direction, if at all, in terms of following winds.

A new era of navigation began in the Mediterranean during the thirteenth century, thanks largely to the advances made by the Maritime Republics.

Tradition assigns the invention of the marine compass to Amalfi, which implies that it was there a magnetized needle was first attached to a circular card, with directions marked on it, and then balanced on a pin or sharp pivot. This early compass did not bear the cardinal points of East, West, North and South, that we know today, but was divided by lines indicating the directions of eight winds, and then further divided until there were sixty-four points. Arab traders have sometimes been credited with bringing the concept of navigating by a needle from China, where its use at sea is documented for an even earlier period, but, according to E.G.R. Taylor, in her history of navigation, the earliest recorded mention of the needle by Arabs is in the middle of the thirteenth century, and then by an Italian name.

Sailors were now able to record detailed sailing directions in a systematic way, and in the mid-thirteenth century these were collected into a single book for the entire Mediterranean – *Lo Compasso da Navigare* – which is preserved for us in a manuscript copy of 1296. This *portulan*, as such books were called, gave bearings and distances, as well as detailed descriptions of local conditions; no longer was it simply a matter of a ship sailing before a following wind.

The next step was to make an accurate 'picture' of these directions, and our oldest known marine chart may have been made in Pisa, where it is now preserved. This *Carta Pisana*, dating from about 1275, shows compass bearings and scale distances. For the first time, with a ruler and a pair of dividers – backed by the necessary mathematical knowledge – a captain could plot his course with some accuracy. cf. 1

It was still necessary for the mariner to gauge the distance he was covering after estimating his speed. Another thirteenth-century invention, the sand-glass, aided in this calculation by allowing him to measure equal intervals of time.

## The Later History of Merchant Ships

From our brief summary of round ships in the fourteenth and fifteenth centuries, just before the discovery of America, one can see that mercantile sailing fleets were mainly composed of rather stocky ships, with ample sides and bulging prows. Making these ships even less suitable were the elaborate castles which weighed down both bow and stern, not to mention the overwhelming size of masts and planking.

All of these technical defects were caused by the ships being constructed on a purely artisan basis. Empiricism prevailed in the field of naval construction, which was based exclusively on the 'secrets' (consisting chiefly of measurements and models) that were jealously guarded and handed down from generation to generation of shipwrights. The skill of these men is undoubted, but they were unable to gather up the various parts of a naval structure into that perfect harmony which is only to be derived from the application of precise longitudinal and transverse force coefficients. This was to be an achievement of the seventeenth century, when science began to contribute something of its own to the art of shipbuilding.

Oceanic navigation had by now led to improvements in sail equipment, just as rapid progress in fire-arms had led to the emergence of new types of ships. These were being built to meet the requirements of the longest possible sea-voyages and the increase in commerce, as well as the ever more powerful armament that was being brought on board.

But the Maritime Republics failed to understand the importance of this technical revolution. Venice, in particular, virtually ignored it at first. The new ships which were to form the navies of the future were not to her liking, both because they departed from ancient tradition, and because the lagoons were not deep enough to receive them.

As a result, the power of the Venetian fleet began to wane, a gradual decline that had begun at the end of the fifteenth century – after the discovery of the Americas. Maritime trade routes turned towards the New World and navigation became predominantly oceanic. Little by little the Mediterranean turned into a closed lake, and its ports, which had once swarmed with activity, became more and more deserted. Meanwhile, the flourishing trade that was to be found on the Atlantic coasts was the source of a continual increase in wealth and power for other maritime peoples and nations.

It was among these other peoples and nations too that the second revolution in navigation would take place. Once outside the enclosed Mediterranean, caught

10    Many of the secrets of galley design, passed from father to son, are lost, but these instructions, dated 1544, by Pre Theodoro de Niccolo of the Venetian Arsenal are still extant

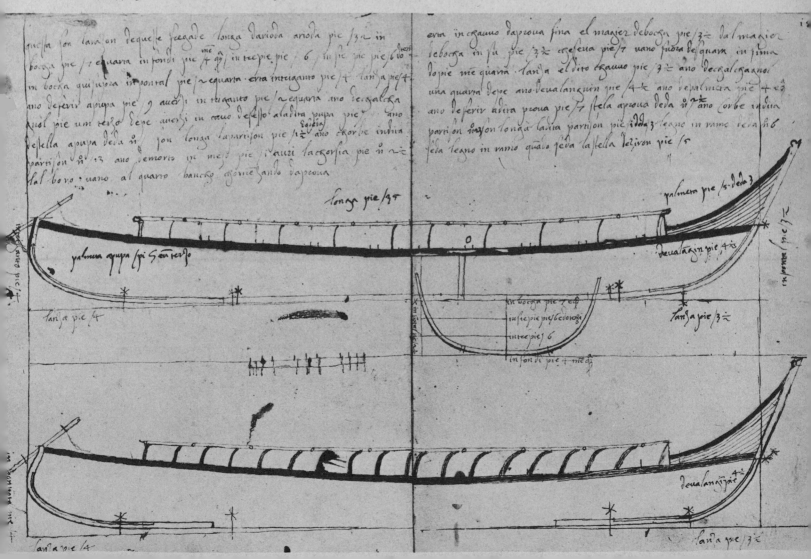

in tidal streams that could put them hundreds of miles out of their calculated positions, the sailors of the Atlantic could no longer rely simply on chart and compass. The voyages of exploration led to the development of instruments which could make precise astronomical observations, allowing the trained navigator to know his position even far out at sea.

*The caravel.* In the fifteenth century, the most noteworthy ship was the caravel, and while no longer in the forefront of shipping, the shipyards of Genoa and Venice built excellent caravels, primarily for commercial use. Perhaps of Catalan or Portuguese origin, the caravel is assured of a permanent place of honour in maritime history through the great voyages of Bartolomeo Diaz, Vasco da Gama and, above all, Christopher Columbus. Lighter and lower in the water than the full-rigged ships of the period, it was more streamlined and faster, and also more inclined to beat to windward because of its lateen sails.

Caravels were the first ships to be used on the great explorations since they were particularly well suited to this kind of task; relatively light, such a vessel could cut its way through the waves of the Atlantic, and it had such a shallow draught that it could carry out reconnaissance close to shore. It was faster than the carrack and, of course, than the heavier and more full-bellied *navis*; the latter, however, with its square sails was easier to handle.

*The galleon.* The most perfect product of Mediterranean shipbuilding remained the galley, but it was unsuited for ocean voyages. The real need was for a type of ship that would meet the requirements of the growing transatlantic trade; one that would combine the virtues of the slender oar-propelled galley with those of the round sail-driven vessel, that is, be both fast under sail and capable of carrying a large cargo. And so the galleon

was conceived. It was shorter than the galley, but less tubby and so faster than the carrack and *navis*. Standing very high on the water, its sides were almost straight from stern to prow. It had three or, more often, four masts: the mainmast, the foremast (with square sails on each, set on top of one another), and one or two mizzenmasts with lateen sails; the larger masts were all fitted with crow's-nests. It had two or three decks, and its tonnage varied greatly, though this was usually considerable. Its castles were high and sturdy, and it was armed with artillery, some of it heavy, often arranged in two tiers on the sides.

The galleon was obviously a very strong ship, and heavily protected – a ship to be used also in battle. But because of the crushing weight of its armament (there were 50 to 80 pieces) and castles, because of its massive construction and the lack of proportion between bottom and topside, and because of the excessive number of men on board, which could rise to 500 or even 800 soldiers and sailors, it was not very seaworthy in a storm, its rudder was capricious, and few ports of the time could accommodate it. Thus, at first, the *navis* and, especially, the caravel were preferred for trade and exploration.

Venice began to build galleons in the first half of the sixteenth century. Documents of that period list one as being 41.30 metres in length, with a keel-length of 30.50 metres, and a beam of 10 metres; that is, an approximate ratio of 4:3:1 (carracks usually had a ratio of 3:2:1).

By this time, however, the New World had been discovered, and this marked the beginning of the Italian navies' decline. Venice avoided the Atlantic, and Genoese fleets continued to operate only within the orbit of the Spanish Empire. Neither was to play a major role in the later development of warships which was to bring about the uncontested supremacy of sail.

---

1  The Roman Empire had finally foundered in the fifth century AD, the sack of Rome by the Goths under Alaric in 410 setting the seal on its demise. Yet the remnants of the Italian people who had succeeded in fleeing the barbarian invaders by taking refuge in coastal outposts such as Venice, Genoa, and Amalfi, not only survived but managed to cling on to the cultural values that ancient Rome had fostered. Centuries later these small communities grew into powerful and independent city states – the maritime republics of Italy. By the fifteenth century, the importance of Genoa as a sea power had already been eclipsed by that

of Venice, greatest of all the republics, but that each was still prestigious is indicated on this detail of a marine chart of 1435. The prominence displayed by Genoa can surely be attributed to the fact that the chart was made for a Genoese patron by Battista Beccaro, himself from Genoa.

The marine chart was evolved by the maritime republics, the earliest known being the *Carta Pisana* from the close of the thirteenth century. Such charts allowed the mariner – equipped with magnetic compass, ruler, and dividers – for the first time to plot his course with accuracy.

2

3

4

2–9 Changes in ship design wrought by the Italian maritime republics are clearly depicted in contemporary paintings. The round ship carrying St Ranier for the Holy Land (6) still exhibits, in the second half of the fourteenth century, the single lateen sail and pair of steering oars known from earlier times in the Mediterranean. By the fifteenth century, due largely to influences from the North, steering oars have been replaced by a single rudder, and the main sails of round ships are now square (2 and 8); removable 'bonnets' for shortening these sails were sometimes ripped away by storms (7). The bulging carrack (9), with characteristic bow and three or more masts, including one with a square headsail, was a further fifteenth-century development from the mixture of northern and Mediterranean traditions.

Warships, too, have changed. The outrigger of Classical times has returned to enable oarsmen to row more efficiently; galley oars are now grouped in pairs (4) or threes (2), allowing more than one rower to pull from a single bench. A slightly later galley, c. 1540, shows the oars still grouped, *a terzaruolo* (5), and the typical arrangement of captain's canopy at the stern, the ship's boat on the port side and the galley hatch on the starboard side.

Naples, not one of the independent republics, enjoyed a brief period of greatness in the mid-fifteenth century. In this fifteenth-century painting (3) a victorious fleet of galleys sails into her harbour past a number of carracks.

5

6

7

8

9

10

10 The transportation of a war flotilla from Venice to Lake Garda constitutes one of the more remarkable feats in naval history. It was accomplished by the Venetians in January 1439 in an attempt to break the blockade of Brescia by the Milanese. After proceeding up the River Adige as far as Verona, the first formidable obstacle was the Gorge of Cerano. In negotiating this S-curve with its powerful currents, a combination of oars, sail and 2,000 oxen was deployed. The climax of the operation entailed manhandling the galleys across mountains rising to 1,050 feet, then dropping 800 feet to Torbole. This fifteenth-century map gives some idea of the terrain.

15

15–18 Fortune did not at first favour Venice. Her fleet, which had been transported to Lake Garda with such effort, was defeated. Another fleet, however, was constructed of timber brought to the lake by wagons, and this was victorious. Finally, after alternating successes and defeats, the lake was given to Venice by the Treaty of Lodi in 1454; the fleet was dismantled and stored in the arsenal at Lazise. By the beginning of the sixteenth century, Venice faced a new enemy in the League of Cambrai, but only one large galley and two small galleys in the arsenal remained serviceable from the ships brought overland from Venice or constructed near by. Facing certain defeat in 1509, the commander filled the large galley with stones and set her afire in the lake, scuttled one of the small galleys less than a mile from the arsenal, and fled to safety in the town of Garda in the remaining small galley.

The remains of the large galley were located recently in the lake at a depth of 88 feet. This remarkable photomosaic (15) shows the remains of the burned hull, approximately 100 feet long, after most of the boulders used to sink her, and masses of mud, had been removed. Two anchors (16 and 17), and examples of the iron bolts which fastened each floor to the keel have been raised. Illustration 18 shows the starboard side of the hulk on the lake bed.

16

17

220

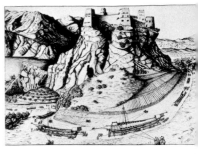

11–14 Reconstruction drawings of the journey: Passing through the Gorge of Cerano (11). The bed of the tributary Rio di Cameras, having first been filled in, is covered over with logs on which to slide the ships (12). In the pass above Lake Loppio huge windlasses and lines of oxen are used to haul the craft upwards (13). The galleys are lowered by means of winches and cables to Lake Garda far below (14).

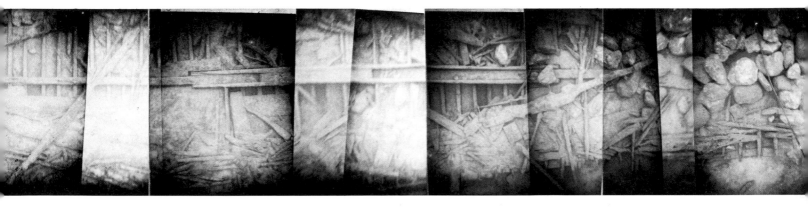

19  In the last great sea battle fought by oared ships, the combined forces of Venice, Spain and the Papal States crushed the Turkish fleet in the Gulf of Lepanto, off the Greek coast, in 1571. The Christian force of about 205 galleys and 6 galliasses faced a fleet of over 280 galleys and galliots under Ali Pasha, but it was reported that 30,000 Turks were killed while the Europeans' losses were 8,000. The importance of the galliasses to the allies' success has been emphasized by contemporary artists, such as the unknown Venetian who painted this scene now in the National Maritime Museum, Greenwich. The galliass was a heavily armed warship, her crew able to fire at the enemy from a great distance rather than having to rush directly into close or even hand-to-hand combat. Her rowers, up to seven men manning each long oar, sat under the protection of a thick deck which supported the heavy artillery.

20

20–21 No remains of a galliass built by the Italian maritime republics has yet come to light, although underwater surveys in the Gulf of Lepanto are planned. The wreck of a sixteenth-century galliass built in Naples was, however, located and excavated by Robert Stenuit: the *Girona* sailed with the Spanish Armada (cf. chapter 10, ills. 15, 16) but was lost in a storm off the coast of Northern Ireland. Nothing of her hull was preserved, but among the items recovered from the wreck site were two rare astrolabes for navigation, one shown at the moment of discovery (20). Another astrolabe (21), pulled from the sea years ago, is thought also to be from an Armada ship.

21

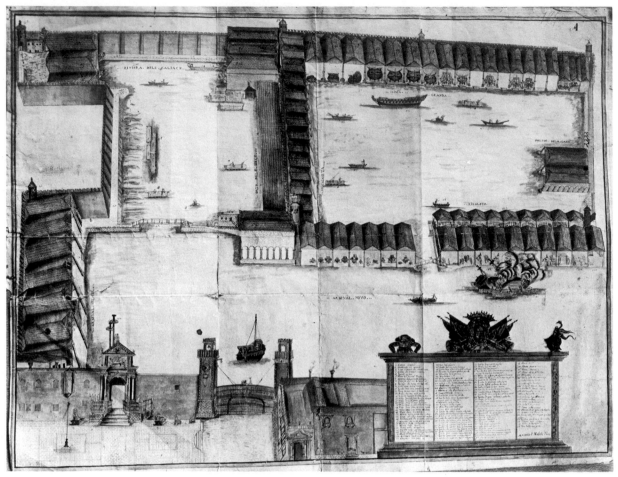

22 The Venetian Arsenal served mainly for the out-fitting of a war fleet; merchant ships were usually built in private shipyards. By the sixteenth century the Arsenal, seen here with its covered docks, had become perhaps the largest industrial complex in Europe.

23 Sawyers, carpenters, caulkers and labourers worked under a foreman shipwright to produce each vessel in the Arsenal. Forests of oak, larch and fir were managed by the Arsenal to insure adequate timber supplies. Rope and sails were also manufactured and stored here.

23

FV FATTO LANNO 1517 SOTTO MISIER ZACHARIA D'ANTONIO GASTALDO DE MARANGONI D'NAVE D'LARSENAL
FV RINOVATO D'LANNO 1753 SOTTO LA GASTALDIA DI FRANCESCO ZANOTTO GASTALDO E COMPAGNI

# 10

# The influence of
# British naval strategy on
# ship design: 1400–1850

ALEXANDER McKEE

# The influence of British naval strategy on ship design: 1400–1850

## The Changing Scene

The period under review may be divided into two main phases: Battleground Channel and Battleground the World. In the first phase only Channel cruise capabilities were required of warships. In the second phase a warship had to be theoretically capable of circumnavigating the globe. The second phase requirement did not just involve a re-design of existing types but introduced quite new problems of crew health, notably victualling, ventilation and protective clothing, and placed a premium upon navigational ability in a time when this was more of an art than a science, the requisite instruments and charts being mostly lacking.

There was also a sub-phase which may be described as Battleground Baltic, underlying both the main phases, just as there was a Mediterranean theatre of war, but both these seas are land-locked and the influence of sea power was mostly localized and even specialized.

These events were accidental only in that they were influenced by geography and affected by birth rates within national boundaries. Mostly, they were acts of will. Very often, they originated with pressure groups rather than the central government. And during the whole of the time under review, with the exception of the last ten years or so when the first efficient rail transport was being introduced into England, transport of both goods and armies by sea was cheaper and more convenient than their transport by land. In effect, the sea was a roadway which never wore out.

The accident of geography favoured England most of all. Her Channel coast (the 'Narrow Sea') lay athwart the route by which all trade must pass between the Mediterranean, France, the Low Countries and the Baltic. Later, when trade became world-wide, the British Isles were situated at the hub where most trade routes converged; and admirably placed to raid those which diverged farther south. This conferred upon a nation so situated actual power to intervene with effect upon the trade of others, as well as the ability to influence events by the threat of such intervention, quite apart from the obvious benefits to English sea trade.

But geography conferred upon the British Isles a further benefit which was so crucial that it affected events involving the entire land mass of continental Europe, even into our own times. The Channel was a moat which gave the English the advantage of having to fight only a one-front war – on the sea. Given a powerful navy, the smallest of armies would suffice for defence. This was not true of the great continental land powers, which were forced to duplicate their war effort. In order to contain or overrun their neighbours they had to raise an expensive professional army (later, a mass conscript army), while at the same time maintaining at least one fleet. When the army of the temporarily strongest power overthrew all its rivals and that power was master of the continent, it was still not master of Europe. England continued to hold out. So, in order to achieve final victory the need now was not for an overwhelmingly powerful land force, but for an overwhelmingly powerful sea force. And so far, no nation in Europe has managed to possess both at the same time.

In this way it was possible for England to exert a disproportionate influence on European and world affairs, even when the birth rate was against her, as for much of the period it was. In Napoleonic times there were eight million English to nearly 30 million French, while the divided German states were individually even weaker than England. In the wars of the twentieth century, there were 80 million Germans to 40 million British, the population of France also being about 40 million. These changes in the European population balance explain why, temporarily, this power or that has tended to dominate the continental land mass and so determined the objective in England's wars.

For clarity's sake, it will be most convenient to describe the evolution of the warship during the period under review primarily through the naval problems of a single power, England. That the ships of other countries are – with certain important exceptions – dealt with mainly by illustration and caption, does not imply that they were inferior. Indeed, except for the Tudor period, England lagged rather than led in ship design, first behind the Dutch and then behind the French. However, the taking of prizes ensured the flow of ideas from abroad, which were often copied, so that over a period the main classes of warship did not differ materially from one country to another although there were special cases. This scheme allows us to take advantage of the fact that we know more about the British ships: partly from the work of nautical archaeologists on several very early vessels; partly from the ample documentation after

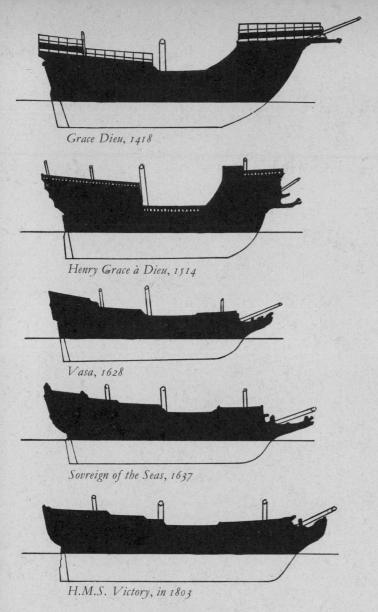

*Grace Dieu, 1418*

*Henry Grace à Dieu, 1514*

*Vasa, 1628*

*Sovreign of the Seas, 1637*

*H.M.S. Victory, in 1803*

*1   Development of the Capital Ship, according to Maj.-Gen. Michael Prynne, from the largely-conjectural 'Grace Dieu' to the well-known 'Victory'*

1700; and partly because of the preservation, afloat or in dry dock, of some actual British warships dating from about 1750 onwards. However, as a catalogue of purely constructional developments would be so specialized as to be almost meaningless, the emphasis will be on use – the purposes for which the ships were built, namely for offensive or defensive action against an enemy.

## Henry V (1410–22)

As the Hundred Years War was drawing to a close, England made her last attempt to dominate by land and by sea both shores of the 'Narrow Seas', a legacy of the Norman Conquest. Her population was fewer than four million, insufficient to provide a continuous line of defence or even to prevent the raiding fleets of the

French from capturing and burning towns on the English side. These were but feeble reprisals for the much greater amphibious operations launched by the English, of which the invasion of Normandy in 1415 was an example. Henry v embarked his army at Southampton on August 19 in a fleet of some 1,500 vessels, many of them hired from the Dutch. They transported to Le Havre a force said to have comprised 20,000 common soldiers, 24,000 of the incomparable English archers, and 6,000 men-at-arms, which on St Crispin's Day crushed a French army at Agincourt.

A year later, Henry, not yet master of the whole of Normandy, ordered the building at Southampton of a monster battleship designed to help maintain sea superiority on his lines of communication, and in 1419 had a similar, but slightly smaller, vessel laid down at Bayonne in France.

The Southampton ship was the *Grace Dieu* of 1,400 tons, launched in 1418. Although it has yet to be established what exactly a medieval 'tun' represented in modern terms, she was, it seems, the greatest ship to be built in England up till then. Her 'retinue' of two balingers, two boats, and three 'Cok-boats' was built at the same time. This shows that she was indeed an enormous vessel, for the tonnage of the two attendant balingers, the *Falconer* and the *Valentine*, was 100 and over. They may well have acted as tugs. Fitting-out seems not to have been completed in time for her to take part in the last great naval engagements of the war and by 1420 she was in reserve, moored up the River Hamble with only a maintenance crew of eight men and a quartermaster aboard. In 1434 she left her moorings 'in the Rode' for a berth above Bursledon, and there, on the night of January 6/7, 1439, she was struck by lightning and burnt out.

The accounts kept by Robert Berd, her Clerk of Works, mention four guns only and a mere 100 lb. of gunpowder. No doubt this was incomplete – for no more than 40 bows were issued to the ship on fitting out – and therefore we cannot know her detailed armament in terms of weapons. But there is no doubt that her main armament consisted of the equivalent of an infantry battalion, equipped in typically English fashion for a combined missile-and-shock fight. Aided by iron and stone missile-throwers stationed in the fighting tops, the task of the archers was to clear the enemy ship's decks; when their fire – so rapid, 'that it seemed as if it snowed', in the words of a French witness – had decimated and disorganized the opposing infantry, the armoured men-at-arms of the shock force would enter and capture the vessel. And as both firing and entering are facilitated by height, the distinctive structural feature of a warship was a great fighting platform forward, projecting well over the bows. Naturally, the larger the ship, the larger and higher the bow platform. The result was a specialized vessel looking somewhat like a seaborne giraffe, and bearing only a superficial resemblance to the very much smaller merchant ships hurriedly con-

*3*

*4*

*2, 3*

*1*

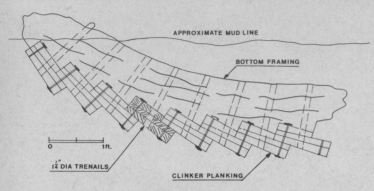

APPROXIMATE MUD LINE

BOTTOM FRAMING

0      1ft.

1¼ DIA TRENAILS

CLINKER PLANKING

*2   A section through the planking of the 'Grace Dieu', drawn by Maurice Young, which shows the unusual triple-skin clinker construction of the lower hull*

verted for war. Above all, the demands of war placed a premium upon size, which sufficiently explains the building of both the *Grace Dieu* and the Bayonne ship, as well as their uselessness for any other sort of enterprise.

That there already existed a doctrine for the employment of English sea-power is established by a contemporary history in verse, entitled *De Politia conservativa Maris*, in which it is stated that 'the true process of English Policy' is to 'Cherish Merchandise, keep the Admiralty; that we be Masters of the narrow Sea'. In short: complete control of the Channel and of Channel trade. The reason being that much of the trade of the then known world, especially that of India, Africa, and Europe, was in foreign hands.

> 'The *Genuois* [Genoese] came in sundry wises
> Into this Land with divers Merchandises,
> In great Caracks, arrayed without in lack
> With Cloth of Gold, Silk, and Pepper black . . .
> The great Gallies of *Venice* and *Florence*
> Be well laden with Things of Complacence,
> All Spicery and of Grocer's Ware:
> With sweet Wines, all of manner of Chaffare,
> Apes and Japes, and Marmusets tailed,
> Nifles and Trifles that little have availed. . . .'

These are tantalizing references, both to the carracks of Genoa and to the galleys of Venice and Florence, for the carrack and the galley (out of which probably developed the galleon) are basic ship types about which comparatively little is known (but see chapter 9). We are in fact much better informed about vessels of the preceding Viking era than we are about medieval ships, although an almost intact example of a specifically Northern type of the Middle Ages, the cog, was discovered during 1962 in the River Weser near Bremen and subsequently dated by dendrochronology to about 1400 (see chapter 8). Oddly enough, apart from having a rudder instead of a steering oar, this ship outwardly resembles a Roman merchantman in general arrange-

ment, although not in hull construction. It seems likely that the bulk of the invasion fleets of Henry v were composed of ships much like this, particularly when one takes into account the fact that it was common practice to requisition all merchant ships, English or foreign, which happened to be in English ports whenever an amphibious operation was contemplated.

It needs to be stressed that the evidence we have concerning the *Grace Dieu* is almost entirely a matter of accountancy; it tells us far more about dockyard costs than ship design. We know that she had at least two masts, a main and a 'mizen', and the general arrangement of towering bow platform and a lower 'summer castle' aft may be inferred from none-too-accurate representations, often on town seals, depicting medieval warships. This absence of any reliable information relating to ship design generally is not confined to the fifteenth century; as far as England is concerned, it applies to the six hundred years from 1066 – when the Norman invasion was carried out in what are clearly Viking craft, about which we now know a great deal, mainly from land evidence – until about 1650. By 1700 we are on firm ground, many shipbuilders' plans and official models, as well as accurate paintings and sketches, having come down to us. From about 1760 actual ships begin to be preserved; indeed, one of them is still in commission. From this time also we have a great many narratives to supplement official despatches, so that we know exactly what life was like at sea, in addition to a full understanding of the ships and of how they were used.

Unfortunately, the developments between 1650 and 1850 were not of a fundamental nature; all the major advances occurred within the 'gap', a period which has yielded virtually no clues. In 1100 the typical war vessel of Northern Europe is a Viking galley – a long, narrow, double-ended, clinker-built open boat, steered by an oar and powered by both sail and oar. Her armament consists solely of fighting men armed mostly with cutting and stabbing weapons for close combat. She is very short-ranged indeed, like all galleys when fully manned, because her shallow draft and pencil-like proportions of approximately 5:1 do not afford much storage space for water and food. Although a Viking 'longship' may exceed 80 feet in length and possess a single mast with square sail, she is still nothing more than a large boat.

By the turn of the sixteenth century the most powerful warship is a genuine ship, of four or five decks, with three masts, carrying as main armament as many as 100 heavy guns. Whereas the Viking craft were in effect light, racing 'shells', clinker-built with overlapping planks, the battleship of 1700 is an enormously strong construction, carvel-built, the planks butted edge to edge, with an inner and an outer skin, heavily reinforced both in the hull and in the decks.

How did this advance take place? What were the intervening stages? From existing evidence we can glimpse the process only dimly, which helps to explain the legend of the 'Bursledon ship' and the controversy which has surrounded it. The first published report appears to have been dated 1859, when it was stated in White's *Hampshire and Isle of Wight Directory*: 'Higher up the river are the timbers of an ancient vessel, finely caulked with moss. Its figurehead was a griffin. It was supposed to have been burnt by the Saxons.' In the 1870s an enthusiastic antiquarian named Crawshay is said to have used explosives in an 'excavation' which proved entirely abortive. In 1899 the Hampshire Field Club removed more timbers and put them on display in a Winchester Museum as relics of a Danish galley. In 1932 Mr G. S. Laird Clowes, Director of the Science Museum, London, examined the wreck and suggested that it might be that of a 900-ton merchant ship of about 1840–50. The defenders of the Danish galley hypothesis retorted that no such ship could have passed upstream later than the completion of Bursledon Bridge in 1800. In 1933 a group of nautical experts which included Dr R. C. Anderson, Mr F. C. Prideaux Naish and his son George (now of the National Maritime Museum) and a young officer of the Royal Engineers, Mr (now Major-General) Michael Prynne, inspected and roughly surveyed the hulk – which is difficult of access – and came to the conclusion that the remains were those of the *Grace Dieu*. In 1947 Mr C. F. Fox denied that the timbers showed any signs of burning and reaffirmed that the vessel was probably one of 'King Alfred's longships or Olaf's Dragons'. In 1952 the timbers, removed to Winchester Museum in 1899 as relics of a Danish galley of *c.* 1000, were dated by Mr A. W. G. Lowther, using the tree-ring method, as probably having been felled 'early in the fifteenth century'.

The wreck lies out in the stream, the bows touching the east side of the deep channel, so that it only exposes at low water of the very high spring tides which occur briefly in spring and autumn, and then not completely; and what is more, for a period not exceeding 60 minutes and usually just after first light or just before last light, with the deep mud discouraging an approach from the shore and the fast spring ebb making progress up-river difficult. This situation implies a large vessel with a draught of about 15 feet, at one time moored out to one side of the stream, although the proposition is not obvious from either land or water. From the air, however, it is perfectly clear. There lies the wreck, utterly unlike a Viking longship in outline, and with the artificial mud-bank which has shaped up around her clearly delineated. This mud-bank resulting from the obstruction to the channel caused by the sunken hull misled all the earlier investigators, without exception, as it did me in 1967. The hull appears to be that of a shallow-draft ship either mud-berthed or run aground on the mud, instead of a large vessel sunk at the side of the deep channel, which would be a normal mooring place. Two aerial surveys made in 1968, when interpreted with knowledge of the sculpturing effects of fast water, show this and, moreover, capture the lines of the stern which

are permanently submerged farther out in the stream; because of a bare 6 inches visibility, they presented an unclear picture even to an underwater survey party led by Mr Maurice Young, a Southampton shipwright, in late 1967.

All this, of course, fits the *Grace Dieu* as to size and tallics with the historical evidence, particularly when one considers that, *pace* Mr Fox, the hull timbers show clear signs of fire. Indeed, this has helped to preserve them, as charred timber will not deteriorate further, being like coal in this respect, almost a fossil. Further, when examined on the spot, the timbers are clearly those of a very large, heavy ship, at least 125 feet on the keel with a beam of perhaps 50 feet.

At the same time, although not a Viking galley, the ghost of the Vikings does indeed pervade the wreck in the River Hamble, and is directly responsible for the controversy. As Dr Anderson's party showed in 1933, the hull construction is most peculiar for a vessel of this size. In principle, it is clinker-built, that is, with planks overlapping, just as in an ordinary boat; although in this case the construction was triple, giving five thicknesses of plank at each overlap. It is as though Viking methods had been modified and developed to meet the special problems involved in building a very large hull; and this may well be the truth of the matter, while still allowing the possibility of some influence from Mediterranean carracks. Unfortunately, all that remains now is the bottom of the hull and, although there may be sundry informative wreckage scattered around and some perhaps even concentrated in an obvious 'eddy hole' downstream of the wreck, further excavation along modern lines may not tell us much more. As this wreck is the only archaeological evidence we have so far for warships of this period, the difficulties of the maritime historian become clear.

## Henry VII (1485–1509)

By the close of the reign of Henry V it was recognized that an aggressive military policy on the continent was unwise and that the aims of England could be achieved at less cost by merely holding the Calais bridgehead, backed by a sufficient fleet. This general policy of limited land war, enabling the resources of a small nation to be concentrated on the sea, was to be adopted by the English until the twentieth century, when it was finally and fatally altered.

A period of exhaustion followed the Hundred Years War and no large warships were built in England until the rearmament programme of 1486–7, which produced two mighty four-masters, the 800-ton *Sovereign*, and the 1,000-ton *Regent*. They were both carracks, with a high, overhanging forecastle developed from the old fighting platform and a lower 'summer castle' at the stern, principally for officers' accommodation. These structures had by now become more an integral part of the ship and less a piece of fancy carpentry. Although the later Elizabethan taunt of 'tottering cage-work' was

229

valid, that cage-work was now solid enough to take a large number of small guns. A few much heavier guns appear to have been put in the waist, on the upper deck, firing through what would now be the deck rails; but the hull itself was not pierced for guns, that revolutionary development being still in the future.

Even further away was the retractable topmast, a safety measure for use in bad weather – not to be introduced for another century. Nevertheless, improvements in masts and sail plan had been effected. The main- and foremast are now square-rigged, while the mizzen carries a lateen sail, and a spritsail could be set under the bowsprit. However, the stern is rounded, with lines not unlike those of the bow, and clinker building is still in vogue. No material evidence, in the form of an identified wreck, exists for this period.

## Henry VIII (1509-47)

The really great advance begins during the reign of Henry VIII. Whenever one researches into military and naval subjects, one is sure to come across his name as the man who started it all. From the building of Southsea Castle to the foundation of the Board of Ordnance, Henry's drive and vision is apparent.

In discussing the great warships built by Henry VIII we must first consider their armament, for this determined their shape. Furthermore, the use to which the weapons themselves were put had to satisfy current tactical doctrine, to which again ship design was required to conform. The dominant type of warship, the 'capital' ship, has from that time on been a sea-transportable emplacement for the major weapon or weapons-system of the day.

The *Grace Dieu* had relied for her striking-power on an infantry weapons-system in which archers (missiles) were integrated with men-at-arms (shock) emplaced as high as possible on a great fighting platform projecting beyond the bow. The striking-power of the *Regent* was embodied in a triple weapons-system, light guns as well as longbows and pikes, emplaced in a higher and more protected castle which had replaced the bare bow platform, and also in the stern castle. No doubt the guns were intended to shatter the castles of an enemy and expose his infantry to a rain of arrows. When numbers of really heavy guns began to be carried aboard ship, their task was not so much to sink the enemy as shatter his wooden defensive walls and shock the defenders, prior to an assault by boarding covered by a hail of arrows from the quick-firing archers.

When the *Mary Rose* was laid down at Portsmouth in 1509 she represented the latest techniques of land warfare as applied by Henry VIII to sea warfare. She was a warship designed to mount a weapons-system evolved around the medium-calibre siege artillery of the day, then the only effective form of artillery. The field artillery still lacked the highly mobile, quick-firing light gun demanded by battle tactics; the hand-gun, which developed from the cannon, was also a clumsy, slow-firing,

inefficient weapon. The 'trayne of artillerie' organized by Henry VIII was well named; in modern parlance, it was all 'tail', and the guns and their supply wagons might take up as much as 15 miles of road. Such a force could not be deployed in mobile, marching warfare because of the short range of the weapons, but, when added to an assault force of archers, men-at-arms and miners it was proving its worth in the static, 'set-piece' battle inevitable when the siege of a fortified town was undertaken. The heavy guns, firing on a small section of wall with much more effect than modern field artillery, would cause a 'breach', upon which the storm troops of the infantry would concentrate, with sections of archers giving covering fire. The defensive answer to the 'punch' of the heavy cannon was to mount a culverin, in effect an anti-cannon gun, which fired a small shot a long way and out-ranged the larger calibre siege pieces. And the answer to that was for the attackers to bring up culverin of their own to knock out the enemy's long-range, high-velocity guns.

It was this complicated, interlocking weapons-system which Henry VIII decided to try out at sea. As the ship capable of carrying it did not exist, such a vessel had to be designed, and the *Mary Rose* came into being; a four-masted carrack of 600 tons, this vessel was rebuilt to 700 tons in 1536, and rearmed. This experimental battleship was so successful that a similar ship, twice her size, was built in 1514. This was the 1,000-ton *Harry Grace à Dieu*, or *Great Harry*, and she was rebuilt in 1540. The dates of rebuilding are important, because it is the rebuilt ships which are depicted in the official Roll of the King's Ships produced by Anthony Anthony. We can see that they are both high-charged carracks with overhanging forecastles, four masts carrying a more advanced rig than their predecessors, square sterns, and a complex of artillery batteries rather than the uniform armament on flush decks with which we are more familiar from much later ships, such as the *Victory* of 1759. They are apparently carvel-built, the planks butted edge-to-edge, and, considering the weight and recoil-action of the artillery on board, must have been designed to be far stronger than their predecessors. For what we see quite clearly now are gun-ports cut in the actual hull of the vessel. The new theory of war involved more than just mounting a few heavy guns in the waist above the hull proper; indeed there is an absolute limit to the amount of weight which can be carried high up in a ship and even the introduction of gun-ports, although bringing the weight lower down, would fall far short of the more satisfactory arrangement in a merchant ship, where the cargo is in the hold. Once again, we find that the 'capital' ship is a specialized vessel, not just an armed merchantman.

True, the *Mary Rose* was lost in battle in 1545, but the cause was a capsize resulting from indifferent handling coupled with open gun-ports low down near the waterline and a failure to secure the guns prior to a turn to port. For posterity, the capsize was a fortunate occurrence, because the *Mary Rose* sank off Southsea Castle, Portsmouth (in full view of Henry VIII and the appalled wife of the Vice-Admiral aboard) at a place where the sea-bed sediments were so light as to engulf part of the hull at once and in a sea area where the 'biological horizon' was extremely favourable to the preservation of organic and other materials. Although the wreck's masts were visible above water, and guns to the salvage value of £100 were recovered, the embedding of the hull in mud and clay must have contributed materially to the failure of all early attempts to salvage her.

In 1836 the almost completely buried remains were discovered by the pioneer inventors of diving gear, John Deane and William Edwards, and in that year and also in 1840 they recovered many of her guns, as well as various artifacts and some timber. They were careful to record by means of scaled watercolour drawings the more important items, and therefore we have a fairly complete record of the salvaged artillery, and the state it was then in (the iron guns have greatly deteriorated since they were raised). The 'Anthony Roll' gives a gun-state for the *Mary Rose*; this not only shows that John Deane recovered less than a quarter of her listed armament, but tells us the precise extent of that armament, which might otherwise have been a matter for conjecture, as we are unfamiliar with many of the Tudor gun names.

The variety of the armament is its most interesting feature. Deane recovered four beautifully made brass guns: a culverin-bastard, a culverin, a demi-cannon, and a cannon royal, the latter firing an 8-inch iron shot. The heaviest piece of the four was the demi-cannon; it weighed three tons and fired a 6-inch iron shot. In 1545, these were the last word in artillery and would have been useful even in the early nineteenth century. The majority of the salvaged guns, however, were of an earlier and quite different type. They were breech-loading bombards, their wrought-iron barrels being constructed of hoops shrunk onto narrow staves, and set in a wooden bed which was secured at the rear end to the deck by means of a 'bitt', thus preventing recoil. The largest of these guns had a calibre of about 8 inches and was more than 13 feet from end to end. They fired stone shot which would splinter on impact to produce a shrapnel-like effect. Although weak compared to the brass pieces, the breech-loading guns had obvious advantages for ship-board use, in that they were fixed and did not have to be run out each time for firing; moreover, the use of spare gunpowder chambers would seem to allow a comparatively high rate of fire. There were also many smaller guns of this type; their purpose was to smash the enemy's fragile upperworks and so expose the soldiers within to the arrows of the English archers, some of whose longbows were recovered in 1840.

The battle of 1545, in which the *Mary Rose* was sunk, together with the naval engagement off Shoreham shortly after, demonstrated the limitations of the carrack in offence. Although easily defended and hard to take,

it was too slow and clumsy to obtain decisive results when confronted, as it usually was on both sides, with an enemy fleet containing a galley force. The carrack was at the mercy of the wind, whereas the oared galleys were independent of it and were besides very much faster and highly manoeuvrable.

The galley possessed only a few guns, in the hull by the bow or mounted on a platform firing ahead over a low, beaked prow, and these were of light construction. Because of the speed of the galley and its independence of the wind, a carrack could only fire a broadside into it so to say by express permission of the galley captain. This awkward situation was probably the reason why Henry VIII, in his rearmament programme of 1538, began to build or buy what are variously described as galleys, galliasses, galliots or galleons. Some of these strange hybrids are depicted in a late engraving of a contemporary painting of the Battle of Portsmouth.

### Elizabeth I (1558–1603)

The need for a 'capital' ship which was both fast and handy doomed the carrack and produced the galleon. The process was aided by the development of artillery and the science of gunnery and occurred at a time when the bow-and-arrow was at last being superseded by the hand-gun. The infantry component was not eliminated but its numbers were reduced, thus obviating the necessity for the embarrassingly high castles which, like unfurlable sails, caught the wind, making the carrack unwieldy besides demanding a deep draught. Now also, for the first time, instead of having to rely on artists' pictures, we have a shipwright's designs to show us what these vessels were really like. A manuscript, attributed to Matthew Baker and dated to about 1586, two years before the Spanish Armada set sail, gives elevations, plans and sections of a number of ships, plus the first recorded instance where the underbody of a ship is compared to the lines of a fish. Set beside a carrack, the galleon gives the impression of a racing yacht, with very fine lines indeed. There is a long, projecting beakhead, a legacy from the galley, while a low forecastle is set back from the bow instead of overhanging it. The stern-castle is now higher than the forecastle, and acts as a navigating 'bridge' with a view forward blanketed only by the sails.

The difference in performance was profound. Admiral Sir William Monson, who as a young man took part in the Armada campaign, pointed out that Henry VIII's fleets never made a proper voyage, 'for his ships were never so far from home but they might return again with a good wind in twenty-four hours' sail; as the others never expected to see the English shore, under four, five, or six months, and many times more.'

Previously confined to mere Channel fighting, war was now being waged farther afield. But while the English had extended their theatre of operations far beyond the 'Narrow Seas' bordered by England, France, and the Low Countries, their over-all policy remained

3 *A map of the Solent area drawn by Baptista Boazia in 1591, showing galleons and a galley. A group of four ships marks the port of Southampton (top centre) with the site of the 'Grace Dieu' wreck in the river Hamble to the east. Up to this time part of the ribs of the 'Mary Rose' could still be seen at Spithead, off Portsmouth (over bows of small ship right centre)*

unchanged. As Sir Walter Raleigh expressed it, 'I take it to be the wisest way, to employ good ships on the sea, and not trust to any intrenchment upon the shore.' That it would come to fighting was certain, because of the glittering trade opportunities opened up in the Americas by the energy and arms of Spain, which that country naturally wished to reserve to herself. Although Spain was now the predominant military power in Europe, her resources were stretched to cover both the Mediterranean and the Atlantic and to provide field armies on the continent. In the words of Francis Bacon, '. . . this much is certain; that he that commands the sea is at great liberty, and may take as much and as little of the war as he will; whereas those that be strongest by land are many times, nevertheless, in great straits; and the wealth of both Indies seems, in great part, but an accessory to the command of the seas.'

Staking everything on the ships and strictly limiting the land forces to mainly local militia seemed at that time a bold policy in view of the renown of the Spanish Army, and the fact that in Henry VIII's day the French had succeeded in putting troops ashore on the Isle of Wight and at various other places. There was then no tradition of an inviolable island, and there were no more than three fortified towns in England, of which Portsmouth was one. In 1588 the matter was put to the test. The King of Spain assembled an international naval and military force. The 'Indian Guard', which convoyed his treasure ships home from the West Indies, was withdrawn for the 'enterprise'; his Mediterranean fleet supplied galleys and galliasses; the Portuguese fleet was added; the city states of Italy supplied their quota; merchant ships were converted to war purposes and mariners recruited from the Low Countries and Germany. And the result of this great effort was a naval force somewhat inferior to the combined royal and private fleets of England. Spain's superiority in superb soldiers was crushing, but she was never given a chance to use them. At the end of 1588 it was possible for the captive King of France to say to his Spanish master, 'It has taken your majesty four years to gather these great fleets, which have been the wonder of the world, and yet it might be said that the Queen of England has triumphed over them all.'

The Armada was not in fact a battle fleet but an amphibious task force which had to collect half of its infantry component in Flanders, before any successful invasion could be launched. The English ships, quite simply, prevented that linking of forces. When they themselves attempted amphibious operations against Spain, they were hardly more successful than the Armada had been. Any detailed study reveals that the basic problems common to all such enterprises at that time were victualling and disease. The arrangements for feeding and supplying large masses of men exceptionally gathered together was rudimentary, because the economy was rudimentary and refrigeration had not been invented. In addition, the ships were not heated and ventilation was poor. The losses from sickness and disease were always far greater than the battle casualties, and when the ships were additionally crammed with soldiers the figures soared even higher. For the short-term local campaigns of the past, the problems had not loomed too large; but on long voyages, and tropic voyages in particular, ship design was a minor factor compared to diet and health.

Recruiting and discipline were also very practical problems. Only in a national crisis are most men prepared temporarily to submit to military or naval routine. As Admiral Monson wrote, 'It is strange what misery

17

15, 16

such men will choose to endure in small ships of reprisal, though they be hopeless of gain, rather than serve her Majesty, where their pay is certain, their diet plentiful, and their labour not so great. Nothing breeds this but the liberty they find in the one, and the punishment they fear in the other.' It was still possible to fight private wars at sea, because governmental control, let alone international law, hardly existed. And many of the developments in ships and guns must have come from the owners of the larger private fleets, who kept no records. Even the Royal Navy was run on a profit-making basis, with the Queen as principal shareholder.

The most important lesson to come from the Armada campaign was that of organization of fleets and of battle control. The customary problems were even graver in 1588 because fleets of the sizes involved were exceptional and few of the ships were standardized. The Armada was very carefully planned and organized, with much thought given to the communications and command system. Even so, the Captain General had to publish a fleet order, when actually in the Channel, to the effect that any captain who did not keep station would be summarily tried and hanged. Two were in fact tried, and one was hanged. And three damaged flagships were abandoned to the English rather than risk breaking up the formation by turning back to rescue them. The English, for their part, had to reorganize actually in the middle of the Channel fighting, in between battles. They were fighting in loose 'gaggles', which were effective in disorganizing the Armada at all the critical points of the passage, where a landing was possible, but they could not crush it outright. Partly, this was because the gun is a poor weapon for sinking battleships, partly because it was difficult to bring the broadside guns of many ships to bear on a particular target simultaneously, when the guns were short-ranged, the ships were powered by the wind, and signalling systems were rudimentary. The gun alone was not enough, but the English dared not board because of the Spaniards' immense superiority in shipboard soldiers.

## The Seventeenth Century

European warships during the time of the Stuarts and the Commonwealth differ most obviously from their predecessors in that the glittering paintwork has been superseded by a most elaborate system of carving and gilding which gives them a fussy appearance and camou- 21 flages the fact that they are only galleons after all, even if larger than Elizabethan ships. The armament has been increased and the lines are not so fine, although the superstructures have been reduced in height. The English ships tend to have rounded sterns below water level, while continental countries retain the square stern; otherwise, there is little difference in their outward appearance. The most important differences were internal. As late as Elizabethan times, much of the longitudinal strength of the hull was given by the wales, thick pieces of reinforcing timber which ran from end to end of the ship. It was a basic rule not to cut gun-ports through the wales, and this led to difficulty in siting the guns. During the seventeenth century, therefore, ships began to be reinforced internally instead, by means of upright beams or criss-cross struts. During this period also shipbuilders began to make models of projected vessels, for prior approval of the design by the Admiralty. Some of these models have survived, as have some of the ship plans. And recently an actual example of such a warship, the Swedish galleon *Vasa* of 1628, was 4 salvaged in a good state of preservation.

The *Vasa*'s elaborate and costly carvings, representing a good deal of excess weight in all the wrong places, can be studied and compared to very similar carvings ashore in Stockholm. This galleon, of Dutch design, had 22–25 continuous decks, and according to contemporary gun-lists had a uniform main armament consisting of 24-pounders on two decks, with the result that the centre of gravity was dangerously high. Theoretically, she was a formidable warship, fast and extremely heavily armed; but these advantages had been bought at the price of stability, and on her maiden voyage in the comparative shelter of Stockholm harbour she capsized and sank.

*4 Longitudinal section through the 'Vasa' drawn by Erich Hofman, showing the rake of the main- and mizzenmasts and the upward curve of the decks aft. The hull was about 150 feet long, with a maximum beam of 37 feet and a draught of just over 16 feet*

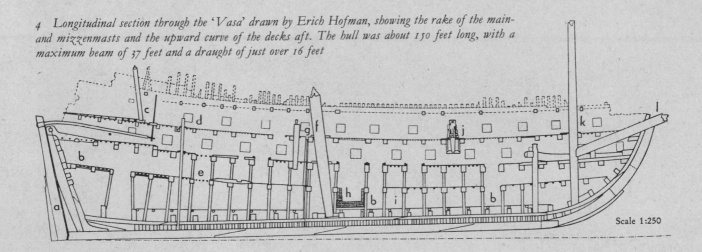

Scale 1:250

However, the freshwater and mud which preserved much of the hull also preserved parts of the bodies of some of her crew and their wives, as well as their clothing and personal possessions; so the raising of the *Vasa* brought to light not merely a ship, mainly of interest to experts, but some part of a shipboard community of the time, which was much more valuable evidence, historically.

The development of fleet tactics is best illustrated by the Anglo-Dutch wars, in which ships and men were very evenly matched in what were exclusively sea battles. Moreover, most of the contests were between opposing fleets, except for raids such as that of 1666, when the British set fire to two Dutch warships and 165 merchantmen in the Vlie, and that of the following years, when the Dutch burnt part of the British fleet in the Medway. The Armada having been an invasion force rather than a battle fleet, the formation adopted had been defensive. Theoretically, the best way for a broadside-gunned fleet to operate was in single line ahead, with clear fields of fire to port and starboard, and it was this formation which became standard mid-way through the seventeenth century. The developments during the second half of the century were mainly concerned with tightening both the formation and its discipline and in working out standard evolutions to be performed on the word of command, transmitted not merely by flags from the flagship but repeated by fast, small craft along the by now lengthy line of battle. Finally, control was further improved by the promulgation of an 'Order of Battle', in which each ship's position in the formation was specified, together with a distinguishing signal for that ship. Much of this had been anticipated by the Spaniards in 1588; the principal difference was that instead of a line-abreast (probably echeloned) formation in depth, there was now a rigid, ruler-straight chain. Breaking the enemy's line thus became a main object, and this was extremely difficult to achieve in any satisfactorily decisive manner because, in order to make use of its broadsides, a fleet had virtually to sidle in sideways towards the foe. To attack head-on meant giving every advantage of gunfire to the enemy until such time as the line was broken; in these circumstances, the head of the attacking line was more likely to suffer.

**The Eighteenth Century**
British warships of the eighteenth century differ in external appearance from those of the seventeenth principally in that most of the gilded flummery has disappeared and the vessels look much more workmanlike. In fact, the trend now is all for strength and seaworthiness, because the sphere of action had become world-wide, in contrast to the local battles in the Channel and the North Sea which had characterized the Anglo-Dutch wars. Nor are we in any doubt as to what changes took place, because during the period 1677–1745 not only were the dimensions of each class of vessel standardized, but thanks to the documents, the plans, and the models

being preserved, the results of the successive 'Establishments' may be studied. Even an exceedingly well-preserved wreck of this period would not tell us much more than we know already.

What happened was, that the size of a ship in proportion to its armament was increased appreciably. The tonnage of the First-Rate line-of-battle ship of 100 guns rose from 1,550 to 2,000 by stages. The guns also increased in size, for any given rating, 12-pounders being replaced by 18-pounders, and 18-pounders by 24-pounders. About mid-way through the eighteenth century the standard battleship became a two-decker carrying 74 guns, but had roughly the same dimensions as previous three-deckers carrying 80 guns. These '74s' were copied from French prizes, and indeed both French and Spanish ships were more often than not superior to British designs. These nations also produced very large four-deckers of 120 guns.

THE LINE
The advantage of a line-of-battle lay in the field of fire for the batteries of broadside guns. The disadvantage was, that weak ships might be opposed to strong ships. Therefore a decision had to be taken as to the types of ship which were fit to lie in the line-of-battle. Ships of the sixth-rate (frigates, brigantines, sloops) of from 300 to 400 tons and carrying 20 guns and 130 men were excluded. An early analysis of British ships by this method (about 1700–1750) gave the following rates:

|  | *Guns* | *Tonnage* | *Men* |
|---|---|---|---|
| First-rates | 100 | 1,700 to 2,000 | 850 |
| Second-rates | 90 | 1,400 to 1,600 | 750 |
| Third-rates | 80 | 1,100 to 1,400 | 600 |
| „ „ | 70 | | 480 |
| Fourth-rates | 60 | 600 to 1,000 | 400 |
| „ „ | 50 | | 100 |
| Fifth-rates | 40 | 500 to 600 | 250 |

At this time, the rating of the ship expressed the minimum number of guns such a vessel could carry; not necessarily the actual number of guns carried at any one time by any particular ship, as this varied considerably. The tonnages given were not the modern displacement tonnages, which would add about 1,000 tons to the given figure for a first-rate. Originally, tonnage was a measurement of cargo capacity, inappropriate for a warship. Later, ratings were computed in a different way, based partly on the calibres as well as the numbers of guns, and smaller ships of 60 guns or less were excluded from the line because they were now too weak.

This increase in size of the larger classes of ship proved a fatal disadvantage to the Dutch, both in war and peace. All their harbours were on the delta of the Rhine and therefore both shallow and subject to silting which was uncontrollable until the invention of the steam dredger. For instance, the maximum high water on the bar at Amsterdam declined from 12 feet in 1700 to 10 feet by 1750. Over-all, Dutch ships had to be designed inside a 16-foot draught, which restricted their size and also dictated the use of comparatively inefficient shallow hulls.

Another result of the demand for warships of world-wide cruising capacity was the introduction, after much experiment, of copper sheathing secured by copper bolts. Lead-sheathing had long been tried, but was too heavy and set up electrolytic action between the lead and the iron bolts used in the hull, as did copper sheathing when secured by iron bolts. Prior to the introduction of all-copper in 1783, the normal practice in fitting out a ship for a tropical voyage was to protect the area below the water-line from ship-worm with a layer of boards on top of tallow and sulphur. These boards were not part of the hull proper and could be stripped off when they became badly worm-holed.

The standard ship was still a three-master, the bona-venture mizzen, or small fourth mast of Tudor times, having given way to one substantial mizzenmast instead. The sail-plan had become much more complicated, because the number of sails had been greatly increased, and the general result was to improve the performance of the vessel when the winds were contrary, while still retaining the efficiency of the square-rig when the winds were fair.

Though the very mixed armament of Tudor times was also well in the past, the range of capabilities was maintained, not by varying the types of gun so much as by varying the types of missile fired. One and the same gun could fire grapeshot, an anti-personnel missile consisting of a mass of musket balls fitted round a coiled iron core; or a canister (a container holding a number of small cannon balls), effective against masts and spars; or chain or sliding bar shot, effective against rigging. Again, the gun could be double-shotted for close-range work. The *Victory*, for instance, had a basically uniform armament, differing only in calibre, flexibility of missile fire being obtained by the use of various types of ammunition. A particularly deadly weapon against boarding, or for sweeping an enemy's decks at close range, was the carronade, introduced towards the end of the century. This was a kind of large, anti-personnel mortar which, being small in proportion to the weight of the shot it fired, could be mounted high up. The *Victory*'s carronades are 68-pounders weighing only 1½ tons, compared to the three tons weight of a 32-pounder cannon.

The warship of 1800 was neater and more utilitarian than its counterpart of Tudor times, with many detailed improvements, but the main object in battle was to subdue the enemy by gun bombardment, then board him under covering fire from small arms. The boarders were now agile seamen instead of armoured soldiers, and the covering fire was given by Marines armed with muskets instead of archers with longbows, but the general principles of ship-to-ship conflict had hardly changed at all; this for the very good reason that guns rarely sink battleships, unlike the mines, torpedoes, bombs and guided missiles of today. On the other hand, the fire danger in wooden ships was extreme, particularly when combined with gunpowder, and the very wide gangways of warships were designed for rapid re-supply of powder charges from the magazines down below, so as to have only a minimum of powder on the actual gun-decks. Being a 'low' explosive, gunpowder merely burns when in the open air; it explodes only when confined, and therefore the most sensitive parts of the ship were the magazines. All were below the water-line and the grand magazine and adjacent filling room were felt-lined and lit by lanterns placed outside, separated from the powder by double glass windows. Here the charges were made up and issued to the hanging magazines, which were the equivalent of the modern ready-use magazines.

By the end of the century England had dropped her claim to the title of mistress of the Narrow Seas, nor was the term any longer meaningful. The Royal Navy had obtained not merely superiority, but actual supremacy, in many oceans. The scale of the effort required may be judged by modern, admittedly peace-time, comparisons. In 1802 the strength of the Navy was 129,000 men, recruited from a population of some 8 or 10 million. In 1968, the strength of the Navy was 94,900 men, recruited from a population now approaching 50 million. In October, 1805, the month of Trafalgar, the *Hampshire Telegraph* reported that 'The total number of ships now in commission, exclusive of cutters and hired vessels, is 698, of which 124 are of the line, 19 from 50 to 44 guns, 139 frigates, and 416 sloops; besides which there are repairing, building, etc. a number of ships, so as to make the total number 903.' In 1968, the strength of the Royal Navy was just over 200 vessels, of which no more than six could be considered as 'capital' ships, compared to the 124 such vessels in 1805, when the population was only one-fifth of what it is today.

## The Nineteenth Century

A distinctively nineteenth-century wooden warship did not emerge until after the Napoleonic wars. An example is the *Albion* class battleship of 3,000 tons, displacing nearly 1,000 tons more than the three-decker *Victory* – and all on two decks. The number of guns carried was fewer, only 90 as against the *Victory*'s 104, but all were 32-pounders, whereas in the *Victory* the 32-pounders were on the lower deck only, the middle deck carrying 24-pounders, the upper deck and quarterdeck 12-pounders. The principle of keeping the greatest weights low down was adhered to by having two classes of 32-pounder cannon, those on the upper gun-deck being shorter and lighter than those on the main gun-deck below. These ships, dating from 1842, were close to the practical limit of size for wooden vessels.

The industrial revolution had given impetus to the habit of scientific thought and calculation in design, as

33

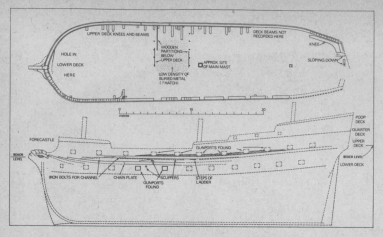

*5 A preliminary survey drawing of the 150 foot-long 'Amsterdam' by Peter Marsden. The conjectural parts are based on existing scale drawings of similar Dutch ships*

temporarily, while other underwater weapons of more lasting importance were to ensure that newspaper headlines of the future would list ships sunk rather than ships taken, as evidence of victory. This transition period was necessarily awkward and unsatisfactory, and many were to look back on the fleets of Trafalgar as representing some classically glorious and romantic peak.

## Merchant Ships of the Period

In comparison, the merchant ships which the warships existed to protect remain less well defined. The State did not require that they be documented and the documents retained for all time. There was also far less standardization, and what there was, usually resulted from the efforts of the designers to circumvent a tax regulation, of which the seventeenth-century Dutch *fluyt* is an example. But it may be said that most merchantmen were small, because of the often limited size of the ports at which they called; that their crews were small also, for economy of wages, so that, even if armed, they could put up little resistance; and that, by about 1800, even the sizes of timber used in their construction were likewise small, because the larger trees were reserved for the building of warships. This was also the reason why the use of iron, first for the heavy 'knees' supporting the decks and then for the complete framing of the hull, was introduced into merchantmen before it was adopted by the navies.

Many merchantmen, particularly those with beakheads, outwardly resembled warships of roughly the same size; and could be mistaken for them at a distance. Examples are the frigate, the hag-boat and the pink, whereas the bluff-bowed cat and barque were clearly traders. Other types were classified more by their sail plans than by their hulls; the difference between the brigantine and the snow, for instance, appears negligible by present perspectives, and eventually both merged into the brig.

There is much scope for the nautical archaeologist in this field, but so far most of the wrecks which have been reported found are Dutch or British Indiamen, comparatively well-known types; one of these, the *Amsterdam*, driven ashore at Hastings in 1748, and discovered in 1969, appears to be in remarkably good condition. Most of the casualties were, however, small coasters, lost at the rate of hundreds every year. Few records of them remain, and even when their wrecks are found, the discoveries are rarely reported, let alone followed up.

31, 32

5

opposed to tradition and rule-of-thumb. In 1836, for instance, the concept of comparing the underwater body of a ship to that of a fish was not merely attacked, but demolished. It was pointed out by a writer in Colburn's *United Service Journal* that 'Ships move under all the inertia of resistance and friction – and are rigid, massive, and heavy bodies. Fishes are exactly the reverse. By means of their air-bladders, and the elasticity of their frames, they contract and dilate, and vary the position of the different parts of their bodies, as they find it needful to lessen any partial obstruction to their velocity; and the scales are admirably placed in a direction to prevent friction, while an oily humour exudes between the squamosities, by which the water is, in a manner, repelled.' More than a century later, science had to learn this lesson all over again, when careful calculations seemed to show that the dolphin could not possibly achieve the speeds which it undoubtedly did attain. It turned out that the dolphin also could vary its streamline shape to that most suited to any particular speed.

By 1850 the world of the old 'wooden walls' was in dissolution. Steam, with its attendant problems of limited range and provision of coaling stations, was vexing Admiralties while delighting Armies with the present of the railway. The breech-loading rifled gun firing high-explosive shells was about to replace the old smooth-bore muzzle-loaders. The iron vessel was about to replace the wooden ships, whose building had denuded the forests of Europe. The ram was about to return

---

1 This carrack, a German example of about 1490, shows many characteristic features of the type, including the dominant fighting castle at the bow supported at the rear on a high 'carrack arch', an immensely strong mainmast with fighting top, and a hull strengthened by massive longitudinal and vertical wales. The rows of

shields along the sides, reminiscent of the Vikings, are another familiar feature, as are the trumpeters at the bow. The stern or 'summer castle' provided a secondary vantage point and also accommodation for the officers. The crew members in the rowing boat show the difference in dress between the sailors and the soldiers.

2, 3 The distorted shape of a carrack on the Seal of John, Duke of Bedford (3), about 1426, and a more realistic picture of this type of ship carved on a bench-end in the Chapel of St Nicolas, Kings Lynn (2), about 1415. Note again the high fighting castle at the bow, the thick main-mast, and the small mizzenmast on the stern castle, which probably served more for steering than for propulsion.

4 The main armament of a fifteenth-century carrack consisted of archers and men-at-arms; such are these armoured infantrymen shown disembarking from their ship which rides on the waters in the background of the drawing. As will be seen, the number of masts has been increased from two to four, and there are three heavy guns mounted in the waist on each side to fire through the deck rails. But there are no gun-ports and there is a fighting top on the mainmast only. Scene from the Pageant of Richard Beauchamp, Earl of Warwick, executed about 1485.

5

6

5–7 The burnt-out wreck of King Henry V's *Grace Dieu*, built at Southampton in 1416–18, still represents the only known remains of a fifteenth-century carrack. Because of fire damage and the curious clinker construction of the hull – a 1400-ton ship built like a rowing boat – the wreck was long believed to be that of a Viking longship. Examination on foot is difficult because the visible timbers expose for only brief periods during the equinoctial spring tides, but the ship was finally identified in 1933 by a team of nautical experts. Recent re-examinations, carried out under water (5), on land (6), and from the air (7), failed to find the stern (which may be out in the river) but did reveal a good deal about the forces acting on the site. Air photographs clearly showed how the hull had caused wide disturbance and resculpturing of the river bed; also a freshwater gulley leading to the starboard side of the wreck – one small item in producing an environment which, while extremely corrosive to metals, has preserved timbers even above the mud-level. A by-product of a trial excavation was the discovery that the 550-year-old ship had been colonized by *Venus mercenaria*, the American clam accidentally introduced into Southampton Water in the late 1950s and now flourishing also up the Hamble River. The study of underwater environments in their relationship to wrecks, pioneered by Anders Franzén with the *Vasa*, has now become a normal part of archaeological enquiry; while over-all study of the site, where air photographs cannot be taken, is beginning to be made by its underwater equivalent, sidescan sonar.

7

8

8　This painting shows the new English Navy in 1520,
gathered to escort King Henry VIII from Dover to his
meeting with Francis I of France on the Field of the
Cloth of Gold. It has been conjectured that these are
not the actual ships which left from Dover, as they were
small, but rather a representation of the five greatest

ships in his fleet at the time; that the four-master leaving harbour is the *Henry Grace á Dieu*, 1500 tons, the gold-clad figure in the waist being the King himself, while the other four-master being boarded from a boat is possibly the *Sovereign*, 800 tons. The three-masters prominently shown are perhaps the *Mary Rose*, 600 tons, the *Gabriel Royal*, 650 tons, and the *Katherine Forteleza*, 550 tons. What is certain, however, is that they are all large carracks carrying a much more formidable armament, with most of the heavy pieces being mounted low down to fire through square ports cut in the sides and at the stern, which is now square instead of round.

241

9

10

9 The Battle of Portsmouth, 1545. The French fleet of 235 ships (left), unable to attack the 60 English vessels anchored in the shallows of Spit Sand (right) have sent forward four galleys as bait. These have been counter-attacked by Lord Lisle in the *Great Harry*, but the *Mary Rose* has sunk while turning out of the navigational channel (centre). The English ships are mainly galleys or galliasses.

10 A unique wrought-iron breech-loading gun with $3\frac{1}{2}$-inch shot and wadding still in the breech, recovered during the 1970 excavations on the *Mary Rose*. Although it appeared to have been 'built-up' by the usual method of shrinking iron hoops onto iron staves, gamma-ray pictures showed that, on the contrary, the barrel had been rolled from a single sheet of wrought-iron and then welded along the seam.

11   A fine X-ray photograph, showing a well-preserved specimen of *Nototoredo norvagica* in a plank from the *Mary Rose*, found 7 feet below the sea bed. The nature of the infestation indicated that considerable changes have occurred in the underwater environment of the Solent. Though the outside of the plank was like cheese, the centre produced sawdust; another sample of decayed timber produced wood shavings which curled.

12, 13   In 1971 much of the buried hull of the *Mary Rose* was uncovered and surveyed. Below a protective clay layer the immensely strong structure, though black with age, appeared quite perfect; the grain of the wood was marred only by the marks left by the Tudor shipwrights 460 years previously. These first pictures, taken under water, show part of the starboard side of the carvel-built hull, near the bow.

11

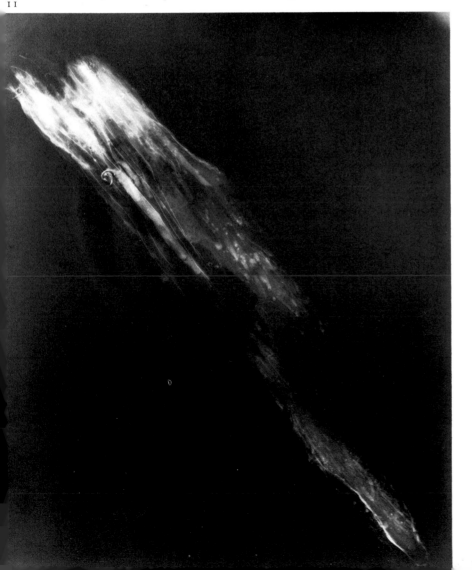

12–13

14

This shippe beynge 29 foot brod, so by the kell 12 foot depe woyld bere in gods 200 tuns in the makyng of whyg [...]
[handwritten caption text, largely illegible]

15

14 An English galleon of about 1586. Although of only about 500 tons, she carried a respectable armament in a fine-lined hull, with a much reduced superstructure. This type of warship could, and did, circumnavigate the globe, whereas the big, heavily-armed carracks of the early Tudor navy operated only in home waters. The picture is from a manuscript described by Samuel Pepys as *Fragment of Ancient English Shipwrightry*, which contains elevations, plans and sections of a number of ships drawn by Matthew Baker, master-shipwright, shortly before the time of the Armada. They are the earliest technical drawings of English warships that have come down to us.

15 A Neapolitan galliass from a tapestry design depicting the defeat of the Spanish Armada, 1588. The type is a cross between a galley and a galleon, and represents yet another attempt to keep some of the fire-power of a carrack without the clumsiness of that

design which made it very difficult to bring the battery guns into action. Small ships of this type had some success, when used as fast auxiliaries, but as a capital ship, the design was a failure. The four galliasses which sailed with the Armada achieved little; two were lost, while a third did not limp back to the Mediterranean until 1589.

16 The most tragic Armada loss was that of the galliass *Girona*, which foundered near Dunluce Castle in Ulster with the surviving crews of two other ships aboard her – 1,300 men in all. There were nine survivors. In 1967 the site was located by Robert Stenuit. The sea bed was both rocky and shallow – the worst conditions possible for the preservation of a four-hundred-year-old wreck. A variety of artifacts was found widely scattered among the gulleys and boulders – valuable in themselves and of considerable historic interest – but no trace of the hull. (See also chapter 9, ill. 20)

17 A scene from the Old Ledger Book of Newport, 1567, depicting the French landings on the Isle of Wight in 1545, with three galleys being supported by the gunfire of a carrack. The arrangement of the carrack's guns is clearly shown – two bronze muzzle-loaders and two iron breech-loaders on the broadside, with two bronze muzzle-loaders at the stern, forming the main armament; and up to three rows of light iron guns on the decks above. Boarding nets have been rigged between the bow and stern castles as a precaution against infantry assault.

18 A Dutch galleon of about 1565 running out of harbour. The four-masted rig of the largest carracks has been retained, but the sterncastle has been reduced in height and the typical overhanging bowcastle has vanished. It is now succeeded by a 'beakhead', perhaps derived from the galley, which serves here as a working platform for men to handle sails and rigging. The truncated remains of the bowcastle form a defensive position only. The main armament is clearly the bronze muzzle-loader of medium size and the emphasis is on a seaworthy, manoeuvrable ship.

19

20

19 An English galleon model of about 1634. Rare in the seventeenth century, such models became plentiful after about 1700, as the builders were then often required to submit both plans and models of the ships they proposed to construct.

20 The first day of the Four Days Battle, 1666, between the English and Dutch fleets, in rough seas which favoured the latter, whose guns were mounted three to four feet higher than the English and so did not have to close their lower-deck gunports. The long, cumbersome line of battle was now standard, since it suited broadside batteries, but it involved complicated manoeuvres to gain the wind and to try to break the enemy's line.

21 A Dutch-built galleon of the French Navy, probably the *Saint Louis*, engraved by Hendrik Hondius in 1626, the year the Dutch-designed *Vasa* was launched in Sweden. The artist has been criticized for exaggerating the length of the beak and figurehead and for the great rake of main and mizzen; but the *Vasa*, which has since been salvaged, attests his accuracy. The picture has also allowed the *Vasa*'s vanished upperworks to be reconstructed with some confidence. By now, the fourth mast (the bonaventure mizzen) has disappeared; instead, the mizzen is larger and carries a square sail as well as a triangular sail. The bowsprit has a spritsail topmast to aid steering.

21

22, 23 An end-on view of the salvaged galleon *Vasa*, showing her rounded stem (23), and the lower part of the solidly constructed stern (22). This Dutch-designed Swedish vessel, located by Anders Franzén after a three-year search, was raised from a depth of 100 feet in Stockholm harbour in 1959, and floated into dry-dock in 1960 – the most stupendous feat in the history of marine archaeology so far. It confounded a wide range of experts, varying from those who believed that the ship no longer existed, having disintegrated after more than three centuries under water, to rationalizers who refused to accept the evidence of contemporary artists, that the main- and mizzen-masts of such vessels were heavily raked and that the sloping decks were continuous. Franzén stuck to facts and to logic. Wrecks did not just fall apart or disappear, he reasoned. Submerged woodwork was consumed by particular organisms, such as the mollusc *Teredo navalis*. If the underwater conditions were such that hostile organisms could not live there, then there seemed to be no reason why wooden ships' hulls could not last for many centuries. And, as he predicted, the Baltic as a whole has indeed proved to be a storehouse for largely intact historic wrecks (see chapter 8).

## 23

24

24 This replica of a carving from the *Vasa* is typical of the large European warship of the time, when heavy decorative woodwork has succeeded the intricate painted patterns of the Tudor period.

25 Once the *Vasa* had been raised, archaeological investigation proper could begin – on land. It was not only the hull that had been preserved, intact almost to the upper deck, but a wide range of items, from ship's fittings and stores to the clothing and personal possessions of the crew. Even the skeleton of a man trapped by a gun-carriage as the ship heeled over, was in good condition, complete with hair, finger-nails and shoes. Examination of the bones revealed something of the racial identity and medical history of the individuals concerned. Most of the crew were Nordic, but some came from farther east, possibly Finland. When removed from their covering of water or mud, their bones turned from white to blue, the result of a chemical change caused by rusting ironwork in the hull near by. The Baltic proved unkind to wrought-iron, very little of which survived after 330 years, whereas pieces in fair condition have been raised from the still older *Mary Rose* at Spithead.

25

26 The sinking of the *Royal George* at Spithead, 29 August, 1782, with the loss of some 900 lives, including those of women and children visiting relatives and friends. The Court Martial found that 'some Material part of her Frame gave way, which can only be accounted for by the General state of Decay of her timbers'. The ship was launched in 1756.

27 The topmasts of the *Royal George* sticking out of the water, as sketched by Rowlandson about two years after the disaster. This obstruction to the main fleet anchorage remained for some sixty years and British inability to remove the wreck was unfavourably contrasted with French salvage feats.

28 The wreck of the *Royal George* during Colonel Pasley's demolition and dispersal operations of 1839–43, which were the first to gain world-wide publicity for the newly discovered underwater world and the odd effects it had on man-made objects. The site was re-located (by the writer) in 1965 and found to be an immense mound resembling a compost heap, but still holding parts of the *Royal George*.

29 Builder's model of the *Royal George*, showing the two white horses of Hanover forming part of the figurehead and the marked 'tumblehome' of the sides. This was to increase stability by placing the guns as near the centreline as possible; similarly, the higher the deck, the lighter were the guns mounted on it.

30 Part of the *Royal George*'s starboard bow, with hawsehole; measuring 38 ft by 27 ft, it was recovered on 16 October, 1839, after the explosion of a cylinder containing 2,300 lb. of gunpowder which had been placed underwater. The approximate position from which it came can be judged by noting the hawseholes on the model.

30

31

31, 32   The wreck (31) of the Dutch East Indiaman *Amsterdam*, built in 1748, is that of a large armed merchant ship contemporary with the *Royal George*, and for which similar copious documentation exists, including a model (32). The historical interest of such ships lies not so much in the hull as in the contents, and what they reveal of cargoes and life at sea for different classes of people at a particular period. The *Amsterdam* was driven ashore near Hastings at the precise point of a geological fault which allowed the hull to sink 30 feet or more into soft clay within 2 to 3 months, so preserving it.

32

33 The *Victory*, like the *Royal George* a first-rate ship-of-the-line, was built in 1759–65 and is still officially in commission and in use for various functions, as well as being open to visitors. She impresses first with her great size and then by the cramped headroom below decks. No plan or model could convey quite such a vivid impression of a wooden fighting and sailing machine, crammed with men.

252

# 11

# Traders and privateers across the Atlantic: 1492–1733

MENDEL L. PETERSON

# Traders and privateers
# across the Atlantic: 1492–1733

Soon after the voyages of Columbus and his immediate successors, the Spanish realized that the wind patterns of the Central and North Atlantic roughly flowed in a clockwise direction. They also discovered the Florida Current and learned to follow it out of the Caribbean Basin through the Florida Straits, and into the Atlantic north of the Bahamas. Other routes, including Columbus's original passage along the northern coast of Santo Domingo and into the open sea continued to be used for some years into the middle of the sixteenth century, but the Florida debouchment came to be the normal one.

Some single ships sailed directly for Spain from the Windward Islands, but from the late 1530s on, the great bulk of the freight was carried in merchant fleets convoyed by armed escorts. The Spanish Crown organized the American trade into a monopoly controlled from Seville. In the earliest period ships sailed from Seville and were required, under pain of severe punishment, to return there; later, Cadiz was made a point of departure for fleets bound for America. The governing authority of the monopoly, the *Casa de la Contratación*, was located at Seville and from that city attempted to control all aspects of the transatlantic trade. The *Casa* prescribed every detail of ship, armament, personnel, and cargo going out and returning. Inspections were thorough, lengthy and irritating to those submitting to them. Long delays occurred in the departure of fleets causing their supplies to be consumed, and at times the weather changed for the worse. Despite this, thousands of ships sailed between Spain and America during the period we are considering, and of these a goodly number, through human error or caprice of nature, were wrecked on the numerous reefs, shoals, and coasts which flanked the great routes from the Caribbean Basin to the Gulf of Mexico. These wrecks are now providing us with a picture of trade and exploration that documents alone could never give.

*1*

### The Earliest Wrecks: Columbus
The history of shipwreck in American waters starts with the very first recorded voyage. In 1492, Christopher Columbus, having made landfall in the Bahamas and explored those islands southward to Cuba whose northern coastline he skirted, lost his flagship somewhere off the northwestern coast of Haiti near the mouth of

a river east of Cap Haitien. The disaster occurred on Christmas Eve, with only an apprentice seaman at the wheel. The ship slid gently onto a shallow sand bar at high tide and with the ebb was left high and dry. Finding he could not re-float his ship, Columbus ordered her to be stripped of all timber, iron, fittings, and supplies; he then put ashore forty-four of his men since there was not room in the *Niña* and *Pinta* to carry them home. A small fort, named Navidad in honour of the day, was established for their safety, but when Columbus returned eleven months later he found not a single survivor. Their disappearance remains a mystery to this day.

The wreck of the *Santa Maria* has not yet been located with certainty. Explorers have searched and claims have been advanced but positive evidence is entirely lacking. The bottom of the ship is probably lying somewhere in the shallows off the Grande Rivière-du-Nord in Haiti. The rest of the structure would have been stripped down to the turn of the bilge for the timber. The floor timbers, some of the futtocks, the keel and keelson with outer and inner planking of the bottom are probably there. In these parts silt piles up fast and if this covered the timber fairly soon after the sinking, the lower planking of the ship would have been protected from the worm and will have survived. The large iron pins which secured the keelson to the keel and clamped the floor timbers would still be in the structure, offering sufficient metal to be detected with a magnetometer. Also remaining would be the cobblestone ballast and perhaps a few distinctive objects lost or thrown into the ballast during the voyage. All of this means that there is likely to be enough evidence to identify the remains – should they ever be found.

*cf. 2*

Columbus's fourth and last voyage left behind two other wrecks. On June 23, 1503, he ran his leaking worm-eaten ships aground on the northern coast of Jamaica to prevent a worse fate. Here, with his ships fast in the mud in shallow water the Grand Admiral and his men spent a miserable twelve months until rescue finally came. The two ships are known to lie near St Ann's Bay and it is very probable that they have in fact been located. Mr Robert Marx, who distinguished himself with his explorations of Port Royal, has discovered the remains of two vessels which fit the description of Columbus's grounded ships and the positions as

*26–30*

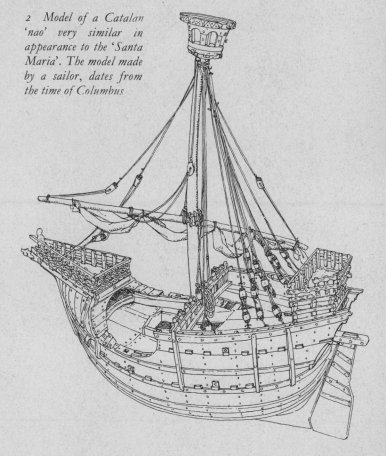

given in his journals. If further excavation confirms the identification, the greatest historical importance will attach to the finds, for they should give us much valuable information concerning the construction of vessels of the late fifteenth and early sixteenth centuries – an era when the documents tell us very little on the subject.

### The Plate Fleet

In the 1530s, the enemies of Spain were so menacing that it became necessary to send armed escorts with the transatlantic trading fleets. In this way the so-called 'Plate fleet' came into being. Larger and more heavily armed ships made their appearance as the flow of wealth from the Americas grew ever greater. Nevertheless, though always threatened, even in times of peace, the Spaniards succeeded in getting large quantities of American treasure back to their country, much of which passed to the creditors of the Spanish Crown. This was to change the whole economy of Western Europe.

There was little the Spaniards could do, however, to protect themselves against the vagaries of the elements. The violent tropical storms which almost annually sweep the Caribbean and Gulf areas could prove fatal to the ships, depending as they did on wind and current. In 1553, a richly laden fleet left Vera Cruz for Spain. In the Gulf of Mexico a tropical storm struck and the fleet was dashed onto the sandy coast of what is now Texas. A

*2  Model of a Catalan
'nao' very similar in
appearance to the 'Santa
Maria'. The model made
by a sailor, dates from
the time of Columbus*

mere handful of survivors finally returned to Mexico to tell of the disaster. Now one of these ships is believed to have been found. The discovery of silver in the form of large discs, a small gold bar and crucifix, wrought iron lombards and swivels, and crossbows are reported. Three astrolabes – for measuring the elevation of heavenly bodies (cf. chapter 9, ills 20, 21) – were among the finds, almost doubling the known examples of this instrument recovered from the sea. If this site yields further finds of consequence, these may well prove to be of the utmost significance, for this, the first fleet disaster of the New World, occurred only seventeen years after the opening of the Mexico City mint and the organization of the regular system of assaying and taxing precious metals. Should any weapons be found at the site, these will tell us how Columbus's ship was in all probability fitted out, since the intervening period had seen little real change in weaponry on the Spanish vessels. An authentic picture of the design, armament, equipment, and cargoes of the earliest Spanish shipping used for trading with the New World may yet emerge from this wrecked fleet.

## Privateers

Archaeological evidence relating to the maritime enemies that preyed on Spanish shipping is scanty. A recent discovery in the Bahamas, however, has provided us with a picture of the size, hull structure, and armament of one of these marauders. A chain of small islands, the Exumas, defines the western side of Exuma Sound which, in the days of smaller sailing vessels, provided a passage for ships making for the open Atlantic. The Spaniards had neglected to settle and fortify the Bahamas as they had Florida, and this eastern flank of the treasure route became infested with pirates and privateers. The numerous islands provided perfect cover for their small, swift, shallow-draft vessels. Near the northern end of the Exuma chain, a small island named on modern charts as Highborn Key provides a protected anchorage on the western side. Here in 1966, while spear-fishing, three Americans, Robert Wilkie, Jack Robinson and Clint Hinchman, found a pile of ballast stones amid a small coral reef lying in about 25 feet of crystal-clear water. On it lay encrusted iron pins, two large cannon, and a dozen or so smaller guns with breech blocks scattered about. Pictures were taken, the site was reported to the Bahamian Government, who issued a licence for working the site. The Smithsonian Institution became interested when the finders consulted me, and on a grant from the National Geographic Society the site was thoroughly explored in the late winter and spring of 1967. For three months they worked with Edward ('Teddy') Tucker and Robert Canton of Bermuda to plot the site, prepare detailed drawings of the timber fragments, and recover the guns and ironwork of the ship. I myself joined the operation for the final phase. After sifting all the evidence we were convinced that here was the wreck of a pirate ship or privateer.

The hull was found to be long and slim, with relatively light timbering and a sharp bow and stern. The two lombards were found in a position which indicated that they were bow chasers so placed to cripple an enemy at some distance. The rails of the vessel had held eleven swivel guns for raking enemy decks at close range while the number of guns carried implied a rather large crew for a vessel estimated to displace around 175 to 200 tons. The sharp-ended hull pointed to a ship designed for speed, probably lateen-rigged, adapted to pursue and capture. The discovery of two anchors lying some 300 feet beyond the seaward end of the wreck would make it appear that the ship had sunk while at anchor. Whether this was the result of battle or of storm damage, or whether the vessel was deliberately scuttled will never be determined. The complete absence of any personal articles, small arms, or remains of food jars strongly suggests that the crew sank the ship after transferring to another vessel. The nature of the guns, and the iron-cored, lead cannon-balls places the wreck most probably in the first half of the sixteenth century, certainly no later than 1580.

## The Ships of the Late Sixteenth Century

While the nature of their business required that pirates and privateers be swift and comparatively small, the ships in the Spanish American trade became larger and larger to accommodate the ever-increasing quantities of cargo. When this trade began, a vessel of 150 or 200 tons was considered large; by the middle of the sixteenth century, ships of 300 to 500 tons were not unusual. The discovery by Teddy Tucker of three separate wrecks in Bermudian waters has provided us with a wealth of information on the hull size, cargoes, armament, and equipment of the Spanish ships engaged in this transatlantic commerce. All lie on the western reefs running out to sea for many miles and constituting a dire hazard for ships approaching the islands from the direction of the Florida Straits.

The earliest of these wrecks has yielded a considerable deposit of timber, probably half of the bottom of the ship. In 1964, under a grant from a private foundation, I explored this site with Tucker and his crew. It was marked by a trail of ballast stones lying on a coral head and extending down into a sand hole. After several hours of pumping out the hole with the 'airlift', the ship's keelson was exposed and the direction of her main axis ascertained. Calm weather fortunately enabled us to uncover the timber systematically, whereupon its full extent was revealed. The vessel's massive structure and the size of the bottom were impressive. The remains, 46 feet long and 28 feet wide, represented about half of the bottom of the hull. The step of the mainmast found in the keelson provided a point from which to estimate the original length of the keel. The floor timbers were 13 inches square, the keelson was 24 × 9 inches, the planking 15 inches wide and 3 inches thick. The keel proved to be 20 inches square. All the surviving timber was

6–8, 15

oak, still comparatively sound. The keelson was clamped to the keel with large iron pins, holding the floor timbers in position while the planking was secured by large oak trunnels. The massive size of the timbers and the length of the section found pointed to a large, flat, fat-bellied vessel perhaps 120–140 feet over-all and displacing 400 tons. This commodious ship was designed to carry large cargoes, but had been stripped of all her contents at the time of the sinking: only a few intact objects, including a brass crucifix, lead cannon-ball, wrought-iron bar shot, encrusted match-lock musket, and a few corroded silver coins, were found. There were also many sherds of the Spanish 'olive jars'. Enough evidence to indicate the period 1570–80. This find has given us not only a graphic picture of the massive timbering of larger ships of the period, but also of the force of the sea during tropical storms – the ship's timbers had been snapped cleanly by the force of the hurricane which had wrecked her.

In 1950, that is several years before the discovery of the wreck just described, Tucker and Canton had found five sand-encrusted iron cannon and a large copper pot full of musket balls in a sand hole between coral heads. Five years later they returned to the site and in the space 34–37 of a few days recovered a rich collection of artifacts which tell us much about the equipment, armament, and furnishings of a small ship of the late sixteenth century engaged in the American trade. The vessel was obviously returning to Spain from America – her very location proved that. The treasure found aboard included gold bullion, silver coins, and jewellery, testifying to the wealth that was then flowing into the Spanish coffers. One piece proved to be the most valuable single object taken from the ocean in modern times. This was a gold 2, 3 pectoral cross set with seven flashing emeralds of the finest colour from the mines of Colombia. More than just a very valuable piece of jewellery, it is an outstanding example of the goldsmith's art of the late sixteenth century. Discovered with the cross was a set of buttons of cast gold filigree set with pearls, some single and some triple. These were probably from the vestments of the high churchman who had owned the cross – a bishop at the very least. Many examples of coins and fine jewellery have found their way into public and private collections, but no bulk gold and silver. For this reason the very few bars of these metals that have been recovered from underwater sites are of particular interest; they throw much light on the transportation of precious metals from the New World to Spain. The Tucker site yielded a fine gold bar weighing over 40 ounces, two round ingots of about 25 ounces, a smaller gold bar of five ounces, and two square sections of bars. All bore marks which showed they had been assayed by the king's agents and taxed. The large bars bore the word 'PINTO', indi- 17–19 cating that the gold was alluvial and had come from the Pinto river area of New Granada.

The Tucker collection gives us a good picture of life aboard ship at the end of the sixteenth and early in the seventeenth century. The officers and wealthier passengers dined from silver and pewter plates and their wine was poured from gilt silver ewers. Pickled fish and beef formed a large part of their diet; the common sailors ate from red-ware bowls and their food was probably much coarser. The ship's armament consisted of cast iron falconets firing ball of about 3 pounds weight with a 38 secondary battery of wrought-iron swivels very similar to those found on the Exuma site referred to above. This constitutes precise archaeological confirmation of what in general the documents tell us. In the last decades of the sixteenth century, cast iron muzzle-loading pieces replaced the wrought iron breech-loading guns in the main batteries of armed ships while the wrought iron breech-loading swivels survived, being short-range pieces where gas pressures did not need to be as high as in the longer-range main battery. To prevent the ship from being boarded, the crew was provided with muskets firing a ball of 80 calibre, the lighter arquebus, the justly famous Spanish sword and boarding axes. Some of the officers wore steel breast-plates. The navigator of the ship used fine brass dividers such as are repre- 10 sented in vignettes on charts of the period and brass-encased, mercury-filled time-glasses of amazing quality 13 and workmanship. One find proved to be part of the ship's surgeon's equipment. This was a fine pewter clyster pump with wooden cylinder, an object which 12 defied identification for some years. Perhaps the most interesting facet of Spanish American trade with which the Tucker collection provides us is revealed by a group of black palm-wood Indian artifacts. These objects, believed to be Carib, include bows, arrows, and a fine staff of office which could also serve as an effective war club. We can thank some ethnologically-minded Spaniard for the preservation to this day of these extremely rare weapons.

The upper parts of the hull and the rigging of these early Spanish vessels will largely elude the underwater explorer in American waters. The natural force of the storms which sank many of the ships, the wave action of the comparatively shallow water in which they lie, and the *teredo* and *limnoria* worms which rapidly devour exposed timbers in the warmer waters of the New World, effectively prevent survivals under water like that of the *Vasa* (see chapter 10). For such information we have mainly relied on contemporary illustrations, many of which appear on title pages of works on navigation 3 and as vignettes on engraved and manuscript charts of 4 the region; these bear out what the documents tell us. Initially, the smaller lateen-rigged ship bore the brunt of the exploring and trading voyages. As ships grew in size in order to accommodate the ever-expanding trade, three-masted vessels with square-rigged fore- and main-mast and lateen-rigged mizzen became common. Smaller vessels, such as dispatch boats which had to move rapidly, continued to use the lateen rig as did the marauders who preyed on the legitimate shipping of Spain and other nations. Undoubtedly, most of the rigs

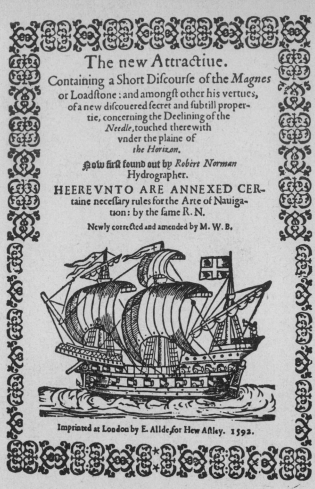

## The new Attractiue.

Containing a Short Difcourfe of the *Magnes*
or Loadftone : and amongft other his vertues,
of a new difcouered fecret and fubtill proper-
tie, concerning the Declining of the
*Needle*, touched therewith
vnder the plaine of
the *Horizon*.

Now firft found out by *Robert Norman*
Hydrographer.

HEEREVNTO ARE ANNEXED CER-
taine neceffary rules for the Arte of Nauiga-
tion: by the fame R. N.

Newly corrected and amended by M. W. B.

Imprinted at London by E. Allde, for Hew Aftley. 1592.

*3   Title page of 'The New Attractive', a work on navigation
published in London 1592, showing a warship of the period*

known at that time in the Old World were applied to ships concerned in the transatlantic traffic. Even the armed galley of Mediterranean invention was used in the patrolling squadrons maintained by the Spaniards for combating corsairs in the Windward Islands and the Bahamas. In the underwater sites of the New World, detached blocks, chain plates, parrels, and other fittings that fell into protective silt and sand, are now beginning to provide us with valuable details of ship's rigging usually omitted from contemporary illustrations.

### The 'San Antonio' (1621)

As the Spanish settlements in America expanded to take in great areas of fertile lands, as farms and ranches grew, and as other activities besides the acquisition of precious metals and gems became an important part of the Spanish-American economy, the cargoes going to Europe became more diverse and began to include more mundane products. No one has ever waxed lyrical about the raw, stinking hides with which the great ships were now filled nor the dirty red logwood, cochineal or sickly yellow raw indigo which flowed to Spain; but these products of forest and farm had, by the end of the sixteenth century, become an important source of income to the American settlements. In addition, exotic woods

such as *lignum vitae* – still used today for the propeller-shaft bearings of steamships – were much sought-after for their tremendous hardness, strength, and resistance to rot. *Lignum vitae* was made into the grooved wheels, or sheaves that were used in the blocks of the rigging and which carried such great strains in the days of sail. So much store did the Spaniards set by this remarkable wood that *lignum vitae* sheaves found on earlier New World shipwrecks usually indicate the vessel's Spanish origin; the English and French, until the second half of the seventeenth century at least, not having access to the wood, used oak for the sheaves of their blocks. Another product which was assuming increasing importance in the export trade to Spain was tobacco, now in great demand in Europe. In the latter part of the sixteenth century, as it was introduced into England, the British sought to make tobacco one of the first money crops in their infant colony in Virginia. In the earlier period, the Spaniards in America held a virtual monopoly.

The discovery by Teddy Tucker off Bermuda of the remains of a third large Spanish vessel furnishes us with archaeological evidence of the importance of everyday goods to the economies of the Spanish American settlements. This ship has been identified as the *San Antonio*,  which set sail from Cartagena, Colombia, late in the summer of 1621 with a cargo of the sort regularly carried from the Spanish Main to Spain: gold in small cakes, silver in coin, and jewellery representing part of the personal possessions of the passengers. The rest of the cargo, however, was of a less romantic nature. As Tucker and I explored the site over a three-year period, an authentic picture of a mixed cargo of those days emerged. Tobacco was found wrapped in bundles. Cochineal – the dyestuff which is the dried bodies of millions of minute insects – had been carried on the ship in the olive jars which constituted one of the standard containers then in use, as red stains on sherds of these vessels showed. The top of a chest of indigo dye appeared to us, as we swam 30 feet deep in crystal-clear water, as a bright blue rectangle in the sand. An area, 30 inches long and two feet wide, was rimmed with rotted wood. The original green colour of the raw dye had been oxidized to the deep blue of the finished product by the oxygen in the sea water. Throughout the site, dark red masses of soggy material were also found; these proved to be bundles of tanned leather dyed and cut thin for the binding of books and or covering boxes used in the leather industry of Spain. Billets of *lignum vitae*, too, lay in various places. These small logs, about 40 inches long, were weathered to a pleasant grey outside; but under the surface the wood proved to be as sound as when it slid into the ocean, a dramatic testimony to the qualities Spanish craftsmen held so dear.

Among the more unusual articles found on the site was tortoise shell. In the days before the invention of celluloid and the other plastics which followed, this shell of bright browns and yellows was prized and commanded a high price in Europe. From it were fashioned

21-25

258

combs, snuff boxes and spectacle frames, and with the advent of the designer Charles André Boule tortoise shell was used to veneer furniture for the very wealthy. Another interesting find was a large quantity of cowrie shells of the variety *Cyprœa moneta*. These small, attractive shells are native to the Indian Ocean basin and have been used since the Stone Age as a medium of exchange, as their scientific name implies. The natives of the coasts of West Africa valued them so highly that just a few would buy a healthy adult slave. The Spanish, after establishing connections with the Far East through Manila, Acapulco, and Vera Cruz, were quick to appreciate the opportunity and shipped these shells home by the millions for use in this despicable trade in slaves. The twenty thousand or so shells on the site were, no doubt, a shipment going to some Spanish merchant for use in West Africa. Mixed with the cowries were small billets of copper about half an ounce in weight; it is to be assumed that these served the same purpose as the cowries. Copper, when sent to Spain from the New World, ordinarily took the form of oval or round ingots of 20–80 pounds weight; small ingots of the metal continued to serve as a form of currency in West Africa until recent times.

While the cargo of the *San Antonio* contained a fine cross-section of the commercial products of the New World, it included also an admixture of treasure that has come to symbolize the Spanish colonies. A beautiful gold ring containing as perfect an emerald as one could wish to see – no doubt a prized possession of one of the passengers on the ship – was found where it had been lost when the forward part of the vessel became flooded as she ran onto a vicious reef. The story of the sinking is well recorded in the Bermuda archives.

The ship ran aground on the southwest reefs of Bermuda on September 13, 1621. Of about 400 tons, she was part of a fleet which had sailed from Cartagena, stopping at Havana as was customary, and had approached Bermuda as part of a small composite fleet. Near Bermuda a storm struck, separating the ships and reducing visibility to such an extent that the islands were not visible even from the outer extremities of the shallow coral reefs. In this situation, the *San Antonio* ran aground just before nightfall. The crew mutinied and, taking the only serviceable boat, rowed ashore, leaving the officers and passengers huddled on the stern, the only part of the ship to remain out of water. During the night the men on board worked feverishly to construct a raft from the timbers of the wrecked ship, and the next day all the remaining survivors were able to get safely ashore, including one Spanish lady 'big with child'. The arrival of these wretched people caused a small 'gold rush' in Somerset on the western extremity of the islands. Within hours the site swarmed with Bermudians salvaging cables, anchors, guns, cargo, and what treasure they could find. According to the records the haul included several cannon, supplies of tobacco (which was ruined) and the personal effects of the un-

fortunate Spaniards. The Bermudians assisted the survivors, and the governor apparently made sincere efforts to comfort and care for them, but when they finally boarded a rescue craft which had been chartered for them they seem to have been relieved of any treasure they had managed to bring from the *San Antonio*.

## English Shipping

As the English established colonies on the continent of North America, new direct routes were opened up from Europe. The old Spanish routes which carried shipping down the west coast of Africa and across the Atlantic on the Trade Winds simply were not suitable for ships wishing to reach the coasts of Virginia and Massachusetts. Although on the southern route the prevailing winds and currents were directed toward the New World, this would have been too great a detour and the English had to take their chances with the head winds and storms of the North Atlantic. The case of the *Sea Venture* which foundered on the coast of Bermuda in 1609 (leading to the settlement of that island and incidentally furnishing William Shakespeare with the theme for *The Tempest*) is a perfect example of the perils and hardships that beset vessels using the northern route. After battling for days against howling winds and battering seas she finally drifted onto the Bermuda coast with a hold full of water and about two hours of buoyancy left. But, as if by a miracle, the ship got stuck between two coral heads which held her upright, enabling the crew and passengers to get ashore safely after the seas had subsided. The *Sea Venture* was en route for Virginia with badly needed supplies and reinforcements of men. The party finally reached their destination a year late in boats built in Bermuda, though many died in the 'starving times' which followed. But the colony hung on tenaciously and by the middle of the seventeenth century its survival was assured. Ships going from England to Virginia would usually stop at Bermuda, which had now been settled permanently and formed a port of call where the crews and passengers could refresh themselves before the final leg of the journey to the coast of North America.

*4 Woodcut of a small armed ship from the title page of 'Nova Britannia' by Robert Johnson, published in London in 1609. The representation of the ship is somewhat more accurate than that in Figure 3*

### The 'Virginia Merchant' (1660)

In 1660 the *Virginia Merchant*, having come from England with immigrants and supplies for Virginia, set sail from Castle Harbor, Bermuda. Almost immediately the ship was struck by a storm which dashed her on the rocky south coast of the island. Here she broke up, parts of the hull sinking under the weight of the ballast, heavy cargo and iron guns of her main battery. The seas carried part of the superstructure ashore, the bowsprit almost entering the door of a house. But even though within hailing distance of the shore, most of the persons aboard died, cut to pieces by the knife-like rocks or drowned by the raging waters. A dozen or so drifted into a small bay with a sandy beach, and were able to save themselves.

It is little more than ten years ago that Teddy Tucker, exploring here, found great sand-encrusted cannon lying in a hole some three hundred yards off the beach. From the hole, too, parts of iron fittings from a ship's rigging were recovered, then some tools including axes, augers, and chisels. Ultimately, it was established that they had belonged to the *Virginia Merchant* Subsequent exploration through the years, in which I participated, have furnished us with a picture of the cargo and equipment of larger vessels serving the English colonies in America in the middle of the seventeenth century. Axes for woodsmen and blacksmiths' tools – mauls, hammers, and tongs – show how important were those crafts to the emerging colony on the fringes of an unfriendly wilderness. Ivory combs, ivory-handled knives, and lead settings for window panes are eloquent testimony to the hunger of the colonists for the small luxuries that reminded them of the comparative comfort and safety of their homeland. The presence of quantities of lead swan- and buckshot serves to remind us of the vital function of the hunter in keeping the struggling colony fed, while cannon-balls, small arms, and other military supplies underline the real dangers of attack the colony still faced from unfriendly savages and hostile Spaniards to the south. One find even reflected the political situation in England. A brass button with the caricature of a king must have been a prized possession of a supporter of the Commonwealth government which was now being displaced by the restoration of Charles II to the throne.

### Port Royal (1692)

The Virginia colony, displeasing as it was to the Spaniards, did not pose a direct and immediate threat to the flow of treasure which sustained the Spanish homeland. It was otherwise when the English began to settle Jamaica. The establishment of Port Royal on the south coast of Jamaica pointed a dagger at the heart of the Spanish Caribbean. Here, encouraged by a liberal attitude toward anyone who attacked the Spanish Main, came buccaneers such as Henry Morgan, followed by the merchants, prostitutes, and tavern-keepers to provide for the freebooters' needs. The city had become the richest in English America by 1692, when it was

5 *Brass button showing a caricature of a king, recovered from the site of the 'Virginia Merchant' wrecked on Bermuda in 1660. The button, which dates from the Protectorate of Cromwell was probably intended to ridicule the concept of monarchy*

destroyed by a terrible earthquake which dumped two-thirds of it into the sea. Operations directed by Mr Edwin A. Link, for the National Geographic Society and the Smithsonian Institution, and later by Mr Robert Marx for the Government of Jamaica, have surveyed the sunken ruins, charting the foundations of buildings and retrieving a tremendous amount of salvage from what is surely the richest deposit of seventeenth-century English and Spanish colonial material on earth.

### H.M.S. 'Winchester'

With a permanent foothold in the central Caribbean, English naval activity in that area increased rapidly and every war in Europe found its reflection in colonial warfare both in the Caribbean and in English North America. At such times of conflict, the English naval forces in America were quickly reinforced and the West Indies saw substantial squadrons of large warships sailing the routes to protect English trade from the enemy and attacking the convoys of the other side.

The War of the Grand Alliance which resulted from the aggressive policy pursued by Louis XIV in Central Europe found France facing virtually all the other powers of Western Europe (the Grand Alliance). This forced England into the Spanish camp, and squadrons of English ships sailed for the West Indies to attack the French there. By and large, however, the naval conflicts degenerated into hunts for prize money. Mismanagement was rife and living conditions in the fleet were abominable even for an age which neglected elementary rules of hygiene at sea. In one instance, the admiral of a squadron and all but one of his captains died of disease during the cruise.

The first wrecked ship in Florida to be seriously studied was found to have run aground and sunk during the War of the Grand Alliance. In 1938 two fishermen reported the finding of a wreck to Mr Charles Brookfield, an ornithologist residing in Elliots Key, Florida. Subsequent investigation revealed many large sand-encrusted cannon lying in five fathoms of water near Carysfort Reef. Realizing that the ship might be Spanish, Brookfield organized a small party and hired a diver, Walter Williamson, who reported that the guns were of iron. In the subsequent operations, these were raised and the site combed for artifacts which might indicate the identity of the lost vessel. Success came with the discovery of an English halfpenny dated 1694 stuck in the crust of one of the guns. Using nothing more than the comparatively crude, open, shallow-water diving helmet of those days, the divers recovered a significant collection of material and were able, with the help of the British Admiralty, to determine that the ship was the

cf. 6 *Winchester*, a Fourth Rate of 60 guns, Captain John Soule, which struck the reef on September 24, 1695, and quickly sank. Brookfield believed that the ship was wrecked by a storm, but an examination of Captain Soule's log in the Public Record Office reveals that she went aground because scurvy had decimated the crew and there simply were not enough men to work the sails. The entire squadron had suffered great losses, and Captain Soule had taken command of the ship only a few days before the accident, replacing the captain who had been transferred to another ship of the squadron, whose commander had himself probably gone sick or died. Soule's log is a dreary chronicle of the deaths of many members of the crew and their burial at sea in the days before the ship ran ashore. Only a handful of men, including the captain, managed to get off the vessel. The collection recovered by Brookfield and his men included a silver porringer, pewter plates, bar- and round-shot, many iron guns, some marked T. W. – ini-

tials of the founder Thomas Westerne of Ashburnam in Sussex – and, most startling of all, fragments of a prayer book still legible after two and a half centuries under the sea. But a final ironical twist is given to the story by the finding in the wreck of a *lime juicer*!

## The Fleet of 1715

The War of the Grand Alliance had come to an end, but it was soon followed by the War of the Spanish Succession and the successful efforts on the part of Louis XIV to place his grandson on the throne of Spain. In the Peace of Utrecht which ended the hostilities, one treaty, that between France and Great Britain, confirmed Philip of France on the throne of Spain and ceded Newfoundland, St Kitts, and the Hudson Bay Territory to the British. In treaties between Great Britain and Spain, the English received Gibraltar and the right to send one ship of 500 tons annually to the trade fairs of Porto Bello and Vera Cruz. With this legal foothold in the door of colonial Spanish commerce, the trade rapidly expanded and the English soon found a way of circumventing the strict provisions of the law, inaugurating a new age of contraband trading with the Spanish. This led to unpleasantness between Britain and Spain, and finally to open hostilities again in the late 1730s.

6 *Official scale model of a British frigate of 48 to 50 guns c. 1695. H.M.S. 'Winchester' was very similar in appearance to ships of this class*

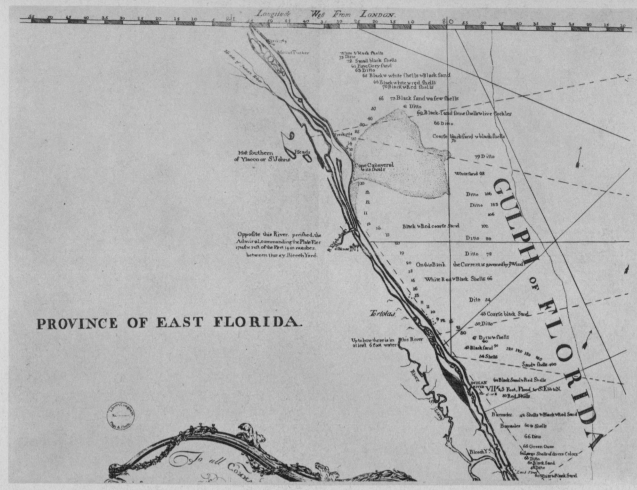

Longitude West From London.

PROVINCE OF EAST FLORIDA.

GULPH OF FLORIDA

7   *Detail of a map of East Florida from a book by Bernard Romans published in New York in 1775. On it the author indicated where the 1715 fleet was wrecked off the mouth of the St Sebastian River*

During the War of the Spanish Succession, which finally ended in 1713, gold and silver had accumulated in the strongrooms of America, the Spanish not daring to send it home during the hostilities. By the summer of 1715, the New Spain fleet and the Terra Firma fleet had reached Central and South America respectively, the trade fairs had been held, and the ships had been loaded for return to Europe. The combined fleet sailed from Havana in July and slowly headed up the Florida Straits toward the debouchment north of the Bahamas. While still in the Straits, a hurricane struck; of the eleven ships in the fleet, only one escaped to sail back to Havana with news of the disaster. Most of the crews and passengers were drowned or dashed to pieces on the reefs. Of the survivors, numbering several hundreds, many died on the beach from injuries, illness and starvation. The Spanish officials at St Augustine and Havana, having rescued whom they could, then took steps to recover the treasure. Full-scale salvage operations started the following spring and continued for almost four years. Probably half of the registered gold and silver was recovered, but since the fleets always carried

quantities of unrecorded wealth being smuggled to Spain, no accurate figure of the final loss can ever be arrived at.

In the course of the naval wars of the seventeenth and eighteenth centuries, all the belligerents commissioned privately-owned warships to augment the regular naval forces. The crews of these ships, having enjoyed the easy life of the privateer, found it difficult when peace came to return to the laborious routine of the peacetime sailor and many became pirates. The disaster to the fleet of 1715, following the end of the War of the Spanish Succession by only two years, aroused the natural cupidity of captains and sailors unable to accept an honest life at sea. Henry Jennings, a Bermudian ship's captain, was one who took action. Sailing from Port Royal with a small flotilla and some 300 men, he attacked the Spaniards' salvage camp which had been established near the site of the disaster. Here were piled up a large number of pieces-of-eight which had been laboriously retrieved by the native divers. Jennings' haul can never be exactly known, but it was probably around 350,000 pieces. The attack was undoubtedly backed by colonial officials and the prize was quietly dispersed. Jennings escaped punishment under a general amnesty granted pirates at Nassau in the Bahamas two years later, and presumably retired to Bermuda. Many of his accomplices were less wise and continued their piratical careers, and this led most of them to the gallows.

Working with native divers, using lung-power and crude pots to trap air under water, the Spanish continued to comb the wreck sites until 1719. After this they were occasionally investigated by ships passing by, but the remains were gradually covered with sand and encrustation and almost forgotten. Charts of the period following the disaster bore laconic inscriptions referring to this fleet. As late as the 1770s, Bernard Romans, working in English Florida, marked the place on a chart accompanying his history of the area.

Treasure lore has always been a part of the life of the Florida sea-coast. For years Mr Kip Wagner, a contractor of Sebastian, Florida, spent his spare time beachcombing for coins and other relics. His finds led him to research work on the documents relating to the lost fleet. Aided by a friend, Dr Kip Kelso, Wagner gathered the information needed for a search. He found divers and other expert team members at the Cape Kennedy Space Center, and was later joined by a group from California with modern electronic equipment. In 1961, after many disappointments, the group succeeded in locating several of the wrecked ships of the fleet. In the years of salvage operations that followed, under licence from the State of Florida, the richest find of Spanish treasure ever taken from the sea was recovered. Silver coins by the thousand, silver wedges, gold ingots, and some 4,000 gold coins were brought up. More important to the historian and the archaeologist is a comprehensive collection of artifacts representing every phase of life in a Spanish treasure fleet of that period. Many naval guns were retrieved along with specialized projectiles such as bar-shot wrapped with flammable tar-soaked rope to form an incendiary missile. Musket balls wired together to produce a deadly, if erratic, projectile, hand-grenades of iron with wooden fuses, swords and muskets, pistols and daggers – standard Spanish weapons for defending the ship from boarders – were recovered. Fittings of the ship's rigging give us details of construction not mentioned in documents or shown in contemporary drawings. Rich collections of Chinese porcelain and jewellery show how prosperous were many of the passengers returning to Spain with fortunes made in the New World. Guadalajara ware from Mexico attests the importance the Spaniards attached to the native crafts. Common red-ware bowls and food jars, and bones of fish and land animals tell us much about the food eaten on the ships and the methods of storing it for the voyage. There were even traces of clothing – shoe soles, buckles and buttons – to help in piecing together the contemporary scene. Every aspect of the American trade of the period and life in the fleet is represented by the assembled finds in a way that no document can so vividly convey.

And if one salient fact emerges from all this evidence, it is that the people who sailed with the fleet of 1715 ate much the same food and lived in much the same way as those who sailed in Spanish vessels a century earlier. The heavy battery of the ships had changed little, the standard weapon being the cast iron, four-wheeled carriage gun, though small arms had improved considerably with the introduction of the flintlock. The documents tell us some of these facts but they have not the dramatic impact of the objects themselves. Years of study will be required for the proper assessment of the materials brought to light by Wagner and his colleagues, and for writing the historical and scientific reports; but when this is done, our knowledge of the history of the period will be greatly enhanced. Carl Clausen, State Archaeologist, is providing professional guidance connected with further study of the sites of the 1715 fleet and other underwater exploration in Florida waters.

## The Fleet of 1733

The disaster of 1715 was a terrible blow to the already tottering Spanish monarchy. The loss of so much treasure almost wrecked the finances of the war-ravaged and debt-ridden nation. But worse was to follow. Just eighteen years, almost to the day, after the loss of the 1715 fleet, another convoy of treasure-laden ships was wiped out by a hurricane. The fleet left Havana on Friday, July 13, 1733. Disaster overtook them two days later in the narrow Florida Straits, the scene of the earlier tragedy, but this time the ships were dashed to pieces on the reefs and beaches of the Central Florida Keys. Accounts vary, but it is believed that eight galleons and thirteen or fourteen other vessels were involved. As in 1715, more than half of the persons aboard lost their lives and again a great deal of valuable material went to the bottom. Rescue and salvage operations were promptly begun and much of the treasure was salvaged; there being no Henry Jennings to raid the salvage camp this time, however, most of it ultimately found its way back to Spain.

In the late 1940s the site of one of the galleons was discovered by Arthur McKee, an experienced helmet diver from Homestead, Florida. Later, Edwin A. Link and I joined McKee in two seasons of diving on the site. A chart presumably prepared by a Spanish navigator when the wrecks were still visible suggests that the ship in question was the flag-ship *Rui*. The site has proved to be virtually a submerged museum. Every aspect of the working and defence of the ship and life aboard, as well as the treasure and cargo carried, is represented. The usual armament of heavy cast-iron guns formed the main battery of the vessel. The hand weapons included the standard 0.70 calibre military muskets, boarding axes or tomahawks, pistols with the Spanish miquelet locks and the ubiquitous Spanish sword. The projectiles included the standard solid iron shot, fixed bar-shot and iron hand-grenades. Chain plates of wrought-iron strap with welded loops for the dead-eyes, blocks, iron hooks, head cringles (the iron rings attached to the head of a sail to lash it to the yard) and parrels represented the fixed and running rigging of the ship. Pewter plates and dishes of majolica as well as simple red-ware bowls tell us how the beef, pork and fish were served. The food could be deduced from identifiable bones, and coffee and cacao beans, while native corn-grinders indicated that the grain had been eaten aboard. Among the small objects of personal use from the chests of the passengers and crew were the usual buckles, shoe soles, brass pins and pewter and brass buttons. The cargo included cochineal and possibly indigo, tanned leather, billets of mahogany, children's toy dishes of Guadalajara ware and Chinese porcelain from the Manila Galleon trade. The treasure, which had been largely salvaged by the Spaniards, comprised the rough silver coins known as 'cobs', in denominations of 2, 4 and 8 reales, a few gold coins and gold jewellery. The manifest shows a large number of silver bars but none have come to light in modern times, and it is believed that the Spanish recovered all of them. One or two of the very rare pillar dollars of new design bearing the date 1732, the first year of issue, were found by McKee. Perhaps the most winsome discovery was a

50 figurine in cast silver, in the whirling attitude of a Flamenco dancer. The dress she wears is still seen in Andalusia today. She exactly fitted onto an onyx base found by McKee the year before.

Since McKee's discovery, several more wrecks of the 1733 fleet have been located and explored. In 1968 a large site was found with the aid of a magnetometer just outside the three-mile limit off Tavernier, Florida. Mr Tom Gurr, president of a salvage organization, has recovered from it articles very similar to those found on the *Rui*. The Spanish chart referred to above points to

42–49 this site being that of the *St Joseph*, one of the galleons of the fleet and probably of English construction. Several objects peculiar to the 1733 sites include a lead water-pump and tank dated 1728, which were probably used to furnish the officers' cabins with water. In the

47 floor timbers of the hull a human skull, the first reported from a site of this fleet, was found. It has not been possible to ascertain whether the skull belonged to a victim of the wreck or to one of the local divers engaged by the Spaniards to recover the treasure.

The salvage collections of the 1733 fleet represent the 42–44 material culture of seafaring Spain during her final decline. The *coup de grâce* came when she lost her last colonies in South America in 1825, but her fate had been determined at least two centuries before by the short-sighted economic policies of her kings and ministers. When Spain was in the first flush of success in her exploitation of the New World her king was able to decree that only vessels of Spanish origin could sail to the American colonies. The ships of the 1733 fleet were almost all built outside Spain. One sea captain who had seen the fleet in Havana harbour before the ill-fated voyage, said that seventeen of the ships were foreign: eleven English, one Genoese, two from New England, one Mexican, one Dutch and one Cuban. What clearer evidence could there be of the drastic decline of Spanish economic power by the early eighteenth century? The years following the disaster saw the rise of British and French trade in America until the Spanish were almost completely excluded from maritime commerce. The English in the colonies of North America had early taken to the sea for a living, and with the establishment of the United States, yankee traders invaded the Atlantic basin in force and a vigorous trade sprang up with the former, previously excluded, Spanish colonies. Gone were the days of the armed convoys bringing to Spain the treasures of gold, silver, gems and the exotic products of tropical America that were the life-blood of the mother country. In their place sailed the great warships of France and England contending for the domination of the Caribbean Basin, and merchantmen from England, France and Holland contending for coffee, cacao, fine tropical woods and dyestuffs – goods highly prized in Europe. The British colonists from the north and later the yankee traders brought lumber, ice (packed in sawdust), and wheat to the hungry plantation markets of the West Indies in return for the sugar which they manufactured into rum; other yankees engaged in that trade in humans which brought Negro slaves to America. Today, with few exceptions, merchant ships still follow those basic routes which the early Spanish navigators pioneered when their country's trade links with America were being forged. If the economists and governing princes of Spain had been as skilled as her navigators, she might still be a major power in world affairs.

---

1 *The Virgin of the Navigators* was painted about 1535 by Alejo Fernandez for the chapel of the Casa de Contratación in Seville, a governing authority set up to control Spain's rapidly expanding trade with the New World which had been initiated some forty years earlier by Columbus's discovery of America. The painting shows the Virgin, whose cloak envelops a group of adoring Spaniards and converted Indians, hovering in the sky above an assortment of ships large and small. The vessel occupying the central position is a fairly accurate representation of a sixteenth-century three-masted merchant ship, with characteristic raised forecastle and high poop, such as the Spaniards used for their transatlantic voyages.

It was the fabled treasure of 'the Indies' that impelled Columbus to set out on his epoch-making voyage across the Atlantic Ocean – only to discover an unknown continent. It was the treasure that he and those who followed in his wake found in the Americas that launched the Spaniards upon the western seaways. Many of their ships foundered in storms or were sunk by pirates and privateers. With the aid of up-to-date equipment more wrecks are being located each decade, and long-lost treasure salvaged. These wrecks and their cargoes throw much light on contemporary maritime activities, corroborating and amplifying the historical record.

2, 3 This magnificently wrought gold pectoral cross set with seven emeralds was among the many objects recovered by Edward Tucker in 1955 from one of three sixteenth-century Spanish wrecks located off Bermuda.

4 Gold pocket watch, complete with all its component parts, found in the ruins of Port Royal, an English settlement in Jamaica which flourished by battening on Spanish shipping in the Caribbean until an earthquake flung it into the sea in 1692. The name of the London maker of the watch is engraved on the case.

5 The richest find of Spanish treasure ever taken from the sea. Coins and jewellery, ingots and artifacts salvaged in the 1960s from ships of a Spanish fleet wrecked by a hurricane in the Florida Strait while on their way from Havana to Spain in 1715.

2

3

4

Modern techniques and equipment have revolutionized underwater archaeology in recent decades, and every year sees the introduction of further improvements.

6 James Mahoney of the Smithsonian Institution, working under water, makes a sketch on heavy plastic of part of an unidentified Spanish ship wrecked off Bermuda prior to 1580.

7 The final drawing, which shows the positioning of the ship's planking, based on the sketch.

8 The author of this chapter adjusts a measuring device on the sea bed at the same site.

9 Among the many objects recovered from the wreck was this brass crucifix, identified as Andalusian, of *c.* 1540.

8

6

7

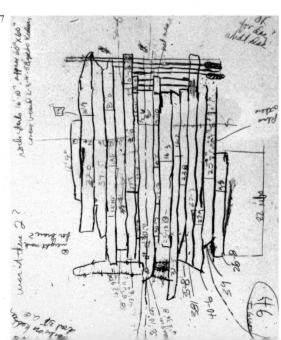

9

10

The name of Edward ('Teddy') Tucker is indissolubly linked with the locating of Spanish shipwrecks in the waters off Bermuda, and the subsequent salvaging operations.

10–13 Among the objects he recovered from one of the wrecks in question, dated to 1594, were: a pair of navigator's brass dividers (10); an apothecary's mortar made of bronze (11); a pewter clyster pump, part of the ship's surgeon's equipment (12) a brass case for a mercury time-glass (13).

11–13

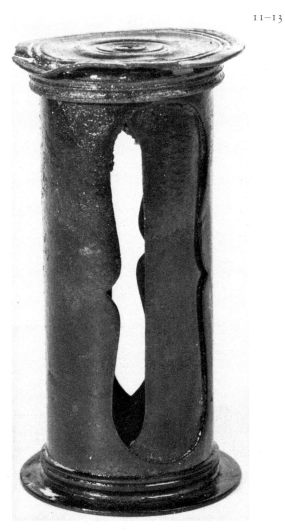

17

18

14   In 1966, on a coral reef off Highborn Key in the Bahamas, the wreck of what is almost certainly a pirate ship or privateer was discovered. These pieces of wrought iron artillery and ship-fittings corroborate the evidence provided by timber fragments of the hull found at the site.

15   A diver at work on the hull timbers of a Spanish ship which foundered near Bermuda prior to 1580.

14

## 19

20

16–20 It was a Spanish vessel wrecked in Bermudian waters in 1594 that yielded the bulk of the 'Tucker Treasure'. A particularly interesting find was a fragment of Japanese porcelain (16); ware of this kind will have come into Spanish possession as a result of Dutch trading via Manila, Acapulco and Vera Cruz. Other objects shown here are gold ingots bearing circular tax-paid stamps (17); stamps in the form of Roman numerals indicating carat weight (18) and others signifying the source of the gold (19); part of a gold bar stamped to show its Pinto river, New Grenada, source (20).

21–23 The *San Antonio*, wrecked in the same area in 1621, has likewise been a rich source of salvage. The cowrie shell (21) was one of a consignment of 20,000; they were used as currency in the African slave trade. The two large pottery vessels, shown with sundry metal objects, were probably used to carry provisions for the voyage (22). In the photograph at the bottom of the page, a diver is seen investigating timber fragments of the ship's hull (23).

21

22

23

24  Beads of various sorts were among the objects found at the site of the *San Antonio* wreck. Above is a selection from these, representing (from top to bottom): steatite facetted beads; trade beads of coral-coloured glass; an aggery bead of red, yellow and blue glass, used in the African slave trade; rosary beads of ivory; rosary beads made from tropical plant seeds, from the South Pacific.

25  Fragments of Spanish majolica ware recovered from the wreck of the *San Antonio*. The passengers' meals were in all probability served on crockery of this kind.

At the end of the seventeenth century the English settled in Jamaica, with a view to breaking the Spanish monopoly of the trade routes in the Caribbean. On the island's south coast had grown up the town of Port Royal, largely a repository for the loot of buccaneers and freebooters. In 1692, at the height of its prosperity, the town was shattered by an earthquake which caused some two-thirds of it to collapse into the sea.

26  This Chinese seventeenth-century figurine of a goddess in white porcelain was recovered from the submerged ruins of the town.

27  A partially encrusted wine-bottle, a pewter plate, pewter spoons, a silver fork, glass tumblers, and bone knife-handles, from Port Royal.

Port Royal, the town that slid into the sea. A huddle of houses on the seashore is all the remains above water of the seventeenth-century British township in the Bahamas, which grew rich by preying on Spanish shipping. Now, after close on three centuries, the sea is in turn reluctantly yielding up some of its spoils, and most of the credit for this must go to Robert Marx acting for the Government of Jamaica.

28 Surface view of an 'air-lift' in operation off-shore, removing sediment from the site.

29 A block of cemented bricks, part of the wall of one of the town's sunken houses.

30 Silver coins, part of a brass key, and the key-hole plate from a chest, recovered from the site. The chest contained more than 500 silver coins such as those shown in the photograph.

In the late 1950s Edward Tucker found some sand-encrusted cannon in a hole in the sea bed off the southern coast of Bermuda. Subsequent exploration revealed further wreckage; this proved to be that of the *Virginia Merchant*, which foundered at this spot in 1660 while carrying immigrants and supplies from England to the newly founded colony of Virginia.

31-33 Among the objects salvaged were an ivory comb in a remarkably good state of preservation (31); a razor hone (32). The strange object at the foot of this page is an iron shot encrusted with the typical black flint pebble ballast of English sites (33).

34

35

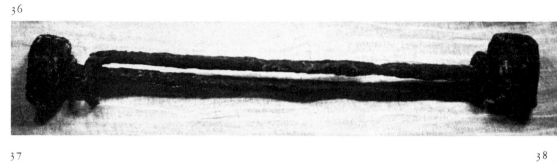

36

37

38

276

## 39

Much valuable information about early ships and their armament can be gleaned from pieces of equipment of various kinds, recovered by divers from the sites of wrecks. Occasionally a chance find will help to identify the ship concerned. In the case of H.M.S. *Winchester*, an English halfpenny dated 1694 was found in the encrusted barrel of one of the guns.

34–37 From the Spanish wreck of 1594 discovered by Edward Tucker in Bermudian waters many weapons were salvaged, including: a sand-encrusted sword (34); incendiary shot (35); expanding bar shot (36); a swivel gun, known as a 'verso' (37).

38 This iron three-pounder falconet was recovered from the site of an unidentified ship, probably Spanish or French, which struck a reef in the Bermudas *c.* 1595. The carriage is a reproduction of the original found with the barrel.

39 The wreck of the Spanish ship *San Antonio* yielded, in addition to much treasure, numerous pieces of the vessel's armament and individual weapons, among them the encrusted daggers, sword hilt and flintlock (Spanish lock) pistol shown here.

40 Some of the 28 cannon retrieved from the wreck of H.M.S. *Winchester*, which in 1695 struck a reef off Florida and sank. In the foreground, the remains of a 15-foot anchor shaft (fitted with a 6-inch ring, not visible in the photograph). These cannon were salvaged as long ago as 1932–35.

41 Among the objects recovered from the *Rui*, one of the ships of a treasure-laden convoy that was dashed to pieces by a hurricane in the Florida Straits in 1733, was this flintlock for a military musket.

42

43

44

On July 13, 1733, a Spanish fleet, laden with treasure, set sail from Havana bound for Spain. Two days later it ran into a violent storm and its entire complement of more than twenty ships was dashed to pieces on the reefs and beaches of Central Florida Keys. The finding of a Spanish navigator's chart, presumably prepared when the wrecks were still visible above water, enabled Arthur McKee to identify a galleon he had discovered in the 1940s as the *Rui*, one of the fleet's vessels. Later, when Tom Gurr, using a magnetometer, located another ship of the 1733 fleet, the same chart served to identify her as the *St Joseph*. In 1968, the author of this chapter assisted Mr Gurr in the salvage work.

45

42–44 Among the objects recovered from the wreck of the *St Joseph* were: gold rings, silver coins and a glass amulet; pots and figurines of black ceramic ware, probably from Mexico; fragments of blue and white painted ware.

45 This modern oil painting, though it does not actually depict the *St Joseph*, gives a good impression of an eighteenth-century vessel of the same type.

46 Some of the planking of the *St Joseph*, as first found and photographed *in situ* by one of the divers.

46

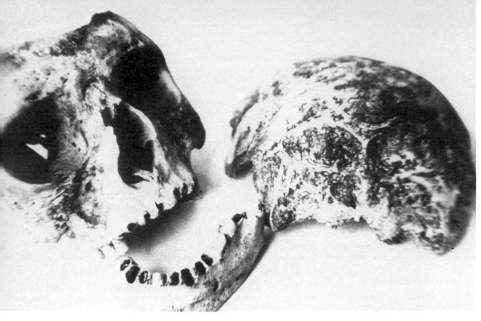

47 This human skull was found in the floor timbers of the *St Joseph*; whether it belonged to a victim of the wreck, or to one of the native divers the Spaniards put to work on salvaging the treasure, is not known.

48 Two encrusted cast-iron cannon, which formed part of the armament of the *St Joseph*.

49 Some of the hull timbers on the sea-bed. The *St Joseph* is believed to have been of English construction, which probably accounts for the solid nature of these timbers and their good state of preservation.

50 This cast-silver figurine of a dancing girl in Andalusian-type skirt is one of the most attractive objects recovered from the *Rui*. The onyx base was found a year before the figure itself.

50

# 12

# Waterways open
# the New World

The North American fur trade

ROBERT C. WHEELER

Ships of the Great Lakes

RICHARD C. van GEMERT

# THE NORTH AMERICAN FUR TRADE
BY ROBERT C. WHEELER

*A new world to exploit.* For five hundred years before Columbus reached the New World, Europeans had known the shores of northeastern North America. The longships of the Vikings had coasted along them, and historians are certain that reticent fishermen from a Catholic Europe had more than once furled their sails and dropped their boats to take a rich harvest of cod from the Grand Banks. In the wake of 1492 came a line of explorer-navigators probing the coast for a passage to the fabled Cathay, a way to the western seas or to a land rich in precious metals.

As knowledge of the region spread and as more fishermen tried their luck off the North American coast, they began to search out landing places to dry and salt the cod. Quickly they discovered that a trinket, a piece of cloth, a worn-out knife or axe would buy fine furs from Indians hungry for items of European manufacture. During much of the sixteenth century, fur trading remained a casual by-product of the fishing industry, confined to brief periods when time was spent in harbours drying fish. It was a case of the Indian seeking out the white man to barter with.

In 1581, however, the initiative in the fur trade passed to the European. A group of French merchants from St Malo began sending vessels up the St Lawrence River to intercept the flow of furs from the interior. Here were the real beginnings of the fur trade in North America, a business enterprise that in two and a half centuries would write an exciting chapter in North American history.

During the sixteenth century and the first decade of the seventeenth, virtually all fur trading was done on the St Lawrence at certain rendezvous points and at annual fairs held in Montreal, Three Rivers and Quebec. Although the European was anxious to move into the interior, the Indian did his best to discourage it. Tribes on the coast and along the St Lawrence quickly assumed the role of middlemen. By 1615 both the Iroquois and the Hurons were engaged in trade with western tribes. Each was supplied by a European wholesaler – the Hurons allied with the French and the Iroquois with the Dutch – as they competed for control of the Great Lakes and Ottawa River routes to the interior. The practice of Indian middlemen was to move westward with the trading frontier.

It must be borne in mind that the impact of European goods upon the Indians was immense. An axe of tempered iron, however dull, was no less than a miracle to a man who had known only stone hatchets; a brass kettle replaced weeks of work invested in making perishable vessels of wood, bark, or pottery. When the Indians demanded guns, they were at first refused, but as with liquor in later years, competition between nations and traders soon erased restraint.

As the Indian became more and more dependent on such European goods, the skills and social disciplines necessary for survival in the wilderness were soon forgotten. As animals were depleted under the relentless slaughter, the Indian faced the painful choice of abandoning his heritage and adopting in some degree the white man's culture or living in pitiful degradation on the white man's charity.

## Explorers, Traders, Trappers, and Voyageurs

Fur trading and exploring were closely related and interdependent. Samuel de Champlain, during the early decades of the seventeenth century, shrewdly turned his exploring efforts to advantage by trading with interior tribes, much to the dismay of the Indian middlemen. So intent was he upon discovering water routes to the west that he encouraged young adventurers to go and live with the Indians, learning their language, customs, and routes of travel. These men became the forerunners of the *coureurs de bois* and the voyageurs, who were to carry French influence from the St Lawrence to the Rockies and from Hudson Bay to the Gulf of Mexico.

*1 Travels of Samuel de Champlain. Sometimes called the father of the fur trade, Champlain was one of the first explorers to probe the interior country west of St Lawrence*

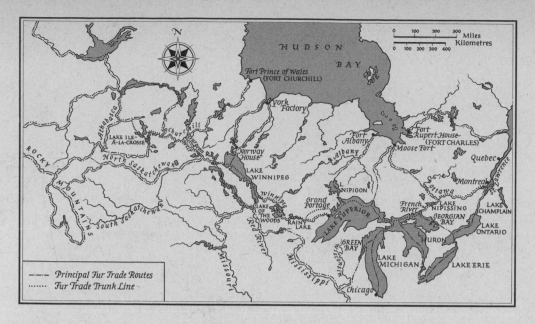

2 *Although trading with the Indians for furs was carried on over much of the North American continent, by far the bulk of it took place within the area encompassed by this map. The area shown, especially the northern half, produced the richest pelts*

Between 1615 and 1760 numbers of French-Canadian woodsmen roamed the Indian country in search of fur. The activities of two of these pioneer-adventurers, Pierre Radisson and Medard Chouart Sieur des Groseilliers who in the mid-1600s traded with Indians in the uncharted country which is now northwestern Wisconsin, were soon to lead to important developments. Hearing of the existence of Hudson Bay from the red man, they were convinced that it would provide the easiest and least expensive route to the interior of the continent. The French ignored their advice, but the English listened and the result was the Hudson's Bay Company, formed in 1670; soon the English had a number of trading posts on the shores of Hudson Bay, all located at the mouths of rivers which radiated out from the bay like spokes of a wheel.

Before long, however, French *coureurs de bois* had worked their way north and were intercepting the Indians who were travelling the rivers with their loads of fur for the English trading posts. They soon spread to the north and west and by 1760 had bartered for furs in the very shadows of the Rocky Mountains.

The end of the French regime on the Plains of Abraham did not relieve the pressures of competition on the Hudson's Bay Company. Scarcely two years after the British had taken possession of New France, independent English and Scottish traders appeared in the Indian country. These 'pedlars' forced the 'Honourable Company' to reach toward the interior with additional posts, even though the Company still enjoyed the enormous advantage of a royal charter which gave it exclusive access to the low-cost sea transportation through Hudson Bay. Eventually the independent operators were forced to combine their resources in the great North West Company, but after thirty years of competition it capitulated and merged with its rival.

By this time, 1821, the United States had achieved effective control over the area south of the 49th Parallel, its legal claim to which had for years been ignored. Many of the North West Company traders there simply joined John Jacob Astor's American Fur Company, often accused of being more British than American in personnel and procedures.

The *engagé* or voyageur was the human packhorse of the fur trade. It was his job to paddle the freighter canoe sixteen hours a day, load it, unload it, and carry both canoe and contents over innumerable portages. The voyageur might be either a 'porkeater', who brought canoes from Montreal to some inland *entrepôt* and returned (eating salt pork on the return leg), or a 'winterer', who prided himself on wintering in the wilderness and sometimes travelled 1,500 or 2,000 miles to the north and west.

### Travel, Communication, and Major Routes

The extension of the fur trade across the upper part of North America was made possible by two factors: the waterway system and the birch tree. Along the chain of hundreds of thousands of lakes and streams to the north and west, altitudes were fairly uniform and no major barriers divided the great continental watersheds. Thus portages between the basins of the Great Lakes, the Mississippi, Hudson Bay, and the Arctic Ocean were relatively short and easy. The portage trails, nearly invisible to all but the Indians and later to the *coureurs de bois*, were chosen with care: one might be quick but risky, another slow but safer. The principal routes were the Ottawa–French River which became the trunk line between the St Lawrence Valley and the upper lakes, the route to the Mississippi by way of Green Bay and the Wisconsin River, the Pigeon and Winnipeg rivers to reach Lake Winnipeg, the Saskatchewan to reach the Rocky Mountains or the Churchill River by way of the Sturgeon Weir. The basic trunk line of the Hudson's Bay Company extended from Fort York on the coast to Norway House near the northern end of Lake Winnipeg. From there smaller lines branched to the Saskatchewan posts, Ile a la Crosse, and the Red River.

The second factor contributing to the success of the fur trade was the birch tree. From its bark the Indians fashioned a craft which could be paddled in the narrowest and most shallow of streams, and which was light enough to be carried over portages around rapids, waterfalls, and other obstructions. Although fragile, the canoe could be mended easily from materials found on almost any lake shore south of the sub-boreal forest.

Travel with the traders, however, was anything but a comfortable experience. Space was cramped, and the traveller was exposed to rain, wind, sun, and insects. Portages were often knee-deep in mire. Food was a monotonous diet of salt pork, lyed corn, and pea soup in the east; in the northwest, pemmican or whitefish. Stops for repairs were frequent. The small roots of the spruce or hemlock tree, called 'wattap', were used to sew the sheets of bark together, and the gum which was applied to the seams was a resinous substance produced by boiling the pitch from spruce trees.

The goods or furs carried over portages at one time were normally two packs, each weighing approximately ninety pounds. The rate of travel varied with the conditions. An average day's run during a three-month trip in the Northwest would be about 33 miles. Pushing hard, with good conditions, an express or 'light' canoe might make as much as 75 or 80 miles. A single square sail was often employed on the larger bodies of water, offering a desperately needed opportunity to rest without loss of too much precious time.

### Fur Trade Craft and their Development

At just what point in time the small craft of the Indian began to undergo change to meet the needs of the white man in the fur trade is not known. Records are scanty, particularly where such mundane details as canoe dimensions are concerned. However, licences for trading made out by French officials in the 1680s generally refer to a canoe with three men. As trade moved farther into the interior, size apparently began to increase: a 1709 manuscript lists canoes 32 feet (French Measure) long, capable of carrying as much as 3,000 pounds, and a 1714 wintering expedition used a canoe able to handle thirty-four bales. The usual size designation of a canoe was by the number of 'places', six-place and eight-place canoes being the most common. A study of eighteenth-century records has, however, convinced Mrs Albert Gerin-Lajoie, working for the Minnesota Historical Society, that 'places' did not refer to the number of men carried but rather to the number of openings between thwarts in the craft.

3, 4    The Montreal canoe, or *canot du maître* (possibly named for one Louis Le Maître, a leading canoe manufacturer of Three Rivers), was built for use on big water, including such lakes as Nipissing, Huron, and Superior, which become wild enough in rough weather to threaten even modern steel steamers. It was ordinarily 35 or 36 feet in length, although some estimates have run as high as 40 feet. Several descriptions indicate that these canoes could carry up to four tons, including eight or nine men with provisions and gear.

The North canoe, or *canot du nord*, was a little brother of the Montreal, designed specifically for inland waters. Ranging from 24 to 28 feet long, it had a shallow draft and a broad beam, namely 18 inches and 4½ feet. Its load was considerably less than that of the Montreal: twenty North canoes were required to carry the contents of twelve *canots du maître*. However, it could be portaged by two men over rough terrain, while its big brother required four. On an average the North canoe carried about one and a half tons, but the size of the load was subject to as much variation as the conditions of travel.

A variation of the North canoe was the express or 'light' canoe. Sometimes this was a smaller craft, ranging from 18 to 21 feet long, built for rapid communication and also for use on particularly difficult northern streams; more often simply a freight canoe, either North or Montreal, lightly loaded and manned by a large enough crew to carry canoe and contents across portages in one trip.

Because birch does not grow on the Pacific slope nor farther north than the head of James Bay, a lack of materials for construction caused hardships as the traders moved farther afield. Many cargo canoes, as standard procedure, carried rolls of bark for patching purposes. Already, however, a solution had appeared. The 1745 journal of one Joseph Isbister, factor of Albany House, contains suggestions that an attempt be made to build a boat of shallow draft which could navigate shoal water and carry more goods than a canoe. We do not know when the first of such boats was built, but by 1779 the craft that came to be known as the 'York boat' was in regular use on the Albany River.

The source of the York boat's distinctive design was probably the Orkney Island fishing boat to which it bore a close resemblance, not surprisingly since the Hudson's Bay Company recruited a large number of its employees from the Orkneys during the eighteenth century. The York boat accomplished the same work as the freighter canoe, but more efficiently. It carried a greater cargo in proportion to the crew; it could safely weather storms that kept canoes bound to the beaches of the larger lakes for days at a time; its sturdy sides withstood floating ice; and it was safer than a canoe under sail, although, like the canoe, it was difficult to manage since it had no keel. Constructed with two sharp ends, it could be easily backed off rocks and sand bars. In short, its only disadvantage in comparison to the canoe was its weight in portaging. It earned its name and reputation by making each year the amazing round trip from Methye Portage to York Fort and back again. By 1810 a typical York boat was carrying almost twice the load of a North canoe, and in the Hudson's Bay Company system it had superseded the canoe for all ordinary freighting purposes. In that year it is reported that the company had only one post where canoes were still made. After the merger of 1821 this trend extended throughout the fur trade area, and the death knell of the great freight canoe had sounded. The York boat, itself,

5

6

was eventually displaced by the steamer and outboard motor, and as far as I know the only true York boat in existence is that displayed at the Lower Fort Garry historical museum a few miles north of Winnipeg; there are reports of one sunk in a lake in northern Canada and the bones of others may be buried in permafrost.

Despite its unusual features the York boat has often been confused with the wooden bateau. Records are available on bateaux from the 1660s in New France, and it seems that the style and size remained constant for a great many years, the addition of one or two knees being the only modifications introduced. The bateau was constructed of pine, was flat-bottomed, double-ended, and had no keel. In size it seldom varied from 25–26 feet long and 22–24 inches deep.

Great numbers of French-Canadian bateaux were in use on the St Lawrence River from as early as the 1680s.

The use of bateaux in the fur trade increased markedly when Yonge Street (now Toronto) was opened up in 1796. Before this time North West Company canoe brigades had gone up the Ottawa and then by way of the French River to Georgian Bay. By the end of the century, however, the company had begun to send fleets of bateaux up the St Lawrence to the Carrying Place, where they were portaged to Lake Ontario. From there the goods were transported to Lake Simcoe and thence to Georgian Bay. In 1960 scuba divers discovered the remains of a number of wooden bateaux on the bottom of Lake George (New York). Bruce Inverarity, former director of the Adirondack Museum, realizing their importance to the history of marine architecture, recovered and preserved several of these rare craft. Following the War of 1812 the increasing use of schooners on the Great Lakes gradually brought an end to the large-scale employment of bateaux.

## Cargo and Logistics

As the fur trade progressed from its simple, almost casual beginnings to a complex continent-wide business, the list of goods traded grew steadily longer and more varied. Certain things, however, remained in demand for two centuries or more; axes, knives, and kettles, among the first items traded, never lost their appeal, the only changes being in size and style.

The business records of the Montreal merchants referred to earlier contain many examples of invoices, illustrating the needs, trends, and operational methods of the trade at various intervals between 1715 and 1775. In these the contents of each bale or 'piece' were listed separately, even including the canvas for packing. Articles such as axes, gunflints, knives, mirrors, scissors, and guns were packed in crates. Barrels were used for liquor, powder, and salt, while lead balls and shot, biscuit, and dried peas were packed in bags. The invoice listed the provisions for the trip, the equipment, the cost of transporting the goods from Montreal to Lachine, the value of the canoe and sail, and even the roll of bark taken along for emergency repairs.

A single bale or crate would contain a variety of goods, while most of the bales in the same shipment had nearly identical contents – offering a preselected variety of goods for display and minimizing the risk of losing the entire stock of any one item by canoe accident.

## Loss of Life and Lading

Accidents were not uncommon. On 23 May, 1800 Daniel Harmon noted in his journal that 'at almost every rapid which we have passed, since we left Montreal, we have seen a number of crosses erected; and at one, I counted no less than thirty!'

A large proportion of accidents took place where rapids had to be passed. Going upstream the voyageurs would usually paddle or pole as far as possible, then portage or line the canoes up. The same procedure was used going downstream, with one important difference: they could, if they chose, shoot or *saulter* the rapids – with, as a rule, only a partial load. There was always room for error, since conditions varied greatly with the level of the water. Detailed eye-witness accounts of such tragedies include a passage from Alexander Henry the Younger's description of a canoe turning over in the year 1800: '. . . I then perceived the man riding upon a bale of dry goods in the midst of the waves. We made every exertion to get near him, . . . but alas; he sank under a heavy swell, and when the bale arose the man appeared no more. . . .' This particular rapid was so dangerous that both the Hudson's Bay Company and the North West Company forbade their brigades to run it.

In travelling on big lakes it was customary to follow a shore-line or a string of islands, and to cross, when necessary, at the narrowest possible place. Often, however, the voyageurs were faced with the choice of paddling for hours along the shore or making a quick 'traverse' from one headland to another, risking sudden and often destructive squalls. Brigades commonly moved out in the calm of early morning, long before daybreak; sometimes they waited weatherbound for days on the shore. For all that, as in the rapids, men and boats frequently went to the bottom.

In the late summer of 1960 the discovery of such a tragedy was made along the old Grand Portage fur trade route. Credit for it goes primarily to Edward W. Davis, the retired head of the University of Minnesota's Mines Experiment Station. In pursuing early fur trade literature, Davis noticed occasional accounts of canoe accidents and he guessed rightly that some of the lost trade goods, especially those of metal, might be found at the bottom of rapids or in the pools below waterfalls where the rushing water had deposited them. He was acquainted with three skilled scuba divers and on their first day of diving for him – at Horsetail Rapids near Saganaga Lake – they located and removed seventeen brass trade kettles, the remains of a bale lost in some accident almost two centuries earlier. When found, eight of the kettles were still nested one inside the other, to conserve vital

*3   Underwater finds were made at the four named points*

cargo space. Davis notified the Minnesota Historical Society, which decided to assume sponsorship of a search project. A second important discovery was made in the summer of 1961 on the same fur trade route northwest of Ely, Minnesota. This site yielded wrought-iron trade axes, ice chisels, spears, beads, thimbles, buttons, vermilion paint, gunflints, an assortment of knives, a unique metal pipe, cloth and various other items.

In 1963 jointly conducted Canadian-American explorations, sharing information and artifacts, were begun through the efforts of the President's Wilderness Committee, composed of members from both countries. Already in 1962 a team from the Royal Ontario Museum had made discoveries in the French River, between Lake Nipissing and Georgian Bay, similar to those made on the Grand Portage route. I was to direct the American phase of the new operation, and Dr Walter Kenyon of the Royal Ontario Museum, the Canadian. The National Geographic Society, the Quetico Foundation, the Hill Family Foundation, the Wilderness Research Center, and others gave financial support.

Until 1966 we simply conducted a systematic search of rapids and waterfalls along the main routes. Westward-flowing streams and rivers were the most productive because west-bound goods recovered were durable hardware while east-bound cargoes were quickly perishable furs, and the majority of accidents occurred when the brigades were proceeding downstream. In the meantime, however, research in early diaries and journals, carried out with the assistance of the Macalester College history department, has revealed the records of more than sixty accidents.

Early in 1966 Kenyon and I decided to concentrate for the first time on a documented accident site. We chose the spot at Portage de l'Isle where Alexander Henry, on August 9, 1800, had lost a canoe, one man and five bales of goods. Within thirty minutes after our Canadian and American divers had entered the waters of the Winnipeg the first group of artifacts was located. Over the next several days the divers continued a search

for additional material, marking positions of clusters of pieces or single items with white styrofoam floats, and plotting locations and relationships of the objects on the bottom for later laboratory study and interpretation.

The material recovered at Portage de l'Isle, which went to the Royal Ontario Museum for preservation and study, included a large mass of iron trade axes, all marked B A R and made in two general sizes, files, beads, two North West trade guns, knives, thimbles, a single engraved tomahawk, and a number of nested heavy tin bowls. Several of these carried the name of the maker, 'Townsend and Compton', a London firm in business between the years 1801 and 1811 – too late for the dishes to have gone down with Henry's goods in 1800. Kenyon has identified the finds of 1966 as having come from two or more different accidents, including Henry's.

The programme of 'whitewater' archaeology, which has evolved from a simple search and salvage operation into one employing sophisticated techniques and equipment, has made a number of distinctive contributions to the study of the fur trade. Trade goods found in Indian graves, on village sites, and occasionally in the excavation of fur post sites, are almost always isolated objects, usually damaged or worn before being buried or discarded. By contrast, our finds have yielded large quantities of unused goods, often lost from the same shipment, allowing the objects to be studied in series.

One of the resulting discoveries has been the unsuspected variety of items supplied by traders. Tools, ranging widely in size and shape within one crate, were apparently designed for highly specialized purposes – suggesting that the Indian of the eighteenth or early nineteenth century was far from a simple savage willing to accept any implement or trinket in exchange for his furs, but a shrewd customer who demanded (and got) merchandise adapted to his specific needs and tastes.

The great quantities of musket balls found will show the approximate calibres of guns used in the trade – again a piece of information not recorded in inventories or bills of lading. A few unique examples of the guns themselves have also been recovered. From masses of objects clustered together we have learned how goods were packaged for shipment, finding old newsprint and pieces of cloth used for wrapping hardware as early as the eighteenth century. Makers' names and trademarks, usually undistinguishable after years of hard usage, have appeared on a number of items, making it possible to date and identify them.

At the same time, our research has given us a more accurate and detailed knowledge of fur trade routes than can be gleaned from documentary sources alone, as well as giving us a better understanding of how traders and voyageurs negotiated the obstructions along the way. The cargoes they lost have much to tell about the fabulous wilderness industry that unrolled the map of North America, determined boundaries, and swayed national policies before the more familiar chapters of Canadian and United States history began.

# SHIPS OF THE GREAT LAKES

BY RICHARD C. VAN GEMERT

*The earliest ships*. During the development of the fur trade in the Great Lakes, it became evident that interior trading posts were as necessary as ample transportation to establish French control of the trade. Near the site of their first fort – Fort Frontenac at what is now Kingston, Ontario – the French elected to insure Indian acceptance of their permanence by a show of naval force. They towed two large barges, painted bright red and blue and bristling with cannon, into Lake Ontario via the St Lawrence River and anchored in the bay near by. Thus, early in 1663, the first vessels of any type other than bateaux or canoes had entered the inland waterway. The French Navy, however crudely represented, was on the Great Lakes.

Shortly thereafter, for conveyance of men and materials across the lake, the French built several small sailing vessels: the 20-ton *Cataraqui*, followed soon after by the 40-ton *Frontenac* and others. These were small versions of large ocean ships, only 50 to 55 feet in length with two square-rigged masts; called barks by some historians, the vessels were probably more like luggers.

On the night of December 25, 1678, the *Frontenac* foundered and sank in a severe gale on Lake Ontario, becoming the first casualty of the Great Lakes. The crew escaped with but little of the cargo, most of which had been intended as equipment for a new ship, the *Griffon*, then being built on Lake Erie. The *Griffon*, herself, was lost the following year on the upper lakes during the return leg of her maiden voyage. Recent attempts to locate the remains of the *Frontenac* have been unsuccessful, but several groups have made unsubstantiated claims for discovering the *Griffon*; the most promising site, containing timbers and keel matching those most probably used in the construction of the *Griffon*, was located under the sandy shore of an island at the northern end of Lake Huron.

Soon after the loss of the *Griffon*, the French were driven from the Great Lakes by Indian uprisings and their remaining vessels were sunk at Fort Frontenac. The next recorded ship on the upper lakes was the 60-foot British schooner *Michigan*, built in 1763, but speculation about other vessels being built on these lakes above Niagara Falls between 1679 and 1763 have been reinforced by two discoveries: wreckage of a ship along with coins dated to 1698 were dredged up in Lake Erie near Erie, Pennsylvania, and near Buffalo, New York, the remains of another old vessel – apparently French – were found in the sands of the shoreline.

Early in the eighteenth century the French regained control of the Great Lakes and built a small fleet of schooners and luggers for the transportation of goods and furs on Lake Ontario (but not, as far as is known, for use on the upper lakes). In poorly made vessels of green timbers, heavily laden with large deck cargoes, sailors were soon to experience the sudden fury of Great Lakes storms which match ocean gales in violence. They faced the added dangers of uncharted waters and attack by sometimes hostile Indians – all in a region of utmost desolation. An eighteenth-century account tells of a ship coming to grief on an uncharted shoal in Lake Ontario; her crew had great difficulty in transferring to a companion vessel which soon after became wrecked at an island where the marooned men died of starvation.

Increasing trade, however, created the need for many more vessels. Their types and quantity were largely dictated by the special geographical characteristics of the area. The stubby, top-heavy craft of the day, for example, were unable to sail into many of the natural harbours because of shoals at their entrances. Thus there was a need for ships large enough to withstand severe gales, yet able to manoeuvre in the confined lakes where it was impossible to run out a storm for days at a time as on the oceans. Necessary changes in ship design covered displacement, size, rigging, and ballast.

Early in the eighteenth century it was discovered that the schooner was ideally suited to the freshwater lakes. With its fore-and-aft rig (the forward edge or luff of its sail set on travellers attached to and sliding upon the mast), the schooner could make much better headway into the wind than the popular square-rigger, and it could manoeuvre in a restricted area. It was to become the standard vessel of the nineteenth century. **6**

## Ships Used in the French and Indian War

The *Halifax*, the first snow of the Great Lakes, was built by the British in 1756 at Oswego on Lake Ontario. The snow was a square-rigged two-masted vessel with a try-sail mast close behind the main mast; it was somewhat wider than the comparable brig. After having first been tried in the late fifteenth century, the snow had become common on the oceans by the eighteenth century, and remained a popular design on the Great Lakes and high seas until the early nineteenth century. **7**

In 1958 I located the hulk of an old vessel whose subsequent excavation, in which Floyd Shearn took part, yielded evidence identifying the ship as the *Halifax*. **4** **22**

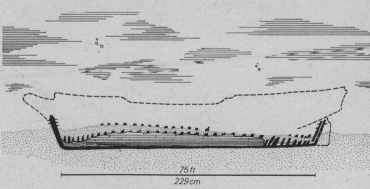

*75 ft*
*229 cm*

*4 Very little of the original hull (dotted line) remained of the 'Halifax' when located. The sand and ballast within the hull, however, contained many artifacts in their original form*

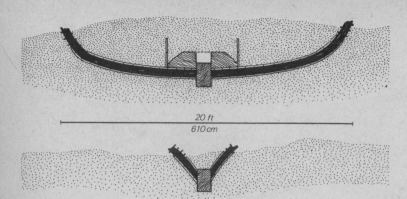

5 *Cross sections of the hull at mainmast (top) and just forward of the stern post show amount of the 'Halifax' remaining*

Keel and ribs were of very heavy timbers bound together with treenails and then faced inside and out with heavy planking fastened with hand-wrought nails. All timbers and planking were hand-hewn oak, still showing tool marks clearly. The hull bore signs of having been repaired on several occasions. A large portion of the keel and ribs near the bow had rotted prior to the sinking, which probably led to the decision by the British Admiralty to abandon the ship rather than attempt still another repair. The deck length of the vessel was 80 ft 6 in.

The antiquities we found within the hulk revealed that internal layout of quarters and storerooms compared closely with those on ocean vessels of the same period. Even the filth and stench of the bilge on the high seas was closely matched on freshwater ships: large quantities of garbage and discarded objects were found

6, 7 *The French fleet of 1756 (upper) comprised three schooners and a sloop. The English fleet (lower) on Lake Ontario had one snow, one brig, two schooners and two sloops*

intermixed with the ballast. The ballast stones were packed within a cushion of sawdust rather than in the traditional brush and twigs usually found; their uncommonly large size was perhaps to facilitate their removal to make space for extra military stores.

Items found on board included shoes, jewellery, coins, pipes, knives, teeth, barrels, rope, and buttons; many of the last appear to be unique and aided greatly in the identification of the ship. Attempts to offset malnutrition were evidenced by the discovery that all bones within the wreck had been broken for the extraction of marrow, highly prized for its nutritional value. In addition, a quantity of small peach stones indicated that hard green fruit was included in the stores so that the crew could eat it, freshly ripened, on the voyage.

The same year as the launching of the *Halifax*, the false keel was initiated. This entailed adding several inches to the bottom of the keel. The invention – probably the result of replacing the lower portion of a keel which had been scuffed off on rocks – was found by the British to increase a vessel's manoeuvrability and greatly decrease her side-slipping motion over the water, thus allowing her to sail faster against the wind. The French soon copied the innovation for its obvious military advantages.

The 'radeau', well known from the last quarter of the century, may well have been developed on Lake Champlain as a sailing, floating fortress about the same time. Rectangular in shape, with protruding vertical sides, it was nothing more than a fancy barge with sails. The awkward craft proved slow and unmanageable during battle and did not have a long history.

Also tried on Lake Champlain, around 1759, was the 'razee'. It was in reality a larger ship which was cut down in size by removing the upper deck works to make a lower, sleeker craft. Fast-moving, with triangular sails, it proved a poor craft for heavy armament and also was short-lived on the lakes.

After two bronze cannon of this period were discovered in 1968, I and two local divers conducted a survey in Lake Champlain for the New York State Department of History in order to identify the site. We found no ships, but located cannon, muskets, swords, tools, and musket balls thrown overboard by the French in an attempt to prevent their capture by pursuing British forces; the ships that had been sunk there had been raised by the British within weeks of their being scuttled. Ironically, nearly all of the items were British-made, having been captured from the British several years earlier at Oswego, New York, and on the Monongahela River.

The locations of the valuable cannon seemed to have been marked for later retrieval by the positioning among them on the lake bed of pairs of anchors attached to opposite ends of cables. The French undoubtedly hoped to return, snag the cables with a grapnel, and then recover their weapons from the shallow water. But they never regained control of the lake.

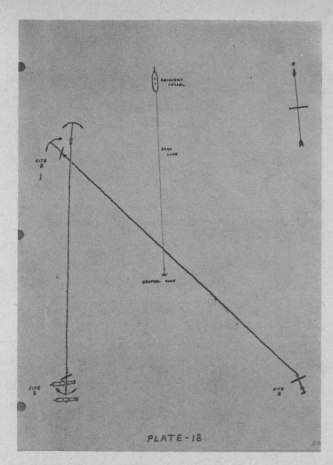

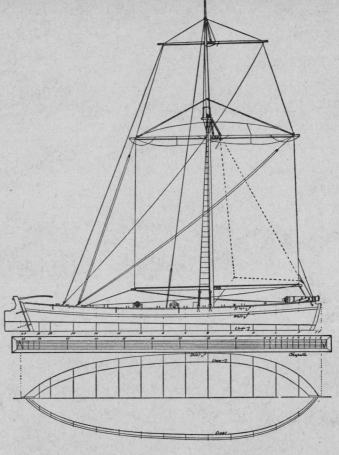

8  *When the French abandoned two cannon for later recovery they employed this elaborate pattern of anchors and cables*

9  *Scale drawing of the salvaged 'Philadelphia'. This vessel was raised intact after having lain for 150 years under water*

17–19  A swivel gun recovered during our survey yielded an unusual charge not known to have existed at such an early date. It had previously been assumed that anti-personnel charges were composed just of loose shot held in a weapon with a wad. Instead we found a series of musket balls packed together in a pouch with powder, and behind this the cannon ball which was to drive it out and explode it. To my knowledge, this is the only swivel gun ever recovered fully primed and ready to fire. Owing to the placement of a cork tampion in the muzzle of the gun, the bore was no more than damp after 200 years at a depth of 30 feet in an exposed area!

### The American Revolution

From 1760 to 1770 few vessels were built by the British forces, for a large fleet remained from the French and Indian War. After 1770, however, the British began again to increase their fleet on the Great Lakes with the launching of several snows, schooners, and sloops. Building activity on Lake Champlain was especially active with the production of two opposing fleets. The American fleet was composed of two schooners, two sloops, three galleys, and eight gundalos. The British had one frigate, two schooners, one gundalo, one radeau, 10  and twenty gunboats and longboats. The Battle of

Valcour Island, in October of 1776, left both fleets shattered and the course of the Revolution altered. Remains of the American fleet, commanded by Benedict Arnold, have since been located and raised from the bottom of Lake Champlain.

During the 1930s the hull of the American gundalo (or gondola) *Philadelphia*, now restored and on display  9  in the Smithsonian Institution, was salvaged from a depth of 35 feet by Captain L. F. Hagglund, who also raised parts of the schooner *Royal Savage* and those of another gunboat. That part of the American fleet which escaped the British was burned at Arnold's Bay where, in 1961, Oscar Bredenberg recovered numerous artifacts including several axes believed to be from the *Congress*.

The gundalo, as represented by the *Philadelphia*, had excellent qualities as a war craft. Although small (53 ft 4 in. long), the vessel was much like a sloop, with one square-rigged mast without the additional fore-and-aft rigged sail common to the sloop of that time. Successful as it was, the gundalo was short-lived and was eventually replaced by the schooner.

The design of war vessels now fell into a regular pattern of sizes and styles. They had the affinity of looking remarkably similar even when in opposing fleets. Standard government vessels on the lakes were

289

10    *The English fleet on Lake Champlain in 1776 was assembled in three months and consisted
of the schooners 'Carleton' and 'Maria', frigate 'Inflexible', gundalo 'Loyal Convert', radeau
'Thunderer', four long boats, 20 gunboats and 40 supply boats*

made up mainly of brigs, schooners, and sloops. The last-named, single-masted fore-and-aft rigged, with a bowsprit and carrying at least one jib, combined excellent speed and manoeuvrability.

The British maintained a fleet upon the inland waters and during the last quarter of the eighteenth century kept control of the lakes even though they had yielded to the colonials upon the high seas. The new democracy was soon to discover that control of the interior went hand in hand with control of the Great Lakes. Jay's Treaty of 1794 forced the British to allow control of the forts on the south side of the lakes to revert to the Americans, greatly alleviating problems between the two countries, and soon the Americans had many small craft on the lakes.

### An Age of Innovation

In 1797 an 80-ton schooner, the *Washington*, was built on Lake Erie. It was later sold, put on wheels and taken around Niagara Falls to be launched in Lake Ontario where it was lost in 1803. This overland transportation of a ship, under crude conditions, was only one of several new developments and experiments at the turn of the century.

The first private yacht appeared on the lakes in 1799 with the launching of the *Toronto*, an ornate and colourfully painted vessel built expressly for the entertainment of visiting royalty. Figureheads and other carved ornaments were popular on vessels of this period, but gradually faded from use after the War of 1812 (none of the original figureheads from the Great Lakes are known to exist today).

About the same time, shipbuilders began to experiment with various woods for their vessels. To use other than proven oak was a distinct challenge, for it was thought to be the only material suitable for the task. The first experiment produced a vessel built completely of black walnut; it was launched at Kingston, Ontario, in 1797. Three years later the schooner *Prince Edward*, built entirely of red cedar, was launched at Belleville, Ontario, to begin an active service including military use in the War of 1812 and commercial use thereafter. Cedar was found to be an excellent material and many years later became a prized wood for marine uses. Its main quality stemmed from its ability to resist rotting in water.

An unusual development came about in 1807 with the launching of the first centreboard schooner. It incorporates a keel blade which can be hauled up into the centre of a craft when entering harbour, and is used only while under full sail; it remains common today. An unidentified vessel believed to be an early example of this type has been excavated in Canadian waters of the St Lawrence River, but work has not been completed and no comprehensive report of the findings has yet appeared.

It was during this period that emphasis on warship design became less marked. The many small schooners and sloops launched at all the major harbours were of single hull construction, as opposed to the warships with their double hulls (inside and outside planking on the ribs). Between 1800 and 1812 a great number of American vessels were launched, and most of these were to be purchased or rented by the American government to play an important role when war erupted again. The brig *Oneida*, the first full-scale warship built by the Americans on the lakes, was launched at Oswego on Lake Ontario in 1809, but she could do little to offset the growing British armada on the lake. In fact, it is surprising that the British forces did not overrun the Americans on the Lakes frontier at the beginning of hostilities, for they greatly outnumbered them in both men and warships.

## The War of 1812

The War of 1812 upon the Great Lakes began a ship-building race which ultimately ended in a stalemate for both sides. Vessels were launched by the hundreds, comprising mainly brigs, schooners, sloops, and luggers, along with many gunboats. Small schooners were most popular with both nations due to their low cost, ease of building, and versatility. The schooner now emerged as the one vessel able to meet the needs of both commercial and government service. A fast sailer, it could overtake and outmanoeuvre all the brigs and frigates. Its shallow draught enabled it to sail into shoal waters to attack and then escape, large ships being unable to follow. As a commercial vessel, it was able to sail into many un-improved ports to load or discharge cargo, needing only a small crew to handle the rigging.

Several brigs were built by the Americans at Sacketts Harbor, New York, in 1813, including the *Jefferson*. It was left to rot in the harbour at the conclusion of the war. In 1960, investigating the wreck of what was thought by many to be an old grain barge, I was able to determine that the old hulk was, instead, the *Jefferson*. Only about 25 per cent of the hull had suffered damage; the complete starboard side from bow to stern and all of the gun ports were still intact.

While plans were being prepared to raise and rebuild the *Jefferson*, a local business group petitioned the State Government and were granted a permit to build a marina on the site. Within weeks the area had been land-filled and built up with docks. Pleas of historians and local residents were ignored. The hull now lies crushed under many tons of rock, a vast amount of unique information about early ship construction on the lakes obliterated. No shipbuilding plans for such early lake-plying vessels are extant today.

The huge British frigate *Canada* and the American frigate *New Orleans* were built on Lake Ontario. On Lake Champlain, the British frigate *Confiance*, and the American *Saratoga* confronted each other at the Battle of Plattsburgh Bay. These frigates matched their ocean counterparts in every way, being first class ships of the line. The sites of several of these vessels have been located by divers and will, it is to be hoped, be excavated scientifically.

*11  Commodore Perry leaves the 'Lawrence' (centre) during the battle for Lake Erie. The message to his fleet flutters atop the broken mainmast. The 'Niagara' (right) was rebuilt in recent years and now stands on display. Only the keel and a few pieces come from the original ship*

Galleys were used on Lake Champlain by both sides during the war. Powered by sail or oars, the galley had been tried first in 1776 by Benedict Arnold in the American fleet and had remained popular owing mainly to its economical construction and proven effectiveness. It usually carried one long cannon and several smaller pieces along with swivel guns. It was between 50 and 75 feet long. Several hulks of galleys have been located, but none has been subjected to professional evaluation.

## The Introduction of Steam

Immediately after the war, the steamer made its debut but did not at once replace the sailing vessel. During the commercial boom from 1820 to 1860, almost every port, river, or bay had at least one shipyard sending vessels of every description and size down the ways at a steady rate. By 1830 most of these sailing ships on the lakes and rivers were schooners. Modifications of the standard design were frequent, however, to meet the specialized demands of the iron, grain, passenger, and lumber trade; in the lumber industry, for example, ships were made to be loaded through the side rather than by way of the deck.

Harbours and canals also played an important role in the development of vessels. The Erie Canal, completed in 1825, led to the development of the Erie Canal barge. Likewise, the construction of the Welland and other canals led to precise specifications for sailing ships of the day: for maximum cargoes, owners wanted their ships to be built to the greatest possible width and draught and still be able to pass through the canal locks. An extreme example of the economic importance of these dimensions was presented in 1829 when Captain Pickering of Sacketts Harbor committed suicide only moments after arriving at the Welland Canal with his new schooner and finding it two inches too wide to pass through the locks.

This was the heyday of sail with sleek little sloops and majestic schooners gliding side by side on the lakes and rivers. Almost everywhere on the horizon of the waterways, one could see bright white canvas. The harbours appeared as a winter forest with hundreds of masts standing amidst tons of cordage. At most shipyards, dozens of ships were being constructed at the same time. The harbours were congested with ships awaiting the towboats to haul them to and from the dock.

Between 1830 and 1840 the steamer had developed into a highly competitive vessel. Steam had proven itself and now had equalled the schooner for speed and dependability. Although the first propeller had been developed and used in 1796, screw-propellers were not perfected for commercial use until 1841 when one was fitted to the steamer *Vandalia*, built at Oswego. So thoroughly successful was the propeller that within a few years most new steamers were built with them as standard equipment. Even the use of metal hulls and masts along with better equipment could not help sail to compete with steam-powered vessels.

The Civil War soon proved, without question, that one steamship could handle three sailing ships of equal size during a naval battle. Its speed and manoeuvrability were far superior and placed the sailers at its mercy during periods of calm. From then on sail gradually disappeared from military fleets.

For cost-conscious businessmen sail too would become secondary as a form of water transport. By 1850 the change was noticeable, with nearly all of the larger craft being built as steamers. In 1870 over three-quarters of the new tonnage of vessels was steamships and by 1900 the last of the sailing craft had been built. Sails were becoming a rare sight in American waters in 1920; by 1935 such craft were unknown for commerce, plans to revive commercially competitive schooners having never materialized. On the Great Lakes today, all the fine old sailing ships are gone. One of the last was the *Lyman M. Davis*, a three-masted schooner burned as a spectacle near Toronto in August, 1933. All of the others have been dismantled, wrecked, or left to rot in the backwaters of harbours. The sound of snapping canvas and wind whipping the rigging is heard no more, and pleasure boats provide the only sail to be seen in the waters of the United States.

26

---

1 The fur trade in North America came into its own when the initiative passed from the Indian to the European during the last two decades of the sixteenth century. Axes, chisels and spears were traded in large quantities to the Indian hunters (who used the chisels and spears in taking beaver and muskrat through the ice in winter) in exchange for rich peltries.

Here one of the Quetico-Superior project divers examines a few of the thirty-six iron axes and twenty-four assorted ice chisels and spears found in the Basswood River, northwest of Ely, Minnesota, in July 1961. The scene owes its golden hue to the shallowness of the river, which allows light to be reflected from the bottom, as well as to the amber tint of the water here.

2 Air view of border lakes between Minnesota and Ontario, the fur traders' waterway. The main fur trade route running through Grand Portage has been described as the 'Voyageurs' Highway'. First knowledge of the routes came from the Indians. Later, pine trees lopped in a special manner were used as markers.

3 'Shooting the Rapids', a painting done in the nineteenth century by Frances Ann Hopkins. Eric Morse, author of *Fur Trade Canoe Routes of Canada: Then and Now*, believes the picture was painted on the Ottawa River just upstream from the modern city of Ottawa, Canada.

4 Hudson's Bay Company freight canoe being portaged as a *canot du maître* (or Montreal canoe). In the days of the fur trade the Montreal canoe was portaged in this manner by four men. The North canoe, a smaller craft used inland from Grand Portage and Fort William, was carried upright by two voyageurs.

5 Hudson's Bay Company men rowing a York boat. This type of craft was first used by the Company on the lower Albany River early in the eighteenth century and came into wide use as operations were carried into the interior near the close of that century. Soon after the merger of the Northwest and Hudson's Bay companies in 1821 the York boat replaced the bark canoes on Canada's rivers and lakes.

6 York boat under sail in northern Manitoba. Sails were frequently used on the larger stretches of water encountered in the fur trade country, such as Lake Winnipeg, Cedar Lake and Ile a la Crosse, to reduce the hard labour of rowing. Many of the York boats were constructed on the upper Saskatchewan River, and were used to carry both furs and pemmican to the Cumberland House and Lake Winnipeg.

7 Remains of two eighteenth-century bateaux found in Lake George by scuba divers. The bateau was a European import used extensively on the St Lawrence River and in the colonies in the seventeenth and eighteenth centuries. Large numbers were employed when the French fur trade was flourishing, in particular between Quebec City and Montreal. This type of craft was also commonly used in military operations to move personnel and supplies.

12 Lead bale seal found at Boundary Falls in 1967. Such seals were used universally in the fur trade to prevent valuable furs and trade goods being tampered with. They are rare· today owing to the fact that used bale seals were often melted down to make musket balls.

13 Fur-trade artifacts recovered at Boundary Falls (Portage de Isle) in 1966 included Northwest trade muskets, wrought iron trade axes, thimbles, knives, beads, tin dishes, an early iron tomahawk, over 5,000 musket balls, and quantities of small (Swan) shot – probably from three separate accidents.

14 Cluster of axes and gunflints found by Canadian divers on the French River. Such concreted lumps when found offer the diver few clues as to the true nature of the objects contained in them.

12

14

15 Nest of seventeen brass kettles found in 1960 at Horsetail Rapids. Once the bales reached the wilderness trading posts the kettles were sold individually to the Indians. When retrieved from the waters of the Granite River some eight or ten were still nested; the others were scattered widely. Those nested were in almost perfect condition.

16 The seventeen brass kettles from Horsetail Rapids laid out. The smallest is 6″ in diameter, the largest 20″.

298

15

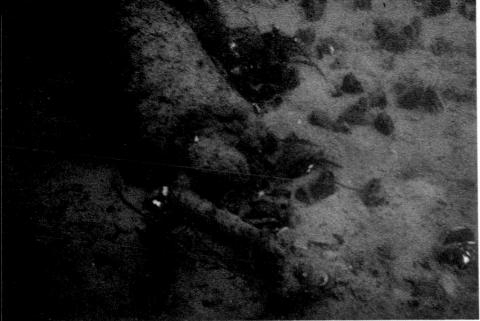

17–19   Swivel-cannon found on the hard bottom of Lake Champlain. When first seen, the cannon lay at a depth of 32 feet (17), but it was not until it was raised that the full extent of the corrosion became evident (18). The weapon, after cleaning, was found to be almost as new (19). The markings indicated that it was of British make and early eighteenth-century date. The bore had been sealed with a cork tompion and remained practically dry for 209 years at the bottom of the lake. Close examination showed that the gun was fully charged and ready to fire. The charge was carefully removed and was found to be a combination small boat and anti-personnel type, in a perfect state of preservation.

20   A pin, beads, and jewellery from the *Halifax*, a British-built snow which sank in Lake Ontario in the late eighteenth century. The pin (of modern pin size) has a head made from a fine strip of wire wrapped about the shaft. The beads, though very small, look larger under water, much as they appear in the photo. The three pieces at the bottom of the grouping are parts of a single item of jewellery. The cut-glass 'gem' is backed by the polished silver reflector (centre) which is then encased in the pewter shell (left). It was probably attached with a loop to the clothing.

21   Top of barrel recovered from the *Halifax*. It shows deep carved numerals which identified not only the contents but the lot number, date, weight, etc. At the top section can be seen the 'broad arrow', the mark of British Government property.

22   Light filters down through the algae and plankton to cast an eerie gloom over the sunken hulk of the *Halifax*. This photo was taken from astern, looking forward past the stern-post supports. The absence of toredo worms in fresh water, along with the lower temperatures, keeps submerged wood in a state of semi-preservation. Exposed iron is subjected to slow but relentless oxidation. This process of eroding the metal fibres is greatly accelerated by the addition of certain chemicals from industrial and municipal pollution.

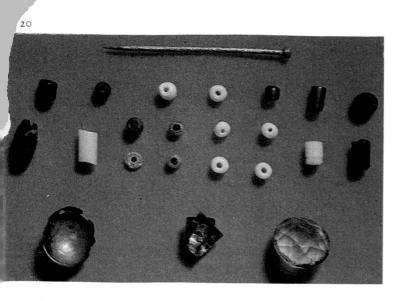

23 The ribs of the brig *Jefferson* break the surface of Sacketts Habor. The vessel measured 110 feet in length by 30 feet in width, and carried a war-time crew of 500. For many years the hulk was thought to be that of an old barge. Upon close examination, however, it was easy to determine that the vessel was in reality an old warship, for under the surface the hull was found to be nearly intact. All of the gunports on the starboard side remained after surviving the elements for more than 150 years.

This survival was brought to a sudden halt when a local group received permission to fill the area with foundation material for a marina. Archaeologists and conservationists pleaded with government officials that they postpone the permit until the vessel could be raised or moved. All to no avail, and the brig is now crushed beneath tons of rock, an untimely fate for a majestic ship.

24 Oswego, N.Y. harbour, Lake Ontario in the late nineteenth century was a maze of rigging, masts and tackle. The schooners in the foreground are typical examples of the sailing ships that plied the Great Lakes for close on 200 years.

25 Lack of room to manoeuvre on the Great Lakes caused many sailing vessels to be driven ashore during severe storms. Once aground, it was not long before masts snapped and hulls broke up under the force of the breakers. Some of the sturdy wooden sailing ships were able to survive this punishment, having been built of solid oak timbers. Of these two vessels wrecked on the rocks at Oswego harbour, the right-hand one has a broken keel.

26 Sleek, powerful lines, topped with towering masts were the hall-mark of most sailing ships that plied the Great Lakes. Pictured here is the *Lyman M. Davis*, one of the last of the line to cruise these inland seas. It was burned as a spectacle near Toronto, Canada, in 1933. Most of the old schooners ended their days in a much less spectacular way by serving as barges. But now even these are gone, and only the memory of the taut canvas and the stout oak hulls that characterized them lingers on.

# Glossary

*No glossary of nautical terms can be wholly satisfactory, since the same word may mean different things in America and England, and even in different parts of the same country, while different words are used to describe the same thing in different countries and areas. For this reason, too, and because they are defined by the authors in their respective chapters, the many different ship types to which they allude are not included. It is hoped, nevertheless, that this brief glossary will be of assistance to those with only a limited knowledge of nautical terminology.*

**after-castle** a castle (*q.v.*) at the rear end of a ship

**'Arab' lateen sail** a rectangular lateen-type sail

**artemon** a steering sail at a ship's forward end (Greek)

**batten** a strip of wood used in shipbuilding to reproduce the curves of a vessel's hull

**beam** the maximum width of a vessel; a horizontal transverse timber forming part of a ship's structure

**bilge** the bottom of a ship's hull

**bonaventure mizzen** the second mizzenmast on four-masters

**boom** a spar to which is attached the foot of a fore-and-aft sail

**bowsprit** a spar projecting forward of a sailing ship's stem

**brace** a rope attached to the boom or yard of a sail, used to control its position; a metal strap used to strengthen the framework of a ship

**brails** small ropes for attaching furled sails to a spar or boom; in antiquity used for furling and shaping the sail

**bulkhead** a vertical partition dividing a ship into sections

**canvas** sail-cloth, hence a vessel's sails

**castle** a tower or defence post on the deck of a ship

**cathead** the projecting timber to which an anchor is held at the ship's bow; tackle used to raise a ship's anchor

**carvel-built** having the planks all flush from keel to gunwale

**carvel planking** smooth seamed planking

**caulk** to stop up the seams between planks

**chine** the angle at which the side and bottom of a hull join

**cleat** short projections of wood or metal, used for a variety of purposes

**clench** bending over and pounding down a bolt or nail

**clinker-built** having lapped strakes of planking

**crow's-nest** a look-out platform at or near the top of a mast

**draft** (*draught*) the depth of water displaced by a vessel

**dug-out** a primitive craft made of a hollowed tree trunk

**dunnage** brushwood or other material used to protect cargo

**flukes** triangular extensions to the arms of an anchor

**fore-and-aft rig** sails fitted in a fore-and-aft direction and secured on their forward side to a stay or mast

**forecastle** a castle (*q.v.*) at the forward end of a vessel; the raised section at the bow of more recent ships

**frames** athwartship timbers forming the internal skeleton of a ship

**freeboard** the distance from the waterline up to the watertight deck

**futtock** one of several members joined to form a frame

**gaff** a spar used along the head of a fore-and-aft sail

**garboard** the first range of planks above a ship's keel

**gunwale** the upper edge of a ship's side

**halyard** rope or tackle used for hoisting or lowering sails and a vessel's other top gear

**hawser** a mooring rope or cable

**helm** a ship's steering gear (*see also* tiller)

**hogging** the arching of a ship longitudinally due to strain

**hogging truss** a cable running fore and aft, to prevent hogging

**keel** the lowest longitudinal timber, forming the backbone of a ship

**keelson** longitudinal floor-timber of a ship, fixed above and to the keel

**knee** a piece of timber having an angular bend, used to join two perpendicular members

**lateen sail** a triangular sail extended by a long tapering yard the lower end of which is brought down to the deck

**mast partner** a fitment at the base of a mast to provide additional support

**mast-step** a socket for the keel of a mast; an attachment for fastening the lower end of a ship's mast to the hull

**mizzenmast** the mast directly aft of the main mast

**outrigger** a framework extending laterally beyond the ship's sides, originally for lending additional support for oars

**parrel** a collar by which a yard is fastened to the mast

**ribs** the curved frame-timbers of a ship, to which the side-planking is nailed

**rigging** the system of ropes used to support the masts and operate the sails

**rove** a small plate or ring on which the point of a nail or rivet is beaten down

**rubbing strakes** heavy protective side timbers on a ship

**scantlings** the hull structure of a vessel as a whole

**scarf** the lapped joint connecting two timbers or planks

**sheet** a rope controlling the after (lower) corner(s) of a sail

**shrouds** heavy ropes that brace the mast athwartships

**spritsail** a small auxiliary sail at the forward end of a ship

**stays** strong ropes to support the mast fore and aft

**stem** a timber forming the front extremity of a vessel.

**stern post** a timber at the extreme rear end of a vessel and extending from the keel to deck level or above

**stock** the heavy cross-bar of an anchor

**strake** one row of planking on the side or bottom of a ship, running from stem to stern on the outside of the hull

**stringer** an inside strake secured to the ribs and supporting the ends of beams

**tabernacle** housing in which a mast may be set up and lowered on a deck

**tack** forward lower part of a sail

**tholes** vertical pins or pegs on a ship's side, for guiding oars

**thwart** the cross seat in an open boat

**tiller** a lever for controlling a ship's rudder or steering gear

**transom** the athwartship timber or structure at the after end of a ship's hull framing

**treenail** a cylindrical wooden pin used for fastening timbers

**trunnel** colloquial term for treenail (*q.v.*); also trennel

**tumble-home** the sloping-in of a vessel's topsides above the point of greatest width

**wales** (*see also* gunwale) horizontal planks or timbers, broader than the rest, extending along the whole of a ship's sides

**yard** a horizontal athwartships spar fitted to the forward side of the mast, to support square sails

**yoke** a board or bar fixed transversely to the head of the rudder and attached by ropes to the tiller; athwartship ends of outriggers used on galleys

# Select Bibliography

## I
## The earliest seafarers in the Mediterranean and the Near East

BASS, G. F. *Cape Gelidonya: A Bronze Age Shipwreck*, trans. Amer. Phil. Soc., new series vol. 57, part 8; Philadelphia 1967.
BÉNÉDITE, G. 'Le couteau de Gebel el-Arak', *Monuments et mémoires publiés par l'Académie des Inscriptions et Belles-lettres, Fondation Eugène Piot* 22 (1916) 1–34.
BORCHARDT, L. *Das Grabdenkmal des Königs Sa' hu-Re'*, vol. II, Leipzig 1913.
BOREUX, CH. *Etudes de nautique égyptienne*, Mem. de l'Instit. Franç. d'Archéologie Orientale du Caire, vol. 50, Cairo 1924.
CASSON, L. *The Ancient Mariners*, New York 1959.
— *Ships and Seamanship in the Ancient World*, Princeton 1971, 3–43.
CLARKE, S. and ENGELBACH, R. *Ancient Egyptian Masonry*, Oxford 1930, 34–45.
COHEN, LIONEL. 'Evidence for the Ram in the Minoan Period', *American Journal of Archaeology* 42 (1938) 486–94.
DAVIES, NORMAN DE G. and FAULKNER, R. O. 'A Syrian Trading Venture to Egypt', *Journal of Egyptian Archaeology* 33 (1947) 40–46.
FAULKNER, R. O. 'Egyptian Seagoing Ships', *Journal of Egyptian Archaeology* 26 (1940) 3–9.
HORNELL, JAMES. *Water Transport; Origins and Early Evolution*, Cambridge 1946.
JANSSEN, J. J. *Two Ancient Egyptian Ship's Logs*, Leiden 1961.
KRAMER, S. N. 'The Indus Civilization and Dilmun, The Sumerian Paradise Land', *Expedition* 6, part 3 (1964) 44–52.
LANDSTRÖM, BJÖRN. *The Ship*, London n.d.
MARINATOS, SP. 'La marine créto-mycénienne', *Bulletin de correspondance hellénique* 57 (1933) 170–235, pls. 13–17.
MORRISON, J. S. and WILLIAMS, R. T. *Greek Oared Ships 900–322 B.C.*, Cambridge 1968, 7–11.
PETRIE, W. M. F. *Prehistoric Egypt*, London 1920, 18–21.
QUIBELL, J. E. and GREEN, F. W. *Hierakonpolis* II, London 1902.
RAO, S. R. 'Shipping and Maritime Trade of the Indus People', *Expedition* 7, part 3 (1965) 30–37.
REISNER, G. A. *Models of Ships and Boats* (Catalogue général des antiquités égyptiennes du Musée du Caire, nos. 4798–4976 et 5034–5200), Cairo 1913

SALONEN, A. 'Die Wasserfahrzeuge in Babylonien', *Studia Orientalia* 8, part 4, (1939).
SÄVE-SÖDERBERGH, *The Navy of the Eighteenth Egyptian Dynasty*, Uppsala Universitets Arsskrift, 1946: 6.
WINKLER, HANS A. *Rock-Drawings of Southern Upper Egypt* I and II, London 1938–39.
WINLOCK, H. E. *Models of Daily Life in Ancient Egypt from the Tomb of Meket-Re' at Thebes*, Cambridge, Mass. 1955.

## 2
## Greek, Etruscan and Phoenician ships and shipping

### General

ALFIERI, N. 'NAVE', *Enciclopedia dell'arte antica* V, Rome 1963, *s.v.*
CASSON, LIONEL. *The Ancient Mariners*, New York 1959.
— *Illustrated History of Ships and Boats*, New York 1964.
— *Ships and Seamanship in the Ancient World*, Princeton 1971.
KOSTER, AUGUST, *Das antike Seewesen*, Berlin 1923.
MOLL, FRIEDRICH. *Das schiff in der bildenden Kunst*, Bonn 1929.
TORR, CECIL. *Ancient Ships*, Cambridge 1895; reprinted Chicago 1964.

### Greece

ADCOCK, *The Greek and Macedonian Art of War*, Berkeley and Los Angeles 1957, 29–46.
AMIT, M. *Athens and the Sea*, Collection Latomus, 74, Brussels 1965.
ANDERSON, R. C. *Oared Fighting Ships*, London 1962
CASSON, LIONEL. 'Hemiolia and Triemiolia', *Journal of Hellenic Studies* 78 (1958) 14–18.
DAVISON, J. A. 'The First Greek Triremes', *Classical Quarterly* 41 (1947) 18–24.
GOMME, A. W. 'A Forgotten Factor of Greek Naval Strategy', *Journal of Hellenic Studies* 53 (1933) 16–24; reprinted in Gomme, Essays in Greek History and Literature, Oxford 1937, 190–203.
KIRK, G. S. 'Ships on Geometric Vases', *Annual of the British School of Athens* 44 (1949) 93–153.
MILTNER, F. 'Seekrieg', Pauly-Wissowa *Realencyclopädia der Classischen Altertums-*

*wissenschaft* Supplement V, Stuttgart 1931, *s.v.*; 'Seewesen', *op. cit., s.v.*
MORRISON, J. S. 'The Greek Trireme' *Mariner's Mirror* 27 (1941)14–44.
— 'Notes on Certain Greek Nautical Terms and on Three Passages in I. G. II 1632', *Classical Quarterly* 41 (1947) 122–35.
MORRISON, J. S. and WILLIAMS, R. T. *Greek Oared Ships*, Cambridge 1968.
RODGERS, WILLIAM L. *Greek and Roman Naval Warfare*, Annapolis and London 1937.
WILLIAMS, R. T. 'Early Greek Ships of Two Levels', *Journal of Hellenic Studies* 78 (1958) 121–30.
— 'Addenda to Early Greek Ships of Two Levels', *Journal of Hellenic Studies* 79 (1959) 159–60.

### Phoenicia and the East

BARNETT, R. D. 'Early Shipping in the Near East', *Antiquity* 32 (1958) 220–30.
BASCH, LUCIEN. 'Phoenician Oared Ships', *Mariner's Mirror* 55 (1969), 139–62, 227–44.
CULICAN, WILLIAM. *The First Merchant Venturers*, London and New York 1966.
DELBRUECK, RICHARD. 'Südasiatische Seefahrt im Altertum', *Bonner Jahrbuch* 155–56 (1955–56) 8–58.
FÉVRIER, J. C. 'L'ancienne marine phénicienne', *La nouvelle Clio* 1–2 (1949–50) 128–43.
GLUECK, NELSON. 'The Second Campaign at Tell el-Kheleifeh (Ezion-Geber: Elath)' *Bulletin of the American Schools of Oriental Research* 75 (Oct. 1939) 8–22, esp. 20.
— 'The Third season of Excavation at Tell el-Kheleifeh', *Bulletin of the American Schools of Oriental Research* 79 (Oct. 1940) 2–18.
HARDEN, DONALD. *The Phoenicians*, London and New York 1962.
MOSCATI, SABATINO. *The World of the Phoenicians*, London 1968.
SCHIWEK, HEINRICH. 'Der Persische Golf als Schiffahrts- und Seehandelsroute in Achämenischer Zeit und in der Zeit Alexanders des Großen', *Bonner Jahrbuch* 162 (1962) 4–97.

### Etruria and the West

BENOÎT, FERNAND. 'Epaves de la côte de Provence', *Gallia* 14 (1956) 32–4.
— 'Nouvelles épaves de Provence', *Gallia* 16 (1958) 30–31.
— *Recherches sur l'hellénisation du Midi de la Gaula*, Aix en Provence 1965, 51–6.

BOSCH-GIMPERA, P. 'Huelva', Ebert, *Reallexikon der Vorgeschichte* V, Berlin 1926, *s.v.*

BOUSCARAS, A. 'Compte rendu des recherches sous-marines année 1964', Bulletin de la société archéologique . . . de Béziers, 4th series, 30 (1964) 5–19.

— 'Recherches sous-marines au large d'Agde (1965). Epave des bronzes de Rochelongues', *Bulletin de la société archéologique . . . de Béziers*, 5th series, 1 (1965) 81–99.

— 'Recherches sous-marines 1966. Epaves [sic] des bronzes', Bulletin de la société archéologique . . . de Béziers, 5th series, 2 (1966) 5–15.

MORETTI, MARIO. *La Tomba Della Nave*, Milan 1961.

PAGLIERI, SERGIO. 'Origine e diffusione della navi etrusco-italiche', *Studi Etruschi* 28 (1960) 209–31.

*Navigation, Construction and Rigging*

CASSON, LIONEL. 'Speed under Sail of Ancient Ships', *Transactions of the American Philological Association* 82 (1951) 136–48.

— 'The Earliest Two-Masted Ship', *Archaeology* 16 (1963) 108–11.

— 'Odysseus' Boat', *American Journal of Philology* 85 (1964) 61–4.

— 'New Light on Ancient Rigging and Boatbuilding', *American Neptune* 24 (1964) 81 ff.

— 'Studies in Ancient Sails and Rigging', *Essays in Honor of C. Bradford Welles* (American Studies in Papyrology, vol. I), New Haven 1966, 43–56.

— 'The Origin of the Lateen', *American Neptune* 31 (1971), 49–51.

COMPERNOLLE, R. van. 'La vitesse des voiliers grecs a l'époque classique (V et IV siècles)' *Bulletin de l'Institut historique belge de Rome* 30 (1957) 5–30.

FROST, HONOR. *Under the Mediterranean*, London 1963, 34–61. Anchors.

KLEINER, GERHARD. 'Die Grabung im Norden des Athena-Tempels', *Istanbuler Mitteilungen Deutsches Archäologisches Institut* 9–10 (1959–60) 87, 91, Miletos anchor stock.

LAVIANO, ALBERTO and COLOSIMO, FRANCO. 'La Testa del Filosofo', *Mondo Sommerso* (January 1970) 22–7.

MOLL, FRIEDRICH. 'The History of the Anchor', *Mariner's Mirror* 13 (1927) 293 ff.

OWEN, DAVID I. 'Excavating a Classical Shipwreck', *Archaeology* 24 (1971) 118–29.

WELTER, GABRIEL. 'Aeginetica XIII–XXIV', *Archäologischer Anzeiger, Jahrbuch des Deutschen Archäologischen Instituts* 53 (1938) 489–81. Aegina anchor stocks.

*The Kyrenia Ship*

KATZEV, M. L. 'Resurrecting the Oldest Known Greek Ship', *National Geographic Magazine* 137 (June 1970) 840–57.

## 3
## Romans on the sea

*Atti del II Congresso Internazionale di Archeologia Sottomarina*, Museo Bicknell, Bordighera 1961.

BASS, GEORGE F. *Archaeology Under Water*, London and New York 1966.

BENOÎT, FERNAND. *L'Epave Du Grand Congloué a Marseille*, Paris 1961.

CASSON, LIONEL. *The Ancient Mariners*, New York 1959.

DUMAS, FRÉDÉRIC. *Epaves Antiques*, Paris 1964.

LAMBOGLIA, N. 'La Campagna 1963 sul Relitto di Punta Scaletta', *Rivista di Studi Liguri* 30 (1964) 229–57.

TAYLOR, JOAN DU PLAT, ed. *Marine Archaeology*, London and New York 1966.

TCHERNIA, M. A. 'Les Fouilles Sous-Marines de Planier (Bouches-du-Rhône) *Comptes Rendus de l'Académie des Inscriptions et Belles-Lettres* (Sept 1969) 292–309.

THROCKMORTON, PETER. *Shipwrecks and Archaeology*, Boston 1970.

TORR, CECIL. *Ancient Ships*, reprinted Chicago 1964. The definitive study of the literary references which concern ancient ships. The new edition contains comments by other scholars.

UCELLI, GUIDO. *Le Navi Di Nemi*, Rome 1950.

WEINBERG, GLADYS DAVIDSON, ed. 'The Antikythera Shipwreck Reconsidered', '*Transactions of the American Philosophical Society*', New Series Vol. 55 Pt. 3, Philadelphia (1965).

## 4
## Greek and Roman harbourworks

AMIT, M. 'Athens and the Sea', *Latomus* LXXIV (1965).

BARADEZ, M. 'Nouvelles Recherches sur les Ports Antiques de Carthage, *Karthago* IX (1958).

BARTOCCINI, R. 'Il Porto Romano di Leptis Magna', *Bollettino del Centro Studi per La Storia dell'Architettura* 13, (1958).

BLACKMAN, DAVID, SCHÄFER, J. and SCHLÄGER, H. 'Un Port de la Basse Epoque Romaine en Grèce Centrale', *Archeologia* 17 (1967) 2–17.

BRADFORD, J. 'The Changing Face of Europe – Classical and Medieval Town Plans', in *Ancient Landscapes*, London 1957.

BRAIDWOOD, R. 'Report on Two Sondages on the Coast of Syria', *Syria* 21 (1940) 183–226.

BRUSIN, G. 'Il Porto Fluviale', in *Aquilea e Grado*, Padua 1956, 94–8.

DE LA BLANCHÈRE, M. Plate VI and harbour state plan, in *Le port de Terracine*, Paris 1884.

— 'Le Port de Terracine', *Mélanges d'Archéologie et d'Histoire* (1881) 322–48.

DRAGATSIS, I. 'Ton en Peiraei Anaskaphon' (in Greek), *Praktika* (1895) 63–71.

DUBOIS, C. 'Observations sur un Passage de Vitruve', Mélanges d'Archéologie et d'Histoire' 22 (1902) 439–67.

— Chapter III ('Port') in *Pouzzoles Antique*, Paris 1907, 249–68.

EUZENNAT, M. and SALVIAT, F. 'Marseille Retrouve Ses Murs et Son Port Grecs', *Archeologia* 21 (1968) 5–17.

FLEMMING, N. C. 'Underwater Adventure in Apollonia', *Geographical Magazine* 31 (1959) 497.

— 'Apollonia Revisited', *ibid.*, 33 (1961) 522.

— 'Archaeological Evidence for sea level changes in the Mediterranean', *Underwater Assoc. Report* (1968) 9–13.

GEORGIADES, A. *Les Ports de La Grèce dans L'Antiquité*, Athens 1907.

GOODCHILD, R. 'Harbours, Docks and Lighthouses', in *Oxford History of Technology*, II (Ed. E. Singer *et al*), Oxford 1956, 516–24.

GUY, M. 'Les Ports Antiques de Narbonne', *Rivista di Studi Liguri*, 21 (1955) 213 ff.

GUNTHER, R. 'Earth Movements in The Bay of Naples', *Geographical Journal* 22 (1903) 121f., 269f.

ISSERLIN, B. S. J. 'Phoenicians in Sicily' *Illustrated London News* (Oct. 18, 1969) 26–7.

— 'New Light on the 'Cothon at Motya', *Antiquity* XLV (1971) 178–86.

JAMESON, M. 'Excavations at Porto Cheli and Vicinity' I, *Hesperia* 38 (1969) 311–42.

JONDET, GASTON. 'Les Ports Submergés de L'Ancienne Ile de Pharos', *Mémoires de L'Institut Egyptien*, 9 (1916).

JUDEICH, W. *Topographie von Athen*, 2nd ed. Munich 1931.

KENNY, E. 'The Ancient Docks on the Promontory of Sounion', *BSA* 42 (1947) 194–200.

KNOBLAUCH, PAUL. 'Neuere Untersuchungen an den Hafen von Ägina', *Bonner Jahrbuch* 169 (1969).

LANCIANI, R. Section LVIII 'The Harbour of Rome and the Commercial Quarters on the Left Bank of the Tiber', in *Ruins and Excavations of Ancient Rome*, London and New York 1897, 509–31.

LE GALL, J. Section 'Les quais', in *Le Tibre dans l'Antiquité*, Paris 1953, 194–204.

LEHMAN-HARTLEBEN, K. 'Die Antiken Hafenanlagen des Mittelmeeres', *Klio*, XIV (1923).

— 'Limen', in *RE* (1926).

LINDER, E. 'La Ville Phénicienne d'Athlit – a-t-elle eu l'un des plus anciens ports artificiels de Méditerranée?', *Archaeologia* 17 (1967) 25–9.

LUGLI, G. and FILIBECK, G. *Il Porto di Roma Imperiale e l'agro portuense*, Rome 1935.

MCCANN, ANNA M. and LEWIS, COL. J. D. 'The Ancient Port of Cosa', *Archaeology* 23 (1970) 201–11.

MEIGGS, R. 'Portus', in *Roman Ostia* Oxford 1960, 149–71.

MOUTERDE, P. R. 'Les Ports Anciens de Méditerranée Orientale', in *Sidon* by A. Poidebard and J. Lauffray, Beirut 1951.

PARIS, J. 'Contributions a L'Etude des Ports Antiques Du Monde Grec' I (Lechaeum), *Bulletin de correspondance hellénique* 39 (1915) 5–16.

— 'Contributions a L'Etude des Ports Antiques du Monde Grec' II (Les Etablissements Maritimes de Delos), *Bulletin de correspondance hellénique* 40 (1916) 5–71.

PICARD, C. 'Sur Quelques Representations Nouvelles Du Phare d'Alexandrie et sur l'Origine des Paysages Portuaires', *Bulletin de correspondance hellénique* (1952).

— 'Pouzzoles et le Paysage Portuaire', *Latomus* 48 (1958) 23–51.

POIDEBARD, A. *Tyr*, Paris 1939.

RAO, S. 'Shipping and Maritime Trade of the Indus People', *Expedition* 7 (1965) 30–37.

ROUGÉ, J. Part I (Sections V–VII), Part II (Section I), in *Recherches sur L'Organisation du Commerce Maritime en Méditerranée sous l'Empire Romaine*, Paris 1966.

SAUMAGNE, C. 'Lungemarine de la Carthage Romaine', *Karthago* 10 (1959) 157–70.

SAVILLE, L. 'Ancient Harbours', *Antiquity* 15 (1941) 208–32.

SCHÄFER, J. 'Beobachtungen zu den Seeseitigen Mauern von Larymna in der Loeris', *Archäologischer Anzeiger* (1967) 527–45.

SCRANTON, R. and RAMAGE, E. 'Investigations at Corinthian Kenchreai', *Hesperia* 36 (1967) 124–86.

SCRINARI, V. 'Porto', in *Encylopedie dell'Arte Antica*, Rome 1965.

SEARS, J. 'Oeniadae, The Ship Sheds', *American Journal of Archaeology* 8 (1904) 227–34.

SHAW, J. 'Shallow-Water Excavations at Kenchreai', *American Journal of Archaeology* 71 (1967) 223–31.

— 'A Foundation in the Inner Harbour at Lechaeum', *American Journal of Archaeology* 73 (1969) 370–72.

STARR, C., Jr. Chapter II, in *The Roman Imperial Navy*, Ithaca 1941.

TAYLOR, J. du PLAT. 'Ports, Harbours and other Submerged Sites', in *Marine Archaeology*, London and New York, 1966, 160–89.

— 'Motya', *Archaeology* 17 (1964) 91–100.

TESTAGUZZA, O. 'The Port of Rome', *Archaeology* 17 (1964) 173–79.

WHEELER, R. E. M. 'The Roman Lighthouses at Dover', *Archaeological Journal* (Second Series) 36 (1929) 29–45.

WHITAKER, J. I. S. Chapter V, 'The Cothon of Motya', in *Motya*, London 1921, 185–93.

## 5
## Ships of the Roman period and after in Britain

BRUCE-MITFORD, R. L. S. *The Sutton Hoo Ship-burial*, British Museum, London 1968.

CUNLIFFE, B. W. 'The British Fleet', *Fifth Report on the Excavations of the Roman Fort at Richborough, Kent*. Society of Antiquaries of London 1968.

FROST, H. *Under the Mediterranean*, London 1963.

HORNELL, J. *British Coracles and Irish Curraghs*, London 1938.

LEWIS, A. R. *The Northern Seas*, Princeton 1958.

MARSDEN, P. 'The County Hall Ship' and 'A Boat of the Roman Period discovered on the site of the New Guy's House, Bermondsey, 1958', *Transactions of the London and Middlesex Archaeological Society*, vol. 21, part 2, (1965).

— *A Roman Ship from Blackfriars, London*, Guildhall Museum, London 1966.

MERRIFIELD, R. *Roman London*, London 1969.

For articles on the Ferriby Boats, see *Mariner's Mirror*, 1947 and 1964.

## 6
## Byzantium, mistress of the sea: 330–641

*Historical background*

AHRWEILER, H. *Byzance et la mer*, Paris 1966.

LEWIS, A. *Naval Power and Trade in the Mediterranean A.D. 500–1100*, Princeton 1951.

PROCOPIOS. *History of the Wars*, trs. H. B. Dewing, London and New York 1914–54.

VRYONIS, S. *Byzantium and Europe*, London and New York 1967.

*Anthedon*

BLACKMAN, D. J., SCHÄFER, J. and SCHLÄGER, H. 'Un port de la basse époque romaine en Grèce centrale', *Archaeologia*, 17 (1967) 12–17.

— 'Der Hafen von Anthedon mit Beiträgen zur Topographie und Geschichte der Stadt', *Archäologischer Anzeiger*, LXXXIII, (1968) 21–98. (Summary in English.)

*Marzamemi church wreck*

KAPITÄN, G. 'Schiffsfrachten antiker Baugesteine und Architekturteile vor den Küsten Ostsiziliens', in *Klio*, XXXIX (1961) 300–02.

— 'The Church Wreck off Marzamemi', *Archaeology*, XXII (1969) 122–33.

*Fourth-century ship at Yassi Ada*

BASS, G. F. and DOORNINCK, F. H. van. 'A Fourth-Century Shipwreck at Yassi

Ada', *American Journal of Archaeology*, LXXV (1971) 27–37.

*Merchant ships*

ASHBURNER, W. *The Rhodian Sea-Law*, Oxford 1909.

CASSON, LIONEL. 'The Size of Ancient Merchant Ships', *Studi in onore di Aristide Calderini e Roberto Paribeni*, I, (1956) 231–38.

JONES, A. H. M. *The Later Roman Empire A.D. 284–602*, II, Oxford 1964, chapter 21.

LOPEZ, R. S. 'The Role of Trade in the Economic Readjustment of Byzantium in the Seventh Century', *Dumbarton Oaks Paper*, XIII (1959) 69–85

*Seventh-century ship at Yassi Ada*

BASS, G. F. 'Underwater Excavations at Yassi Ada: A Byzantine Shipwreck', *Archäologischer Anzeiger*, LXXVII (1962) 537–64.

— 'Underwater Archaeology: Key to History's Warehouse', *National Geographic Magazine*, CXXIV (1963) 138–56.

— 'The Asherah: A Submarine for Archaeology', *Archaeology*, XVIII (1965) 7–14.

— *Archaeology Under Water*, London and New York 1966, Chapter 8.

— 'New Tools for Undersea Archaeology', *National Geographic Magazine*, CXXXIV (1968) 402–23.

— 'A Byzantine Trading Venture', *Scientific American*, CCXXV (1971), 23–33.

— 'Underwater Archaeological Expedition to Turkey', *National Geographic Society Research Reports*, *1964 Projects*, 21–34.

BASS, G. F. and DOORNINCK, F. H. van. 'Excavations of a Byzantine shipwreck at Yassi Ada, Turkey', *National Geographic Society Research Reports*, 1964 Projects, 9–20.

DOORNINCK, F. H. van. 'Reconstitution d'un navire byzantin du VIIe siècle', *Archaeologia*, 17, (1967) 38.

KATZEV, M. L. and DOORNINCK, F. H. van. 'Replicas of Iron Tools from a Byzantine Shipwreck', *Studies in Conservation*, XI (1966) 133–42.

*Pantano Longarini ship*

THROCKMORTON, P. and KAPITÄN, G. 'An Ancient Shipwreck at Pantano Longarini', *Archaeology*, XXI (1968) 182–7.

*Greek fire*

MERCIER, M. *Le Feu Gregeois*, Paris 1952.

PARTINGTON, J. R. *A History of Greek Fire and Gunpowder*, Cambridge 1960.

*Later Byzantine warships and naval warfare*

*Chronicles of the Crusade*, ed. Henry G. Bohn, London 1848, 115–16.

CONSTANTINUS PORPHYROGENITUS, *De Caerimoniis*, II, Chapters 44 and 45.

DAIN, A. *Naumachica*, Paris 1943.

DOLLEY, R. H. 'The Warships of the Later Roman Empire', *Journal of Roman Studies* XXXVIII (1948) 47–53.
— 'The Rig of Early Medieval Warships', *Mariner's Mirror*, (1949) 51–5.
— 'Naval Tactics in the Heyday of the Byzantine Thalassocracy', *Atti dell' VIII Congresso di Studi Bizantini*, I (1953) 324–39.


## 7
## Scandinavian ships from earliest times to the Vikings

ARBMAN, HOLGER. 'Der Årby-Fund', *Acta Archaeologica* XI (1940).
— *The Vikings*, London and New York 1961.
BRØGGER, A. W. and SHETELIG, H. *The Viking Ships*, 2nd ed. Oslo 1971.
ESKERØD, A. N. 'Early Nordic Arctic boats', *Studia Etnographica Uppsaliensis* XI (1956).
MARSTRANDER, S. *Skjebergs Helleristninger* I and II, Oslo 1963.
NICOLAYSEN, N. *Langskipet fra Gokstad*, Christiania 1811.
ROSENBERG, G. 'Hjortspringfunnet', *Nordiske Fortidsminder* III (1937).
SHETELIG, H. 'Skibet', *Osebergfunnet* I, Christiania 1917.
SHETELIG, H. and JOHANNESSEN, FR. *Kvalsundfunnet og andre norske myrfund av fartøyer*, Bergen 1929.
— 'Das Nydamschiff', *Acta Archaeologica* I (1930).


## 8
## The Vikings and the Hanseatic Merchants: 900–1450

THORVILDSEN, K. 'Ladbyskibet', Nordiske Fortidsminder VI-I (1957).
ÅKERLUND, H. *Fartygsafynden i den forna hamnen i Kalmar*, Uppsala 1951.
— *Die Bremer Hanse-Kogge*, Bremen 1969.
ANDERSON, R. C. 'The Bursledon Ship', *Mariner's Mirror*, 20 (1934).
CRUMLIN-PEDERSEN, OLE. *Cog-Kogge-Kaag-*, *Handels- og søfartumuseet paa Kronborg*, Aarbog, 1965 (English summary).
— 'Das Haithabuschiff', *Berichte über die Ausgrabungen in Haithabu*, 3 (1969).
FLIEDNER, S. 'Die Bremer Kogge, nr. 19', *Hefte des Focke-Museums*, Bremen (no date).
HASSLÖF, OLAF. 'Sources of Maritime History and Methods of Research', *Mariner's Mirror*, 52 (1966).

HEIDE, G. D. van der. 'Zuyder Zee Archaeology', reprint from *Antiquity and Survival* (no date).
HEINSIUS, P. *Das Schiff der hansischen Frühzeit*, Weimar 1956.
LIENAU, O. *Die Bootsfunde von Danzig-Ohra aus der Vikingerzeit*, Danzig 1934.
MCCUSKER, JOHN J. Jnr. 'The Wine Prise and Mediaeval Mercantile Shipping', *Speculum*, XLI, (1966).
OLSEN, OLAF and CRUMLIN-PEDERSEN, O. 'The Skuldelev Ships (I) and (II)', *Acta Archaeologia*, XXIX (1958) and XXXVIII (1967).
— *Fem Vikingeskibe fra Roskilde fjord*, Roskilde 1969.
PHILIPSEN, J. P. W. 'The Utrecht Ship', *Mariner's Mirror*, 51 (1965).
TIMNISWOOD, J. T. 'English Galleys, 1272–1377', *Mariner's Mirror*, 35 (1949).


## 9
## The Maritime Republics: Medieval and Renaissance ships in Italy

ANDERSON, R. C. *The Oared Fighting Ship: From Classical times to the coming of steam*, London 1962.
BRAGADIN, MARCANTONIO. *Repubbliche Italiane sul mare*, Milan 1951.
GUGLIELMOTTI, ALBERTO. *Vocabolario Marino e Militare*, Rome 1889.
— *Storia della Marina Pontificia*, Rome 1886–1893 (10 vols).
LA GRAVIÈRE, JURIEN DE. *Les dernières jours de la marine à rames*, Paris 1885.
— *La Guerre de Cypre et la bataille de Lepante*, Paris 1888.
LANE, FREDERICK C. *Venetian Ships and Shipbuilders of the Renaissance*, London 1934; French edition, Paris 1965.
LEVI, CESARE AUGUSTO. *Navi Venete da codici, marmi e dipinti*, Venice 1892.
NANI, JACOPO. *Istituzioni navali per il servizio dell' Armata Sottile*, Venice 1937.
NANI MOCENIGO, MARIO. '*L' Arsenale di Venezia*, Rome 1938.
— *Storia della Marina Veneziana da Lepanto alla caduta della Repubblica*, Rome 1935.
RANDACCIO, CARLO. *Storia navale universale antica e moderna*, Rome 1891.
RODGERS, WILLIAM LEDYARD. *Naval Warfare under Oars: 4th to 16th Centuries*, Annapolis, Maryland 1939.
TAYLOR, E. G. R. *The Haven-finding Art*, London 1956.
VECCHJ, AUGUSTO VITTORIO. *Storia generale della Marina militare*, Florence 1892.
VOCINO, MICHELE. *La Nave nel tempo. Iconografia della nave dalle origini ai nostri giorni*, Milan and Rome 1927.
— *La nave nel tempo*, 3rd ed., Milan 1950.
ZENI, CIRO GIOVANNI. *Con i remi e con le vele*, Milan 1957.

## 10
## The influence of British naval strategy on ship design: 1400–1850

VINGIANO, GIUSEPPE. *Storia della nave*, Rome 1955.
ANDERSON, ROMOLA and R. C. *The Sailing Ship*, London 1947.
ARCHIBALD, E. H. H. *The Wooden Fighting Ship*, London 1968.
BATHE, BASIL W. *The Man-of-War*, London 1968.
CHRELIUS, BENGT. *Vasa, The King's Ship*, London 1962.
CLOWES, G. S. LAIRD. *Sailing Ships*, London 1932 and 1962.
CLOWES, WM. LAIRD. *The Royal Navy*, London 1897.
ENTICK, JOHN. *A New Naval History*, London 1757.
FRANZÉN, ANDERS. *The Warship Vasa*, Norstedts 1966.
LANDSTRÖM, BJÖRN. *Sailing Ships*, London 1969.
LEWIS, MICHAEL. *The History of the British Navy*, Harmondsworth 1957.
LLOYD, CHRISTOPHER. *The Nation and the Navy*, London 1954.
LONGRIDGE, C. NEPEAN. *The Anatomy of Nelson's Ships*, London 1955.
MCKEE, ALEXANDER. *History Under the Sea*, London 1968.
MONSON, ADMIRAL SIR WILLIAM. *Naval Tracts*, London 1902.
MORDAL, JACQUES. *25 Centuries of Sea Warfare*, London 1965.
VARENDE, JEAN de la. *Cherish the Sea: A History of Sail*, London 1955.
WARNER, OLIVER. *The Navy*, Harmondsworth 1968.


## 11
## Traders and privateers across the Atlantic: 1492–1733

BLAIR, CLAY. *Diving for Pleasure and Treasure*, Cleveland, Ohio 1960.
CRILE, JANE and BARNEY. *Treasure-diving Holidays*, New York 1954.
ESQUEMLING, JOHN. *The Buccaneers of America*, New York 1967.
GAGE, THOMAS. *The English American*, London 1656.
HAMILTON, EARL J. *American Treasure and the Price Revolution in Spain, 1501–1650*, New York 1965.
HARING, CLARENCE HENRY. *The Buccaneers in the West Indies in the XVII Century*, London 1910.

— *Trade and Navigation Between Spain and the Indies in the Time of the Hapsburgs*, Cambridge, Mass. [no date], (Harvard Economic Studies XIX)

LINK, MARION CLAYTON. *Sea Diver, a quest for history under the sea*, New York 1959.

— 'Exploring the Drowned City of Port Royal', *National Geographic Magazine* 117 (1960) 151–83.

PETERSON, MENDEL. 'Forms of New World Treasure', *The Numismatist*, January 1964.

— *History under the Sea*, 3rd ed., Washington 1969.

— *The Last Cruise of H.M.S. 'Loo'*, Washington 1955.

— 'Numismatic Objects Recovered from an Early Seventeenth Century Wreck Site', *The Numismatist*, June 1961.

— 'Ordinance Materials Recovered from an Early Seventeenth Century Wreck Site', *Journal of the Company of Military Collectors and Historians*, XIII, No. 3, (1961).

— 'The Significance of the Bermuda Treasure Find', *Life*, January 9, 1956.

TUCKER, TEDDY. *Treasure diving with Teddy Tucker*, Bermuda 1966.

VAZQUEZ de ESPINOZA, ANTONIO. *Compendium and Description of the West Indies*, Washington 1942.

WAGNER, KIP (as told to Taylor, L.B., Jr). *Pieces of eight: recovering the riches of a lost Spanish treasure fleet*, New York 1966.

## 12
## Waterways open the New World

### THE NORTH AMERICAN FUR TRADE

ADNEY, EDWIN T. and CHAPELLE, HOWARD I. *The Bark canoes and skin boats of North America*, Washington 1964. 'Fur Trade canoes', 135–53.

BREBNER, JOHN B. *The explorers of North America, 1492–1806*, New York, 1955.

CONFERENCE ON UNDERWATER ARCHAEOLOGY, ST PAUL, 1963: *Diving into the past* . . . St Paul, Minnesota Historical Society, 1964.

DAVIES, KENNETH G. ed. *Letters from Hudson Bay, 1703–40.* London, 1965.

DEWDNEY, SELWYN H. and KIDD, KENNETH E. *Indian Rock paintings of the Great Lakes*, Toronto, 1962.

FRASER, SIMON. *Letters and Journals, 1806–1808.* Edited with an introd. by W. Kaye Lamb. Maps by C. C. J. Bond. Toronto, 1960.

GATES, CHARLES M. ed. *Five fur traders of the Northwest* . . ., St Paul Minnesota Historical Society, 1965.

GLOVER, RICHARD. 'York boats', *The Beaver*, Outfit 279, no. 4 (Mar. 1949) 19–23.

— 'Salvaging the Last of the York boats', *The Beaver*, Outfit 266, no. 2 (Sept. 1935) 10–11.

GUILLET, EDWIN C. *Pioneer travel in upper Canada.* Toronto, 1966.

HALL, BASIL. *Travels in North America, in the years 1827 and 1828*, Philadelphia, 1829. 2 vols.

HARMON, DANIEL W. *A journal of voyages and travels in the interior of North America* . . ., Toronto, 1911.

HEARNE, SAMUEL, and TURNOR, PHILIP. *Journals of Samuel Hearne and Philip Turnor.* Ed. by J. B. Tyrrell . . . Toronto, 1934.

HENRY, ALEXANDER. *New light on the early history of the Greater Northwest* . . . New York, 1897. 3 vols.

HUDSON'S BAY COMPANY. *Cumberland House journals and Inland journal, 1775–82*, ed. by E. E. Rich . . ., London, 1951–52. 2 vols.

INNIS, HAROLD A. *The fur trade in Canada* . . . rev. ed., Toronto, 1956.

MACGREGOR, JAMES G. *Peter Fidler: Canada's forgotten surveyor, 1769–1822.* Toronto, 1966.

MACKAY, DOUGLAS. *The honourable company* . . ., Indianapolis, 1936.

MORSE, ERIC W. *Canoe routes of the voyageurs* . . ., Ottawa, 1962.

NISH, CAMERON, ed. and trans. *The French regime.* Englewood Cliffs, N.J., 1965. v. 1 only.

NUTE, GRACE L. *The voyageur's highway, Minnesota's border lake land*, St Paul, Minnesota Historical Society, 1965.

RICH, EDWIN E. *The History of the Hudson's Bay Company, 1670–1870.* London, Hudson's Bay Record Society, 1958–59. 2 vols.

UMFREVILLE, EDWARD. *The Present State of Hudson's Bay* . . . Toronto, Ryerson Press, 1954.

WALLACE, WILLIAM S. ed. *Documents relating to the North West Company* . . . Toronto, 1934.

— *The pedlars from Quebec, and other papers on the Nor'-Westers*, Toronto, 1954.

### Manuscripts

Canada. Public Archives, MG 18, L4, Packet 18, p. 25.

Montreal merchants records. Originals in the Chateau de Ramezay with microfilm copies in the Public Archives of Canada and at the Minnesota Historical Society.

Montreal. Superior Court. Judicial archives.

Quebec. District Court. Judicial archives.

### SHIPS OF THE GREAT LAKES

DIGBY, WILLIAM. *The British Invasion from the North* . . . New York 1887.

GILCHRIST, HELEN. *Fort Ticonderoga in History*, Fort Ticonderoga Museum 1923.

HADDEN, JAMES M. *Journal kept in Canada and upon Burgoyne's campaigns in 1776, '77* . . . New York 1884.

LOSSING, BENSON J. *The Pictorial Fieldbook of the War of 1812* . . . 2 vols, New York 1869.

ROOSEVELT, T. *The Naval War of 1812* . . . New York 1882.

WATER, F. F. van de. *Lake Champlain and Lake George*, New York 1946.

# Sources of illustrations

*Page numbers appear on the left, italic numerals refer to in-text figures, roman numerals to half-tone illustrations*

*The maps in this book were drawn by Hanni Bailey*

## Chapter I

13 *1*. Pictogram on tablet from Mesopotamia; second half of 4th millennium BC. After V. Gordon Childe
*2–4*. Nile boat depicted on Amratian vase (2), rock carvings from Wadi Hammamat of 'Egyptian' (4) and 'Mesopotamian' (3) boats; 4th millennium BC. From Hans A. Winckler, *Rock Drawings of Southern, Upper Egypt*, 1938. Courtesy the Egyptian Exploration Society
*5*. Sailing boat depicted on a late Gerzean period vase; *c*. 2900 BC. British Museum, London

14–15 *6*. Map of the Mediterranean, Egypt, Mesopotamia and the Indus valley.

15 *7*. Hieroglyphic sign on a fragment (Berlin inv. no. 20037) from the Sun Temple of Ni-user-re, Abusir; *c*. 2500–2350 BC. After L. Keimer, 'L'Hieroglyphe' in *Annales du service des antiquités de l'Egypte*, 43, 1943
*8*. Modern boat of ambatch wood. After drawing in *Annales du service des antiquités de l'Egypte*, 43, 1943

16 *9, 10*. Reliefs from the tombs of Abibi (9) and Ipi (10), Saqqara; *c*. 2500 BC. Cairo Museum

17 *11*. Warships incised on 'frying pans' from Syros, Cyclades; 3rd millennium BC. After Arthur Evans
*12*. Clay model boat from Palaikastro, Crete; *c*. 2600–2300 BC. Heraklion Museum

18 *13*. Map inscribed on clay tablet from Mesopotamia; *c*. 1500 BC. University Museum, University of Pennsylvania

19 *14, 15*. Model of funerary barque from Meket-re's tomb in Thebes, *c*. 2000 BC (*14*). Constructional details of similar models (*15*): V and U in Cairo Museum, T in Metropolitan Museum, New York. From H. E. Winlock, *Models of Daily Life in Ancient Egypt*

20 *16*. Plan of the hull of a boat from Dashur; *c*. 2000 BC. Cairo Museum. After Reisner, *Models of Ships and Boats*, Cairo 1913

21 *17*. Drawing by Björn Landström based on relief at Deir el-Bahari; *c*. 1500 BC. Courtesy International Book Production, Stockholm
*18*. Relief from Medinet Habu; *c*. 1190 BC. Courtesy the Oriental Institute, University of Chicago

22 *19–21*. Paintings of Mycenaean ships on a pyxis from Messenia (*19*), a stirrup vase from Asine, House G (*20*), and a stirrup jar from Skyros (*21*); *c*. 1200–1100 BC. *19* and *20* drawn by W. Dodds after Kourouniotes, and Froedin and Persson, respectively. *21* after Hansen

22–23 *22*. Wall painting from tomb 162 of Kenamon, Thebes; 14th C. BC. Drawn by N. de G. Davies. Courtesy the Egypt Exploration Society

24 *23*. Plan of the Cape Gelidonya wreck site. Drawn by C. K. Williams

25 *1*. Diver at work on the Cape Gelidonya wreck. Photo Herb Greer and Peter Throckmorton

26 *2, 3*. Clay model boats from Fara (2) and Eridu (3); *c*. 3000 and *c*. 4000 BC. respectively. University of Pennsylvania Museum, Philadelphia. Photos George Quay
*4*. Boat representation on a Gerzean vase; 4th millennium BC. University of Pennsylvania Museum, Philadelphia. Photo George Quay
*5*. Carved ivory knife handle, probably from Gebel el-Arak; 4th millenium BC. Louvre, Paris. Photo M. Chuzeville

27 *6*. Wall painting from a tomb at Hierakonpolis; 4th millennium BC. From Quibell and Green, *Hierakonpolis II*, London 1902, courtesy Bernard Quaritch Ltd
*7*. Fragment of painted linen from El-Gebelein; 4th millennium BC. Museo Egizio, Turin. Photo Giustino Rampazzi. Courtesy the Soprintendenza alle Antichità (Egittologia)

28–29 *8*. Uruk cylinder seal; end of the 4th millennium BC; Iraq Museum
*9*. Akkadian seal; *c*. 2000 BC. Iraq Museum, Baghdad
*10*. Relief on a terracotta amulet from Mohenjo-daro; 3rd millennium BC. National Museum of Pakistan, Karachi. Photo courtesy George F. Dales
*11*. Detail of an incised 'frying pan' from Syros, Cyclades; 2500–2200 BC. National Museum, Athens. Photo Peter Clayton
*12*. Silver model boat from Ur, Mesopotamia; 3rd millennium BC. Iraq Museum, Baghdad
*13*. Lead model boat probably from Naxos, Cyclades; 3rd millennium BC. Ashmolean Museum, Oxford
*14*. Clay model boat from Mochlos, Crete; 2800–2000 BC. Archaeological Museum, Heraklion. Photo Hirmer Fotoarchiv
*15*. Relief from the tomb chapel of Ka-pu-re, Saqqara; *c*. 2500–2200 BC. Photo University of Pennsylvania Museum, Philadelphia
*16*. Relief from the tomb of Sahu-re, Abusir; 2494–2345 BC. Agyptisches Museum, Berlin. Photo Staatsbibliothek, Berlin
*17–18*. Model boats from the tomb of Meket-re; *c*. 2000 BC. Cairo Museum. Photos Egyptian Expedition, the Metropolitan Museum of Art, New York

30 *19*. Model boat from the tomb of Meket-re, Thebes; *c*. 2000 BC. Metropolitan Museum of Art, New
*20*. Wall painting in the tomb chapel of the sculptor Ipuy Thebes; 13th C. BC. Photo Wim Swaan. Courtesy Paul Elek Productions Ltd

31 *21*. Detail of a painted relief in the Mastaba of Ti, Saqqara; 2494–2345 BC. Photo Jean Mazenod
*22*. Three engraved Minoan gems; 1600/1400 BC. British Museum, London. Photo Eileen Tweedy

32–33 *23*. Detail of a relief in the tomb chapel of Ukh-hotep, Meir; 20th C. BC. Photo Bildarchiv Foto Marburg
*24*. Bas-relief from Deir el-Bahari, Thebes; *c*. 1500 BC. Photo John Webb
*25*. Stone anchor from Cyprus; between 1400 and 1200 BC. Courtesy the Director of Antiquities and the Cyprus Museum
*26*. Papyrus ship log from Memphis; 1239 BC. Papyrus Leiden I 350 verso Col. I–IV. Rijksmuseum van Oudheden, Leiden
*27*. Funerary boat of Sesostris III from Dashur; 1878–1843 BC. Field (Columbian) Museum of Natural History, Chicago

34 *28*. Mural from tomb of Rekh-mi-re; 15th C. BC. Copy by N. de G. Davies. Egyptian Expedition, the Metropolitan Museum of Art, New York
*29*. Ingots from the Cape Gelidonya wreck; *c*. 1200 BC. Photo Herb Greer

35 *30*. Diver chiselling ingots on the Cape Gelidonya wreck. Photo Herb Greer and Peter Throckmorton

36 *31*. Bronze swage from the Cape Gelidonya wreck; *c*. 1200 BC. Bodrum Museum, Turkey. Photo Herb Greer. Courtesy the University of Pennsylvania Museum expedition
*32*. Bronze tools from the Cape Gelidonya wreck, before cleaning. Bodrum Museum, Turkey. Photo Reuben Goldberg
*33–36*. Merchant's cylinder seal (33), two scarabs (34, 35) and stone balance-pan weights (36) from the Cape Gelidonya wreck. Bodrum Museum, Turkey. Photo Peter Dorrell. Courtesy the University of Pennsylvania Museum expedition

## Chapter 2

38 *1*. Rope fragments found at Tell el-Kheleifeh; 8th–4th C. BC. Photo American Schools Oriental Research. Courtesy the late Dr Nelson Glueck

41 *2*. Vase painting by Aristonothos; *c*. 660 BC. Palazzo dei Conservatori, Rome

42 *3*. Fragment of a Geometric krater from Elis; *c*. 720–700 BC. Courtesy P. G. Themelis
*4*. Ship representation on an Attic krater; *c*. 750 BC. Louvre, Paris
*5*. Ivory plaque from the sanctuary of Artemis Orthia, Sparta; *c*. 600 BC, National Museum, Athens

43 *6*. Ship incised on Ficoroni *cista*; before 300 BC. Villa Giulia, Rome
*7*. Graffito on a vase from Veii; early 7th C. BC. Villa Giulia, Rome
*8*. Etruscan vase painting; *c*. 580 BC. British Museum, London

44 *9*. Attic red-figure volute-krater by the Talos painter; 5th C. BC. Palazzo Jatta, Ruvo

*10*. Drawing largely based on the so-called Lenormant relief (ill. 5). After J. S. Morrison and R. T. Williams, *Greek Oared Ships*, 1968

45 *11*. Fragmentary marble eye, found in Piraeus; probably early 5th C. BC. Staatliche Museen zu Berlin

46 *12*. Etruscan grave relief from Bologna; late 5th C. BC. Giardino Margherita, Bologna

47 *13*. Ship representation on a coin from Aradus; *c*. 350–325 BC. British Museum, London

48 *14*. Detail of a relief from the Palace of Sennacherib; *c*. 701 BC. British Museum, London

49 *15*. Engraving on a Phoenician gem from Tharros, Sardinia; *c*. 500 BC. Cagliari Museum
*16*. Representation of an anchor on a coin from Apollonia; 4th C. BC. British Museum, London
*17*. Anchor stock found off Cap d'Antibes; early 6th C. BC. After Lagrand, from *Gallia*, 16, 1958

51 *18–19*. Reconstruction plans of the Kyrenia ship; 4th C. BC. Drawn by Helena Wylde and Joachim Höhle

53 *1*. Hull of the Kyrenia wreck on the sea bed in 1969; 4th C. BC. Photo © National Geographic Society

54 *2*. Detail of the François vase from Chiusi, painted by Kleitias; *c*. 570 BC. Museo Archaeologico, Florence. Photo Hirmer
*3*. Detail of an Athenian Geometric funerary vase; *c*. 760 BC. Metropolitan Museum of Art, New York, Fletcher Fund 1934
*4*. Painting on a late Geometric Attic spouted krater; *c*. 700 BC. Royal Ontario Museum, Toronto
*5*. Trireme carved on the so-called Lenormant relief; *c*. 400 BC. Acropolis Museum, Athens. Photo Deutsches Archäologisches Institut, Athens

55 *6*. Relief from the northeast gate at Karatepe (after restoration); *c*. 700 BC. Photo Halet Çambel, Ankara
*7*. Ship representation on a coin trom Sidon; second quarter of the 4th C. BC. British Museum, London. Photo Ray Gardner
*8*. Seal from the royal palace at Persepolis; *c*. 485–465 BC. Courtesy the Oriental Institute, University of Chicago

56–57 *9*. Wall painting from the Governor's Palace at Til Barsib; *c*. 700 BC. Aleppo Museum. Photo Hirmer
*10*. Painting on an Attic cup; late 6th C. BC. British Museum, London. Photo Eileen Tweedy
*11*. Odysseus and the Sirens, painting on red-figure Attic vase; early 5th C. BC. Courtesy the Trustees of the British Museum, London
*12*. Detail of a wall painting from the Tombe delle Caccia e delle Pesca, Tarquinia; *c*. 520–510 BC. Photo Scala
*13*. Wall painting from the Tombe

58–59 *14*. Egyp[...]
trireme[...]
seum, C[...]
*15*. Gre[...]
warship[...]
Courtes[...]
Museum[...]
*16*. Cyp[...]
model; [...]
Museum[...]
Cesnol[...]
*17*. Att[...]
Photo [...]
ità dell[...]
*18*. Tw[...]
Sicily; [...]
DeVri[...]
*19*. Les[...]
harbou[...]
BC. F[...]
di C[...]
*20*. [...]
5th [...]
logi[...]
*21*. [...]
va[...]

313

316

# Index